THE GREAT AN

ALSO BY PHILIP JENKINS

Laying Down the Sword

Jesus Wars

The Lost History of Christianity

God's Continent

The New Faces of Christianity

The Next Christendom

Hidden Gospels

THE GREAT AND HOLY WAR

*How World War I Became a
Religious Crusade*

PHILIP JENKINS

HarperOne
An Imprint of HarperCollinsPublishers

HarperOne

THE GREAT AND HOLY WAR: *How World War I Became a Religious Crusade*. Copyright © 2014 by Philip Jenkins. All rights reserved. Printed in the United States of America. No part of this book may be used or reproduced in any manner whatsoever without written permission except in the case of brief quotations embodied in critical articles and reviews. For information address HarperCollins Publishers, 195 Broadway, New York, NY 10007.

HarperCollins books may be purchased for educational, business, or sales promotional use. For information please e-mail the Special Markets Department at SPsales@harpercollins.com.

HarperCollins website: http://www.harpercollins.com

HarperCollins®, 🅗®, and HarperOne™ are trademarks of HarperCollins Publishers.

FIRST HARPERCOLLINS PAPERBACK EDITION PUBLISHED IN 2015

Library of Congress Cataloging-in-Publication Data
Jenkins, Philip
The great and holy war : how World War I became a religious crusade / Philip Jenkins. — First Edition.
          pages   cm
          ISBN 978–0–06–210514–1
1. World War, 1914–1918—Religious aspects. 2. World War, 1914–1918—Religious aspects—Christianity. 3. Nationalism—Religious aspects—History—20th century. 4. Nationalism—Religious aspects—Christianity—History—20th century. 5. Messianism.
6. Eschatology. I. Title.
          D639.R4J56   2014
          940.3'1--dc23   2013041013

15 16 17 18 19 RRD(H) 10 9 8 7 6 5 4 3 2 1

940.31
Jen

Contents

LIST OF MAPS

A Note About Terminology

Throughout this book, I refer to ideas about the end times, or "eschatology." In particular, the apocalyptic vision tells a story of increasing chaos, marked by war, plague, famine, and disaster, culminating in a divine act of judgment that ends the existing world order and begins a wholly new creation. In Western cultures, those ideas are commonly associated with the New Testament book of Revelation, which in its Greek original bears the name Apocalypse. Yet such ideas are by no means a Christian preserve, as they originated in Judaism and are the common inheritance of Islam. I will therefore use the term "apocalyptic" without limiting it to its Christian context.

I will also use "millenarian," another term that stems from the New Testament, to describe Christ's utopian thousand-year rule on earth. Yet many societies throughout history have imagined an imminent revolutionary crisis after which the purged world will enjoy an unprecedented era of peace and prosperity. The fact of being human, and knowing the circumstances of birth, means that societies naturally assume that any new age must be born amidst blood and peril. Despite its Christian roots, then, we can refer to millenarian impulses in other faiths and traditions.

In speaking of the early twentieth-century world, I use the term "India" in its larger sense at that time, namely the British-dominated territories of South Asia, including the modern nation-states of India, Pakistan, and Bangladesh.

The legend of the Angel of Mons, as imagined in a 1920 painting

From Angels to Armageddon

*The war was another plastic work that totally absorbed us, which reformed
our forms, destroyed the lines, and gave a new look to the universe.*
—MARC CHAGALL

*In the day when heaven was falling, the hour
when Earth's foundations fled . . .*
—A. E. HOUSMAN

IN 1914, WELSH FANTASY writer Arthur Machen unwittingly
invented a legend. In the compact twelve hundred words of "The
Bowmen," he told a story set during the Allied retreat across France
that August, when British forces made a heroic stand against the
advancing Germans at the village of Mons. When a soldier jokingly
calls on Saint George for help, he is shocked to find that he really
has invoked an army of English archers from the great fifteenth-
century Battle of Agincourt, who rise to protect their descendants.
"The singing arrows fled so swift and thick that they darkened the
air; the heathen horde melted from before them." This intervention

saves the Allied cause, leaving Germany, "a country ruled by scientific principles," to determine what kind of gas or secret weapon the British might have deployed.[1]

Machen's fiction ran out of control. He was soon meeting people who claimed to have participated in the battle and seen the visionary bowmen, or witnessed arrow wounds in German corpses. Hawkish critics were appalled at Machen's unpatriotic attempts to describe the tale as a mere fiction. Denying his authorship, they claimed that he had acted only as an intermediary in leaking the story, which must have come from the highest political or military circles. Why was he conspiring to suppress the truth? Religious and occult writers further elaborated the tale over the next few months until the bowmen morphed into an angel or angels, and in that form the story won global fame. Through the war years, the Angel of Mons was regularly depicted in propaganda posters and works of art, and it inspired musical compositions. Machen was at once amused and bemused. "How is it," he asked, "that a nation plunged in materialism of the grossest kind has accepted idle rumors and gossip of the supernatural as certain truth?"[2]

Religion and the War

MACHEN'S REMARK ABOUT GROSS materialism fits many accounts of the First World War, by authors both at the time and subsequently. The war, we often hear, marked the end of illusions, and of faith itself. In this account, the ideals and chivalry that rode so high at the start of the conflict perished miserably in the mud of France and Belgium. They vanished in a world of artillery and machine guns, of aircraft, poison gas, and tanks, as hell entered the age of industrialized mass production.

A striking commentary on the war was offered by Britain's Harry Patch, the last soldier actually to have fought in the war's trenches and who died in 2009 at the age of 111. He felt the war had not been worth a single life (although he might have shot the kaiser, if the opportunity had arisen), and he had no criticism of anyone who had deserted. He recalled seeing half-savage dogs fighting over biscuits taken from dead men's pockets and wondering, "What are we doing that's really any different? Two civilized nations, British and German, fighting for our lives." In summary, he commented, "What the hell we fought for, I now don't know." That last line epitomizes what many modern people think about the war. All that butchery, they believe, took place for narrow national rivalries and selfish imperial interests.[3]

In such a picture, religion and spirituality seem irrelevant, except as the window dressing offered by states invoking divine justice before sending their young men off to slaughter. Each side cynically appropriated God to its own narrow nationalist causes. As J. C. Squire's despairing rhyme noted,

> God heard the embattled nations sing and
>   shout,
> "Gott strafe England!" and "God save the
>   King!"
> God this, God that, and God the other thing.
> "Good God!" said God, "I've got my work cut
>   out!"[4]

But such a wholly secular account makes it impossible to understand the mood of the era and the motivations of states and policy makers. For one thing, contemporary enthusiasm for the war was much greater than we might imagine from what Harry Patch wrote with ninety years of hindsight after the event; it would be instructive to read anything he might have written during the conflict itself. In recent years, historians of the Great War have paid special attention to the attitude of frontline combatants, to try to understand just why they were prepared to withstand the dreadful conditions so long, and the greatest surprise is how thoroughly many reflected the attitudes that we might think of as elite propaganda.

Even when they were writing in diaries or journals that were never intended to be read by official eyes, soldiers expressed very standard views about God and country and the virtues and vices of the respective sides. The words of ordinary British soldiers show how many really did believe they were engaged in a war for righteousness's sake, in issues such as the defense of outraged Belgium. German or French soldiers likewise needed little urging to see their war as a desperate defense of national survival, while the letters of ordinary Russian soldiers regularly asserted their belief in "Faith, Tsar, and Fatherland," in that order. Judging from the abundant evidence of letters and diaries, soldiers commonly demonstrated a religious worldview and regularly referred to Christian beliefs and ideas. They resorted frequently to biblical language and to concepts of sacrifice and redemptive suffering. The sizable Jewish minority in the respective armed forces turned to their own religious traditions.[5]

Contrary to secular legend, religious and supernatural themes pervaded the rhetoric surrounding the war—on all sides—and these clearly had a popular appeal far beyond the statements of official church leaders. If the war represented the historic triumph of modernity, the rise of countries "ruled by scientific principles," then that modernity included copious lashings of the religious, mystical, millenarian, and even magical. Discussions of the Great War, at the time and since, have regularly used words such as "Armageddon" and "apocalypse," although almost always in a metaphorical sense. Yet without understanding the widespread popular belief in these concepts in their original supernatural terms, we are missing a large part of the story. As Salman Rushdie remarks, "Sometimes legends make reality, and become more useful than the facts."[6]

The First World War was a thoroughly religious event, in the sense that overwhelmingly Christian nations fought each other in what many viewed as a holy war, a spiritual conflict. Religion is essential to understanding the war, to understanding why people went to war, what they hoped to achieve through war, and why they stayed at war. Not in medieval or Reformation times but in the age of aircraft and machine guns, the majority of the world's Christians were indeed engaged in a holy war that claimed more than ten million lives.

Acknowledging the war's religious dimensions forces us to consider its long-term effects. In an age of overwhelming mass propaganda and incipient global media, nations could not spend years spreading the torrid language and imagery of holy warfare without having a potent effect, although not necessarily in any form intended by the nations responsible. Often, too, these messages appealed to audiences quite different from the expected ones. In consequence, the war ignited a global religious revolution. However thoroughly Eurocentric the conflict might appear, in the long term, it transformed not just the Christianity of the main combatant nations but also other great faiths, especially Judaism and Islam. It destroyed a global religious order that had prevailed for the previous half millennium and dominated much of the globe. The Great War drew the world's religious map as we know it today.

Holy War

THE CONCEPT OF SANCTIFIED warfare is familiar enough in history; but can we legitimately describe the events of 1914 as a holy war in anything like the same sense as the medieval Crusades or Europe's confessional wars of the sixteenth and seventeenth centuries? Surely, we might assume, the Great War was a highly material conflict fundamentally concerned with great power rivalries, with economic grievances and imperial ambitions.

The crusading analogy is instructive, because in those earlier ages, too, historians can find plenty of reasons for the campaigns beyond the religious ideology of the time. Depending on one's interpretation, we might suggest that Crusaders fought because of land hunger, population pressures, or a desire to escape from restrictive state mechanisms. A great many combatants fought out of simple greed or because more powerful neighbors forced them to participate, and they gave next to no thought to the weighty issues supposedly motivating the holy cause. Yet most scholars are comfortable in accepting the wars' religious justifications at their face value and asserting that Christian warriors really thought they were engaged in a holy struggle against enemies of their faith. This was certainly true of governing elites and, as far as we can reconstruct their views, of many humbler followers. And the same argument can be made about their distant descendants at the start of the twentieth century—descendants who themselves sometimes boasted the archaic title of Crusaders.[7]

The issue of definition is critical. To speak of a holy war, it is not enough to find national leaders deploying a few pious rhetorical flourishes or claiming that God will see the nation to a just victory. Instead, the states involved must have an intimate if not official alliance with a particular faith tradition, and moreover, the organs of state and church should expressly and repeatedly declare the religious character of the conflict. Not just incidentally but repeatedly and centrally, official statements and propaganda declare that the war is being fought for God's cause, or for his glory, and such claims pervade the media and organs of popular culture. Moreover, they identify the state and its armed forces as agents or implements of God. Advancing the nation's cause and interests is indistinguishable from promoting and defending God's cause or (in a Christian context) of bringing in his kingdom on earth. Speaking of such a conflict in religious terms does not preclude the state having other motives or causes, such as naval rivalries or struggles over natural resources. Nor does it demand that each and every participant support these goals, or indeed treat them seriously.

Beyond this, the holy war framework defines attitudes to the role of the armed forces and the conduct of combat operations. That nation should broadly accept the idea that military action has a sanctified character, equal or superior to any of the other works approved by that religion. The nation is struggling against an enemy that defies or violates the godly cause, so that such a foe is of its nature evil or represents satanic forces. Death in such a righteous cosmic war represents a form of sacrifice or martyrdom, elevating the dead soldier to saintly status. The state and the media might even claim that the nation and its armed forces are receiving special supernatural assistance.

By these criteria, we can confidently speak of a powerful and consistent strain of holy war ideology during the Great War years. All the main combatants deployed such language, particularly the monarchies with long traditions of state establishment—the Russians, Germans, British, Austro-Hungarians, and Ottoman Turks—but also those notionally secular republics: France, Italy, and the United States. More specifically, with the obvious exception of the Turks, it was a Christian war. With startling literalism, visual representations in all the main participant nations placed Christ himself on the battle lines, whether in films, posters, or postcards. Jesus blessed German soldiers going into battle; Jesus comforted the dying victims of German atrocities; Jesus personally led a reluctant kaiser to confront the consequences of his evil policies. Apart from the obvious spiritual figures—Christ and the Virgin—most combatant nations used an iconography in which their cause was portrayed by that old Crusader icon Saint George, and their enemies as the Dragon.

When in November 1914 the Ottoman Empire formally declared war, the regime's language was powerfully religious—was

not the emperor also the caliph of all Islam? The sultan-caliph proclaimed that

> right and loyalty are on our side, and hatred and tyranny
> on the side of our enemies, and therefore there is no doubt
> that the Divine help and assistance of the just God and the
> moral support of our glorious Prophet will be on our side to
> encourage us. . . . Let those of you who are to die a martyr's
> death be messengers of victory to those who have gone before
> us, and let the victory be sacred and the sword be sharp of
> those of you who are to remain in life.[8]

Yet these words seem pallid when set against the fevered pro-
nouncements emanating from Berlin and Paris. Swords and prophets, divine guidance and holy martyrdom? In Christian Europe,
such notions were already clichés. If Russia or Germany or Britain
had been Islamic states in 1914, would their rhetoric have differed
significantly?

I am not arguing that each combatant nation in the war possessed anything like the same degree of religious zeal, or that any
nation entered the war exclusively because of a religious cause, in
the sense of seeking to destroy the heretics or infidels in an opposing state. In two crucial cases, though—Germany and Russia—
religious motivations were so inextricably bound up with state
ideology and policy making that it is impossible to separate them
from secular factors. Each of these Christian empires, in its way,
regarded itself as a messianic nation destined to fulfill God's will
in the secular realm. Each, moreover, had networks of allies that
were destined to clash with each other, making it virtually certain
that the whole continent would be dragged into conflict. The war
began as a clash of messianic visions. Other states, such as France or
Britain, might initially have had no such religious motives, but once
at war, those themes became increasingly powerful. At a very early

stage in the war, also, the full panoply of holy war rhetoric came to dominate media and propaganda in all the combatant states.

Enemies of God

IN EACH OF THE combatant powers, holy war ideas produced a substantial and diverse literature, in high and low culture, in literature, art, and film. One of France's greatest modern writers was Paul Claudel, who portrayed the struggle in his 1915 play *La Nuit de Noël de 1914* (*Christmas Eve 1914*). His play depicts the gathering of the souls of French people killed by the Germans, including soldiers but also many civilians slaughtered in German mass executions. All are among the blessed, martyrs in a holy Catholic struggle against German aggression and against that country's pagan worship of naked state power. At the Battle of the Marne, says Claudel, French armies stood flanked by Saint Genevieve and Joan of Arc. Even so, France's best hope was the Virgin Mary, who had led their armies so often through the centuries. As a dead soldier reports from beyond the grave,

> It's not a saint or a bishop, it's Our Lady herself, it's the Mother of God-made-Man for us, who endures the violence and the fire. She's the one we saw burning at the center of our lines, like the virgin of Rouen once upon a time. She's the one they're trying to slaughter, the old Mother, the one who gives us her body as a rampart. At the center of our lines, she's the one who stands as the rampart and the flag against Black Luther's dark hordes.[9]

The play culminates in a Midnight Mass conducted in this heavenly setting, with the noise of the German shelling of Reims Cathedral substituting for the customary midnight ringing of bells.

Reims Cathedral hit by German artillery fire, September 20, 1914

For both sides, the Great War was a day-and-night conflict against cosmic evil. When the United States entered the conflict in 1917, Randolph McKim, Episcopal rector of Washington's Church of the Epiphany, proclaimed that

> it is God who has summoned us to this war. It is his war we are fighting. . . . This conflict is indeed a crusade. The greatest in history—the holiest. It is in the profoundest and truest sense a Holy War. . . . Yes, it is Christ, the King of Righteousness, who calls us to grapple in deadly strife with this unholy and blasphemous power [Germany].[10]

American clergy produced some alarming assertions of cosmic war rhetoric. One prominent American liberal was Congregational minister Lyman Abbott, for whom the war was a literal crusade. In his best-known article, "To Love Is to Hate," he declared an explicit Christian duty to hate imperial Germany and all its works. American preachers frankly accepted the literal and material aspects of the sacred conflict, which was no mere spiritual battle. Even Albert

Dieffenbach, a liberal Unitarian with a proud German heritage, had no doubt that Jesus himself would join the fray directly if he could: "There is not an opportunity to deal death to the enemy that [Jesus] would shirk from or delay in seizing! He would take bayonet and grenade and bomb and rifle."[11]

Another Congregationalist, Newell Dwight Hillis, took holy war doctrines to their ultimate conclusion, advocating the annihilation of Satan's earthly servants and the extermination of the German race. In 1918, he urged the international community "to consider the sterilization of the ten million German soldiers, and the segregation of their women, that when this generation of German goes, civilized cities, states and races may be rid of this awful cancer that must be cut clean out of the body of society." America's Liberty Loan Committee distributed a million and a half extracts from Hillis's book.[12]

God's Mailed Hand

ACTIVISTS IN MOST COUNTRIES spoke the language of Christian warfare, but the German approach to the war still stands out for its widespread willingness to identify the nation's cause with God's will, and for the spiritual exaltation that swept the country in 1914. We are not just dealing with a few celebrity preachers.

Of course, any statement about national mood has to be made with care. A generation of scholars has combated the myth that European nations experienced total national solidarity in support of the coming war. More people had doubts than we would guess from the media of the time, and those doubts were more openly expressed as time went by. Yet having said this, educated and elite opinion in Germany in 1914 assuredly did have a deeply patriotic and pro-war tinge, and that ideology had a strong religious coloring. The constant repetition of such ideas in propaganda over the following years made them absolutely commonplace.[13]

German artillery passing through the Brandenburg Gate, summer of 1914

Germany's Protestant preachers and theologians frankly exulted in the outbreak of war. Christian leaders treated the war as a spiritual event, in which their nation was playing a messianic role in Europe and the world. Educated Christians saw the spiritual exhilaration that greeted the war as a foretaste of eternal bliss. War, it seemed, was a heavenly revelation, even a New Pentecost. Regularly appearing in the texts of the time is the word *Offenbarung*, "Revelation" (this is the German title of the book known in English as Revelation). So is *Verklärung*, "transfiguration" or "glorification," the word that preachers commonly used to describe the war's effects on the national mood. As Thuringian minister Adam Ritzhaupt asked, "When did peacetime ever offer us the heavenly exaltation that we are feeling in war?"[14]

Allied propagandists had no difficulty in finding embarrassing sermons and essays by German leaders that assumed their empire was engaged in a sacred war. In 1914, one notorious pastor, Dietrich Vorwerk, praised the God who reigns on high, above "Cherubinen und Seraphinen und Zeppelinen" (Cherubim and Seraphim and Zeppelins). Vorwerk even rewrote the Lord's Prayer:

Our Father, from the height of heaven,
Make haste to succor Thy German people.
Help us in the holy war,
Let your name, like a star, guide us:
Lead Thy German Reich to glorious victories.
Who will stand before the conquerors?
Who will go into the dark sword-grave?
Lord, Thy will be done!
Although war's bread be scanty,
Smite the foe each day
With death and tenfold woes.
In thy merciful patience, forgive
Each bullet and each blow
That misses its mark.
Lead us not into the temptation
Of letting our wrath be too gentle
In carrying out Thy divine judgment.
Deliver us and our pledged ally [Austria-
    Hungary]
From the Evil One and his servants on earth.
Thine is the kingdom,
The German land.
May we, through Thy mailed hand
Come to power and glory.[15]

However tempted we may be to consign such militaristic pastors to the demagogic fringe, we find near-identical sentiments from some of Germany's greatest thinkers and theologians, and this at a time when the country plausibly could claim cultural and spiritual leadership of the Christian world. But in all the main combatant powers, holy war views were advocated by the most respected mainline clergy. Clerics who deviated from these doctrines—and many did, as individuals—found themselves persecuted or forced into silence.

In modern times, radical Muslim clergy and activists have often cited religious justifications for violence, to the extent that many Jews and Christians even doubt that Islam is a religion, rather than a militaristic doomsday cult. Yet Christian leaders in 1914 or 1917 likewise gave an absolute religious underpinning to warfare conducted by states that were seen as executing the will of God, and they used well-known religious terms to contextualize acts of violence. Modern Shiites recall the bloody sacrifice of the Battle of Karbala; Christians spoke of Gethsemane and Golgotha. Christians then, like Islamists today, portrayed their soldiers as warriors from a romanticized past, with a special taste for the Middle Ages. Both shared a common symbolism of sword and shield. Both saw heroic death as a form of martyrdom, in which the shedding of blood washed away the sins of life and offered immediate entry to paradise.

We have no problem granting the title of "crusade" to the medieval Christian movements to reconquer Palestine, because that was the ideological framework that contemporaries used to justify their cause. Why, then, should we deny holy war status to the conflict of 1914-18?

Believing Worlds

RELIGIOUS THEMES RESONATED POWERFULLY with ordinary people. The war took place in a world in which religious faith was still the norm, even in advanced and industrial nations, and even more so in mainly rural and peasant societies. Religious language and assumptions were omnipresent, on the home front and at the front lines, as part of the air people breathed. All those religious interpretations, all that willingness to believe tales of angels and apparitions, did not spring into life overnight in August 1914. Rather, they were deeply embedded in prewar culture, to a degree that must challenge familiar assumptions about the impact of Enlightenment and scientific ideas on ordinary Europeans. And the experience of war greatly intensified perceptions of the religious dimension, in an age when death was such a familiar fact, when so much effort was devoted to analyzing the vagaries of providence and fate.[16]

Around the world, the stirring events of the war created a spiritual excitement that burst the bounds of conventional religion, and also transcended individual faith traditions. A public thirst for spiritual manifestations would be obvious throughout the war years. Although the Mons story is now largely forgotten, the Catholic world still venerates the miraculous apparition at Fátima in Portugal in 1917, when the Virgin brought comfort and counsel to a tormented continent. Each nation had its myths and legends, its battlefront apparitions and miracles, and these were widely accepted. Russians knew that the Virgin had appeared to their forces in 1914 at Augustovo; the French likewise credited the Virgin with their survival from invasion. French wartime mythology included the legend known as "Debout les Morts!" (Let the dead arise!), which told how outnumbered forces had been saved not by angels but by French soldiers risen from the dead. Time and again we hear of soldiers on all sides convinced that their long-dead comrades still literally marched into battle alongside them.[17]

If the hunger for spirituality was limitless, the ability to keep that new wine within the constraints of the old institutional bottles was strictly limited. As Machen himself noted, an age in which intellectual elites preached materialism had few safeguards against the onslaught of mystical speculations. Looking at the proliferation of visions and revelations, we might be tempted to think that governments were actively promoting such tales to strengthen morale and benefit the war effort. To the contrary, though, both states and churches spent a good deal of time actively trying to *suppress* popular claims. When the British fought a victorious campaign in Palestine, the media naturally wanted to trumpet a new crusade and the fulfillment of ancient prophecy. An appalled British government used draconian censorship powers to stamp out any such talk, which would potentially enrage the empire's Muslim subjects. Churches struggled against the popular assumption that any soldier who perished in the good fight automatically won salvation as a martyr, regardless of his personal life or moral behavior. Myths and supernatural tales manifested themselves despite official efforts, rather than because of them.

The First World War was a golden age for the fringe, for the esoteric, mystical, and occult. Spiritualism reached new heights—how could it not when so many wanted to contact their lost loved ones? Esoteric ideas fascinated the powerful and educated as much as they did ordinary subjects. When we find a political leader or general dabbling in the occult, we might dismiss that as personal eccentricity, but in the war years, such interests were commonplace. The German general who led the invasion of France in 1914 had strong occult interests, as did Erich Ludendorff, who was virtually the empire's dictator in the second half of the war. So did Aleksei Brusilov, Russia's most effective wartime general, and so did many other prominent figures in all the combatant nations. These alternative currents collectively represented a rival orthodoxy to the mainstream faiths, closely overlapping official religions. For those other believers, as for mainstream Christians, such ideas gave an overwhelming spiritual dimension to worldly conflict and aroused expectations of gigantic cosmic changes lying on the horizon.

Rumors of Angels

APOCALYPTIC IDEAS EXERCISED A special power. Throughout history, secular disasters have repeatedly driven revolutionary eras of religious change and visionary expectation, but rarely have the four horsemen of the Apocalypse—war, famine, death, and plague—rampaged so freely as they did between 1914 and 1918. If names like Golgotha and Gethsemane offered a vision of unimaginable suffering, they also betokened resurrection and supernatural victory over the forces of evil and death. And ultimately they belonged to a broader Christian narrative in which the struggle against evil concluded with a monumental final battle, ushered in by signs and wonders. On all sides, the great authors and thinkers of the age recognized that they lived in the time of what Thomas Hardy called "The Breaking of Nations." Hardly less than the war itself, the influenza pandemic evoked visions of the imminent end of days and the twilight of the existing world order. Taken together, war, epidemic, and globalization made for an overpowering historical devil's brew.[18]

Remarkably often, angels featured in contemporary tales and legends, as at Mons. Angels had a special role in the apocalyptic scheme and feature prominently in the biblical book of Revelation. Michael in particular leads the cosmic hosts in the final war against Satan. Even before 1914, angelic images were a mainstay for Europe's most progressive cultural figures. This is not surprising, as successive war scares over the previous decade had placed imminent war and catastrophe firmly on the cultural agenda. In Germany and Russia, France and Italy, young artists and writers understood the fragility of the social order and filled their creations with images of angels and Antichrist, of cosmic war and apocalypse. Leading prewar modernists organized in the famous Blue Rider school, which is actually a mistranslation of the German original: it should refer to a horseman, harking back to Revelation. As the movement's manifesto proclaimed in 1912, "We stand before new pictures as in a dream, and we hear the apocalyptic horsemen in the air. . . . Today is the great day of the revelations of this world." Angels likewise featured in nationalist and military mythology as the nations' symbolic guardians in the conflicts to come. German patriots had a special devotion to the archangel Michael. When the German Empire launched its all-or-nothing final offensive against the Allies in 1918, the operation was naturally code-named Michael.[19]

The apocalyptic vision took pride of place in popular culture. In 1916, D. W. Griffith's blockbuster film *Intolerance* combined the biblical image of the fall of Babylon with a futuristic vision of angels appearing over the war's battlefronts to end war and usher in an era of millennial peace. The same year brought Vicente Blasco Ibañez's novel *The Four Horsemen of the Apocalypse,* the war's global bestseller. The triumphant Hollywood adaptation of this work actually depicted the four horsemen on screen, as well as the Beast of Revelation and the Angel of Prophecy. How else could one understand the cataclysm if not in such cosmic terms? Hearing so much supernatural talk from the wounded British soldiers under her care, skeptical nurse Vera Brittain wondered what would happen if the imagined angelic protectors of British and German forces encountered each other over no-man's-land. Who would win, the Angel of Mons or the kaiser's Michael? It sounds like a page from a superhero comic book. But such mockery was rare in these tortured years.[20]

After Armageddon

A WAR THAT BEGAN with angels ended with Armageddon. While historians acknowledge the explosion of patriotic passions and God talk in 1914, they rarely acknowledge just how strongly these persisted throughout the war years and actually reached new heights during times of crisis and threatened ruin. The most intense era of spiritual excitement probably came in late 1917, when apocalyptic hopes ran high. As signs of the end times accumulated— the crescendo of slaughter on the western front, two revolutions in Holy Russia, the vision at Fátima—the British triumphed in their lengthy campaign against the Turks in Palestine. When General Sir

Edmund Allenby entered Jerusalem in 1917, American evangelical Cyrus Scofield exclaimed, "Now, for the first time, we have a real prophetic sign!" [21] Scofield was so significant because his hugely popular version of the Bible has done so much to shape evangelical thought up to the present day, especially in framing ideas about the end times and the Rapture. The following year, Allenby won his decisive victory near the hill of Megiddo, in a battle that the world's media commonly termed "Armageddon."

Of course, those millenarian hopes never materialized, and the failure or betrayal of those dreams would have catastrophic consequences for the secular world. By 1918, surrounded by the legions of bereaved and the millions of maimed, it seemed blasphemous to speak of bringing in the kingdom of God or living in the end times. But the apocalyptic impulse could not simply be dismissed as if it had never existed. As in earlier ages, the failure of apocalyptic hopes, the Great Disappointment, could be expressed in various ways. If some renounced their hopes, others found grounds for rededication, as expectations were transferred into the secular realm. In political terms as well as religious, the modern world was born in a spiritual conflagration.

That messianic and millenarian mood underlies the great revolutions that swept the world in the immediate aftermath of the war, even those that adopted the most ferocious anticlerical and antireligious rhetoric. Insurgent movements imagined future glories in terms of the triumph of history and science, of the state or race, rather than the kingdom of God. In other ways, though, the aspirations of the war years endured: the quest for communal unity and strength, enforced by the purging of unworthy elements, and pervasive themes of sacrifice and blood.

Wartime dreams and expectations found new forms of expression that often bypassed the mainline churches. In Europe, this spiritual meltdown led directly to the interwar rise of extremist and totalitarian movements, as the shifting role of churches in national affairs opened the way to pseudo religions and secular political cults. These movements freely exploited supernatural hopes and fears to justify totalitarianism and state worship, aggression, and scapegoating. They offered a new world, to be achieved by whatever means proved necessary. As Michael Burleigh describes in his studies of European religion, both Nazis and Communists drew freely on popular millenarian traditions, and mimicked the rituals and iconography of the discredited churches. The two nations with the most aggressive ideologies of holy nationhood and holy struggle in 1914 were Germany and Russia, both of which would by the 1930s claim a vanguard role in new messianic movements seeking global dominance.[22]

The sleep of religion brings forth monsters.

New Christian Worlds

THE SPIRITUAL UPHEAVAL OF the war years had lasting consequences, to the point of constituting a worldwide religious revolution. If we look back at the history of religions worldwide over the past century, a number of major themes transcend the boundaries of individual faiths. One is the secularization that has overtaken large sections of the West, especially in Europe, and the sharp decline of Europe's role as the deciding force in global religion. At the same time, we witness the corresponding rise of non-European religions. Islam has become a global force, and so have non-Western forms of Christianity. Besides secularization in Europe, any account of twentieth-century religion would also note the rise of decidedly anti-secular forces across much of the rest of the globe, including in the United States: charismatic, fundamentalist, traditionalist forms of faith. Around the world, we also see the efflorescence of esoteric and mystical ideas that we often summarize as New Age. All these trends bear the imprint of the war years—of what Andrew Preston has aptly termed "Christendom's ultimate civil war."[23]

Christianity began its most radical transformation since the time of Martin Luther. In 1914, Christianity was obviously rooted most firmly in Europe and its overseas offshoots, with all that implied for its cultural and political outlook. As Hilaire Belloc declared, "Europe is the Faith, and the Faith is Europe." The respected World Christian Database suggests that the world in 1914 had a global total of some 560 million believers: 68 percent lived in Europe, with a further 14 percent in North America. This Christian world had a geography that had been familiar for five hundred years: a tripartite division of Protestant, Catholic, and Orthodox, based overwhelmingly in Europe and North America, with some ancient outliers in the Middle East. No less familiar in historical terms was the close alliance that in most countries bound churches to the state. That Christendom model was by no means uniform, but in large swaths of what we can still unabashedly call the Christian world, churches clung limpet-like to their affiliation to the state.[24]

That world changed very rapidly. One whole branch of Christianity—the Orthodox—entered an era of appalling crisis, as the Christian world suffered its worst period of persecution in several centuries. The faith's very existence stood in peril in Russia, which had hitherto accounted for almost a quarter of the world's Christians. For the first time in centuries, European Christianity was forced to reverse its expansion, as the faith faced a rigid new frontier not too far east of Warsaw. In 1914 the Orthodox outnumbered Pentecostal and charismatic Christians by better than a hundred to one; today, Pentecostal/charismatic believers outnumber the Orthodox by three to one. But even those mainstream Catholic and Protestant churches not devastated by Communist persecution had to come to terms with a new political world, as the ancient church-state alliance was widely replaced by new forms of separation and independence.

Apart from the Russian crisis, the war terminated other phases of Christian history, while beginning vital new chapters. In the Middle East, the war was a near-terminal experience for Christian communities that could trace their religious roots to the Roman Empire—the Armenians, but also Greeks, Assyrians, Chaldeans, and Maronites. As remaining Christians struggled to survive in the new environment, they developed new political ideologies that would dominate the politics of the region into the current century.

Wartime catastrophe in one region coincided closely with the phenomenal takeoff of prophetic and charismatic native Christianity elsewhere, as black Africa began its historic rise to a central place in the Christian world. By 2030, at the latest, Africa will be the world's largest Christian continent, and most of its major churches will to some degree trace their origins to the spiritual explosion of the First World War years. While one door was closing for the church, a second massive portal was swinging open. Noting the parallels, a providentially oriented historian might suggest that God was taking the faith in a radically different direction and ending the North Atlantic captivity of the church. But a different, secular interpretation is also possible, in terms of the global effects of a world war.[25]

Rethinking Christianity

AS CHRISTIANS SOUGHT TO cope with this alarming new world, they were forced to find new bases for their faith. Most urgently, they had to reconsider the ambiguous blessings of the alliance with the secular state, which offered material rewards but at the same time required frequent compromises of principle. When churches in Germany and other nations that saw themselves as the apex of Christian civilization worshipped a God enthroned among the zeppelins, surely that proved that faith in Europe had taken a catastrophically wrong turn, succumbing to a vulgar cult of worldly power and military might. This situation was acute in Europe, where churches had an intimate and long-standing bond with states, but American clergy yielded nothing to their foreign counterparts in their willingness to transform the cross into the bayonet.

For some of the greatest Christian thinkers of the era, the war raised unsettling questions about the proper relationship between faith and the surrounding culture. Since the Enlightenment, Christian churches had struggled to determine their correct relationship to the secular state. Now, Christians confronted a state-centered modernity rooted in nationalism and militarism, which demanded that religious bodies conform to these troubling values. Many European churches succumbed to these temptations, which undermined their credibility and eventually opened the gates to secularization and pervasive skepticism. The question remains whether, in the long term, the alliance with states poisoned Christian life more lethally than did the overt persecution of atheist or Muslim regimes.

But if the holy war furor had demonstrated the scale of the moral crisis, the solution for thinkers between the world wars was not clear. Should modern-day believers shun the state and the wider culture and seek to withdraw from it, or try to reshape political entities in their own interests? Should they become more distinctive and separate in their beliefs and orthodoxies, or more accommodating to the wider culture, to the outside world? Should Christians even take up arms to resist tyrannical regimes? If the nation-state itself proved so shaky a rock, Christians might fare better as the spiritual force in a supranational united Europe that rose above older rivalries. By what authority should or could Christians live in such a world?

However agonizing the process, post–Great War churches had to abandon the traditional thought world of Christendom to return to their own resources, spiritual and intellectual. In different societies, this meant exploring ancient forms of faith, from the stern neoorthodoxy of learned Protestantism to scriptural fundamentalism, and to the widespread charismatic revival. Especially in the United States, prophetic and premillennial ideas surged. Although these ideas and movements often grew at the fringes of the churches of the day, some enjoyed spectacular success, experiencing their greatest expansion from the 1960s onward. By the end of the century, such alternative ideas would arguably constitute a new Christian mainstream, supplanting what were once "mainline" churches.

Remaking Judaism

OTHER RELIGIONS FACED PROBLEMS similar to those we have already seen within Christianity, in terms of their accommodation to states and secular cultures. Across the faith spectrum, believers had seen worlds perish. As the crisis of war discredited state alliances, believers were driven to challenge ideas of assimilation and assert new identities. Among Jews and Muslims, too, we see a revolutionary shift in attitudes to states, a new self-definition of faiths in opposition to the wider culture, and a quest for independent sources of authority and authenticity. In all the great faiths, we trace the rapid global spread of new religious styles, often claiming to return to a past of imagined purity. And as for Christians, much of the story would take place in lands far removed from the traditional centers of faith. As old assumptions perished, faiths had to find new maps—both literal and figurative—to guide their conduct.

If the twentieth century redrew the geography of Christianity, then the consequences for Judaism were still more sweeping. Obviously, Jews had not been able to depend wholly on friendly nation-states before the war, but in several countries, at least, they created workable arrangements. The crisis of war in 1914 raised hopes that the enthusiastic patriotism of Jews would lead to full recognition of their membership in the national community, to a full recognition of Jewish rights. As the war dragged on, though, anti-Semitism grew across the continent, with a venomous element of conspiracy theory. In 1916, the German government carried out a "Jewish census" to examine charges that Jewish soldiers were shirking their frontline responsibilities. For patriotic Jews, this act was a vicious betrayal that called into question everything they had taken for granted about their German loyalties. In Russia, meanwhile, the enemies of the revolution blamed the Bolshevik victory on Jewish plotting, and that theme became a mainstay of the European Right. The Jewish position in Europe seemed ever more dangerous. With theories of benevolent assimilation in ruins, writers and thinkers were driven to seek alternatives, to redefine their identity as Jews. Jewish scholars who, before the war, had lauded secularism now rediscovered much older aspects of faith, including Hasidism and Kabbalism.

But the war also created new opportunities in the form of the Balfour Declaration and the subsequent growth of Zionism—events that would have been inconceivable except in the millenarian excitement of 1917–18. As Geoffrey Wheatcroft remarked, "The First World War changed everything: without it, there would have been no Russian Revolution, no Third Reich, almost certainly no Jewish state." We might add, no modern Judaism in anything like the form in which we know it.[26]

After the Caliphs

FOR MUSLIMS, TOO, THE war changed everything. Modern political leaders look nervously at the power of radical Islam, and especially those variants of strict fundamentalism that dream of returning to a pristine Islamic order, with states founded on rigid interpretation of Islamic law, sharia. Of special concern are the extreme Islamist movements, sometimes associated with states like Saudi Arabia and Pakistan but often autonomous. Terms such as "jihad" provoke nightmares in Western political discourse. All these concepts were well known a century ago, but it was the crisis during and immediately following the war that brought them into the modern world. What we think of today as modern Islam—assertive, self-confident, and aggressively sectarian—is the product of the worldwide tumult associated with the Great War. Islam certainly existed in 1900, but the modern Islamic world order was new in 1918.

The most shocking single development for Muslims was the effective end of the caliphate. Although historic Islamic societies had never been strictly theocratic, the normal assumption was that religious authority would be backed up by a state and a sovereign. The caliph was the successor to the order created by Muhammad and the guarantor of the global unity of the *umma,* the Muslim community. Even as most Muslim societies had increasingly fallen under the sway of European Christian states, the Ottoman Empire survived into the twentieth century, and with it the caliphate. The war, though, destroyed the Ottoman realm, along with those religious structures.[27]

How could Islam survive without an explicit, material symbol at its heart? Later Muslim movements sought various ways of living in such a puzzling and barren world, and the solutions they found were very diverse: neo-orthodoxy and neo-fundamentalism, liberal modernization and nationalism, charismatic leadership and millenarianism. For many Muslims, resurgent religious loyalties trumped national or imperial allegiances. Armed Islamic resistance movements challenged most of the colonial powers in the postwar years, and some of those wars blazed for a decade after the fighting ended on the western front. That wave of armed upsurges would be instantly recognizable to an American strategist today, who is so accustomed to the idea of a turbulent Arc of Crisis stretching from North Africa through the Middle East, and into Central and Southern Asia. And for Muslim insurgents, these struggles bore the holy sanction of jihad warfare. Beyond armed resistance, activists developed specifically Islamic structures and institutions, with contours that are very familiar today.

Out of the political ferment immediately following the war came the most significant modern movements within that faith, including the most alarming forms of Islamist extremism. So did the separatism that eventually gave birth to the Islamic state of Pakistan and the heady new currents transforming Iranian Shiism. From this mayhem also emerged what would become the Saudi state, dominating the holy places and rooted in strictly traditional notions of faith.

Changes within Islam in turn had their impact on those other faiths with which Muslims had long interacted. In the enormous Indian empires, this meant Hinduism. Hindus found themselves confronting a more militant Muslim faith unwilling to tolerate easy compromises, reluctant to see themselves as a portion of a broadly defined Indian continuum. Hindus shared the same exposure to global trends as Muslims and reformulated their faith accordingly, seeking a return to basics. As Islam became more definitively and historically itself, so did Hinduism. For Hindus, as for Jews and Christians, the war began a process of redefinition and self-assertion. As for other religions, many of these changes were benevolent, in fostering a cultural and spiritual reawakening, but there were also real political dangers. In the long term, the divisions that emerged in the Great War would culminate in the ghastly Hindu-Muslim violence in 1947, which slew millions.

For Christians, Jews, Muslims, and Hindus, the war opened opportunities for wholly new political structures, and for new expressions of faith. In some regions especially—in the Middle East, Africa, and South Asia—the war transformed patterns of religious belief and sometimes of religious demography. Although at the time those other faiths and regions seemed marginal to a Eurocentric world, their importance would grow enormously as the century progressed. Hardly noticed by the West, new religious worlds were coming into being.

WITHOUT APPRECIATING ITS RELIGIOUS and spiritual aspects, we cannot understand the First World War. More important, though, the world's modern religious history makes no sense except in the context of that terrible conflict. The war created our reality.

CHAPTER ONE

The Great War
The Age of Massacre

Le feu tue.
(Firepower kills.)
—MARSHAL PHILIPPE PÉTAIN

THE GREAT WAR TOOK place in a world where many educated people thought that religion was destined to fade rapidly before the growing strength of science and technology. Yet the scale of violence in that war was so incomprehensibly vast that only religious language was adequate to the chore of describing it, or justifying it.[1]

The full horror of the war was obvious in its opening weeks. In the summer of 1914, French forces struggled to prevent what looked like a near-certain German victory, in which the invaders would shortly capture Paris and impose a humiliating peace settlement, much as actually occurred in 1940. On one single day, August 22, the French lost twenty-seven thousand men killed in battles in the Ardennes and at Charleroi, in what became known as the Battle of the Frontiers. (This was the day before the Battle of Mons, with its supposed miracle.) A French NCO reported, "Heaps of corpses, French and German, are lying every which way, rifles in hand. Rain

German soldiers setting off for the war in 1914

is falling, shells are screaming and bursting." Sounding as if he was sketching a project in a geometry class, a French officer recalled that "thousands of dead were still standing, supported as if by a flying buttress made of bodies lying in rows on top of each other in an ascending arc from the horizontal to an angle of 60 degrees." [2]

To put these casualty figures in context, the French suffered more fatalities on that one sultry day than U.S. forces lost in the two 1945 battles of Iwo Jima and Okinawa combined, although these later engagements were spread over a period of four months. One single August day cost half as many lives as the United States lost in the whole Vietnam War.

During August and September 1914, four hundred thousand French soldiers perished, and already by year's end, the war had in all claimed two million lives on both sides. The former chapel of the elite French military academy of Saint-Cyr systematically listed its dead for various wars, but for 1914 it offered only one brief entry:

"The Class of 1914"—all of it. The vast majority of dead, of course, were not professional soldiers: they were peasants and laborers, industrial workers and shop assistants. They also included a major portion of the French literary world of the day, including poet Charles Péguy and Alain-Fournier, author of the beloved coming of age novel *Le Grand Meaulnes*.[3]

Confronted with such horrors, it would be amazing if contemporaries had not believed they were entering some apocalyptic era. How could anyone understand such hideous numbers except in supernatural terms?

The Harvest of Memory

TO DESCRIBE THE CONSEQUENCES of the Great War in statistics is an overwhelming temptation, but these numbers quickly become numbing. In all, perhaps 60 million were mobilized and served in uniform, and that at a time when global population was around a quarter of what it is today. Of those, some 10 million became military fatalities. Germany lost 2 million war dead, France 1.4 million, Austria-Hungary 1.1 million, Italy almost 700,000. Russia lost 1.8 million dead in the war itself, although it is difficult to distinguish this catalog of slaughter from the still worse massacres that occurred in the prolonged civil war that began in 1918. The British Empire as a whole, including India, Canada, South Africa, and Australia, lost 1.1 million. The United States lost 114,000 military fatalities, almost all in the single year of 1918. In terms of American fatalities, the six-week-long Meuse-Argonne battle of that year remains the bloodiest battle in the nation's history. Figures for the dead take no account of the many millions more left maimed, blinded, or otherwise gravely wounded in body or mind. For each fatality, each man wounded or crippled, there was a corresponding blow to a family: the ranks of the widows and fatherless swelled.[4]

Although the Great War was more merciful on civilian populations than the second cataclysm of 1939–45 would be, millions of noncombatants did perish, chiefly in the massacres conducted by the Ottoman Turks. In Europe, too, the war hit civilian populations, as distinctions between the home front and the "real" fronts of war shrank distressingly. Some communities suffered direct attacks from aircraft or naval forces, but by far the most powerful weapon of assault was that of food. Both sides tried to starve their neighbors, hoping to drive their enemies into submission by hunger. Combining the effects of massacre and famine, the war claimed perhaps seven million civilian dead, and those figures just refer to the years 1914–18. For many parts of the world, particularly in Russia and the Middle East, much of the killing was yet to come, in what we dubiously call the "postwar" period. Nor do those statistics take account of the influenza epidemic, which took more lives than bullets and shells had done over the previous four years. Between 1918 and 1922, typhus killed three million in Russia, Poland, and Romania.[5]

The Good War?

THE SHEER SCALE OF the conflict means that it has left a potent heritage in later memory and popular culture. The war's horrors have become a central reference point in debates over war and peace, military values and unquestioning obedience. Nobody needs to explain terms like "the trenches" or "Verdun" because their symbolic associations are so inexhaustibly rich.

But in order to understand the abundant religious interpretations prevailing at the time, we need to excavate through the later strata of ideas and myths that have accreted over the decades. In particular, we must challenge the familiar idea that the war was a spasm of blundering savagery lacking any intelligible rationale or purpose, and that only the naïve would believe that either side had any moral cause or motivation worthy of the name. Recalling Barbara Tuchman's book *The Guns of August,* many believe that the great powers stumbled into war in 1914, carried away by the unstoppable momentum of an international arms race. Each nation had become so dependent on precise mobilization timetables and train schedules that they could not reverse the unintentional rush to doomsday. In this view, no side, no nation, could claim to be fighting for the right, in stark contrast to the war that erupted in 1939. The conflict was, so to speak, a war about nothing.[6]

Many nations remember the war chiefly as an exercise in futility, and an object lesson in the virtues of pacifism. This was the message of such classic films as *All Quiet on the Western Front* (1930) and *La Grande Illusion* (1937). Generations of English speakers took the same point from cherished war poets like Wilfred Owen and Siegfried Sassoon. In British and American mythology, the war was vastly worse than it need have been because of the stellar incompetence and official callousness that supposedly marked military strategy and tactics. This interpretation appears in films like *Oh! What a Lovely War* and Stanley Kubrick's *Paths of Glory* as well as the 1980s British television comedy series *Blackadder.* It is well expressed in Harry Patch's comment that the "politicians who took us to war should have been given the guns and told to settle their differences themselves, instead of organizing nothing better than legalized mass murder."[7]

This pessimistic attitude has become controversial in recent years as British governments have announced plans to commemorate the war's centennial, focusing wholly on such bloody massacres as the Somme and Passchendaele. No plans exist, apparently, to commemorate overwhelming Allied victories like the Battle of Amiens in 1918 or the succeeding Hundred Days battle, which some historians claim as the greatest achievement in a millennium of British military history. So thoroughly have subsequent generations rejected the patriotic interpretations prevailing during the Great War itself that in 2001 Britain unveiled a Shot at Dawn Memorial to commemorate soldiers executed for cowardice or desertion in those years. These presumably were martyrs for decency and humanity in a world gone insane.[8]

Yet the Western Allies did have grounds for believing they were fighting a war that was just and good, if not exactly holy, and that perception went far to shaping religious interpretations of the struggle at the time. Despite the popularity of the moral equivalence theory, we can in fact make a plausible case for German responsibility in starting the war. Since the 1960s, German historians have shown that the kaiser's regime had devised elaborate plans for aggressive war against France and Russia at least, and the only real issue was exactly when the imperial armies would strike (1912 would be too early, but on no account could they wait until 1917). In the immediate prewar years, German leaders were actively debating how best to prepare their people for the inevitable struggle between *Slawentum* and *Germanentum,* "Slavdom" and "Germandom."[9] Now, not everyone accepts the argument for German responsibility, and as far back as the 1930s, critics stressed the aggressive and reckless behavior of other countries, particularly Russia. Yet even allowing for these rival charges, Germany still remains the most convincing candidate as chief perpetrator.[10]

In terms of the conduct of the war, too, the Germans in 1914 bear some resemblance to their heirs in 1939. At the high tide of its military push in September 1914, German officials drew up a sweeping program of war aims that threatened the permanent annexation of French and Belgian territories and the destruction of French defenses and fortifications, and further demanded reparation payments that would cripple France for the foreseeable future. Scholars argue at length whether such ambitions predated the war or they just emerged ad hoc as opportunities arose following the initial victories. But whatever the answer, the German demands of late 1914 were extraordinarily aggressive by the standards of recent decades.[11]

While its Western schemes remained in the realm of aspiration, the Second Reich really did succeed in imposing comparable terms on a defeated Russia in 1918, in the Treaty of Brest-Litovsk. Under this arrangement, Russia would be pushed far east of its current borders, losing its teeming subject peoples to German control. Russia would have lost fifty million of its people and three hundred thousand square miles of territory. The country would also have lost its industrial base, forfeiting most of its coal and iron reserves. These plans also neatly foreshadowed the ambitions of the Third Reich in 1942. If not an actual Carthaginian peace, in which one side seeks to annihilate the other, Brest-Litovsk was a close modern parallel. It also gives an idea of the kind of peace that the Germans would have inflicted on a defeated Britain or France, or even the United States. The German proposal for alliance with Mexico included renewed Mexican sovereignty over Texas, Arizona, and New Mexico.

The War of the Beast

THE FACT THAT A German flag might have flown over European provinces previously subject to Russia or France need have meant little in itself, provided that local subjects continued to live their everyday lives much as they had always done. But in critical ways, the experience of German occupation in the First World War foreshadowed the conditions of the Second.

Certainly, German would-be conquerors of 1914 operated under rules very different from Hitler's Wehrmacht, and many of the atrocity tales soon proved to be bogus. Today, we cringe when we look back at the outrageous charges of an American anti-German pamphleteer like Newell Dwight Hillis, a Congregationalist minister:

> **Think of the catalogue! Babies nailed like rats to the doors of houses! Children skewered on a bayonet midst the cheers of**

marching Germans—as if the child were a quail, skewered on
a fork! Matrons, old men and priests slaughtered; young Italian
officers with throats cut and hanging on hooks in butchers'
shops; the bombing of Red Cross hospitals and nurses and the
white flag; everything achieved by civilized man defiled and
destroyed.[12]

(We have already met Hillis advocating the extermination of the
German race.) Equally dubious is the portrayal of German behavior
in such successful films as *The Heart of Humanity* and D. W. Griffith's
Hearts of the World. In both, Germans are stereotyped as ruthless,
lecherous brutes, and both depicted rape or near rape as best they
could without trampling contemporary standards of obscenity.

One of the most successful propaganda images of the era concerned the young Canadian soldier reportedly crucified in the
trenches near Ypres in April 1915. After the Germans captured a
young sergeant, "he was found transfixed to the wooden fence of a
farm building. Bayonets were thrust through the palms of his hands
and his feet, pinning him to the fence. He had been repeatedly
stabbed with bayonets, and there were many punctured wounds
in his body." The tale of hellish German behavior echoed around
the world and was widely reported in newspapers and pamphlets.
It also became the subject of propaganda posters and featured in
an American propaganda film, *The Prussian Cur*. On a larger scale,
Western nations believed the legend that the Germans were ren-
dering corpses for industrial purposes, turning human flesh and fat
into tallow. The florid atrocity tales of these years would have a
disastrous unintended consequence in the 1940s, when Allied policy
makers, not wishing to be duped a second time, initially refused
to credit emerging accounts of the Holocaust. (The corpse factory
legend is indeed bogus, but the story of the crucified Canadian does,
oddly, have a basis in fact.)[13]

In retrospect, claims about German war atrocities have not been

German atrocities committed during their invasion of Belgium in 1914 continued to shock Allied public opinion throughout the war. This painting is one of the War Series by American realist painter George Bellows (1918).

treated too seriously in Anglo-American popular memory, and they fade into insignificance when we set aside the events of Hitler's war. But Wilhelmine Germany, too, had its share of atrocities, when whole regions and populations were treated as pawns to be sacrificed to the war effort.

The German treatment of Belgium was abominable. At the height of their invasion in August and September of 1914, the Germans slaughtered six thousand civilians in Belgium and northern France, most (falsely) on the suspicion of being *francs-tireurs* (snipers) or saboteurs. Commonly, nervous soldiers entering a town heard what they took to be gunfire, which might or might not have come from their own lines. They responded by burning and bombing houses, taking hostages, and executing prisoners. The German army earned worldwide condemnation by sacking the historic city of Louvain. They torched the library and its collection of rare books and manuscripts, and soldiers carried out random mass shootings. While such a crime would scarcely have earned a footnote in Russia in 1942, this was appalling by the standards of an earlier era—at least, when inflicted on white Europeans.[14]

Throughout the war, the Germans treated their occupied populations dreadfully, in Belgium and elsewhere, imposing forced labor and supplying starvation rations. In 1916, the Germans deported seven hundred thousand Belgians to work in their farms and factories, transporting many in cattle trucks. When the Germans withdrew to a new defensive line in northern France in the winter of 1916–17, Operation Alberich, they engaged in a scorched earth campaign that prefigures German withdrawals from Ukraine a generation later.[15]

If events had developed differently, the Germans might have established their rule securely over the vast regions of eastern Europe granted to them at Brest-Litovsk. In that case, they probably would have created there a servile society foreshadowing the Nazi era. In occupied Poland and the Baltic, German overlords already had a strong ideology of racial supremacy. The influential General Erich Ludendorff had far-reaching plans for the full-scale Germanization and ethnic cleansing of conquered eastern Europe, with the Crimea as a German colony. He also regarded Jews as the source of most evils in the modern world.[16]

In a counterfactual world of German victory, Germany would never have fallen to Hitler, not because the country would somehow have retained its moral moorings but because it would already have won everything the Nazis promised. Germany would have held total mastery of Europe and almost infinite *Lebensraum* in the east, complete with millions of serfs. If the Second Reich had succeeded, Germany would not have needed a Third. If Germany had won the Great War, Hitler would have been superfluous.

No side in this war had a monopoly of atrocities. The Germans denounced the British for a catalog of atrocities that included the use of devastating dum-dum ammunition, and they reasonably regarded the British blockade of food supplies as a severe crime against humanity. The Russians, moreover, were no strangers to massacres and ethnic cleansing, particularly of Poles and Jews in their western border regions, which inflicted casualties far higher than anything the Germans ever caused in Belgium. Yet for all this, the moral differences between the two world wars are considerably less than is widely accepted today, and the Good War rhetoric more appropriate.

Apocalypse Soon

ADDING TO THE WAR'S shock value was its unexpected course and duration. Although a European or even global war as such was not surprising of itself, few predicted the conflict would last as long as it did, would rage at that intensity, or would wield anything like as much destructive power. Nor did most foresee that its scope would extend to most of the inhabited world.

Accounts of the outbreak of war commonly stress the great and lasting peace that had prevailed for many years before 1914, making the sudden violence appear startling. In fact, war scares involving the major powers had been almost annual events for twenty years beforehand, and the main question was which particular constellation of alliances might be involved. After the formation of the Anglo-French Entente in 1904, the most likely clash involved Germany on the one hand versus some combination of rival powers. The number and severity of crises accelerated, with a dangerous confrontation between the Russians and the Habsburg Empire in Bosnia in 1908–1909. Just two years later, Europe came close to war over the control of Morocco.[17]

Awareness of approaching menace was not confined to professional diplomats. For twenty years before the outbreak of war, novelists had speculated about the coming of a European conflict, creating a popular fantasy genre. Sometimes these forecasts were accurate in identifying the chief participants, with a German-British clash as the war's centerpiece. The 1903 thriller *The Riddle of the Sands* imagined a German plot for a surprise naval assault on eastern

England. In 1908, H. G. Wells's *The War in the Air* foresaw a near-future global war fought by vast air fleets, in a multisided high-tech conflict between the United States, Germany, the British Empire, and an East Asian confederation.

But if few were surprised by the outbreak of a major war in 1914, its chronology was a different matter. Any knowledge of recent history suggested that a coming war would involve an intense spasm of violence, but in a short space of time. Obvious models for a likely conflict would be the Austro-Prussian War of 1866—the Seven Weeks War—or even better, the Franco-Prussian conflict of 1870, in which the vast majority of actual maneuver warfare and combat was over within a month or so. The war of 1914, surely, would be just that, a whirlwind affair of a single season. Like its recent predecessors, moreover, it would rage chiefly through the high summer, presumably culminating in a grand decisive battle. In fact, it would unfold very much like the later struggle of May and June 1940. If the Franco-Prussian War was a reliable guide, then the coming conflict would probably claim some hundreds of thousands of fatalities, rather than multiple millions. Religious believers set no such restrictions on the casualty list, in a cosmic struggle that would engulf the world, but they too thought in terms of a swift and devastating judgment. The war of 1914 simply would not leave a 1915 for anyone to bother about.[18]

But of course it did leave a 1915, and subsequent years as well. The war lasted far longer than most had reason to expect, and it soon became apparent that it would be much bloodier. It would also involve technologies hitherto unsuspected by anyone, except for the most far-sighted readers of H. G. Wells.

Whatever the underlying rivalries, the immediate cause of the war was the perennial tensions in the Balkans.[19] In June 1914, an assassin killed an Austrian archduke in Sarajevo, leading Austria-Hungary to demand humiliating concessions from Serbia. Russia intervened to defend Serbia, drawing the tsar's French allies into

German soldiers setting off on what the graffiti on the train
announce as an excursion to Paris

the messy situation. Germany, in turn, supported Austria. As expected, Germany began its westward campaign on August 3, violating Belgian neutrality. This act provoked Britain into joining the war on the side of France and Russia. In contemporary parlance, the French-British-Russian grouping constituted the Allies, or the Triple Entente, confronting the German-Austrian Central Powers (Mittelmächte). Other combatants were drawn in over the next two years, the Turks and Bulgarians on the German side and Japan, Italy, and Romania in the Allied cause.

Initially the war seemed to be following the predictions of a short, sharp struggle on the lines of 1870 as the German army implemented its ambitious Schlieffen Plan. If all went according to plan, the German operation would take six weeks, and at first their prospects seemed excellent. But the German assault went awry. Through August and September, French and German armies fought a titanic series of battles with names scarcely known in the Anglophone world—Namur, Sambre, Ardennes—which together

German infantry advance. As the war opened in August 1914,
both sides hoped for a war of rapid movement.

made up the Battle of the Frontiers. By the start of September, the
Germans stood on the edge of victory, with Paris just thirteen miles
from their front lines. And yet they failed to encircle and destroy
the French forces, to draw their foes into a decisive *Kesselschlacht*
(cauldron battle). Instead, the French organized a heroic resistance
at the Marne, recovering to the point that by September 9 they
were themselves on the verge of surrounding and annihilating the
invaders, who were forced to withdraw. Two million fought at the
Marne, a quarter of whom became casualties. The French lauded
the victory in supernatural terms, as the Miracle of the Marne.[20]

For secular historians, the Marne marked a key turning point in
world history, in preventing the Germans winning a swift victory,
forcing both sides into a long-drawn-out struggle. By December,
winter was setting in and the rival armies dug in, literally.

The Trenches

CONTRARY TO EXPECTATIONS, THEN, the war entered a
static phase of entrenched warfare that lasted, broadly, through the
German collapse in the fall of 1918. At their height, the trench sys-

tems would run for a length of 475 miles. Along that span, though, the trench lines did not move more than a few miles in either direction between 1914 and 1918. The resulting Edge City was home to several million fighters, making it, grotesquely, one of the world's largest urban centers.

Trench warfare has, rightly, left ghastly memories, but the phenomenon deserves some explanation if we are ever to understand why nations could ever get into this situation, and why they could not extricate themselves. Why did the competing sides allow themselves to be trapped in a seemingly eternal vortex of slaughter and squalor? According to a common stereotype, First World War generals were utterly lacking in imagination and forced their troops to dig themselves into holes in the ground from which they could hardly ever emerge. They and their enemies took turns in repeatedly launching futile attacks against impregnable fortifications, with inevitably dire consequences. In the British comedy series *Blackadder*, a junior officer despairs when he discovers the top-secret plan being unveiled by his high command. As he asks, "Now, would this brilliant plan involve us climbing out of our trenches and walking slowly toward the enemy, sir? . . . It's the same plan that we used last time, and the seventeen times before that." One definition of insanity is repeating the same act over and over again and expecting different consequences.[21]

The evils of the war—and its static quality—are epitomized by Ypres, the picturesque medieval town in the Belgian region of Flanders, which became the setting for five separate battles between 1914 and 1918. The five battles combined inflicted a million and a quarter casualties, including dead, wounded, and missing. For the British and Canadians, the haunted name of Ypres still symbolizes the pointless mass sacrifice of a generation of young men in Flanders fields. Within a fifty-mile radius of Ypres, we find such other names of accursed memory as Neuve-Chapelle, Loos, and Vimy. The fact that so much action occurred around one small town demonstrates

One of the war's iconic images: British casualties of
German gas warfare, April 1918

how little the front actually moved in this time. The war utterly destroyed the town itself, while the surrounding countryside was subjected to such repeated bombardments by both sides—by artillery
and poison gas—that the soil and water were thoroughly poisoned.
Much of the area resembled a lunar landscape.[22]

Ypres also witnessed the first use of military technologies that
initially seemed uniquely frightening, and indeed served chiefly as
terror weapons. One, of course, was poison gas. From late 1914,
various combatant powers had experimented with different kinds
of chemical weaponry, including tear gas, but in April 1915, at the
second battle of Ypres, the Germans attacked with chlorine. The
Allies soon organized themselves to respond, and the British recip-
rocated at Loos that September. By 1917, both sides were using the
still more lethal mustard gas. The gas weapon contributed mightily
to the war's nightmare quality.[23]

In a sense, all wars involve the same roster of horrors, but what
made this conflict different was the unimaginable scale on which
they were inflicted. From countless memoirs, we might turn to

Harry Patch, the last British veteran of the struggle. Naturally, he was most affected by the carnage, as men all around him died brutally: "It wasn't a case of seeing them with a nice bullet hole in their tunic, far from it." They were blown to pieces. In the words of a French Jesuit who served as an army sergeant at Verdun, "To die from a bullet seems to be nothing; parts of our being remain intact; but to be dismembered, torn to pieces, reduced to pulp, this is a fear that flesh cannot support and which is fundamentally the great suffering of the bombardment." British veteran Henry Allingham recalled spending a night in a shell hole: "It stank. So did I when I fell into it. Arms and legs, dead rats, dead everything. Rotten flesh. Human guts. I couldn't get a bath for three or four months afterwards." Animal corpses also abounded. The British alone used a million horses and mules in the war, and a quarter of those died violently. A million German horses died.[24]

Patch likewise stressed the lingering memories of the overpowering stench, a sickening mix of rotting corpses, latrines, unwashed bodies, and the creosote used to prevent infection. The only relief was in the sweeter smell of tobacco, as ubiquitous cigarettes continued their conquest of the planet. The stench of war is a dominant theme of many war memoirs, and of contemporary observations. When the Germans marched west in 1914, a U.S. correspondent remarked on "the smell of a half-million unbathed men, the stench of a menagerie raised to the nth power. That smell lay for days over every town through which the Germans passed." Describing his Flanders battle positions in 1915, German officer Rudolf Binding noted, "One is overcome by a peculiar sour, heavy, and penetrating smell of corpses. . . . Men that were killed last October lie half in swamp and half in the yellow sprouting beet-fields. . . . Nobody minds the pale Englishman who is rotting away a few steps farther up. . . . Such is a six months old battlefield." An observer at Verdun claimed that the reek of putrefaction was so bad as almost to make the sweet smell of gas shells seem preferable.[25]

The only thing conceivably worse than the smell was the eardrum-shattering noise of battle. At Passchendaele, the only analogy Patch could find for the artillery fire was "non-stop claps of thunder. It took your breath away. The noise was ferocious. You couldn't hear the man next to you speaking." Such remarks are such a familiar part of wartime memoirs that we sometimes fail to register just how devastating the constant barrage of noise could be, both physically and emotionally. Repeated exposure to shellfire reduced strong men to quivering wrecks who would seek any means of escaping the situation, even if that meant risking charges of desertion and facing a firing squad. After several days under incessant bombardment at this front, another German soldier remarked, "The torture and the fatigue, not to mention the strain on the nerves, were indescribable." He could have been speaking for millions more.[26]

The conditions of the war naturally angered and brutalized the participants, a point that needs stressing in light of the acts of chivalry and humanity that certainly did occur. Ypres was the front where British and German soldiers began the celebrated Christmas Truce of 1914, emerging from their trenches to fraternize, drink, and even play friendly games of soccer. (The unofficial peace spread along much of the front, and French forces participated widely.) This has become one of the best-remembered moments of the First World War, a moment frequently depicted in films, fiction, and popular songs. The brief moment sends an optimistic message about wars and ideological struggles, which supposedly result from rows between governments and elites, while ordinary people maintain their basic human decency.[27]

Actually, it is all too easy to romanticize such moments, and chivalrous gestures were often rebuffed. The Germans rarely honored British attempts to apply gentlemanly standards to combat, dismissing them as the *Sportsidiotismus* of overgrown children. Prolonged contact further discouraged friendly relations and made both sides even harsher in their treatment of the enemy. Soldiers' letters

The war's brief shining moment: fraternization
during the Christmas Truce of 1914

on both sides show that surrenders often were not accepted, and
prisoners were massacred on the battlefield. One British officer recalled the surrender of a German unit at the Somme:

> And I must say that they fought most stubbornly and bravely.
> Probably not more than 300–500 put their hands up. They
> took it out of us badly, but we did ditto, and—I have no
> shame in saying so—as every German should in my opinion
> be exterminated—I don't know that we took *one*. I have not
> seen a man or officer yet who did anyway.[28]

Breaking Through

HOWEVER SAVAGE THE NEW patterns of combat, the practice of
trench warfare betokened neither incompetence nor despair, nor a
refusal to contemplate innovation. In different forms, it was used by
many armies throughout history, often as a preparation for success-

ful attacks. The Great War, after all, ended when Allied armies used those notorious trenches as the basis for triumphant assaults that crushed their German foes in 1918.

The fundamental problem that armies faced in this era was that the rise of the machine gun had decisively shifted the always-delicate balance between offense and defense to the massive advantage of the defender, who could hold his position indefinitely. Initially, the French and British were slow to learn critical lessons about the superiority of defense, and a series of offensives in 1915 resulted in disasters that came close to justifying the *Blackadder* stereotype. Loos especially was an object lesson in what happened when an army advanced without enough artillery over uncut barbed wire: thousands died for a zero gain of ground. The French also believed, quite wrongly, that a courageous and determined advance could overcome well-placed machine guns. In the Artois offensive that spring, an officer reported seeing three hundred French soldiers lying dead in a neat line. "At the first whistling of bullets, the officers had cried 'Line up!' and all went to death as in a parade." Even after Allied armies abandoned their romantic illusions about plucky fighting spirit and gallant frontal assaults, they still had to face the practical problems of finding weapons and tactics sophisticated enough to restore the advantage to the attackers.[29]

But invent and innovate they did. Technological innovation surged during the war, to a degree that makes nonsense of the familiar cliché of the army commanders as hidebound reactionaries who could not wait to get back to the cavalry charges they knew and loved. We see this from the rapid evolution of chemical warfare after 1915, not to mention the development of tanks. Even those elaborate trench systems were heroic triumphs of engineering and mining, which we should properly regard as monuments to scientific achievement quite as significant as the aircraft that dominated the skies above them. Ultimately, the war would be won by the side that best mastered the use of artillery, to ensure that no effective enemy positions remained to harass one's own advancing forces. This not only meant designing and mass manufacturing shells that could penetrate enemy fortifications but also ensuring that they exploded predictably according to plan. It also demanded something like a scientific revolution in the technology of aiming and coordinating heavy guns. Technological innovation had to go together with a total reorganization and rationalization of industrial society, and an unprecedented mobilization of civilian labor. Not until 1917 would either side achieve real success in these areas.[30]

In the meantime, the different armies somehow had to break through the enemy lines, although with the virtual certainty that this would mean intolerable casualties. And at least until 1918, that horrific decision had to be taken by the Allies rather than the Germans—not because British and French commanders were more inept or sadistic than their rivals but because of basic strategic realities. By the end of 1914, the Germans occupied most of Belgium and portions of northeastern France, which they defended by intricate fortifications. The French lands occupied were not large in absolute terms, but they were enormously significant economically as well as symbolically. In the peace settlement of 1871, France had lost most of its two historic provinces of Alsace and Lorraine, and the amputation of those regions still caused national agony forty years later. A new peace settlement might involve the reduction of French sovereignty over still more borderlands, bringing the German frontier ever closer to Paris itself.

The British likewise faced an existential threat. As long as the Germans occupied Belgium and parts of the northern French coast, they posed a constant threat of an amphibious assault on England and a quick strike at London. In order to remain an independent nation, Britain could accept no settlement that left that coast in German hands; Germany would accept no settlement that did not. The September 1914 wish list of German war aims envisaged Belgium and the Netherlands becoming de facto members of the

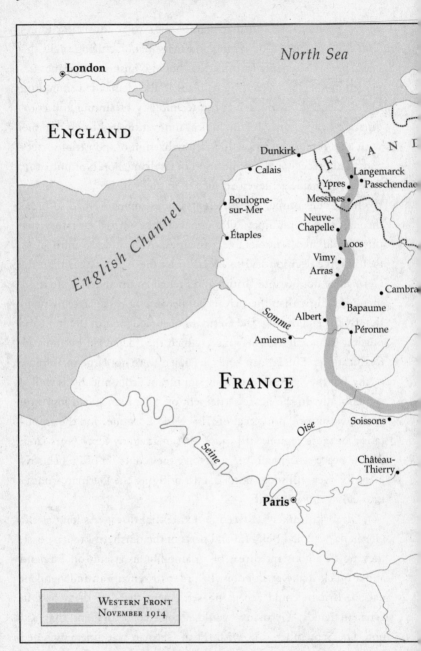

North Sea

London

ENGLAND

F L A N D I

Dunkirk
Calais
Langemarck
Ypres · Passchendae
Messines
Boulogne-
sur-Mer
Neuve-
Chapelle
Étaples
Loos
Vimy
Arras
Cambra
English Channel
Bapaume
Somme
Albert
Péronne
Amiens

FRANCE

Oise
Soissons

Seine
Château-
Thierry

Paris

WESTERN FRONT
NOVEMBER 1914

GERMANY

BELGIUM

•Louvain

sels⊙

Meuse

ons   Namur•

harleroi•   Sambre

Rhine

ARDENNES
FOREST

Moselle

LUXEMBOURG

Sedan•

ARGONNE
FOREST

Meuse

Reims   LORRAINE

Verdun•

CHAMPAGNE

Marne

Saint-Mihiel•

ALSACE

Rhine

German Empire, ensuring that British coasts would be permanently indefensible.

If Germany merely held its gains without adding another inch of French soil, both England and France faced the near-certain prospect of being reduced to client states of Germany. In order to win the war, the Germans just had to sit on their recent gains and defend them, so that they could win the war by standing still. By 1916, moreover, they possessed sixteen thousand machine guns on the western front alone. The French and British had no option but to maintain their attacks, and the only place to do that successfully was in the main theater of operations, on the western front, in and around places like Ypres. The war would be one of siege and reduction rather than movement and maneuver.

War in the East

WITH SO MUCH BLOODSHED under way on the western front, it is hard to believe that eastern Europe was the scene of comparable or even greater violence. Throughout the war, though, the eastern front was twice the length of the western, and more men were involved in fighting.

When the Germans contemplated war in 1914, they recognized two main foes, namely the modern and efficient French army and the vast Russian forces that were in the middle of a sweeping modernization. The Russian threat played a key role in driving the Germans to launch a preemptive war in 1914. The nightmare scenario was that the Russians would invade eastern Prussia, devastating the landed estates that supported the German officer corps. It was a critical event when, in late August, the Germans took the initiative and destroyed a powerful Russian force at Tannenberg in East Prussia. In this epochal German victory, the Russians suffered eighty thousand dead, as against just five thousand Germans. (The disgraced Russian commander shot himself.) Tannenberg made a national hero of the German commander Paul von Hindenburg, who came to dominate the empire from 1916 onward. Hindenburg's chief of staff, Erich Ludendorff, effectively directed the war effort in those years.[31]

But the Russians remained in the fight and maintained their pressure on Germany's ally, Austria-Hungary. In 1915, the two empires fought in the Carpathians, focusing on the besieged fortress of Przemyśl, near the present-day border between Poland and Ukraine. The resulting combat was particularly bloody because of the wasteful usage of large armies of peasant conscripts, who fought in conditions of bitter cold and hopelessly inadequate logistics. Apart from gas and shells, fighters faced death from frostbite and starvation. Nor could prisoners expect much mercy. The Russians spared few who surrendered, and the Germans and Austro-Hungarians followed suit. A modern historian calls the Carpathian winter war "the Stalingrad of World War I . . . one of the most ill-conceived campaigns of the war." Given the fierce competition for this title, that is a stunning evaluation.[32]

German assistance allowed the Habsburg armies to win a convincing victory over the Russians in the Gorlice-Tarnów campaign of 1915, but at frightening cost. The Romanov and Habsburg Empires each lost over a million casualties, making this campaign bloodier than Verdun or the Somme.

The Age of Massacre

THE ENORMOUS SCALE OF the war's casualties was partly a matter of new military technologies, but it also reflected changed attitudes to human life. A number of unsettling cultural influences were reshaping attitudes to the conduct of warfare, and these encouraged the view that enemy populations could and should be wholly removed. One factor was the imperial experience, which most of the combatant powers now shared, and the values they now brought back to European soil. For a century before 1914, it was an open secret that Europeans in Africa and Asia did not observe the rules of war that might prevail with their white neighbors, so that victorious armies rarely took prisoners.[33]

By the standards of the time, civilized Europeans knew such violence could not properly be visited on fellow whites, but restraints slackened when soldiers believed that they were fighting for the survival of their nation and race. The popularity of social Darwinism promoted a view of warfare as a struggle between races, in which weaker populations might be destined to perish, to be removed for the benefit of stronger stocks. That was quite separate from the religious idea that enemy nations were serving diabolical forces and viciously impeding the coming of God's earthly reign. The language of racial purification and extermination was already appearing in this war, although not as centrally as it would in the 1940s.[34]

Just as colonial habits of fighting lowered the value placed on human life, so also did the influence of warfare in eastern and southeastern Europe. Centuries of struggle between races and religions in this region had created vicious traditions of ethnic cleansing and atrocities against civilians. An international commission investigating atrocities in the Balkan Wars of 1912–13 declared that in the Balkans, above all, "it has become a competition, as to who can best dispossess and 'denationalize' his neighbor." Several combatant nations had recent experiences in these regions, including Italy and Austria as well as Russia and Turkey. Other nations, too, became involved during the continuing Balkan struggles that merged with the larger world war. In consequence, fighting on these fronts had a barbaric quality that will be familiar to anyone who knows the Balkan experience in the 1940s, or indeed in the 1990s. By 1918, Serbia alone had lost over a quarter of its 1914 population. Although he may not have needed much training in the art of savagery, one war correspondent in the Balkan theater was Leon Trotsky, later to be a notoriously ruthless commander in the Bolshevik Revolution. Like his counterparts in the Balkans, Trotsky had no compunction about executing prisoners in the thousands, slaughtering hostages, or punishing entire populations by devastating their crops and homes.[35]

The Dead Marshes

JUST AS EUROPEANS THOUGHT they were getting used to what was now the normal conduct of warfare, 1916 and 1917 brought new transformations and a drastic escalation of the scale and savagery of combat. Already the battles of 1914 were almost looking like an age of relative innocence.[36]

The year 1916 witnessed the epic slaughter of Verdun, a battle of many undesirable superlatives. As Alistair Horne remarks, it was the longest battle in history and created "the battlefield with the highest density of dead per square yard that has probably ever been known." That February, the Germans launched a massive offensive to capture the key fortress that was the centerpiece in one of the world's most powerful networks of military fortifications. However, their aim was not so much to win any piece of ground as to force the French to defend the place at all costs, to begin a battle of attrition that would kill millions of France's best and strongest young citizens—in the language of the time, to bleed the country white. The resulting battles were focused on a narrow front of fifteen miles, where the intensity of destruction beggared belief. In five months, the two sides fired a combined total of twenty-three million shells. By May, it seemed as if the Germans would win their objective and France might be forced out of the war, but the French held their positions. When the battle ended in December, it had inflicted eight hundred thousand French and German casualties.[37]

In order to relieve pressure on the French line at Verdun, Gen-

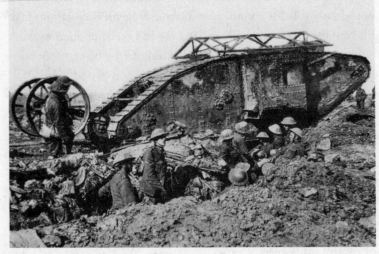

A British tank in action at the Somme, September 1916

eral Douglas Haig planned an offensive on the river Somme, which would begin with one of the greatest artillery bombardments in history. So confident was Haig of the devastating effects of the shelling that he hoped his infantry would have little to do but pick through the shattered remnants of the German army. The plan went horrifically wrong. Many British shells failed to explode, and those that did were simply inadequate to penetrate deeply entrenched German positions. Nor was the wire cut as it should have been. British infantry were mowed down by machine guns, and the massacre continued long after British commanders should have realized the new situation. By the end of that dreadful July 1, British and empire forces had lost almost sixty thousand casualties, and nineteen thousand lay dead, in the worst military disaster in British history. The Somme battle continued until November, with an eventual loss of over a million casualties on both sides, and all for virtually nothing in terms of territorial gains or losses. Six hundred thousand Allied casualties gained six miles of French ground. The Somme battle left uniquely dreadful memories because of the overwhelming images of Flanders mud, after heavy rains saturated a landscape already torn up by artillery bombardment. Soldiers fought and died in a literal sea of mud, and actual death by drowning was a serious danger.[38]

While the casualties were escalating, the nature of warfare was changing swiftly and horribly. Nowhere is this more obvious than on the Somme, which British historians often depict entirely in terms of the catastrophic first day. What such a portrait misses is the uncomprehending shock that the Germans themselves encountered as the British unleashed the full horrors of total industrial warfare over the following months. By this point, not only had the British corrected the errors in their artillery, they were deploying aircraft, poison gas, and, soon, tanks. Moreover, the Allies were learning to use these weapons in concert. The battle killed one hundred seventy thousand Germans, quite apart from other casualties.

The psychological effects defied the capacities of human language. One observer was Ernst Jünger, author of perhaps the finest account of the war, *Storm of Steel*. Arriving on the Somme in August, he gazed with awe:

> Ahead of us rumbled and thundered artillery fire of a volume we had never dreamed of: a thousand quivering lightnings bathed the western horizon in a sea of flame. . . . Because of racking pains in our heads and ears, communication was possible only by odd, shouted words. The ability to think logically and the feeling of gravity, both seemed to have been removed. We had the sensation of the ineluctable and the unconditionally necessary, as if we were facing an elemental force. . . . Abandon all hope![39]

Another German officer wrote, "Somme. The whole history of the world cannot contain a more ghastly word." When Corporal Adolf Hitler arrived on the Somme in September, he encountered a scene "more like hell than war." At the time, that was scarcely an original observation, as this language was commonly used both of the Somme and Verdun. German writers spoke of "the hell of Verdun" or referred to Moloch, the hungry pagan god who feasted on young human lives. Poet Rudolf Binding was despairing about this "final battle":

> **War beats us into pulp**
> **In horrible clouds of smoke.**[40]

There was an overwhelming temptation to frame the Somme in supernatural or mythological terms. His "hideous" memories of the battle contributed powerfully to the scenes of war and desolation later penned by the twenty-four-year-old officer J. R. R. Tolkien, who was at the front from July through late October. In *The Lord of the Rings,* hobbit Sam Gamgee is horrified to look into a bog in the Dead Marshes and reports, "There are dead things, dead faces in the water," he said with horror. "Dead faces!" Frodo Baggins explained,

> "They lie in all the pools, pale faces, deep deep under the dark water. I saw them: grim faces and evil, and noble faces and sad. Many faces proud and fair, and weeds in their silver hair. But all foul, all rotting, all dead." . . .
> "Yes, yes," said Gollum. "All dead, all rotten. Elves and Men and Orcs. The Dead Marshes. There was a great battle long ago."

Sam was Tolkien's composite tribute to the ordinary British soldiers who had served under him, to the millions of real-life counterparts of Harry Patch.[41]

Together, Verdun and the Somme killed over a million soldiers. More disturbing than any single story of combat or massacre is the planning process of each side, the lethal mathematics under which each power operated. Each regime looked at its own population, calculated how many military units that figure might generate, and projected how many million soldiers each side could lose before the process of attrition would force it to withdraw. As France's Marshal Joseph Joffre declared in 1915, "We shall kill more of the enemy than he can kill of us." Soon, generals would be scrutinizing their regular casualty reports and worrying that particular units were not losing men at the expected rate: Did those formations have a problem with morale or leadership?

Nations were planning, calmly and rationally, on sacrificing multiple millions of their own people.

The War at Home

THIS WAS ALSO A catastrophic time for the home fronts of the struggling nations, a statement that runs contrary to the general Anglo-American stereotype of the war. While a vast corpus of literature in English recounts the evils of the front line and the trenches, the civilian experience is usually told in terms of military production, not to mention the despairing fears of families awaiting news of loved ones. But any war is a matter of logistics and supplies, and ensuring that enemies no longer have the wherewithal to continue the fight. In the Great War, that meant seeking to cut off all useful supplies to enemy nations, all war materials, and in the context of the time, that also meant food for civilian populations. The Germans tried to sink enough Allied shipping to starve Britain into submission, while the vastly superior British navy ensured that Germany could not import the food it needed to maintain its population. This was a war of food and fuel.

The Germans failed and the British succeeded. Despite some anxious times in 1917, British civilians never came close to real starvation, but their German and Austrian counterparts assuredly did. In 1916 and 1917, Central Europe suffered a disastrous famine that claimed perhaps a million lives, in a close parallel to the celebrated Irish famine of the 1840s. For Germans, the last months of 1916 were the *Kohlrübenwinter* (turnip winter). Normally, turnips were fed to cattle, but they now provided desperate people with their last resort. We can argue about the immediate cause of the disaster. Immediately, of course, the Allies were to blame for cutting food supplies, but scholars also cite official German decisions to concentrate food supplies on soldiers and war workers at the expense of everyone else, who became dispensable.[42]

But however we interpret the food shortages, they had a cascading effect as they left people vulnerable to a range of debilitating diseases, including scurvy and dysentery. Also, famine and general weakness prepared the way for the later influenza pandemic. Still better, from the British point of view, increasing desperation in German cities in 1917 provoked Reich authorities to strike harder at British supply routes through unrestricted submarine warfare. This meant targeting U.S. shipping, a strategy that would inevitably bring that nation into the war. The blockade persisted for several months after the 1918 Armistice, an additional insult that infuriated even moderate Germans.[43]

However little trace the great blockade has left in the Anglo-American mind, the event was deeply traumatic for Germans. The famine goes a long way to explaining the fury of ordinary people at their defeat after the immense costs they had suffered, not just frontline soldiers but ordinary women and children. This awful experience also explains German cynicism about any Allied claims about war crimes and atrocities. For Germans, nothing their own forces had ever done in Belgium or elsewhere came close to the mass murder of civilians perpetrated by Allied navies.

THE WAR MARKED THE end of a world. Whichever side eventually triumphed, the old international order was shattered, and empires and nations would be utterly remade, through a process of extraordinary mass violence, of blood and famine, and through the construction of astonishing futuristic weaponry. In a Western world in which most educated people had at least some background in Christian teachings, religious language and imagery inevitably provided a structure to comprehend the global changes.

NEUVE-CHAPELLE — Le Champ de Bataille — Le Christ des tranchées
The Christ of the trenches

The Christ of the Trenches. In this 1915 postcard, a shattered crucifix produces an image of Christ gazing in agony over the battlefield.

CHAPTER TWO

God's War
Christian Nations, Holy Warfare, and the Kingdom of God

In a world gone pagan, what is a Christian to do? For the world is gone pagan. Members of the body of Christ are tearing one another, and His body is bleeding as it once bled on Calvary, but this time the wounds are dealt by His friends. It is as though Peter were driving home the nails, and John were piercing the side.

—WILLIAM TEMPLE

THE COMBATANT POWERS USED many rationales to justify their involvement in the spreading war and its enormous human toll. Variously, they spoke of national interest and honor, of self-defense and even national survival. Persistently, though, on all sides, governments, media, and cultural figures presented these arguments in highly religious forms. Although modern memory recalls Christmas 1914 for the great unofficial truce in the trenches, a splendid moment of peace and sanity, contemporaries offered quite different and more cosmic interpretations. This was the setting of Paul Claudel's dream of divine vengeance in his violently anti-German play *Christmas Eve 1914*. Another celebrated French author of the time was Louis-Ferdinand Céline (Louis-Ferdinand Destouches), a decorated war hero who was at that time recuperating from severe battle wounds. He was baffled to see how seriously so many of his contemporaries took the rhetoric of sacred war. "Decidedly," he wrote, "I found myself embarked on an apocalyptic crusade." Every combatant nation produced similar expressions of sanctified nationalism, reaching as far as Claudel in their identification of God's will with national interest. This was God's Great War.[1]

God's Wrath

GIVEN THE DREADFUL CONNOTATIONS that the war has acquired over the years, it is difficult to imagine Christian leaders at the time responding to these actions with anything other than grief and revulsion. Nor did they have an excuse for failing to appreciate the nature of the war. Paris was never more than a hundred miles from the hardest-contested sections of the western front, which on occasion crept much closer to the city. Journalists could visit the front and return in a day, and then circulate stories and images worldwide via telephone and telegraph. Even facing all the heavy-handed devices of military censorship, readers could still interpret the ghastly casualty lists released regularly. There was no reason not to know what was happening.

From the earliest days, some religious leaders spoke resoundingly against the war's horrors and in some cases against the institution of war itself. In the Anglo-American world, we hear antiwar sentiments from most of the traditional peace churches, from Quakers and Mennonites as well as many of the emerging Pentecostal denominations. Reluctantly and grudgingly, some nations granted conscientious objector status to such believers. Generally, though, the fact that we can identify the opponents of war so readily indicates just how scarce and exceptional they were.[2]

By far the most significant center of Christian antiwar activism was the Vatican. Although the popes had no doubts about the legitimacy of just wars in theory, the incumbents in this era were deeply troubled by this particular conflict. Reputedly, the war's opening battles so distressed the reigning pope, Pius X, that they contributed to his death on August 20, 1914. His successor, Benedict XV, took office on September 3, a nightmare moment in European history. Throughout his papacy, Benedict spoke and acted as modern observers might have expected a Christian leader to do.[3] Within a week of his accession, he condemned "the appalling spectacle of this war that has filled the heart with horror and bitterness, observing all parts of Europe, devastated by fire and steel, reddened with the blood of Christians." War was "the bane of God's wrath," and all participants should hasten to achieve peace. In November, he protested,

> There is no limit to the measure of ruin and of slaughter; day by day the earth is drenched with newly-shed blood, and is covered with the bodies of the wounded and of the slain. Who would imagine, as we see them thus filled with hatred of one another, that they are all of one common stock, all of the same nature, all members of the same human society? Who would recognize brothers, whose Father is in Heaven?

In 1916, he lamented "the suicide of civilized Europe."[4]

Benedict did all that he practically could to promote peace, seeking to prevent the conflict spreading. In 1914, he urged at least a temporary Christmas ceasefire so the cannon should not be booming on the night that angels sang, exactly the policy that soldiers implemented unofficially on the front lines. In August 1917, he offered a peace proposal that, when we consider how events actually played out, sounds like an extremely attractive alternative. Benedict called for a peace without victors or losers. Rival states would cease fighting and restore all the territories they had conquered, leaving disputed claims to arbitration. European nations would disarm, using the money saved for social reconstruction. Although the proposal failed in its goals, the warring powers treated it as a serious basis for negotiation. Benedict even favored ending military conscription, which in the European context of the time would have constituted a social revolution.[5]

So starkly does the Vatican policy stand out from other Christian voices at this time that it demands some explanation beyond the simple fact of Benedict's saintly character. But he was also in the unusual position among European religious leaders of not being associated with a nation-state or empire. In 1914, the Vatican was a beleaguered territory marooned within the new nation of Italy, but not beholden to either Italy or any other state. Benedict, then, had the luxury of being able to consider the whole European picture, at a time when the war was forcing tens of millions of Catholics to try to kill each other. Generally, when religious leaders had a primary identification with a state—as most did—they not only abandoned words of peace and reconciliation but advocated strident doctrines of holy war and crusade, directed against fellow Christians.

Wars for Christ

MODERN-DAY CHRISTIANS KNOW THAT earlier generations of believers fought what they defined as holy wars, but they assume that these actions occurred at a primitive stage of the faith, in what can be safely dismissed as the Middle Ages. In fact, theories of Christian warfare were anything but ancient history in the early twentieth century, especially in those countries with current or recent memories of established churches.

Still, in 1914 most of Europe's Christians lived in nations that accepted some form of the centuries-old ideology of Christendom, in which a properly guided Christian state followed in the paths desired and planned by God. To varying degrees, Christianity enjoyed official status in most major states, certainly in the conservative Catholic realm of the Austro-Hungarian Empire, but also in Protestant countries like England or Denmark, where the Reformation had made the monarchy and the state the supreme authority over the church. Germany, too, had a strong tradition of church-state ties. Before unification in 1871, each German state or kingdom had its own established church, and that decentralized system survived under the Reich that emerged in 1871. The German monarchy, though, was rooted in the Prussian tradition of intimate alliance with the Lutheran church, to the point that the kaiser occupied the political-clerical role of *summus episcopus,* "highest bishop." To varying degrees, churches acted as agencies of their respective states, which gave financial support and controlled appointments. Service in the state, more particularly the military, involved taking religious oaths not to the nation but to the monarch. Across Europe, great national events were also religious occasions and took place in cherished cathedrals or other sacred places, whether in Westminster Abbey or in Saint Petersburg's Peter and Paul Cathedral.[6]

But while we might expect clergy to support their nations at war, in practice they went far beyond any simple endorsement and became vocal, even fanatical, advocates. Often they presented sophisticated arguments for holy warfare, which drew heavily on both biblical tradition and Christian history. Nor did it make the slightest difference whether a given country actually formalized its relationship with the church through some form of establishment. Yes, it was natural enough for clergy to espouse the cause of a government that paid their salaries, but some of the most egregious holy war advocates enjoyed no such privileged position. In England, those non-Anglican Protestants collectively known as Nonconformists yielded nothing to Anglicans in their support for the war effort. And although Catholics were subject to the transnational spiritual

authority of the Vatican, believers in individual countries were just
as bellicose as their Protestant counterparts. While Christians differed in the sides they identified with the divine will, war enthusiasm transcended denominational labels.[7]

So modern and technological does the First World War seem in
many ways that it is easy to forget how firmly embedded political-
religious concepts were in the consciousness of the Christian nations. Protestant countries especially looked to biblical doctrines of
national chosenness, to promises that victory and prosperity awaited
those peoples who faithfully followed their divine covenants. Well
into the nineteenth century, even the most modern nation-states
spoke the language of divine providence and divine favor, seeking God's blessing in times of war by national displays of piety, by
officially proclaimed days of fasting, prayer, and humiliation. For
England, the Crimean War of 1854–56 was the last conflict to call
forth such communal assertions of belief, which also featured on
both sides of the U.S. Civil War. Days of prayer had a much longer
afterlife. In England, New Year's Day 1916 was such an occasion
for wartime prayer and intercession, which was marked by virtually
all churches, both established and Nonconformist, as well as Jewish
congregations.[8]

Through the nineteenth century, too, Christians showed themselves ready to go to war over religious grievances. Central to European politics was the fate of the decaying Ottoman Empire, a source
of perpetual tension between England, France, and Russia. Continuing controversies surrounded the control of Jerusalem's holy
places, the shrines associated with Christ's life and resurrection, and
the very same issue that had ignited the First Crusade as far back
as 1095. But even in the modern era, Christian powers—especially
Russia—demanded control of these sites and regarded the continuing Muslim role as intolerable. The issue of the holy places sparked
the Crimean War, which has been described as "the last crusade."[9]

Christian nations demanded the right to protect fellow believ-

ers under infidel rule. When the Ottomans savagely suppressed insurrections in Bulgaria and their Balkan territories in the 1870s,
the Christian powers expressed horror, and some threatened armed
intervention—effectively, yet another last crusade. Russia invoked
its treaty rights to protect Christian populations within the empire,
raising the prospect of a general European war that would have
foreshadowed the breakdown of 1914. Outside Russia, too, the
media and publics of Christian states often showed deep concern
over the holy places and, to a much larger extent, the fate of persecuted fellow believers. The French, for instance, used the protection of Middle Eastern Christians to justify establishing a sphere of
influence in what would become Syria and Lebanon. In 1898, as the
new Kaiser Wilhelm II was beginning to assert German power in
Europe, he made a sensational and messianic-tinged visit to Jerusalem, showing that his empire, too, claimed an interest in safeguard-
ing the Christian heritage.[10]

Yet even acknowledging these other claims, Russia does stand
out for the strong, indeed overwhelming, religious content of its
policies. However much diplomatic historians may regard issues like
the holy places as thin excuses to justify imperial expansion, that approach underplays the religious and even theocratic strands in Russian state ideology. This does not mean that Orthodox Christians
were somehow more belligerent or less critical than their Catholic
or Protestant counterparts, but Russian political conditions still, in
1914, bound church and state together much more intimately than
in the West. The Russian tsar ruled a population of some 160 million, including sizable minorities of Catholics, Jews, and Muslims,
but the great majority of the people followed the Orthodox faith
of the imperial regime. The Orthodox Church operated in intimate alliance with the imperial authorities, from which it drew its
power and wealth. From the time of Peter the Great, in 1700, the
church's ancient patriarchate ceased to function, leaving the church
as a virtual arm of government. It was supervised by a Holy Synod

appointed by the tsar and under the authority of a cabinet-level imperial official. Orthodox Christianity shaped every aspect of daily life, from the annual round of feasts and fasts to the compulsory religion lessons in schools.[11]

Far from being an archaic survival, the Orthodox political presence was if anything growing more marked in the early twentieth century. This was a time of widespread spiritual revival across the empire, with an upsurge of mystical sects and apocalyptic speculations. Although the revival affected broad sections of Russian society, it was particularly marked among the country's educated elites, from whom the empire drew its administrators and policy makers. In 1914, as in the 1850s, plenty of tsarist officials had sincere religious motivations, and they saw no hypocrisy in identifying the projection of Russian power with the greater glory of Christ's Orthodox Church. Much of Russian imperial history was a narrative of huge territorial advances justified by the liberation of Christian peoples held in subjection by the Ottomans and other Muslim states. Nineteenth-century Russians kept alive the Byzantine apocalyptic tradition that prophesied the liberation of Eastern Christians at the hands of a messianic emperor, a new Constantine.

The causes of monarchy, empire, and church were all one, and they merged into a messianic vision of the tsarist regime, which was destined to liberate Constantinople. For many Orthodox thinkers, moreover, rival Christian churches, Catholic and Protestant, were only in the most technical sense fellow believers or brothers, and as such they deserved little more political consideration than did Muslims or Jews. Such attitudes affected Russian policies toward Catholic Austria-Hungary in its confrontation with Orthodox Serbia. They also ensured that once war began, the Central Powers would readily be depicted as the Antichrist or the Beast, the foes of Holy Orthodox Russia. Religion mattered crucially in European politics in the age of coal and steam, of the Maxim gun and the Krupp cannon.[12]

A Run on the Bank of God

IN WESTERN NATIONS, TOO, religious themes pervaded the rhetoric of war and by no means only during the first excited weeks. In Britain, certainly, religious enthusiasm merged enthusiastically with patriotic fervor in the summer of 1914. One of Britain's authentic religious heroes of the war was military chaplain Geoffrey Studdert Kennedy, who noted wryly that the initial declaration of war sparked "a run on the bank of God."[13]

Especially in its early days, it is painfully easy to find British writers reading the war in bloodthirsty religious terms, and some clerics in particular offer a great deal of low-hanging fruit for any modern writer seeking gory sound bites. The most frequently cited example was the Anglican bishop of London, Arthur F. Winnington-Ingram, who in 1915 wrote to a newspaper, declaring the church's explicit duty "to mobilize the nation for a holy war." In a notorious sermon, much quoted by later historians, he urged British forces to

> kill Germans—do kill them; not for the sake of killing, but to save the world, to kill the good as well as the bad, to kill the young as well as the old, to kill those who have shown kindness to our wounded as well as those fiends. . . . As I have said a thousand times, I look upon it as a war for purity, I look upon everyone who died in it as a martyr.

Beyond his speeches and sermons, Winnington-Ingram took his warrior obligations very seriously, to the point of making regular visits to forces at the front.[14]

Such extreme language distressed some responsible observers: Prime Minister Herbert Asquith called Winnington-Ingram "an intensely silly bishop." But from the outset, holy war language was commonplace, even among clerics who before the war had shared the pro-German sympathies so widespread among British elites. Beginning with denunciations of German barbarism, preachers soon passed to condemning German culture as radically anti-Christian, and even demonic, making war a Christian obligation. Albert Marrin's history of the English church in the war traces the evolution of rhetoric "from Just War to Apocalyptic Crusade." While admitting that commercial rivalries and simple greed might play their roles in the war, Carlisle's bishop John Diggle saw the conflict chiefly in otherworldly terms:

> But in this war there move and work spirits deeper, stronger, more revolutionary than any or all of these—spirits of good and evil, powers of heaven and principalities of hell, invisible spirits of goodness and wickedness of which men are the instruments and the world the visible prize. . . . This present war is essentially a spiritual war; a war waged on earth but sustained on either side by invisible powers.

Another bishop saw the Allies as "predestined instruments to save the Christian civilization of Europe from being overcome by a brutal and ruthless military paganism."[15]

The vogue for medieval imagery across Europe in the prewar period made it natural to portray contemporary soldiers as knights in armor, and as Crusaders, often under angelic protection: Machen's medieval bowmen clearly belonged to the same moral universe as the modern-day British regulars they defended at Mons. In 1916, British prime minister David Lloyd George declared that "young men from every quarter of this country flocked to the standard of international right, as to a great crusade." For clergy, particularly, this was no metaphor, no "as to"; this was a crusade against God's enemies, and that British view influenced other English-speaking nations. In 1916, Cecil B. DeMille's film *Joan the Woman* borrowed the medieval legend of Joan of Arc to frame the contemporary

Allied war effort on the western front, presenting the later story as quite literally a reincarnation of its predecessor. The Crusader concept powerfully influenced the monuments that the British in particular crafted for the war dead after 1918.[16]

To the credit of the English churches, some of their most prominent leaders and thinkers were more restrained in their interpretation of the war. While virtually all supported the decision to go to war, they were well aware of the dreadful consequences. They justified the policy in terms of secular values of honor and humanitarianism, buttressed by traditional notions of just war, rather than holy war. In 1917, Randall Davidson, archbishop of Canterbury, declared himself still "absolutely persuaded of the rightness, the inevitableness for men and women of honour, of what we did nearly three years ago, when duty and loyalty and truth compelled us to enter in [the war]." The word "inevitableness" suggests a weary acceptance of fate and duty, rather than any exaltation in crusading for God's kingdom. Another important Anglican thinker was William Temple, who would serve as archbishop of Canterbury in the Second World War, and whose reservations echoed Davidson's. Like him, though, he accepted the justice of the cause, "which there was, at that time, no way of serving except the soldier's way." The greatest tribute to such nuanced Anglican leaders was that their moderation attracted the fierce hatred of hyper-patriotic tabloid newspapers like *John Bull,* which became viciously anticlerical. However tempting it may be, though, to commemorate such thinkers, they always constituted a small minority, speaking against their times.[17]

Hurrah and Hallelujah

IN BRITAIN, AS IN all the warring nations, we easily find assertions that a particular country in question was pursuing God's will, and such declarations shade into vulgar, aggressive chauvinism.

German soldiers hailed as heroes as they head off to the war

Yet for all the abundance of such statements, one Western country above all stands out for the power and consistency of religious-based militarism, and that was Germany. The country's position in global and military affairs at the time forces us to pay special attention to religion's role here above all in driving the international conflict, rather than just responding to it.[18]

A great many Germans greeted the outbreak of war with an ecstatic response that was clearly religious as well as patriotic. (If the upsurge was nothing like as unanimous as some claimed at the time, it was still a deeply impressive movement.) The "spirit of 1914" became a defining moment in German history, a conservative and patriotic riposte to the French revolutionary spirit of 1789. Germany briefly experienced what some saw as the first signs of a national religious revival. During the opening months of the war, Germany's churches were fuller than they had ever been, even in working-class areas notorious for secular and anticlerical politics.[19]

Particularly stirring was the vision of unprecedented German unity. This was the hour of the *Burgfrieden,* the "civil peace," in which all factions agreed to stand together in support of a divine cause, regardless of ideology. For writers immersed in the Christian tradition, that unity had obvious scriptural precedent. Preachers and theologians appropriated the famous words of the book of Acts describing how the apostles were overcome by a mighty wind from heaven and inspired to speak to a crowd of people of all nations. This New Pentecost was a European parallel to the famous Pentecostal movement that had surged across the Anglophone world in the previous decade. For true believers, the Spirit was again sweeping the world, pouring spiritual gifts on true believers. A preacher in Bremen recalled the German mood of 1914: "The spirit of God came upon us. It was a New Pentecost. A great roar came from heaven. . . . Didn't we hear the divine words?" God's voice in history, he claimed, echoed through the imperial statements and war communiqués of that triumphant opening week of war. Instead of the biblical list—Parthians, Medes, Elamites, and the rest—Gustav Freybe of Hannover listed the hearers of his own day as

> villagers and city dwellers, conservatives and freethinkers, Social Democrats and Alsatians, Welfs and Poles, Protestants and Catholics. . . . The apostles of the Reich stood together united on the fourth of August [1914], and the Kaiser gave this unanimity the most appropriate expression: "I see no more parties. I see only Germans." [20]

Note that even at this time of effervescent excitement, Jews are missing from the list.

For a time, even Rudolf Binding—later to earn fame as the author of one of the most pessimistic memoirs of the war experience—shared in the national mood. In August 1914, he published a poem in the *Frankfurter Zeitung,* about his departure for what he termed the holy war. Adapting the common pseudo-medieval language of the time, he wrote,

> I am a sacred rider
> I do not seek the Cross or Grail
> But nevertheless am blessed a thousand times
> As a warrior of righteousness.[21]

One reason why German churchmen were so ecstatic, so Pentecostal, in their attitudes compared to Allied thinkers was that up to the start of 1916 their forces were clearly winning, and they had less need for modesty or reflection. But the explanation must lie deeper than this, as these leaders continued throughout the conflict to present stark justifications for war and conquest, incorporated into quite a sophisticated *Kriegstheologie,* a "theology of war." The same themes emerge repeatedly in sermons right through 1918. The war was "a struggle of faith," "a struggle between light and darkness," "a war for God against Antichrist," "the final hour of decision," and—of course—a holy war. Much of what was said echoes what we hear in Britain, and at least part of the difference can be attributed to different mechanisms of censorship. But even when we make that allowance, German clerical statements were significantly more warlike in both degree and volume.[22]

Serious scholars and academics said and wrote things that the Western Allies widely quoted as evidence of German aggression and fanaticism, and we naturally tend to doubt them because they fit so naturally into the propaganda themes of the time. In the United States, one potent argument in favor of intervention was the now-forgotten bestseller *Hurrah and Hallelujah* (1916), by the Danish scholar J. P. Bang, who presented an anthology of hyper-patriotic statements by German thinkers, especially religious leaders. But propagandists did not have to dig too deeply to find hair-raising quotes from sermons and lectures of the era, and Bang's examples were accurately quoted and translated. Even the silly-sounding title *Hurrah and Hallelujah* was authentic, and it was appropriated from Protestant cleric Dietrich Vorwerk, whom we have already encountered hymning celestial zeppelins.[23]

Holy war language poured from the nation's Lutheran pulpits, from ordinary clergy as well as church leaders. Pastor Franz Koehler offered a detailed rationale for understanding the war as a spiritual revival and listed its benefits. War was a cure for individualism and selfishness; it presented the highest moral test; it gave abundant opportunities to practice Christian virtues; it taught holy zeal; it led believers from death to life. In his "Sword-Blessing," Koehler hymned "World War, you transfigure our nature, like the Word and the Spirit. . . . Come, Sword, you are to me the Revelation of the Spirit." In such paeans, speakers gave little thought to the destructive power of war or the losses that would be a necessary sacrifice in the greater cause. Leipzig professor Franz Rendtorff announced, "Bless this war, if it brings to our people the religious uplifting which makes us unconquerable!" Early German victories, reputedly over impossible odds, enhanced this sense of divine blessing.[24]

Such opinions transcended denominational lines, remarkably so given the ambiguous position that Catholics enjoyed in the united Germany. The German-speaking peoples as a whole were neatly divided between Catholic and Protestant populations, but this balance was not reflected in the Reich created by Bismarck's unification in the 1870s. Although it had strong Catholic minorities, the new Germany was predominantly Protestant, with a heavy Lutheran tone (Germany in 1914 had some forty million Protestants and twenty-four million Catholics). When war broke out, German Catholics found their nation confronting nations with deep Catholic roots, in France and Belgium. German Protestants made no secret of their suspicion about Catholic dual loyalties and developed a lively paranoid mythology about the pope's pro-Allied leanings. Anti-Catholic sentiments were further strengthened by the visible role of Catholic clergy in leading resistance to the German occupiers.[25]

In reality, German Catholics lacked nothing in patriotic zeal in 1914. The more devout showed a special zeal in pursuing war against a France that was so intimately linked to secular and anti-clerical politics, and a heretical Russia. So enthusiastic was Catholic bishop (later cardinal) Michael von Faulhaber in his support for the country's armies that in 1916 he was awarded the Iron Cross. One prominent Catholic voice was Engelbert Krebs, an academic theologian who would live long enough to be a persistent critic of the Nazis' abuse of state power. In 1914, though, he supported the holy war cause. Like Protestant clergy, he preached on the moral revolution that the war had wrought:

> The seed must die to bring forth fruit—this lesson was once again acknowledged by everyone. And had it not been acknowledged, Germany would be destroyed today . . . with an iron fist our army is turning back our enemies from the borders that they wickedly attacked.[26]

Militia Christi

LIKE THE BRITISH AND the other powers, German cultural leaders made great use of medieval imagery in their war propaganda, with all the attendant knights and angels. We glimpse this historical fascination from some of the titanic monuments erected shortly before the war and dedicated amidst vast public celebrations. The Kyffhäuser Monument (1896) commemorates the crusading emperor Frederick Barbarossa, who supposedly lies sleeping until he will reawake to lead his empire once more. In late 1913, Germany dedicated a still more grandiose shrine recalling the Battle of the Nations a century previously, when the German states defeated Napoleon Bonaparte. This

Knightly images in modern warfare. In this 1915 appeal to subscribe to the Austro-Hungarian war loan, a heroic mailed knight defends civilians from Allied assault.

site, with its gigantic, heroic, and knightly statues, so prefigures the motifs of German propaganda in both world wars that it becomes a visual prophecy of those later events. Presiding over the whole is a forty-foot-high figure of the archangel Michael, whose name we will encounter again in the story of the war.[27]

But for all these appeals to the past, the religious themes that emerged so powerfully in 1914 represented a strictly contemporary ideology, rather than a bizarre recrudescence of medieval fanaticism, and its origins dated back decades rather than centuries. Listening to the patriotic sermons of these years, we might suppose that a militaristic state was co-opting a naïve church establishment for its own purposes. In fact, the church itself—particularly the Lutheran Church—had been an ardent supporter of nationalism and militarism long before 1914, and Niall Ferguson has stressed the strictly Protestant roots of the movements that created the nation's aggressive and expansionist mood. It is not easy to tell exactly who was co-opting whom.

Among the most fervent advocates were Germany's best-known

theologians and religious scholars. During the nineteenth century, Germany had produced some of the greatest Christian scholarship—at universities such as Göttingen and Tübingen, while Marburg and Erlangen enjoyed worldwide fame at the turn of the century. By 1914, Christian intellectual endeavor was manifested by brilliant Bible scholars and theologians such as Adolf von Harnack and Wilhelm Herrmann, and sociologists like Ernst Troeltsch. Von Harnack was the symbol of the most advanced cutting-edge historical criticism of the Bible and Christian history, the heir of the dazzling German scholarship of the previous century. For a foreigner, an American or Englishman, to be ignorant of von Harnack was to forfeit any claim to share in contemporary discussions of Christian history or theology. Herrmann, meanwhile, was a legendary leader of liberal Protestantism, demanding that believers ground their faith in the life of Christ, as understood through both faith and history, rather than in abstract philosophy.[28]

In 1914, though, von Harnack, Herrmann, and others signed aggressively propagandist statements and manifestos that lauded Germany's war effort. For both sides, the Great War involved heroic propaganda endeavors intended to convince neutral nations of the justice of the respective causes, and religious and intellectual leaders played a central part in this process. In September 1914, while battle raged on the Marne, an awe-inspiring group of twenty-nine German church leaders and theology professors signed an *Aufruf . . . an die Evangelischen Christen im Ausland,* an appeal to foreign Protestants. Insisting on Germany's right to defend itself against "Asiatic barbarism," the signatories and their kaiser invoked divine aid in the struggle. Besides von Harnack and Herrmann, the *Aufruf* was supported by such figures of global fame as church historians Adolf Deissmann and Friedrich Loofs, philosopher Rudolf Eucken, preacher Ernst Dryander, and Wilhelm Wundt, the pioneering psychologist of religion.[29]

In October, the same religious figures joined dozens of other German scholars, scientists, and artists in signing a new *Aufruf,* a manifesto aimed at the international world of culture and science. The document placed the full weight of German intellectual prestige behind the war effort, and in the process, made a number of assertions, some of which were debatable, others blatantly false. Reasonable people could disagree whether Germany sought or provoked the war, but the signatories were on shakier grounds when they cited the myth of Germany's "fictitious defeats" (if they were fictitious, why weren't the Germans in Paris?). The manifesto dismissed claims that the Germans had behaved atrociously or illegally in Belgium, which they certainly had.[30]

Such remarks read oddly in the context of von Harnack, who owed his cosmic reputation to his insistence on applying rigorous criteria of evidence and historical truth to accepted stories, even those surrounded by the sanctified antiquity of the church. But his critical facilities vanished when faced with the assertions of a twentieth-century secular regime. Ironically, one of his best-known works was *Militia Christi,* a historical analysis of early Christian pacifism. In 1914, von Harnack presented the German armed forces as a quite literal Militia Christi.[31]

People who sign petitions and manifestos often regret their actions and easily find excuses in terms of the fevered atmosphere of the time, or the overwhelming pressure from friends and neighbors: everybody was doing it. In the case of the 1914 manifesto, a few of the secular signatories actually did withdraw their names after reconsideration. But the great majority of the scholars remained firm, and by no means all could pass themselves off as absentminded professors, as some consistently upheld their role as public propagandists for radical militarism.

Von Harnack himself was extremely well connected to the kaiser's court, serving as a privy counselor from 1902 until the fall of the empire. In 1911 he gained the prestigious post of president of the senate of the Kaiser Wilhelm Foundation, making him the overlord of Germany's academic world, with its world-renowned research institutes. In 1914, he helped draft the kaiser's famous speech declaring that he saw only Germans, not parties.[32] Dryander had served the kaiser as tutor, and he occupied the key position of court preacher. Troeltsch was quite consistent in his fervor, lamenting that he and his fellow intellectuals could only attack the enemy with their words: "Oh, if the speaker of this hour only were able to transform each word into a bayonet, a rifle, a cannon!" Even the well-known liberal newspaper *Die Christliche Welt* (*The Christian World*) accepted the justice of Germany's military position, including the illegal invasion of Belgium, although with nothing like the crude jingoism that ruled the nation's pulpits.[33]

German Christians

CHRISTIAN PASSION FOR WILHELM'S war was not an immediate response to German popular passions, nor a reflection of some mystical feature of the supposed national character. Rather, it reflected the growth of theories over the previous forty years, which had established some controversial and dangerous themes in the heart of German spiritual life. For Germany's Protestant intellectuals, the language of holy war was the logical conclusion to a century of theological endeavor, which took the core biblical theme of national chosenness to extravagant messianic heights.

Conventional labels fail us here. Although we might describe hypernationalist views as reactionary, they actually grow out of the *liberal* theologies that dominated German Protestant thought at this time, in the *Kulturprotestantismus* associated with von Harnack. Since the Enlightenment, German Protestantism had rejected unquestioning reliance on such traditional sources of religious authority as the Bible and early church tradition: incisive German scholarship presented the Bible as a strictly human artifact, rooted in the interests of successive historical societies. German theology was dominated by the liberal tradition of Friedrich Schleiermacher, who taught that the church's creeds and historic doctrines had to be subordinate to the inner experience of God as understood by the individual believer, through the knowledge of Christ.

For liberal Protestants, the God presented in the Bible was only one limited perception of the deity, who became better understood through the progressive workings of history. The church likewise existed in history and had to be adapted and modernized for successive generations and cultures. Such an approach is liberal in its openness to changing ideas and standards, but the lack of any external absolutes allows the church to be swept along with contemporary political obsessions. In the German case, liberal Protestantism allowed itself to identify wholly with the emerging Wilhelmine Reich and came close to state worship, if not war worship.[34]

The creation of the Reich in 1870–71 transformed Europe, stirring epochal hopes and fears, and exciting thinkers who saw the new state and its *Kultur* as the highest manifestation of human progress. In its intellectual life, Germany had a real claim to lead the world, and its progressive social policies genuinely did lead to a vast improvement in the lives of ordinary people. Over the next forty years, nationalist thinkers demanded that the Reich expand within Europe and overseas, and some, like Heinrich von Treitschke, framed their ambitions in racial and anti-Semitic terms that can be characterized as proto-Nazism.[35]

Lutheran leaders gave a special German emphasis to understanding the workings of God in history. Nationalist-minded Protestant thinkers stressed that nations and races were divine concepts, and the Bible showed that God might use a people to fulfill his purposes, following the example of the ancient Hebrews. Given the sudden and near-miraculous quality of its creation and its rise to glory among the old nations, the German Reich demanded attention as the highest accomplishment of the Christian political order, and something very like the kingdom of God. Germany was a holy nation, with the need and right to expand, and Germans were conscious of a special national and racial "sense of mission," *Sendungs-bewusstsein,* so that the actions of that state could be a holy necessity. For Lutheran theologian Friedrich Gogarten in 1915, "The German people and German spirit [*Geist*] are, in our most sublime conceptions, the revelation of eternity." Reinhold Seeberg developed a sweeping theology of German imperialism, which he based on the German *Volk*'s will to survive and expand, its *Lebensinstinkt* (life instinct), which went far beyond mere rational calculations.[36]

In this visionary framework, war itself was a means of working out God's purposes in history, with Protestant-ruled Germany fulfilling the medieval-sounding role of Hammer of God. Force and violence were, after all, normal and familiar parts of nature, and the obvious means by which God fulfilled his purposes in the world. After the Reich's ultimate victory, German Christianity would reach its full potential as the spiritual light of the world. Troeltsch saw the German state and its army as the earthly means used by God to bring about the kingdom of God on earth. God indeed "protects and asserts the national incarnations of the divine spirit," and the Reich was a historical incarnation of the Spirit of God.[37]

Christian political thought has always been ambiguous about the exercise of state power, as exalted ideals of the Christian nation have often come into conflict with concerns about using the weapons of this world. German Protestants of this generation, though, had remarkably few qualms about presenting violence and warfare as legitimate tactics for a Christian state. Through its *Zwei-Reiche-Lehre* (two-kingdoms doctrine), Lutheran theology taught that the two kingdoms, earthly and heavenly, each had its own moral codes and ways of being. Although Christians lived in both simultaneously, it was impossible to apply the absolute demands of New Testament ethics to each: the state simply could not be expected to operate according to such standards. A state that turned the other cheek in the face of aggression or invasion would soon cease to exist. Even a nation made up almost entirely of devout Christians could never act politically according to strict Christian moral teachings. Potentially, this approach justified cynical state actions that seemed to violate Christian teachings or commonly accepted moral standards. In 1914, the doctrine overrode objections to the treatment of Belgium.[38]

Although the Christian nation might conduct a holy war, its real head must be God itself, and clergy vied with each other in identifying the Almighty ever more closely with the worldly high command. German war preaching was unabashed in applying Christian language and concepts to the nation and the state, and gave religious underpinnings to the personality cult surrounding Kaiser Wilhelm. One Berlin cleric appropriated titles normally applied to the kaiser in declaring God "The All-Highest Lord of War and Peace." Walter Lehmann spoke of the German God, and presented Germanism as the soul of Christianity. Ludwig Ihmels, a distinguished theology professor at Leipzig, proclaimed that unconditional loyalty to the imperial throne was as holy as the gospel. Such language revived Old Testament images of God as Lord of Hosts, but preachers also struggled to present Jesus himself as the true war leader, which meant struggling against generations of imagery of "gentle Jesus meek and mild." For Germans, Jesus was instead "the born hero and standard-bearer for our time, and our Volk."[39]

MOST MODERN CHRISTIANS FIND it scandalous that their predecessors should have joined so wholeheartedly in the patriotic movements that led Europe to catastrophe a century ago. Yet as we examine the mainstream assumptions of the greatest churches at the time, we repeatedly see just how close to the surface of the Christian and biblical tradition such patterns of state alliance and militancy actually lie, and how easily ideas of the church militarist emerge in times of crisis. A study of history, up to and including the twentieth century, must make us question any attempts to dismiss such uses of Christianity as a crude distortion of the faith.

Poster for the film *Pershing's Crusaders,* a documentary about
U.S. forces in France, spring 1918

CHAPTER THREE

Witnesses for Christ
Cosmic War, Sacrifice, and Martyrdom

*During the last four years more men have taken up their cross and
followed the Great Leader through Gethsemane to a sacrificial
death than in any previous age of the world's history.*
—LYMAN ABBOTT

IN OTHER NATIONS, TOO, faith-based militarism had a long
history, although one quite distinct in its origins from the German
intellectual history and political setting. In Germany, Protestant
churches coexisted happily with imperial rule and hoped to benefit
from the state's continuing political expansion. In such an environment, Christians spoke powerfully for their nation and their armed
forces. But similar ideas also flourished in societies that had nothing
like the cozy established church model that prevailed in Germany or
Britain, and where church-state relations were poisonous. In other
settings, Christians had a special interest in proving their patriotic
and pro-war credentials as a way of reasserting the political position
and privileges they had lost over previous decades.

Whatever the local agendas, Christians in all combatant
nations—including the United States—entered wholeheartedly
into the spirit of cosmic war. None found any difficulty in using

fundamental tenets of the faith as warrants to justify war and mass destruction.

Under the Sacred Heart

ALTHOUGH THE CHRISTIAN FAITH was clearly based in Europe, that is quite different from declaring Europe a Christian continent, any more than the United States today is a Christian nation, and active nonbelievers and secularists flourished. Even those countries that gave a favored role to a particular church recognized in practice that the denomination might have only a tenuous hold on the mass of the population. From the 1880s, church power was under attack in several major nations, from rival believers or secularists. The German *Kulturkampf* (the original "culture war") raged through the 1870s, pitting the newly formed German Empire against the Catholic Church. Elsewhere, established church power came under attack, either from the stance of radical Protestant faith, as in Great Britain, or from secularism and anticlericalism, as in France and Italy.[1]

For a generation before 1914, France was the scene of the most acute church-state confrontation, as attitudes to religious belief and practice became fundamental to political ideology. France's republican tradition was profoundly secularist, and radicals regarded the Catholic Church as the soul of reaction. Still, the church maintained a strong social position, particularly in provincial communities, and even in the 1890s Catholics still claimed the loyalty of the overwhelming majority of French people. The two sides, Catholics and secularists, almost represented two rival nations that maintained an ongoing cold war, and on occasion, they came close to armed hostilities. Hatred reached new heights during the Dreyfus affair of the 1890s, when a Jewish army officer was falsely convicted of treason. The resulting scandal split France into two armed camps: conservative, monarchist, Catholic on the one side, and republican, secularist, and Masonic on the other. At the start of the twentieth century, republican governments severely limited church power, and in 1905, France passed a Separation law that established the principle of state secularism. Fervent believers remained in a kind of internal exile. They focused their hopes on new forms of religious devotion such as the Sacred Heart of Jesus, a traditional French image that epitomized Christ's burning love for humanity. The doctrine and the image came to signify rejection of official secularism.[2]

Even the Paris skyline epitomized the religious battle, the struggle of dueling histories. In the 1870s, conservatives supported the building of the great church of Sacré-Coeur (Sacred Heart), which was intended to show the city's contrition for the murder of the archbishop of Paris and other Catholic clergy during the Paris Commune of 1871. (The building was completed in 1914.) Secularists and anticlericals countered with the Eiffel Tower of 1889, a shrine to science and rationality, steel and electricity, and a commemoration of the radical revolution of 1789.

Facing the threat of national ruin in 1914, France entered the war determined to put aside the internal struggles of the previous generation, just as Germans proclaimed their own civil peace. French Catholics happily accepted the vow of President Raymond Poincaré to lead the French into a *union sacrée,* in which different ideologies would join together to defeat the German nemesis. But here, as elsewhere, older divisions helped shape church responses to the war, encouraging Christian leaders to give full sanction to the national cause. After all, a country fighting a holy war needs an official religion, even an established church. Pious believers who had spent decades troubled about the confrontation between their church and nation were now thrilled to find the causes were absolutely united. Provided the nation survived, this was a unique opportunity to restore the glories of Catholic France.[3]

Particularly in the war's first few months, French Catholics freely spoke the language of crusade, all the more so as Catholic France was battling for survival against a predominantly Protestant Germany. (Not until 1916 did Protestant Britain play a large enough role in the conflict to make such declarations embarrassing.) For Catholic thinkers like Jacques Maritain, Lutheran theology had not just demoralized Germany but converted it to a new anti-Christian ideology of aggressive imperialism, which demanded some entirely new title like "Germanism." Its adherents were savages barely worthy of the name of human.[4]

Few French observers denied that the country's preservation from conquest in 1914 was remarkable, but for Catholics, the victory at the Marne was a straightforward and literal miracle. National salvation was directly attributed to the fervent prayers of Catholic believers, above all at Paris's Sacré-Coeur. Pamphleteers noted the coincidence of dates, that the key turning point of the battle that saved Paris occurred on September 8, the Feast of the Virgin's Nativity. Again, when Claudel presented his medieval-sounding vision of the Virgin and saints saving Paris, he was summarizing the standard popular mythology of Catholic France. One contemporary missal shows the German soldiers approaching the Paris skyline in which can be seen those banners of Catholic identity, the churches of Notre Dame and Sacré-Coeur—but also the secularist shrine of the Eiffel Tower.[5]

The Marne gave the country more than its share of martyrs, to provide still more ammunition for the sacred cause. One was poet Charles Péguy, a former socialist, anticlerical, and Dreyfusard who converted to Catholicism and then perished heroically at the front. His admirers often cited the prewar lines of his "Eve":

> Blessed are those who die for carnal cities
> For they are the body of the City of God . . .
> Blessed are they who die in a just war
> Blessed the ripened grain, the harvested wheat.[6]

Also in 1914, Catholic France was granted a powerful new symbol when the Germans shelled Reims Cathedral, a place of immense patriotic significance over and above its religious role: this was the historic site of the coronation of French kings through the centuries. The German attack wrecked some medieval statues of angels, including one of a beatifically smiling angel. When the figure's head was recovered, *L'Ange au Sourire* (*The Smiling Angel*) became a material image of French culture and endurance, and yet another confirmation that angels were watching over the Allies. The building itself earned the title of Martyr Cathedral.[7]

Although deeply patriotic and utterly committed to the war effort, French Catholics despaired of peace until and unless the national government ended its silly pretense that this was not a Catholic country, and they urged that France formally dedicate itself and its armed forces to the Sacred Heart. In 1915, the French bishops campaigned for such a national consecration, as each parish was to read a document formally repenting of national sins, including official secularism and *laïcité*. Catholic activists petitioned that the Sacred Heart be added to the republican tricolor flag, and ordinary families sewed patriotic flags, suitably Catholicized, to send to their menfolk at the front.[8]

The debate over France's religious identity reached new heights during 1916, the year of Verdun. Late in that year, a young countrywoman named Claire Ferchaud claimed a series of visions in which she learned that France's survival depended on national rededication and the addition of the Sacred Heart to the flag. She was taken sufficiently seriously to be granted audiences with senior church authorities, and even with President Poincaré. Church leaders decided to reject the authenticity of her visions, but not because of any doubts of the underlying spiritual mission that the nation faced. French Catholics had all the heavenly support they needed in saints like the warrior Martin of Tours, whose holy day fell on November 11—the day that would mark Allied victory. Most evocative of all was Joan of Arc, whose cult reached new heights during the war, and who would finally achieve canonization in 1920.[9]

If France really had been officially a Catholic country and the whole debate over separation and secularism had never occurred, it is hard to see how the nation's public rhetoric could have been more fully permeated with religious language and imagery than it actually was.

Americans Present Arms

THE UNITED STATES, OF course, was no more officially a Christian country than was France, but here, too, Christians enjoyed an overwhelming predominance in the population. And here, too, a holy war ideology became social orthodoxy to an extent that is amazing if we think of the nation's composition at that time. Millions of Americans had strong vested interests in avoiding war, certainly if any U.S. intervention would be on the Allied side. People of Irish and German ancestry had little taste for allying with the British Empire, while Poles and other eastern Europeans—especially Jews— had come to America to flee Russian oppression. Many American churches also had a historic orientation toward peace and national isolation. Across the religious spectrum, most Christians (and Jews) expressed clear antiwar views when the European conflict broke out in 1914, and churches still spoke out against war during the national debates over intervention that were so central to the 1916 election campaigns. By the time the United States actually did enter the war in April 1917, though, not only were religious calls for holy warfare clearly in the ascendant but the nation's rhetoric sounded very much like that of England or Germany three years before, and some of the most militant voices were penitent former pacifists.[10]

Just how American clergy became such fire-breathing advocates of a crusade against Wilhelm's Germany was the subject of Ray

Abrams's 1933 book *Preachers Present Arms,* a minor classic of American religious history. Abrams himself was writing at a time when the antiwar reaction had set in with a vengeance, and he is incredulous that so many educated believers could have fallen for the view that the Great War was in any sense just. He saw the massive shift to pro-war sentiment as a naïve concession to cynical manipulation by Allied agents, in association with militarist forces within the U.S. government. For Abrams, American clergy gave way to "propagandism" and media-incited panic in a kind of mass hysteria reminiscent of the colonial-era witch hunts.[11]

Abrams's analysis is multiply problematic. As I will suggest, America too had its own autonomous tradition of religious-based justifications for violence, which needed no external manipulation. Also, Abrams lacked comparative perspective. In more senses than one, he was a strict isolationist, who saw American circumstances purely on their own terms, with no sense of just how passionately other churches around the world were galvanizing themselves into crusading mode at just this time. By 1917, the growing savagery of the war had vastly escalated the rhetoric among European combatants, whose opinions easily made their way to the United States and stirred public opinion. America was joining a war that was already being cast in eschatological terms.

But whatever the reason underlying the national mood, Abrams compiled an astonishing anthology of militarist rhetoric from Christian leaders. What is remarkable is not the words of any one or other clergyman but the overwhelming weight of sentiment, and the degree to which these individuals had thought through their concepts of the church militarist. This was not just a matter of adding a few colorful touches to a plea to buy Liberty bonds. Churches with historic British orientations were among the most militant, especially the Episcopalians, but denominational loyalties made little difference to bellicosity. Henry Churchill King, president of Oberlin College, felt that "it is neither a travesty nor exaggeration to call this war on the part of America a truly Holy War." No less dedicated were members of other denominations with powerful traditions of pacifism and internationalism, including Quakers. Yale theology professor Henry Hallam Tweedy fully justified clergy participation in the struggle: "When the greatest crime in all history was perpetrated and the World War began, it was natural and necessary that the ministry of all lands should buckle on the Christian armor and take its place in the fighting ranks."[12]

Tweedy portrayed warfare in romanticized medieval guise, so that his hearers are to buckle on armor and take up the sword, rather than deploy their bayonets or their mustard gas. Other clergy, though, went beyond general statements about the virtues of this particular war to commend its ugly specifics, and some preachers even waxed lyrical on the glories of the bayonet. As Abrams says, "To ignore [the bayonet's] use Christians could not; defend it they ultimately must; glorify it they frequently did." Methodist minister George W. Downs fantasized about going over the top with other soldiers, as "I would have driven my bayonet into the throat or the eye or the stomach of the Huns without the slightest hesitation."[13]

To Love Is to Hate

SOME OF THE MOST extreme advocates of Christian warfare came from the country's strong movement of progressive Christians, those who extolled human potential to build a better world free of social injustice. During the lead-up to war, though, it was exactly these thinkers who most urgently supported U.S. intervention in what they saw as the global cause of Christianity. Although they approached the concept in different ways from their German counterparts, Americans too saw the war as a means of advancing God's earthly kingdom. The same men and women who favored social crusades at home—against poverty, bad housing, and alcohol—also demanded military interventions overseas. One militant propagandist was Lyman Abbott, a prestigious Congregational minister who identified strongly with social reform and liberal theology. During the war, though, he devoted himself to the cause of defeating Germany. His 1918 tract *The Twentieth Century Crusade* asserted that "a crusade to make this world a home in which God's children can live in peace and safety is more Christian than a crusade to recover from pagans the tomb in which the body of Christ was buried."[14]

Readers found such warlike images not just in sermons and denominational newspapers but also in mainstream mass media, including the emerging field of motion pictures. Already by 1916, cinema represented an enormous cultural force, with the capacity to reach audiences worldwide, and viewing publics showed an inexhaustible appetite for war-related themes. One of the war's greatest commercial successes was the British documentary, *The Battle of the Somme*, released that August while the battle was in progress and reportedly viewed by millions in Britain alone, and far more around the globe.[15]

For American attitudes at this time, we can turn to Thomas Ince's film *Civilization,* which was in its time one of the most colossal productions ever released from Hollywood, at a then-staggering cost of $1 million. The film is powerfully antiwar, a plea "that a shocked and appalled world may henceforth devote itself more earnestly in the cause of peace." It is "dedicated to that vast, pitiful army whose tears have girdled the universe—the mothers of the dead." But although avowedly pro-peace in its content, it offered a devastating picture of specifically German violence and echoed the analysis coming from so many contemporary pulpits. The film focuses on Ferdinand, an officer in an imaginary kingdom looking uncannily like the German Reich. He becomes a Christ figure when he is executed for refusing to sink a ship carrying civilians. Emerging from Ferdinand's dead body, Jesus himself appears to intervene with the evil emperor, whom he takes on a tour of the

A patriotic U.S. print shows Kaiser Wilhelm as a satanic figure sitting on a mountain of skulls. "Über Alles" recalls the German patriotic song "Das Deutschlandlied."

battlefields to observe the carnage he has inflicted. The horrified emperor agrees to make peace, and a new era begins. If the film is neutral, it is definitely neutral on behalf of the Allies, and it assumes that peace can only come through the intervention of Christ. In the absence of that direct intervention, it would be necessary for his faithful servants to take up arms in his cause—to fight for Christ.

Fighting the Devil

IN WHATEVER COUNTRY WE look at, we find strikingly similar interpretations of the war. We can see this from two themes in particular, namely the framing of the nation's enemies as anti-Christians, if not actually as the Antichrist, and also the potent concepts of martyrdom and redemptive sacrifice that pervaded wartime language.

Countries at war generally demonize their opponents, if only because dehumanization makes it easier to kill them. This process became much more intense, and much uglier, when the rise of democracy and mass media forced governments to arouse broad popular support. Building on skills developed during the growth of newspapers and advertising, propaganda reached new heights during the Great War. But when warring countries share a religious ideology, dehumanization must also include dechristianization. This is a familiar Christian dilemma, dating back to the Middle Ages, when the church suppressed groups that it deemed heretical, and it did so by denying their Christian credentials as the prerequisite for making them the targets of armed violence. Church leaders thus described the faith of their rivals as so fundamentally flawed or sinister as no longer worthy of the name of Christianity. In fact, they did something closely akin to the process of *takfir* by which modern-day Islamists proclaim fellow believers as de facto infidels, who can therefore become subject to violence and jihad.[16]

During the Great War, clergy varied greatly in how they handled the dilemmas of inter-Christian warfare, and some tried to preserve humane standards even as national hatreds were so much in evidence. Even those who denounced enemy regimes in the harshest terms encouraged their followers to remember that individual foes might well be faithful Christians and brothers. Generally, though, pastors from all combatant nations implemented something like *takfir* as they zealously denounced enemy nations as ungodly, unchristian, even as Satan or the Antichrist. All sides did it, using the religious resources and prejudices at their disposal: Arthur Machen's heavenly bowmen destroyed Germany's "heathen horde." According to context, Protestants denounced Catholics, and vice versa; Protestants and Orthodox likewise berated each other's betrayals of the true faith. Self-styled Christian nations also declared themselves engaged in a holy struggle against atheist or secularist regimes like the French. "Can God find pleasure in our opponents?" asked a German preacher. "France denies him, England laughs at him, Russia forgets him." Any approach was preferable to confronting the realities of inter-Christian strife.[17]

Philippine poster showing German soldiers crucifying a prisoner, as American soldiers come to his rescue. The reference is to the story of the crucified Canadian.

Protestant countries deployed the Bible's language of condemnation directed against enemies and evildoers, villains who over the centuries had often acquired diabolical aspects. German preachers focused their rage on the British, whose decision to enter the war in 1914 seemed an unaccountable act of sabotage against the divine plan, and they overtly declared it a Christian duty to hate such enemies. In its war on Germany, Britain was attacking the heart of Protestantism, and thus of authentic Christianity. In the words of one German denominational newspaper, "It is England that has let loose the wild lust of conquest of heathen Asiatics against the people of the Reformation." The reference is to British reliance on the Muslim and Hindu soldiers of its Indian army, a theme that vanished when Germany allied itself with the Muslim Ottoman Empire. German propagandists portrayed Britain as evil or actively satanic, using such familiar literary parallels as King Richard III, or Mephistopheles himself. For cathedral preacher Gerhard Tolzien, writing in 1916, Germany's enemies were "murderers," "monsters," "beasts in human form." Significantly, given his pivotal role in policy making, Kaiser Wilhelm himself became ever more personally convinced as the war progressed that England was more or less in league with the devil.[18]

Other countries pursued their own tactics. Former American president William Howard Taft believed that "Germany has mistaken the Devil for God." Among British clergy, mainstream Anglicans focused on what they saw as German paganism, the nation's slavish state worship, and the frank revival of ancient pagan cults among some intellectuals. Hereford's Bishop Percival denounced "a brutal and ruthless military paganism." Bishop Winnington-Ingram believed that Germany had so succumbed to the cynical cult of military strength and power politics that it had abandoned Christ for the Norse war god Odin, making the war "a struggle between two gospels." Other Allied thinkers extended this concept to suggest that while Christian nations venerated the four Gospels, Germany instead worshipped the books of modern-day authors who extolled power and violence, including Friedrich Nietzsche, Prussian ultranationalist Friedrich von Bernhardi, military strategist Carl von Clausewitz, and Heinrich von Treitschke. Allied propagandists regularly denounced Germany's unholy trinity of Nietzsche, von Bernhardi, and von Treitschke.[19]

A few clergy even condemned whole enemy populations—who were overwhelmingly fellow Christians—as deserving death. As we have seen, one notorious advocate was the prestigious American Congregationalist minister Newell Dwight Hillis. In his 1918 tract *The Blot on the Kaiser's 'Scutcheon,* Hillis paraded every propaganda charge then in circulation, both plausible and ludicrous, with a prurient emphasis on sexually tinged sadomasochistic tales. He then proposed a final solution for the German nation responsible for such crimes: "In utter despair . . . statesmen, generals, diplomats, editors are now talking about the duty of simply exterminating the

German people." American eugenic laws already ordained painless medical sterilization for "confirmed criminals and hopeless idiots." So why not Germans?[20]

Martyrs

MUCH OF THE CHRISTIAN war theory in these years would resonate mightily with modern-day Islamist thinkers, particularly the idea that any believers fighting in a properly declared jihad were ipso facto martyrs. They would find nothing surprising in the widespread Christian belief that this held true of soldiers killed fighting in the Great War, those who, in the words of German pastor Johannes Reetz, had been promoted from lower to higher postings.[21]

The soldiers of England, Germany, France, and the other nations practiced a faith based on redemptive suffering, following an exemplar whose innocent sufferings purified and liberated the whole world. Beyond being martyrs, then, Christian soldiers were thought of as sacrificing their lives for a godly cause. They became identified with Christ himself, suffering torments for the salvation of the world. Often, religious thinkers turned to the New Testament language of sowing and harvest, so that a grain of wheat must be buried in the earth before it could achieve new life culminating in the great harvest. Death was the doorway to life.[22]

The language of suffering, sacrifice, and redemption thoroughly penetrated popular discourse about the war, in the works of essayists or poets, in newspapers, and in political speeches. British war leader David Lloyd George declared,

> The stern hand of Fate has scourged us to an elevation where
> we can see the great everlasting things which matter for a
> nation—the great peaks we had forgotten, of Honor, Duty,

Patriotism, and clad in glittering white, the great pinnacle of Sacrifice pointing like a rugged finger to Heaven.

In *Mein Kampf,* Hitler singled out Lloyd George as a rhetorical genius, whom he imitated in his own speeches.[23]

These sacrificial ideas became a mainstay of sermons. In 1916, a French Christmas carol imagined an army waiting in the trenches "and like the child in the stable / it awaits that critical hour / to sacrifice itself [*s'immoler*] on the altar." Some of the most vivid examples come from the war's very rich visual heritage, which is so readily found in the illustrated magazines that were such a mainstay of popular media in all major countries and languages. At Christmas 1914, a widely reproduced British print represented Christ taking in his arms a dying British soldier. Usually these magazines produced their own prints and cartoons, but sometimes they adapted celebrated paintings of the time. Other much-reproduced British military images of the war years bore titles such as *The Great Sacrifice, The Greater Reward,* and *Greater Love Hath No Man.* That final phrase also appeared regularly on Russian military graves, implying that the dead man had laid down his life for his friends. In practice, though, this commitment to suffering and sacrifice meant serving in uniform, taking up weapons, and inflicting death upon others. So constantly do such accounts portray soldiers undergoing sacrificial death that it is sometimes hard to tell who, if anyone, is actually attacking, rather than merely dying nobly. Somebody, surely, must be firing the shells and wielding the bayonets.[24]

Over the past century, the term "sacrifice" has become a standard part of media vocabulary in reporting on warfare, so that every fallen soldier has "made the supreme sacrifice" for his country. In the Great War context, though, Western publics were far more closely attuned to Christian usage, and the explicitly religious use of sacrificial terminology was standard: it was much more than a mere euphemism. Pastor and popular novelist Harold

Bell Wright declared that "a man may give his life for humanity in a bloody trench as truly as upon a bloody cross. The world may be saved somewhere in France as truly as in Palestine." Soldiers could be Christ, and so could whole nations. Lyman Abbott described how each of the combatant powers had taken its sacrificial role in turn, culminating when "America offered her life that she might save England, France, and Belgium." "Crucified Belgium" was a familiar term. German preacher H. Francke explicitly compared the mistreatment of his nation by the Allies to the sufferings inflicted on Christ himself: "As Jesus was treated, so also have the German people been treated." For both sides, the war was an immense, continent-wide Good Friday.[25]

In various forms, the crucifixion theme was a mainstay of wartime propaganda imagery, used variously to stir hatred against the enemy or to persuade people to enlist or buy war bonds. Apart from the crucified Canadian and other prisoners supposedly murdered in this grotesque way, Anglo-American posters often depicted disheveled but glamorous young women crucified by the Germans. Over and above the religious content, such images appealed to contemporary views of the sanctity and innocence of womanhood, and thus accused the perpetrators of violating all known standards of chivalry, honor, and true masculinity. Not incidentally, posters of this kind were also eye-catching in presenting seminude young women. On occasion, the female crucifixion victim was a symbolic figure representing a whole nation, a Serbia, Poland, or Armenia.

Ideas of suffering and sacrifice had a special resonance for Catholics, whose faith focused on the reenactment of Christ's sacrificial death in the Mass. That event gave great charismatic power to the priests who were alone permitted to perform the ritual. Eucharistic imagery dominates Catholic war literature, of whatever nation. In 1915, pseudonymous French author René Gaëll published the popular book *Les Soutanes sous la Mitraille* (*Cassocks Under Machine-*

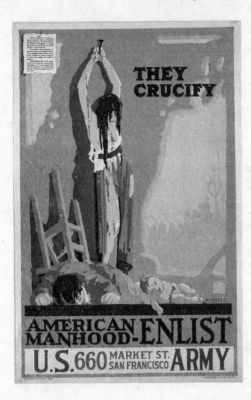

A U.S. Army recruiting poster uses the imagery of crucifixion so common in wartime atrocity propaganda. Appealing to a sense of chivalry—and perhaps to generate prurient interest—such posters often depicted attractive young female victims.

Gun Fire), which appeared in English translation the following year. The book depicts France's priests as the heroes and martyrs of a war that is at once Christian, Catholic, and patriotic, in a death struggle against the barbarians of "sacrilegious Germany, which profanes weakness and slaughters Catholic temples." Victory would come only through "sacrifices [*immolations*] and voluntary sufferings"— the original English translation gives "holocausts" rather than sacrifices. Although Christians will shed their blood, this should be seen as "the red seed of battle, an eternal seed of victory and redemption." God, who requires us to suffer and die, also "gives us the superhuman joy of having been chosen to be heroes of freedom, and martyrs for violated rights." [26]

Similar ideas run through Claudel's *Christmas Eve*. The play begins with the two dead soldiers, Jean and Jacques. Jean realizes that they are now with God: "Just one second made me a Christian and one of the blessed." Jacques replies, "Now, I am pure, Jean, and without sin. It's your blood that made me this white robe." They summon the souls of the civilians murdered by Germans, especially the children:

> Come, holy innocent souls. Come, witnesses of Jesus Christ. Come, tender lambs immolated by cruel Herod, not for the slightest wrong that you have done, but for the hatred of the God of which you stand as image.

These were martyrs and saints, just as much as the missionaries killed by native tribesmen, as much as the martyrs of China, as much as the heroes of faith in the time of the Roman emperors. "Just as Christ gave his life for you, you have given yours." [27]

A similar rhetoric of blood sacrifice manifested itself in Ireland, where a decades-long nationalist struggle against British rule culminated in the great Easter Rising of 1916 and the subsequent war of independence. But however much Irish nationalists opposed the Allied war effort, their language reflected a worldview identical to that of the warring powers. One of the movement's leaders was Patrick Pearse, who was obsessed with ideas of redemption through blood. These ideas were rooted in Catholic thought but also drew on neo-pagan racial mysticism. In 1913, he had written, "Bloodshed is a cleansing and sanctifying thing." Two years later he praised the war, declaring, "The old heart of the earth needed to be warmed by the red wine of the battlefields," because "life springs from death." He believed firmly that "one man can free a people, as one man redeemed the world." Following the logic of his teaching, on Easter Monday 1916, Pearse joined other nationalists, Catholic and secular, in a suicidal rising against British power;

the revolt was of course intended to symbolize the nation's death and resurrection.[28]

Protestant nations had their own images of modern-day martyrs, usually associated with overseas missions, and they readily adopted the blood-drenched imagery of Catholic propaganda. For the English-speaking world, by far the greatest martyr image was Nurse Edith Cavell, executed in 1915 for helping Allied soldiers escape occupied Belgium. Her death was a welcome gift to Allied propaganda, which made her a literal martyr and saint. Successive accounts made the already ugly circumstances of her death even more gruesome. Reportedly, her refusal to wear a blindfold meant that she fainted before the firing squad and was shot while lying on the ground. Apart from the obvious religious imagery of martyrdom, the Cavell story was powerful in portraying a (supposedly) innocent woman. Already in 1916, a popular Australian film was portraying *The Martyrdom of Nurse Cavell*. Canada gave her name to one of its towering western peaks, which was conveniently located near Angel Glacier. The Church of England commemorates the anniversary of her death—a recognition short of canonization, but still potent. The Germans had no doubt of the damage the case had caused them internationally. When Adolf Hitler visited a conquered Paris in 1940, he ordered the destruction of two highly offensive statues—one depicted Nurse Cavell.[29]

None of the Allied sentiments about sacrifice and martyrdom would have surprised soldiers from the Central Powers. At the time of Verdun, German Catholic clergy regularly compared the sacrifice of frontline soldiers to that of Christ. One of Germany's celebrated war writers was Walter Flex, who died in 1917 of wounds received on the eastern front. His popular verses presented the war as a Last Supper, in which "from German blood is Christ's wine prepared / And in the blood of the purest works the power of the Lord / who strides through the holy transformation." "The sacrifice of the best of our people is only a repetition willed by God of the deepest miracle of life . . . the death of Christ." Like other writers of the time, Flex absolutely merged the cause of Christianity with that of his nation; his epitaph quoted from his Prussian Military Oath: "He who swears on Prussia's flag has nothing left that belongs to himself." As for American thinkers, sacrifice was the prerequisite for glorification and resurrection: "To fight, to die, to be resurrected, that is the essence of being. From out of your death [in the war] the nation will be restored." Predictably, the Nazis loved Flex's work, with its mystical vision of German blood and military sacrifice, and celebrated his writings—which is the main reason why he has so dropped from the memory of later generations.[30]

So common was the language of sacrifice and martyrdom as to cause multiple difficulties, both secular and religious. The martyrdom idea could be deeply dangerous when it affected attitudes to the scale of military losses. It was one thing for an individual to decide to sacrifice his life for others, but on occasion commanders steeled themselves to accept the mass bloodshed of inferiors in the great cause. In Italy, for example, the high command committed their infantry to "a necessary holocaust" with the goal of "redeeming" Italy's natural frontiers. This fanatical mind-set contributed to Italy's appalling rate of wartime casualties and a repeated series of crushing defeats.[31]

The constant stress on martyrdom also raised serious theological problems for the churches, in eroding distinctions between spiritual and secular causes. Yes, Christians could agree that the war was holy and that soldiers were following Christ. But in pouring praise upon the battle dead, newspapers and popular orators ventured into controversial theological terrain, suggesting that the act of sacrifice washed away previous sins, and automatically gave an instant place in paradise. Military valor trumped all other virtues, including faith, and conveyed something like heroic sanctity. Church leaders demurred but were in a difficult position because they did not want to appear to be minimizing military heroism. In 1917, the World Evangelical Alliance rejected the notion of automatic salvation through glorious death in a pamphlet on *The War and Sacrificial Death*.

The theological argument was obvious enough, but it is remarkable that the case had to be made and that it should prove so controversial. The language of sacrifice and martyrdom—of immolation and holocaust—was the common currency of war.[32]

A British Easter card shows the risen Christ walking alongside two British soldiers. The image recalls the New Testament story of the two apostles meeting Christ on the road to Emmaus (Lk. 24:13–35).

CHAPTER FOUR

The Ways of God
Faith, Heresy, and Superstition

The soldier has got religion; I am not sure that he has got Christianity.
—NEVILLE TALBOT

IN 1916, THE INEFFABLE Bishop Arthur F. Winnington-Ingram made a statement about the war's spiritual impact on combatants. "Those who were serving at the front," he declared, "would return with their souls purged and purified by what they [had] experienced." The words appalled Siegfried Sassoon, then serving with near-suicidal courage at the Battle of the Somme and subsequently one of Britain's most admired war poets and memoirists. In his poem "They," Sassoon portrayed a bishop welcoming the returned heroes who had stood face to face with Death, who had led the attack on the Antichrist. Surely, after such transfiguring experiences, the boys would never be the same! Grimly, the soldiers agree that their lives have changed irrevocably, but not in any noble way. Bill has been blinded, George has lost his legs, others are mortally wounded or syphilitic. To which reports, the militaristic cleric can make no useful reply: "And the Bishop said: 'The ways of God are strange!'"[1]

Reading so many high-octane orations about cosmic struggles, modern readers might wonder about the relationship between the pious hopes of the preachers and the audiences they were trying to reach. Really, we may ask, what did ordinary soldiers want from the war, except the chance of escaping from it with life and limb intact? When preachers and professors called for a crusade, did anyone on the ground—or in the trenches—actually believe these sixty-year-old fire-eaters? Outside the seminaries and the bishops' palaces, did anyone pay much heed to the propaganda barrage about the diabolic nature of the enemy, all the God-fueled patriotism? From London to the western front, seemingly, you needed to travel a hundred miles and about a thousand years.

Certainly, some contemporary soldiers expressed their contempt for the religious rhetoric of war. Sassoon dismissed God as "a buffoon, who skulks somewhere at Base with tipsy priests to serve him." For moderns, such mockery seems entirely appropriate, and the long-term cultural consequences would seem entirely predictable. From this perspective, surely, the churches must have tarnished their credibility beyond saving with those who might once have been their followers, who became disenchanted with religion and prepared to consider secular and indeed radical solutions to the world's problems. Reviewing the evils of the bloody year 1916, British Jew Israel Zangwill noted:

> **The world bloodily minded**
> **The Church dead or polluted**
> **The blind leading the blinded**
> **And the deaf dragging the muted.**[2]

But the religious aspects of the war were much more complicated, and more extensive, than this reading might suggest. Religious ideas, very broadly defined, directly influenced the lives of ordinary people in all the combatant nations, including the men serving in the armed forces. To modern eyes, they were amazingly open to accepting and repeating these exalted interpretations of the war and the demonization of the enemy.

Had the soldier—or the civilian—"got" Christianity? It very much depends how we define the limits of that faith. Supernatural and spiritual interpretations of current events often manifested themselves outside the mainstream churches. In Europe in 1914, as in the modern United States, it is not possible to understand the range of religious belief just by looking at the churches' official teachings, because conventional belief was accompanied by a vast penumbra of occult and mystical belief that had a wide influence across classes. If in retrospect these ideas seem to us bizarre or deluded, we might well ask whether they were any more lunatic than the official policies of governments and military commands at the time. Official propagandists were so successful not because they were trying to create ideas of cosmic confrontation but rather because they exploited ideas that were already thoroughly diffused in the culture at large.

A Believing World

COUNTLESS POPULAR CULTURE DEPICTIONS have taught later generations to be keenly aware of the gap separating wartime propaganda from the attitudes of soldiers at the front, who on occasion felt more kinship for the enemies in the opposing trenches than for the blowhard warmongers safe at home. Nor were ordinary soldiers necessarily pious, especially when so many came from urban and industrial settings long influenced by socialist and anticlerical militancy. Berlin, the setting for so many declarations of God's German partisanship, was notorious for its dismal rates of church attendance among the working classes. The church likewise struggled for respect in Italy's thriving Red Belt. Even in England, evangelical writers assumed that servicemen could make themselves unpopular by ostentatious piety, so that praying visibly attracted mockery, or worse. Compulsory church parades in the British army gave skeptics still greater opportunities for blasphemous parody. In 1919, the British churches commissioned a despairing report on *The Army and Religion,* which noted the common impression that "Christianity and the churches have failed, are out of it, are disliked, and not for righteousness's sake."[3]

But not only were European publics at the time highly attuned to religious and particularly Christian ideas but so were soldiers at the front, the George and Bill of Sassoon's poem. Of course, levels of practice and belief varied enormously across Europe and were certainly declining in some countries: France, particularly, suffered a sharp decline in practice in the decade or so before the outbreak of war, during the intense church-state political crisis. Generally, though, rates of church identification and participation still remained high across Europe in 1914. Protestant countries especially had successfully promoted popular religious education as part of the general increase in literacy that had marked the later nineteenth century. British levels of church membership reached all-time historic highs in the decade or so before the war. As in many other countries, British clergy responded to urban and industrial growth by developing innovative social missions, which were making real progress in recolonizing the areas lost to radical secularism or indifference.[4]

However counterintuitive this might seem in light of later events, the Russian church in 1914 looked like one of the Christian world's major success stories. The country was in the midst of a general religious revival, with rising levels of literacy among peasants and a publishing boom in devotional literature. The church had even made serious inroads among industrial workers, under the leadership of a series of charismatically led reform movements preaching a kind of social gospel activism. Levels of religious practice reached unprecedented heights in the cities and industrial areas. The church could also claim a thriving cultural life and intellectuals and artists were suffused in its imagery and traditions, even if they rejected its political authority. Many proclaimed themselves "God seekers," *Bogoiskateli.* The Orthodox Russia that entered the war looked as if it was beginning an epoch of cultural achievement equal to any in its history.[5]

Quite apart from formal religious participation, Christian values and worldviews permeated European public discourse well into the mid-twentieth century. Just because people were not going to church—especially to the state-approved churches—did not mean that they had rejected faith. Describing England, Michael Snape adapts the concept of "diffusive Christianity," the dominance of broadly Christian ideas even for people who might not have consciously defined themselves as religious, including those urban and industrial classes the churches might occasionally have given up for lost. Plenty of people still thought of themselves as Christian and applied a Christian worldview, even if they despised the clergy and never set foot inside a church, and that would also be true in Germany or France. In each of the combatant powers, religious terminology was part of the cultural air that people breathed.[6]

Moreover, despite the strength of anticlerical politics in much of Catholic Europe, secularization was still a strictly limited phenomenon in this era. Most European countries were far more likely than England to have large rural and peasant populations that remained closely tied to the traditional church, and these groups supplied the great majority of those nations' armies. Peasants still constituted 80 percent of Russia's population, and most of that country's newly emerging working classes were close to their peasant roots—and often to their historic faith. Across Europe, we can heartily endorse Snape's remark about England that "the idea of redemptive sacrifice was second nature to the population, whether they realized it or not."[7]

Even a good number of those often-maligned army chaplains

won the respect of the soldiers they served by sharing their privations and dangers, giving credibility to the spiritual messages they preached. Some became legendary. Britain's Tubby Clayton was famous for the meeting house he maintained at the front, under the sign ALL RANK ABANDON, YE WHO ENTER HERE, and this operation became the basis of a significant postwar movement. In Catholic ranks particularly, less celebrated clergy kept up their church's reputation by their efforts to reach and comfort the wounded and dying.[8]

The war in turn brought a new and intensely elevated sense of the presence of death and the potential for spiritual action. This mood reached into some surprising quarters, affecting even the most hardened skeptics. One influential wartime book was H. G. Wells's *Mr. Britling Sees It Through* (1916), an account of the British home front as it affected one intellectual's family. So successful was it that American isolationists despairingly cited *Mr. Britling* as one of the most effective forces driving U.S. public opinion toward intervention in 1916–17. (In mobilizing Anglophilia, the film of *Mrs. Miniver* offers a close parallel in the 1940s). But *Mr. Britling* carried a religious message that was incredible given Wells's reputation as the apostle of scientific materialism and the deadly foe of organized faith. After losing his son, Mr. Britling—a clear surrogate for Wells—experiences a classic religious conversion:

Religion is the first thing and the last thing, and until a
man has found God and been found by God, he begins at no
beginning, he works to no end. He may have his friendships,
his partial loyalties, his scraps of honour. But all these things
fall into place and life falls into place only with God. Only with
God. God, who fights through men against Blind Force and
Night and Non-Existence; who is the end, who is the meaning.
He is the only King. . . . It was as if he had been groping all
this time in the darkness, thinking himself alone amidst rocks
and pitfalls and pitiless things, and suddenly a hand, a firm

strong hand, had touched his own. And a voice within him
bade him be of good courage. . . . God was beside him and
within him and about him. . . . Then after a time he said:
"Our sons who have shown us God . . ."[9]

An embarrassed Wells spent the rest of his life denying that he
had gone Christian, asserting unconvincingly that by "God" he had
meant something like the spirit of history. In the mood of the time,
religion had a bad habit of catching even the most unlikely victims
unawares. And if even a Wells could be so transformed, then it is
scarcely surprising to find a general revival of faith among those
who had not distanced themselves from the churches.

Faith at War

IN LIGHT OF THIS, it is not surprising to find so many expressions of faith among the war's fighting soldiers.[10] In their diaries
and letters, Protestant soldiers—American, Canadian, British, or
German—made frequent reference to the Bible, either from reading
the text or (often) from recalling childhood memories. The psalms
were a popular favorite, perhaps because these were so often read
and memorized in schools or Sunday schools, but their emphasis on
God's mighty hand controlling events also seemed highly comfort-
ing in the circumstances. For those passing through the valley of the
shadow of death, the 23rd Psalm had a special appeal. Soldiers rarely
cited the Bible's harsh or military texts, such as the wars of Joshua
or the Maccabees, but they turned time and again to the Gospel
of John. Here, they found a reassuring vision of Christ's absolute
power, his unconditional offer of resurrection and survival after
death. Soldiers responded to the image of Christ as faithful leader
of a small band of loyal companions. Christ himself declared the
most stringent demand that could be placed on a soldier: when you

must, you lay down your life for your friends. It was an apt gospel for comrades, for pals.[11]

Going beyond specific texts, soldiers inevitably resorted to exalted biblical language when dealing with events of this unimaginable magnitude. In his study of U.S. forces in the war, *Faith in the Fight,* Jonathan Ebel showed how spontaneously U.S. servicemen interpreted violence and mass death in religious terms, how freely they drew on the standard Christian vocabulary of suffering and redemption as a means of salvation. Biblicizing also gave a cosmic meaning, even a grandeur, to acts of extreme violence and mass killing. When German forces lost thousands of young men at Ypres in 1914, the event inevitably became known as the *Kindermord bei Ypern,* from King Herod's Massacre of the Holy Innocents, recounted in the New Testament. In 1925, Britain erected a monument to its wartime Machine Gun Corps, with the biblical inscription "Saul hath slain his thousands, but David his tens of thousands."[12]

As literate Christians described the events of the war or the landscapes of destruction, they turned naturally to the Bible and later spiritual classics. Even slightly educated continental Europeans thought readily of Dante's *Inferno,* so that the phrase "Abandon hope" became commonplace in battlefield recollections. Less steeped in Dante, English speakers thought rather of John Bunyan's *The Pilgrim's Progress,* which enjoyed near-scriptural status in that era, and two of the book's scenes recur countless times in letters and memoirs. Gazing over the fields of mud, minds turned naturally to Bunyan's miry slough of despond, or to the valley of the shadow of death: "Now I saw in my dream, that at the end of this valley lay blood, bones, ashes, and mangled bodies of men, even of pilgrims that had gone this way formerly." As Paul Fussell comments, both valley and slough became "inevitable clichés of memory" for soldier-pilgrims struggling through the wartime wilderness.[13]

Such otherworldly imagery appealed even to those soldiers who had learned to be deeply skeptical of official statements by governments or the high command. English war poet Wilfred Owen, for instance, was anything but a passive follower of official orthodoxies, but when describing the utter destruction of the no-man's-land between the trenches, he turned to both the Bible and *The Pilgrim's Progress*:

> It is like the eternal place of gnashing of teeth; the Slough of Despond could be contained in one of its crater holes; the fires of Sodom and Gomorrah could not light a candle to it—to find the way to Babylon the Fallen.[14]

The constant problem was reconciling religious teachings with the everyday tasks of warfare. British veteran Harry Patch, the product of a church school, reported trying to serve faithfully while obeying the commandment "Thou shalt not kill." He made his squad pledge to avoid firing fatal shots where at all possible and to aim at legs rather than bellies. Patch hated situations when the mere demands of survival forced him to ignore the pleas of the wounded, and he framed the situation in biblical terms: "But we weren't like the Good Samaritan in the Bible, we were the robbers who passed them by and left." Was a Christian soldier a contradiction in terms?[15]

God on the Battlefield

WITHOUT NECESSARILY TURNING TO the biblical text, Catholic combatants were at least as likely to interpret their experience in spiritual terms and to seek supernatural aid for themselves and their country. Catholics were after all taught to believe in the intrusion of the supernatural into the secular world, in the charismatic power

BELGIAN + RED CROSS

DONATIONS MAY BE SENT TO THE HON. TREASURER.
THE RHT. HON. THE LORD MAYOR OF LONDON,
OR TO THE PRESIDENT, BARON C. GOFFINET.
28, GROSVENOR GARDENS, S.W.
COPIES OF THIS POSTER MAY BE OBTAINED FREE F EACH FROM 28, GROSVENOR GARDENS, S.W.

This 1915 appeal for the Belgian Red Cross depicts Allied nurses as literal angels, complete with wings.

attached to special people and places. Throughout the French trench system, soldiers built their own chapels, commonly dedicated to the Virgin Mary. Shrines and grottoes proliferated across France, and pilgrimage surged in popularity, especially to the Marian shrine of Lourdes.[16]

Catholic sensibilities attracted Protestants and others. The war brought together millions of mainly young men who otherwise might never have encountered each other, and soldiers from allied nations borrowed each other's spiritual ideas and practices. The regions of Belgium and northern France that now constituted the western front were traditionally pious Catholic areas, and servicemen not raised in that tradition often admired the spiritual landscape created over the centuries, where holiness endured even through the worst violence.

Much commented on were such public symbols of faith as the calvaries (representations of the Crucifixion) and other shrines. When the communities were destroyed in the course of war, some of these sites survived, albeit damaged, and they made for evocative landmarks. Catholic or not, passing armies noted the figures of Christ standing in the ruined wilderness and developed stories of their miraculous survival. Now, soldiers neither noted nor commemorated the many places where figures of Christ and the saints had been shattered beyond recognition, but that still left plenty of miracles to go around. As Robert Graves recalled,

> [This] made most of the English soldiers in the purgatorial trenches lose all respect for organized Pauline religion, though still feeling a sympathetic reverence for Jesus as our fellow sufferer. Cross-road calvaries emphasized this relationship.[17]

German Protestants likewise fell under the influence of Catholic fellow soldiers, whether those of their own nation or of the Austro-Hungarian Empire.

The pressures of war drove some to still more explicitly spiritual interpretations. Jesuit Pierre Teilhard de Chardin wrote in 1917 that

> through the war, a rent has been made in the crust of banality and convention. A window was opened on the secret mechanisms and deepest layers of human development.

In the words of the oft-quoted English poem "Christ in Flanders,"

> This hideous warfare seems to make things clear.
> We never thought about You much in England—
> But now that we are far away from England—
> We have no doubts, we know that You are here.

A German student who served at Verdun wrote similarly that "here we have war, war in its most appalling form, and in our distress we realize the nearness of God." [18]

For every observer like Sassoon who saw religious claims about the war as a blasphemous parody, we easily find many others whose experiences drove them to different forms of religious conversion. While at an army hospital in 1918, Lieutenant C. S. Lewis was surprised to find himself enjoying the essays of G. K. Chesterton, the greatest Christian apologist in contemporary England: at that stage, Lewis was a convinced atheist. Encountering Chesterton, though, began the process that led to Lewis's postwar conversion and his distinguished role in Christian thought. Sometimes war experiences inspired a deeper commitment to one's original faith, but in Britain, the war and its immediate aftermath witnessed many conversions to Catholicism. [19]

Theists in the Foxhole

A FAMOUS SAYING HOLDS that "there are no atheists in the foxhole," but that is quite different from saying that the stress of war produces orthodox believers. Actually, much of the religious and spiritual interest in the various armies existed on the fringes of Christianity, as soldiers freely integrated elements of both Christian and occult beliefs. To adapt the title of Walter Flex's popular war novel, they became wanderers between both worlds. [20]

Soldiers encountering violence on such a scale resorted to supernatural explanations to make sense of it. Some found that the worldview offered by orthodox religion gave satisfactory answers, but many did not, especially those whose prewar contacts with the churches had been minimal or actively hostile. Under the stress of combat, some developed a powerful belief in a kind of fate or destiny, a notion of design that might or might not involve any kind

of personal deity. Once-popular American poet Alan Seeger, who
served in the French Foreign Legion, celebrated this military fatalism in his poem "Maktoob." He tells how he took a fragment of the
shell that had killed his friend and made it into a ring. He then persuaded a Muslim soldier to write on it the Arabic word *maktoob,* "it
is written," the phrase commonly used in North Africa to indicate
acceptance of the relentless fate commanded by God. For Seeger,
this "wisdom of the East" taught a mighty spiritual lesson:

> **Learn to drive fear, then, from your heart.**
> **If you must perish, know, O man,**
> **'Tis an inevitable part**
> **Of the predestined plan.**

Such informal theologies were commonly accompanied by a
florid world of rituals and superstitions, again divorced from any orthodox Christian belief, but nonetheless powerful. Soldiers followed
what Paul Fussell has termed "a plethora of very un-modern superstitions, talismans, wonders, miracles, relics, legends, and rumors." In
the words of frontline officer Marc Bloch—later to become one of
France's greatest historians—"The prevailing opinion in the trenches
was that anything might be true, except what was printed." [21]

So prevalent were fatalism and superstition that frontline armies
seem to have lived in an alternate spiritual universe more akin to
the Middle Ages than the era of tanks and aircraft. Accepting such
worldviews was much easier for the millions of soldiers who came
from peasant households where folk magic and traditional beliefs
still reigned. In 1917, folklorist Hanns Bächtold-Stäubli published
a scholarly analysis of *German Soldiers' Customs and Beliefs,* which
makes for astonishing reading. As he remarked, war and the threat
of death did a marvelous job of focusing the minds of ordinary men
who were suddenly willing to pay avid attention to quite outlandish
prophecies and folk beliefs. [22]

For both soldiers and their families, the main concerns were natural enough. How would the war develop and when would it end? Answers to both questions lay in such ancient signs as the state of the moon and sun, the flights of birds, all as interpreted by widely circulating verses and pamphlets. As one German rhyme interpreted the years preceding the war,

1911 ein Glutjahr	A Year of Fire
1912 ein Flutjahr	A Year of Flood
1913 ein gut Jahr	A Good Year
1914 ein Blutjahr	A Year of Blood

Numerology came into its own, as soldiers tried to calculate the war's end by adding together the digits in special dates such as the beginning and end of the war of 1870–71. One popular attempt cited by Bächtold-Stäubli predicted the end of the current war as November 11, 1915—an impressive coincidence in terms of the month and day, although off by three years on the actual year. The prophecy again demonstrates the widespread expectation that such a war could not conceivably last more than a year or so, which helps to explain the stupefied despair that resulted as it dragged on into its fourth and fifth years.[23]

Both at the front and at home, people sought omens, signs that foretold either safety or death, and a few of these became widely famous. Such was the Golden Virgin of Albert, a town cursed with a wonderfully strategic location. Medieval stories told of the discovery of a miraculous statue of the Virgin, which attracted pilgrims through the centuries, and a great golden statue stood atop the basilica. In 1898, the pope had declared it "the Lourdes of the North." German shellfire damaged the building in 1915, and although the statue began to lean to the horizontal, it remained attached to its base. Allied soldiers developed the legend that the statue's fall would mean the end of the war and—probably—their own defeat, leading commanders to order the figure reinforced by wire. The Germans in turn believed that the side that actually brought down the Virgin would lose the war and aimed their guns away from the basilica accordingly. Both legends proved wrong when, in 1918, British artillery destroyed the figure, shortly before winning their decisive victory on the western front.[24]

While knowledge about the future was useful, soldiers needed immediate spiritual protection to give them a chance of seeing the war's end. Here, orthodox religion offered some protection, but ordinary people turned to their own resources when the churches failed. Fighting men had a powerful hunger for protective amulets and talismans, which were believed to ward off danger. As Paul Fussell remarks, "No frontline soldier was without his amulet, and every tunic pocket became a reliquary." To the despair of the Protestant clergy who distributed Bibles and New Testaments among the forces, soldiers collected and treasured these items not as sources of wisdom and inspiration but as talismans. American soldiers in particular wanted a Bible in their pockets when they advanced into battle. Even if they bothered to open the books to read the actual Bible text, plenty of them were looking for protective spells rather than inspiration. Like countless other Christians throughout history, Protestants of all nations turned to Psalm 91, the ancient defense against violence and evil ("A thousand shall fall at thy side, and ten thousand at thy right hand; but it shall not come nigh thee. . . . For he shall give his angels charge over thee").[25]

Catholics in this era had access to a much richer arsenal of protective supernatural resources, in the form of rosaries and holy medals. A German soldier tasked with burying the dead noted that most of the soldiers bore a medal of the Immaculate Virgin. Devout Catholics wore the scapular, a pair of simple holy images worn over the chest and back and tied together with light woolen cloth over the shoulders. As scapulars were believed to give protection, from 1914 they became hugely popular among the soldiers and sailors of all the fighting nations. Whether French or German, Irish or Austrian, Catholic groups sent scapulars and holy images to the fighting forces, and anecdotal evidence suggests these were widely accepted, even by individuals whose peacetime politics might have been strongly antireligious. Protestants too developed a real affection for crucifixes and the protection they could afford. French Catholic papers delighted in reporting miracles attributed to scapulars and sacred images—of units escaping casualties during artillery barrages, of vital supplies kept safe by the Sacred Heart. Orthodox Russians, Romanians, and Serbs followed their own traditions of supernatural intervention, commonly by the Virgin or the saints.[26]

Even these resources proved inadequate for believing families who sought to equip their menfolk with still stronger spiritual weapons. Bächtold-Stäubli tells of German mothers and wives pronouncing ritual verses and spells before sending men to the front, or giving them a *Schutzbrief,* a heaven-sent letter of protection, in a model that would not have been out of place in the Thirty Years War.[27]

Souls in Khaki (and Gray and Blue)

HARRY PATCH RECORDED A classic story of a supernatural encounter at the front. Falling into a trench, he found a mortally wounded British soldier "ripped shoulder to waist with shrapnel." He begged Harry to shoot him, to end his agony. Harry held his hand as he died, and in that final minute, "he only said one word: 'Mother.' I didn't see her, but she was there. No doubt about it. He passed from this life into the next, and it felt as if I was in God's presence. I've never got over it. You never forget it. Never."[28] The abundant memoirs of the war record many such episodes, when even highly secular individuals report moments of epiphany, of what they believed to be passages between worlds. Surrounded by death and loss, it was natural for soldiers to make sense of such events through storytelling, and these stories escalated into legends of religious or spiritual significance.

In one telling case, we can actually see a routine battle casualty in the process of becoming a martyr and near saint. In 1917, journalist Arthur Copping published his reverential book *Souls in Khaki* about the work of his own evangelical Salvation Army movement among British forces. He tells a moving story of two sailors holding on to a piece of wreckage after their ship is sunk during a disastrous naval action in 1914. It soon becomes obvious, though, that the small piece of wood could not support them both. One of the pair, a Salvationist, tells his friend, "Goodbye mate. Death means life to me. But you are not converted, so keep hold and save yourself." Abandoning the spar, he goes to his death. Retold in testimony at Salvationist meetings, the story became a staple of evangelical folklore, and it still circulates today. As Copping investigated the story, he soon unearthed bewildering and contradictory versions of the sacrificial death of the heroic sailor Brumpton. Copping's frank account makes it obvious that we can say nothing with confidence about this affair except that a Salvationist sailor probably did perish in that particular incident. Rather than discrediting the central legend, though, Copping accepts the diversity of accounts as actually confirming Brumpton's Christian heroism. Such legends circulated as folktales, or rather what scholars call FOAF-tales: stories attributed to a "friend of a friend." [29]

Although Brumpton's story demands no belief in the supernatural, it shows how easily legends could arise and flourish when they conveyed truths that people wanted to hear, when they seemed to teach appropriate moral or spiritual messages. So abundant are occult stories, in fact, that it is difficult to do more than to divide them into a general typology. Sometimes, as with the Angel of Mons, the stories were on a vast historical canvas, and each country generated comparable legends: French forces saw Joan of Arc. Other stories were much more local and individual. What they had in common was that they helped fill a need of the people telling or hearing the tale. Even if they did not really believe it, it was encouraging to think that angelic or supernatural armies might conceivably come to their aid in the ultimate crisis. Obviously nobody recounted tales of mystical forces or ancient kings coming to help the enemy.

Naturally enough, too, legends arose most prolifically at times of extreme stress, during great offensives when the fate of whole armies stood in danger. During the great German spring offensive of 1918, British nurse Vera Brittain was stationed at the army base at Étaples. She noted how British units "began to suffer from a curious masochism, and as in 1914, turned from their usual dogged reliance upon their own strength to the consolations of superstition and the illusions of fatigue." Wounded soldiers told of the ghostly appearance of a dead officer who had once promised to help his men in their time of trouble, and he duly returned during the 1918 debacle. That account in turn provoked a series of other ghost stories, all reporting the reappearance of comrades who had died at the Somme two years before: "And it's our belief they're fighting with us still." [30]

One very popular legend in wartime France was known as "Debout les Morts!" (Let the dead arise!). Originally, a French lieutenant in 1915 reported being surrounded by Germans when a wounded comrade shouted that phrase. Several badly wounded men stood to arms and fought off the foe. Soon, though, the story evolved to claim that dead French soldiers had arisen to join the fight. The French unit was greatly helped by finding plenty of grenades, apparently supplied by the dead themselves. Patriotic writer Maurice Barrès worked to circulate the story, but as had happened with Arthur Machen the previous year, the tale ran away from him. "Debout les Morts!" became an accepted part of national mythology because it told people just what they wanted to hear. The legend was also politically perfect, offering something to both sides of France's enduring culture wars. Apart from the obvious Catholic Christian theme of Resurrection, the phrase also recalled the opening of the socialist/secularist anthem, the Internationale: "Debout, les damnés de la terre!"—"Arise, wretched of the earth!" [31]

If supernatural military aid was not feasible, people might still hope for crucial information from the beyond, and many wartime legends concerned omens and auguries. One recurring theme was that of the Warning Voice, the unearthly and untraceable speech that warned of the death of individuals or the disasters that would accompany a major offensive. We hear of heavenly visions: French soldiers reported flaming swords and tricolor stars in the skies, not to mention apparitions of saints and angels. British narratives told of crosses, like the one that supposedly heralded the bloody beginning of the Somme offensive in 1916. More prosaically, the British knew that anyone dreaming of a bus did not have long to live. [32]

One widespread tale reported the mysterious deeds of the Comrade in White, the spectral figure who appeared in the worst of the battle to assist wounded and dying soldiers, often in what was appropriately termed no-man's-land. The Comrade story became famous through its treatment in popular books, and through a painting that was widely reproduced as a print. There was always some debate about how far the Comrade should be taken as Christ or an angelic figure, which was the interpretation generally pressed in home-front versions of the tale. In this view, Christ was extending his aid to human fellow sufferers who shared his calvary. Front-line tales were more open-ended in understanding this anonymous friend, but however the Comrade was understood, these stories held out a degree of comfort to soldiers who dreaded being abandoned to a lonely death. [33]

Most persistently, there were the countless premonitions, the final proofs that individual lives were in the hands of a larger destiny, and these tales were endlessly repeated and reprinted. If there is a generic wartime ghost story, it might be that of one Private Reynolds, serving at Gallipoli, who awoke with a start, reporting a dream in which he had seen his mother reading an account of his death, together with the exact place and time. Reportedly, the premonition was fulfilled precisely to the minute. Changing the name and uniform, the story could easily have been American, German, Italian, or French. Catholic soldiers might perhaps have introduced an explicitly Christian figure, such as an angel.[34]

We see this process at work in a story reported in a mainstream Irish newspaper, in which a soldier in France reported encountering a nun who passed on a prophetic message. The war would not end, she warned, until humanity renounced its sins and fell before God in worship. Intrigued, the soldier tried to find the nun at the local convent but was told that no such woman was known there. He eventually recognized a picture of her, only to be told that this was a long-deceased mother superior, a woman of noted holiness. What matters is less that somebody told this story and more that it was published, and this at a time when official censorship was suppressing any materials that might contradict the standard narrative of the war—that it would continue until victory, not just until the people of all nations practiced Christian piety. The story does not suggest that any one nation, Allied or Central Powers, was in less need of repentance than any other.[35]

Such mythologies found a hospitable home in Russia. Russian soldiers had their distinctive body of legends about miraculous apparitions of the Virgin and angels, which circulated in prints and broadsheets with print runs in the hundreds of thousands. In 1917, Sofia Fedorchenko recorded a rich collection of popular customs and beliefs in her book *The People at War,* with a familiar array of mysterious beings, fairies, and goblins as well as omens and portents. If the British had the Comrade in White, Russians knew the White Horseman, and that anyone who looked him in the eye would survive the battle. As if these domestic resources were not enough, Russian media also printed Western stories, including images of the Virgin of Albert. Modern media powerfully reinforced medieval beliefs.[36]

Faith at Home

ON THE HOME FRONTS too, as at the front line, we often find expressions of collective behavior that appear to have a very strong religious content, although it is all but impossible to assign them to any familiar kind of tradition or denomination. Sometimes quite pagan or archaic in their character, they suggest the strength of the popular ideas that surface with such regularity in the war years. This is the impression we get from the mainly Catholic German city of Freiburg, the subject of one of the best modern case studies of the Great War as it was experienced in a single locality. Like their counterparts throughout Europe, local clergy expressed alarm at the "growing rash of prophecies, chain letters, omens, card-reading, and occult practices." [37]

In German-speaking lands, one such manifestation was the iron nail statues, *Nagelfiguren,* which began to appear in 1915. In medieval Austrian custom, travelers beginning a journey would hammer a nail into a statue to seek good fortune. This practice now revived on a near-industrial scale, with an upsurge of warlike figures depicting medieval knights, shields, or Teutonic warriors, and ordinary people showed their support for the war effort by driving nails. Beginning in Vienna, these spread to Germany, where they appeared in the thousands, with figures of crosses, eagles, and heroic individuals. The fashion culminated in September 1915 with Berlin's forty-foot-high wooden statue of Field Marshal von Hindenburg. Seeing a potential money spinner, the authorities allowed individuals to hammer nails into Hindenburg for a healthy fee, much as an American town sells donors the right to have their names inscribed on bricks on a sidewalk at a new library or public building. A hundred marks bought a gold nail, five marks for silver, one for iron. The Hindenburg statue alone reputedly earned millions of marks. One historian writes of Germany's wartime "nail epidemic." [38]

The giant "nail figure" of Field Marshal Paul von Hindenburg,
erected in Berlin in 1915

But the element of civic (or national) pride gave way to a startling outbreak of what looked like superstition. Religious believers around the world are well acquainted with the ancient practice of using a symbolic object such as a cloth or amulet to touch a holy figure, in order to access some of its power. In a Christian context, the nailing obviously suggested a kind of symbolic crucifixion, with Hindenburg as Christ figure. This statue in particular also aroused concern for its magical connotations, as families participated less to fund the war effort than to purchase protection for their men in the army, much as they might have done at an ancient pagan shrine. A woman with four sons hammered four nails and prayed for their safety.

The Hindenburg statue represents a juxtaposition of ancient and modern, scientific and superstitious, that we often find in the war years. In itself, it was a triumph of modern marketing, aimed at supporting a modern scientific war (other popular statues portrayed U-boats). But the response suggests strong undercurrents of supernatural and mystical belief of a kind that seems surprising in the urban West of this time. It was not that these visceral ideas were new, rather that the peculiar circumstances of the war allowed them unprecedented public expression.

A Gigantic Psychological Experiment

REPORTING THE CULT OF the Hindenburg statue, French academics mocked this near idol worship and asked, "Is German *Kultur* regressing to African fetishism?" In all nations, though, educated and largely Christian populations were enthusiastically following spiritual practices that seemed primitive. The vogue for prophecy is suggested by the vast surviving body of pamphlets and books from all the fighting nations. This literature drew heavily on biblical sources but also referred to such venerated seers as Nostradamus and Saint Malachy. The British devoured such titles as *The Great War in the Divine Light of Prophecy: Is It Armageddon?, Prophecies and Omens of the Great War,* and the 1916 publication *Why the War Will End in 1917.*[39] French readers wanted to know what the seventh-century Saint Odile had to say about the war's end. They read pamphlets promising to reveal "how at this very moment is being accomplished the end of the German Empire, as announced by several famous prophets."[40]

Spiritualism and mediumship found a vast new popularity in the war years. Originating in mid-nineteenth-century America, the spiritualist movement soon became a global sensation. For its devotees, spiritualism was a whole alternative scientific system in which gifted individuals explored the afterlife, usually by means of séances. The battlefields of the Great War offered endless material for psychics and occult researchers at a time when there was never a shortage of deaths, or of young men cut off in the prime of life. People had a keen interest in the nature of death and postmortem survival, and many heard hopefully the assurance of British spiritualist Wellesley Tudor Pole that "the transient conditions of so-called death [*sic*] are becoming more harmonious than ever before." Pole and his like asserted that families could protect soldiers in the field by meditation and the projection of positive energies.[41]

Stories of ghosts and miraculous communications from the newly deceased now proliferated, often resulting from friend-of-a-friend legends like those of Brumpton the sailor. A British compendium of such otherworldly wartime encounters suggested the sheer scale of the surging folklore: "A fulfilled prophecy . . . foresaw own death . . . A true vision . . . prophetic dreams," not to mention many "communications from soldiers who have 'died.'" (The quotation marks are in the original.) These tales were regular fodder for general media outlets at the time, quite apart from the numerous specialized magazines catering to occult or spiritualist audiences. The English-speaking world supported the *Occult Review, Harbinger of Light*, the *International Psychic Gazette*, the *Psychical Research Review, Azoth, Light*, and the *Two Worlds;* Germany had the *Psychische Studien, Zeitschrift für Psychische Forschung*, and the *Zentralblatt für Okkultismus*. So much evidence of the supernatural emerged from the war that, in the words of British spiritualist Hereward Carrington, "a gigantic psychological experiment is being undertaken in Europe." In 1918, Arthur Conan Doyle published a survey of spiritualist doctrines under the ambitious title *The New Revelation*.[42]

The fact that so many supernatural tales inevitably had a frontline setting did not of itself mean that soldiers necessarily believed them. However much the soldiers accepted a ghostly or supernatural universe, the trappings of spiritualist mythology with all its mediums and séances belonged to the home front, not the battlefront. Reading the popular spiritualist writers of these years, like the British authors Hereward Carrington and Wellesley Tudor Pole, the main focus of the cases they recount is always the bereaved families who reportedly receive visions and communications telling them of what their sons and brothers had suffered. In fact, the best-known account of spiritualist experiments by British soldiers themselves appears in E. H. Jones's popular 1919 memoir *The Road to En-Dor,* which reports the deeds of two fraudulent mediums who used their supposed powers to escape from Turkish captivity. Soldiers didn't do such things—but their families emphatically did.[43]

Through their memoirs and poems, many individuals have emerged as the distinctive voices of the First World War's armies—Wilfred Owen and Robert Graves, Ernst Jünger and Walter Flex, Henri Barbusse and Erich Maria Remarque. At the time, though, in the English-speaking world one name stood out above all as the most celebrated voice from the trenches, entirely for things that he presumably did not say. In September 1915, Raymond Lodge was killed at the Battle of Hooge, near Ypres. Over the following months, mediums reported that Raymond was seeking to communicate with his family and particularly his father, Sir Oliver Lodge, a distinguished physicist who specialized in electromagnetism. A trained scientist, Sir Oliver applied many tests before determining that the mediums were reporting faithfully what Raymond was trying to say, including his descriptions of the afterlife and his prophecies about the material world. As an (apparently) documented scientific case study of the postmortem survival of the dead, Sir Oliver's narrative of the case, *Raymond,* made it a sensational success when it appeared in book form in 1916.[44]

Although there were enough such books to represent a whole genre, this case commanded the greatest attention, and the book went through twelve editions by 1919. In 1917, an Anglican chaplain to British forces wrote, "The chief interest among the masses for the moment centers round the possibility of communion with the departed, such as is dealt with in *Raymond.*" Through this book and several counterparts and imitators, the fundamental claims of spiritualism became something like international orthodoxy into the 1920s. Far too much smoke was swirling for there to be no fire at its heart.[45]

Although founded on the experience of mass death, the alleged spirit messages were strikingly nonpolitical. British ghosts, for instance, had little to say on the church's doctrines of holy war or the conflict's rights and wrongs, and rarely expressed resentment toward the nation's enemies. But such stories did contribute powerfully to a more general belief in supernatural forces and the absurdity of thinking that material bodies represented the limits of reality. "Death," as spiritualists usually punctuated the word, was an illusion, or rather a transition. It was no great leap from such accounts to seeing the supernatural dimensions of earthly conflicts.

CONDEMNATIONS OF THE MAINLINE churches are never hard to find in this era, but they should not mislead us into imagining a wholesale abandonment of religious ideas. However we label them—esoteric, occult, mystical, or merely superstitious—supernatural themes not only survived the war but flourished. For mainstream churches and governments, the problem was not that Europeans and Americans were abandoning God but that they were pursuing radical spiritual ideas, both messianic and millenarian, and those passions threatened to take secular forms. The ways of God were far stranger than most could have imagined, or wished.

CHAPTER FIVE

The War of the End of the World
Visions of the Last Days

Every day just now, the false, the unreal, the superimposed things
are falling from us. New ideas, new hopes are emerging, and with
them some vision of the eternal truth at the back of things.
—WELLESLEY TUDOR POLE

IN SEPTEMBER 1916, D. W. Griffith released his film *Intolerance*, which still astounds by its scope and ambition. Griffith addressed the theme of intolerance as it had manifested in several eras of history, from ancient Babylon and the time of Jesus through the European religious wars, and on to the United States in his own day. After the twin climaxes of the fall of Babylon and Christ's Crucifixion, a final scene shows trench warfare on the contemporary western front. Suddenly, though, a celestial vision ends the fighting. As soldiers see angels appearing in the skies, they lay down their arms, initiating a utopian postwar world of harmony and innocence. *Intolerance* brought the contemporary war into the apocalyptic framework familiar throughout Christian history (the fall of Babylon is a key moment in the book of Revelation).[1] The film suggested that Europe was so far sunk in slaughter that it could only be rescued by something like divine intervention. In its sensitivity

Several combatant powers saw the war as the struggle of the knight and the dragon, evoking the war in heaven portrayed in the book of Revelation.

to eschatological themes, Griffith's film was speaking precisely to a widespread mood at the time, in Europe as well as North America.

It is easy to see the churches' responses to the war as a credulous surrender to popular passions and official propaganda, but their actions must be understood in terms of the irresistible cultural pressures surging long before 1914. Even before the first shells fell, all the main Western societies were thoroughly imbued with apocalyptic and millenarian beliefs, so that a cosmic struggle was neither more nor less than what they expected. The pervasive nature of apocalyptic ideas offered both opportunities and perils for governments, and for mainstream churches. At first sight, we might think that such ideas would have a natural appeal for governments seeking to mobilize their people for war. Girding a people for Armageddon should make for determined and ruthless warriors, which is why the biblical book of Revelation has so often provided the scriptural justification for Christian wars. But to borrow a suitably New Testament image, such rhetoric is a two-edged sword. People who believe the end times are at hand might see little point in waging human wars or in supporting the claims of any earthly government at all, including one's own. Holy warfare was quite acceptable, provided that elites kept their ability to declare the acceptable limits of religion.[2]

The End Times

CHRISTIANS HAVE AN ANCIENT fascination with the book of Revelation, which portrays a sequence of world-destroying catastrophes culminating in a perfect age of divine rule on earth. In both Protestant and Catholic versions of the Bible, Revelation appears as the final book, suggesting that it is in a sense the ultimate point of the story. Yet in different eras apocalyptic thought has enjoyed varying degrees of popularity, not to mention respectability. From the late nineteenth century these ideas experienced a worldwide vogue, as believers tried to make sense of the sweeping changes they witnessed around them—the collapse of old social assumptions, the rise of gigantic cities and mass society, and the spread of seemingly miraculous technology. Across cultures and denominations, the resulting mood of expectation was peaking just as the war began.[3]

Despite the abundance of end-times themes in the Bible, the book is by no means clear on the nature or sequence of those events: Will the massacres and cosmic warfare come before or after the blissful utopia when Christ would reign on earth, the millennium? By the end of the nineteenth century, the tendency in the English-speaking Protestant world was definitely toward premillennialism, the theory that matters would get very much worse before any divine intervention could be expected. One of this era's most influential students of doomsday was Anglo-Irish preacher John Nelson Darby, who taught a theory of dispensationalism. According to this view, the Bible taught a sequence of different dispensations, each with its own covenant between God and humanity. The nightmares and cosmic battles of Revelation will be followed by the last and greatest dispensation, which is Christ's millennial kingdom. (Darby also popularized the then-novel idea that Christ's saints would be rescued or raptured before the final cataclysm.)[4]

Dispensationalism was popularized worldwide by the reference Bible published in 1909 by American Cyrus Scofield, one of the most influential religious texts of the twentieth century. *The Scofield Reference Bible* offered a complete scriptural text with luxuriant annotations and cross-references. It explained how every individual portion of the book presented a single and coherent theological system that culminated in the approaching end times, and Armageddon was very close. Scofield's system seems so familiar today through popular evangelical writings (such as Hal Lindsey's 1970s bestseller *The Late Great Planet Earth* or the Left Behind series of Tim LaHaye and Jerry Jenkins) that it is difficult to imagine how startling it must have been to a contemporary audience.[5]

Scofield's text appeared just in time for believers to respond to European developments in the summer of 1914. As one Pentecostal journal headlined the outbreak of war, "The nations of Europe battle, and unconsciously prepare the way for the return of the Lord Jesus." When an older prophecy book was reissued in 1915, the editor remarked, "Armageddon has now become a household word." In the words of evangelical pastor Reuben Torrey, observing the world's conflicts, "The darker the night gets, the lighter my heart gets."[6]

Fundamentals

FURTHER STIRRING POPULAR HOPES and fears of the end of the world were the sweeping revival movements of the early twentieth century, which resonated not just through the United States and Great Britain but also around the imperial worlds. These movements spread rapidly following the widely publicized Welsh national revival of 1904 and reached fever pitch after the San Francisco earthquake of 1906. Within months of the earthquake, a revival in Los Angeles launched the Pentecostal movement, which missionaries soon carried around the world. Although the Pentecost story is taken from the New Testament book of Acts rather than Revelation, the passage clearly had a last-days context. The text that became the charter of the new movement quotes the Old Testament prophecy:

> And it shall come to pass in the last days, saith God, I will pour out of my Spirit upon all flesh: and your sons and your daughters shall prophesy, and your young men shall see visions, and your old men shall dream dreams.

However amazing the miraculous signs and wonders might be in their own right, they mattered because (in this interpretation) they betokened the imminent end of the age. And the Pentecostal revival reportedly produced countless manifestations that seemed impossible to interpret except in supernatural terms—the healings, the speaking in tongues, and (most striking perhaps in this age) the generous interracial collaboration. Pentecostal believers soon organized into formal denominations such as the Assemblies of God (1914).[7]

But religious excitement ranged far beyond Pentecostal ranks. Around the world—in Russia, West Africa, and elsewhere—many Christian churches were in the midst of powerful revival movements in the years around 1914, and the most vigorous of all arose in the United States. A mighty evangelical revival found its anthems in such legendary hymns as "The Old Rugged Cross" and "In the Garden" (both from 1912). The movement placed the language of blood and atonement, sacrifice and national righteousness, firmly on the nation's cultural and political agenda. Activists intervened forcefully in secular politics through campaigns to enforce public morality and alcohol prohibition. Also, 1910 marked the World Missionary Conference at Edinburgh in Scotland, which raised hopes of converting the world to Christianity within a generation, and thereby creating the conditions for Christ's coming. Already by 1918 observers were mapping America's Bible Belt.[8]

Between 1910 and 1915, moreover, antimodernist American evangelicals published a multivolume manifesto of *The Fundamentals,* those basic points of doctrine that anyone had to believe before they could be considered a true Christian. These works gave their name to the emerging fundamentalist movement, which defended its views with a militant and confrontational style. And at least in some versions of the fundamentals, believers were required to accept a very specific concept of the future of the world, in "Christ's personal, *premillennial* and imminent second coming."

Apocalyptic ideas boomed as the United States entered the war, with Germany or the kaiser as the Antichrist. Revivalist Billy Sunday characterized the war simply: "It is Bill [Kaiser Wilhelm] against Woodrow [Wilson], Germany against America, Hell against Heaven." Even an American Quaker, John L. Carver, lauded "this present war of unselfish sacrifice to save humanity from the reign of the Beast." Such rhetoric could not fail to influence the mainline churches. In May 1918, twenty-five thousand believers, mainly Baptist and Presbyterian, attended the Philadelphia Bible conference on Christ's return. So rampant were such ideas that leading evangelicals were forced to damp down speculation. In 1918, *A Textbook on Prophecy* surveyed the country's prominent Protestant clergy on the simple question "Is the kaiser the Antichrist?" In the event, a majority denied the suggestion, citing specific ways in which Wilhelm failed the criteria spelled out in scripture, but the debate shows just how centrally such concerns were being debated in this critical year.[9]

These speculations alarmed secular authorities to a degree that seems astonishing today. In 1918, when federal and state authorities were deeply concerned about pro-German subversion and sabotage across the United States, much of their activity focused on suppressing one densely packed theological rant, namely *The Finished Mystery*. This was a continuation of the apocalyptic writings of Charles Taze Russell, a founder of the Watch Tower movement (later the Jehovah's Witnesses). The movement spent decades warning that the world would end precisely in 1914, a spectacularly lucky example of selecting an auspicious date. Surviving the disappointment of the world's continued existence, Russellites turned their attention to denouncing human governments and their nationalistic acts, and to condemning the ongoing war. The German government was said to have financed the publication of *The Finished Mystery* so that it could be distributed free in large quantities in several Allied nations. Mere possession of the book for sale was enough to merit prosecution under the draconian U.S. Espionage Act, and Russellite leaders received harsh prison terms in the affair.[10]

Threshold of Apocalypse

BECAUSE DISPENSATIONALISM HAS HAD such an enduring influence through the twentieth century, the movement's rise is a familiar theme in Anglo-American religious history. But speculation about the end times ran far beyond the bounds of the United States and was not confined within evangelical and charismatic faith. Germany likewise demonized its enemies in apocalyptic terms. In his study of apocalyptic themes in German thought (itself an inexhaustible topic) Klaus Vondung devotes special attention to "the Apocalypse of 1914." If Americans had Billy Sunday, Germans had the bestselling poet Ludwig Ganghofer, an acerbic right-wing nationalist who viewed England simply as "Babylon, the great Whore."[11]

Apocalyptic expectations flourished among Roman Catholics,

who in 1914 represented by far the largest segment of the Christian world, almost half the whole. Although Catholics generally lacked the Protestant obsession with biblical minutiae, they had their own clear ideas about the mysterious figures of the book of Revelation, which they understood in the context of the Virgin Mary. Revelation's chapter 12 describes the awesome figure of the Woman Clothed with the Sun, "the moon under her feet, and on her head a crown of twelve stars," who gives birth to a messianic ruler. In the narrative, she is the holy and heavenly counterpart to evil female figures like the Scarlet Woman and the Whore of Babylon. Reading Mary as the Woman Clothed with the Sun—as we presumably should—neatly associates the Virgin with the end times, as her appearance in the text marks the beginning of some of the most violent and phantasmagoric portions of Revelation. This includes the war in heaven that pits Michael and his angels against the Red Dragon.[12]

Catholic devotion to Mary burgeoned during the nineteenth century, and the celebrated Marian apparitions often had these cosmic implications. Although the apparition at Lourdes in 1858 was the most famous, another and more controversial event had occurred at La Salette near Grenoble, France, in 1846. The basic format of this event was familiar—the Virgin reportedly appeared to two shepherd children, and mighty miracles followed—but the witnesses' stories of what they had seen were widely challenged, and their accounts developed significantly over time. The core of the message, though, was that the Virgin was troubled by the terrible sins that afflicted the world, and unless they were corrected, human misdeeds would provoke divine punishment. By the early twentieth century, La Salette's true believers accepted that the Virgin had predicted many catastrophic events for the world, including apostasy from the faith, the decay of the church, social upheavals, and wars that would destroy Paris and other great cities.[13]

So accurately did these predictions catch the flavor of French affairs from the 1840s onward that the La Salette prophecies naturally attracted attention among Catholics during the Great War. One of France's most famous Catholic writers was Léon Bloy, whose thoughts on the opening of the war were collected in a 1916 book entitled *On the Threshold of the Apocalypse*. Like Claudel, Bloy saw Germany as a manifestation of all that was anti-Christian, if not actually of Antichrist, and saw German invaders as apocalyptic forces.[14]

These French themes were popularized worldwide through the work of Spanish author Vicente Blasco Ibañez, whose 1916 novel *The Four Horsemen of the Apocalypse*—one of the war's literary triumphs—depicted the Miracle of the Marne. A 1918 translation took the popular title on to new glories in the English-speaking world, particularly given its strong anti-German slant. In the United States alone, the book sold half a million copies in its first year of publication, and it easily topped the bestseller charts. But for Blasco Ibañez, apocalypse was far more than merely a colorful synonym for mass destruction. In an extended scene set in August 1914, the Russian mystic Tchernoff explains the conflict explicitly in terms of the Revelation expounded to Saint John:

> The four horsemen of the Apocalypse! . . . Already they were in the saddle! Already they were beginning their merciless gallop of destruction! The blind forces of evil were about to be let loose throughout the world. The agony of humanity, under the brutal sweep of the four horsemen, was already begun!

Like Bloy, Blasco Ibañez identifies the Beast with German militarism.[15]

Worshipping the Name

ORTHODOX CHRISTIAN READERS ALSO cherished the Apocalypse. Orthodox churches have never felt so comfortable with the book of Revelation as their Western rivals and give it a lower status within the canon, although they too have often fallen under its spell. At the turn of the century, Russia was an international byword for mystical and messianic ideas. When Blasco Ibañez needed a character to expound mystical teachings, he naturally invented a Russian, much as a novelist in the 1970s would invoke an Indian guru.

Russia's contemporary religious revival spawned extremist sects devoted to investigating mystical truths. One in particular, the so-called name worshippers, bore a close resemblance to the Pentecostal revival in the contemporary West in its promise of charismatic power and its rejection of conventional authority. Since the Middle Ages, Orthodox mystics had sought to achieve ecstatic union with God by means of the repetition of holy names. At the start of the twentieth century, the movement experienced a broad revival under the title of "name worship," *Imiaslavie,* which taught that the divine names—especially the Jesus Prayer—gave the power to heal and to cast out demons. By 1913, name-worshipping monks dominated the Russian monastery at Mount Athos. Horrified by this extravagance, Russian authorities sent gunboats and marines to storm the holy site. The name worship controversy, and the prospect of bringing the divine presence into human reality, had a profound effect on Russian culture. The debate continued to split the Russian church until the time of the Bolshevik Revolution and beyond.[16]

When Russia entered the war, its religious world was passionately divided over these familiar themes of charisma, worldly power, and the imminent hope of a divine intervention in human affairs. Depicting the expectations of July 1914, Anna Akhmatova—perhaps the country's greatest poet—imagined a pilgrim prophesying:

> Beware of terrible times . . . the earth
> Opening for a crowd of corpses
> Expect famine, earthquakes, plagues,
> And heavens darkened by eclipses.

Издыхающiй многоглавый Австро-германскiй змѣй.

This 1914 Russian poster depicts the rulers of Germany and Austria-Hungary as the diabolical seven-headed dragon foretold in the book of Revelation.

Faith offered the only hope in such times, with the dream that "the Mother of God will spread / a white shroud over these great sorrows." When Moscow observed a solar eclipse in the following month, this apparent heavenly sign filled the newspapers, and also became a popular theme for the city's flourishing artistic community. That September, the Virgin and Child reputedly appeared to Russian forces waiting to engage the Germans at Augustovo, in one of the war's most often-cited miracles.[17]

Russians, quite as much as Western Christians, were on the watch for the prophesied forces of evil, and Orthodox believers were quite as immersed in nightmares of the Antichrist as were any American evangelicals. By far the most influential writer on the topic was Vladimir Soloviev, an old friend of Fyodor Dostoevsky and possibly the model for one or more characters in *The Brothers Karamazov*. Soloviev's 1900 "A Story of the Antichrist" imagined a near-future Europe locked in a death struggle against the Islamic world, before falling prey to a newly united axis of East Asian powers. Out of the resulting chaos comes the biblical Antichrist, in a vision that would often reappear in Russian—and later European—thought. Among other consequences, Russian Orthodox nightmares would contribute powerfully to the emergence of anti-Semitism in the immediate postwar period.[18]

Russians had no difficulty assimilating Kaiser Wilhelm to the Antichrist. One poster from 1914 depicted a monstrous fire-breathing dragon figure with seven crowned human heads and billed as the "Austro-German serpent." The image clearly identifies German and Austrian royal leaders with "the scarlet colored beast, full of names of blasphemy, having seven heads and ten horns" in Revelation's chapter 17. (The artist reaches the magic number of seven by including the kingdoms incorporated into the German Empire—Saxony, Bavaria, Prussia, and the rest). *The Antichrist* was also the title of a widely distributed Russian film depicting the kaiser's notorious atrocities.[19]

Dreams of the End

ESCHATOLOGY HAD A BROAD appeal across nations and societies. Images of a forthcoming ultimate battle predominated in the years immediately before the war, partly because of the series of war scares between 1906 and 1912 (Bosnia, Morocco, and the rest). These end-times ideas appealed to progressive avant-garde figures at least as much as to traditionalists. The early twentieth century was an effervescent time of cultural innovation and experiment, the era of such artistic movements as cubism, futurism, symbolism, Dadaism, and expressionism, and they all emerged in what was quite self-consciously a prewar atmosphere. The key innovators not only knew that war was coming soon but that they were liable to be conscripted to fight and die in any coming conflict. However much they espoused radical or anticlerical political views, artists and writers ransacked their religious pasts in search of images and symbols that would allow them to come to terms with this fate. Movements pledged to cultural iconoclasm produced an era of great religious art, writing, and music, drawing overtly on biblical and liturgical themes.[20]

The imagery of apocalypse proved so overwhelmingly attractive that distinctions between mainstream faith and radical modernism often seem paper-thin. One of the heroic young poets of the German expressionist avant-garde was Georg Heym, whose famous poem "Krieg" (War), is an apocalyptic nightmare. For Heym, writing about 1911, war was a monstrous figure arising from a long sleep in order to cast hellish fire and brimstone on a great modern-day city, a Gomorrah. Read on its own, "Krieg" sounds weirdly prophetic, but in the context of the three or four years before the actual outbreak of war, its themes were absolutely routine: apocalypse was a German literary and artistic genre. Among visual artists, expressionist Ludwig Meidner earned fame for his paintings of burning cities and his sequence of so-called apocalyptic landscapes. As he recalled, from 1912 onward

> I unloaded my obsessions onto canvas day and night—Judgment days, world's ends, and gibbets of skulls, for in those days the great universal storm was already baring its teeth and casting its glaring yellow shadow across my whimpering brush-hand.[21]

These works culminated in his 1916 piece *The Last Day*.

Russia, meanwhile, produced the greatest urban apocalypse of the era. Andrei Bely's 1912 modernist novel *Petersburg* resembles the work of Joyce or Proust in its daring experimentation and its enormous influence on later literature. (It appeared in full-length book form only in 1916.) Bely's interest in Russian apocalyptic was already long-standing, and it was reinforced by his acquaintance with the venerated Austrian occultist Rudolf Steiner. The novel depicts prewar Saint Petersburg as a society on the verge of explosions, literal and metaphorical. It is a city under the eye of angels, where the devil walks the streets, and whose people await conquest and obliteration by an Asiatic horde. The statue of a horseman is a pervasive symbol, obviously suggesting one of the four horsemen of Revelation. Only in whispers can Bely's characters discuss the real issue at hand: "the Second Coming of Christ." Petersburg is a city living at the end of the world.[22]

Although Bely apparently never met the painter Wassily Kandinsky, the work of the two men so often echoed each other's interests in angels and imminent judgment. In 1912, Kandinsky edited the legendary manifesto *Der Blaue Reiter,* which cultural historians regard as an epochal movement in European modernism, bringing together the most innovative German and Russian artists of the day. But we lose the religious significance of the name when we use too literal a translation of the school's German name, terming it "The Blue Rider." As we have seen, it actually refers to a blue *horseman,* and the movement was born as a protest against a gallery's decision to reject a Kandinsky painting of the Last Judgment. That cosmic finale lay at the heart of European modernism. The movement's founders included Franz Marc, who in 1913 painted his *Animal Destinies (Tierschicksale).* He later acknowledged this contorted violent work as a "gruesome and overwhelming" premonition of the coming world war. On the back of the canvas, Marc quoted the Buddhist text "And all being is flaming agony." Once war came, Marc devoted his skills to the imperial cause, adapting Expressionist styles to designing radical new forms of camouflage to protect German artillery from the inquisitive eyes of enemy pilots. He perished at Verdun.[23]

Another angel-obsessed member of the school was Russian painter Natalia Goncharova, who in 1910 created her stunning image of the archangel Michael, the leader of the heavenly hosts in Revelation's final battles. Although an advanced modernist, her work draws heavily on Russian icon traditions. In 1915, she designed sets for Sergei Diaghilev's planned ballet *Liturgy,* which was to feature such ancient images as the six winged seraphs, with music based on Orthodox Christian liturgical themes.[24]

Quite aside from these fairly conventional religious traditions, occult and esoteric beliefs also exercised a profound influence. Another of Russia's avant-garde heroes of the day was the composer Alexander Scriabin, an enthusiastic devotee of Theosophy, which we shall explore in more detail shortly. In the years before the war, Scriabin devoted his attention to composing his *Mysterium,* a titanic multimedia and multisensory event to be held in the foothills of the Himalayas, with the aim of unleashing Armageddon and initiating a new era in world history.[25]

The Spiritual Unrest

HOWEVER MUCH THEIR PROGRESSIVE views set these cultural figures at odds with virtually all churches, most felt no discomfort in drawing so freely on biblical themes. Often, though, they could imbibe their views wholeheartedly from esoteric forms of spirituality without using orthodox religious sources. These alternative ideas influenced some of the most significant cultural and political leaders of the time.

The boom in the occult and esoteric was part of a larger fascination worldwide with phenomena that at first sight seemed primitive or irrational. The nineteenth century had been a thrilling era of scientific progress, bolstered by ideologies of rationality and progress, but from the 1890s, these themes came under systematic attack. New approaches are sometimes bracketed together under the convenient title of "vitalism," the idea that living organisms function in ways beyond what can be determined by conventional sciences of physics, chemistry, or biology, or any form of materialism. Some theorists postulated a higher principle of life, an energy or a vital spark. Applied to ordinary life, vitalism exalted intuition, impulse, and experience over intellect and reason; it exalted the primitive and spontaneous. And if a life force existed independent of the body, then it was likely to survive beyond the death of any individual. Artists and writers enthusiastically explored the unconscious and the primitive, seeking inspiration in the non-European cultures that globalization had made familiar in the West. Some of the finest cultural landmarks of the early twentieth century drew on these primitive or exotic themes, from Picasso's paintings to Stravinsky's 1913 ballet *The Rite of Spring*.[26]

Esoteric interests actually drew support from the daring achievements of science and technology, and from the very modernity that at first sight they seemed to reject. If mainstream science proved the existence of mysterious invisible powers such as electromagnetic forces, radio waves, and radioactivity, that gave added plausibility to claims for paranormal powers and psychic intuition, clairvoyance and spiritual healing. If scientists had now split the atom, perhaps matter itself could be disintegrated and reconstructed. In such a vision, future research might someday reveal that spiritualism and mediumship drew on forces just as real as those that permitted radio transmissions.[27]

So broad was the interest in such themes that cultural critics spoke of a fundamental transformation of human consciousness, much as others would preach during the 1970s. In his 1910 book *The Spiritual Unrest,* American journalist Ray Stannard Baker proclaimed the death of the old materialism. The result was an explosion of contemporary interest in "consciousness, the self, the relation of mind to mind, telepathy, the strange phenomena of double or multiple consciousness, hypnotism." Spiritual forms of healing excited such interest that even as rational-minded an observer as William James remarked in 1907,

> It is quite obvious that a wave of religious activity, analogous
> in some respects to the spread of early Christianity, Buddhism,
> and Mohammedanism, is passing over our American world.

He could easily have extended his comment to Europe, where strictly comparable trends were also in vogue.[28]

The "unrest" found its best-known public face in Theosophy, which excited modernist thinkers and creative leaders on both sides of the Atlantic, and which would be the ancestor of most esoteric movements of the age. This Anglo-American concoction was created in the 1870s by Helena Blavatsky, yet another Russian guru. Rooted in Hindu and Buddhist ideas, Theosophy claimed to transmit the ancient teachings of various lost civilizations and races, most not known or recognized by mainstream historians but passed on through visions and trances. Theosophy and its offshoots told the story of a planet vastly older than orthodox historians would ever accept, a world in which successive races had risen and fallen, usually through the purest Darwinian means of conflict and combat, cycles of racial vigor and degeneracy. For true believers, the idea that civilizations collapsed in bloody cataclysm was something like a law of history. Theosophy was messianic, drawing on the Buddhist view of successive bodhisattvas as godlike charismatic leaders who guided the world's spiritual development. Buddha and Jesus were spiritual masters of earlier eras, and early-twentieth-century Theosophists dreamed that another such world teacher would appear imminently, to lead the world into a utopian Aquarian Age. Robert Graves remarked how wartime audiences have a special taste for books about Jesus, as they seek both consolation and inspiration. In the Great War, the most popular title in this genre was George Moore's *The Brook Kerith* (1916), which had a distinctly esoteric and Asian flavor. Moore portrayed a Jesus who survives the Crucifixion only to recoil from the preaching of the emerging Pauline church, and who eventually joins a group of Buddhist monks evangelizing the Judean countryside.[29]

Across Europe and North America the ferment of new ideas and millenarian visions led to the creation of numerous study groups, sects, and secret societies, combining Theosophical ideas with Masonic models of organization and gradual initiation. For Americans, the year 1915 was the pivot of so many radical and experimental movements that the resemblances to 1968 are overwhelming. This was the year of political tumult and radicalization, gender liberation, radical cultural experimentation, and innovative forms of racial organization. As in 1968, the year was also marked by a startling upsurge of new religions, of occult and mystical sects—of New Thought and Rosicrucianism, believers in lost continents and new messiahs. It was in 1915 that the very term "New Age" entered popular parlance, in order to describe a package of beliefs very much like those of the late twentieth century.[30]

Far from being incidental trivia surrounding the war, such esoteric ideas could achieve real political significance. Most people know the notorious story of the monk Rasputin who used his charismatic powers and reputation as a healer to achieve a sinister dominance over the court of the Russian tsar. Indeed, his very name has become synonymous with evil. But it would be wrong to dismiss such a case as a freakish manifestation of superstition when supernatural and mystical ideas—focused especially on healing—also manifested themselves so strongly in all the most advanced nations. In the realm of psychology, which is often seen as a key marker of modernity, Carl Jung's followers ostentatiously investigated the alchemical and occult. No less than their evangelical or Catholic fellows, esoteric believers too had a lively faith in the possibilities of prophecy and the imminent end times. As spiritualist Wellesley Tudor Pole asked in 1914, "Can anyone still doubt that this is the ending of the age? That the great conflict now raging is the one prophesied from time immemorial?"[31]

These themes reached mass audiences through the broad interest in spiritualism and through the very lively publishing industry catering to interests in the supernatural and astrology. One of Germany's main esoteric publications was the Leipzig-based *Zentralblatt für Okkultismus,* the most popular of a large range of contemporary magazines and as close as the alternative world came to a mainstream German voice. In its 1916–17 volume, at the height of the war, the *Zentralblatt* published two hundred articles on subjects as diverse as prophecy and famous seers, presentiments of death, dream visions, telepathy, hypnosis, vampire beliefs, spiritual healing, Norse and pagan German beliefs, and alchemy. Many authors gave their writing a strictly contemporary relevance, with pieces on "What the War Will Bring," "The Kaiser and the World War," and "War and Occultism." A piece on "War Prophecies" included very specific predictions about the fate of England and Nostradamus's supposed foretelling of the sinking of the *Lusitania.*[32]

Other Worlds

NEUTRAL SWITZERLAND ILLUSTRATES THE diversity and power of Europe's religious and esoteric thought in these years. The German-speaking environment placed Switzerland in close touch with the most advanced intellectual developments of the age, but it also offered a refuge from war and propaganda. In 1916, for instance, progressive German and Austrian artists exiled in Zurich gave birth to the Dada movement. Some of the leading cultural figures were themselves Swiss, others were refugees or transients, but in the same short period this small country was home to such spiritual innovators as Karl Barth, founder of neoorthodox Protestantism; radical Christian socialists like Leonhard Ragaz; Rabbi Abraham Isaac Kook, a founding father of modern ultra-Orthodox Judaism; occult entrepreneurs like Rudolf Steiner; and psychologist Carl Jung.

So diverse were these various figures, they seem scarcely to have occupied the same planet, never mind the same small European country. Although the different figures virtually never interacted with their near neighbors—Kabbalists did not pass time with Barthians, or Barthians with occultists—they were responding to the same global crisis. The interpretations they developed shared common themes, especially about the evil effects of alliances between religious institutions and existing states. They could agree easily enough on the now-obvious truth of the fall of humanity, the limitations of human reason and science, and the triumph of sin and ignorance in the current world order. Each, also, would transform the postwar world, far beyond what anyone could have guessed at the time.

Jung himself illustrates the overwhelming power of apocalyptic ideas in these years among cultural leaders far removed from mainstream church teachings. By 1914, he was facing a profound spiritual crisis brought on by his schism with Freud, and by the catastrophe of the war itself. He claimed to have received repeated auguries of the coming conflict, with three visions of imminent disaster. In the first, in October 1913,

> I saw the mighty yellow waves, the floating rubble of civilization, and the drowned bodies of uncounted thousands. Then the whole sea turned to blood. . . . That winter [1913–14] someone asked me what I thought were the political prospects of the world in the near future. I replied that I had no thoughts on the matter, but that I saw rivers of blood. . . . Soon afterward, in the spring and early summer of 1914, I had a thrice-repeated dream that in the middle of summer an Arctic cold wave descended and froze the land to ice. . . . All living green things were killed by frost.[33]

Living in Zurich, Jung spent the following years in self-examination, while his theories of the collective unconscious led him to explore occult and mystical teachings from different cultures through history. In 1916, Jung wrote the mind-stretching *Seven Sermons to the Dead,* reputedly as the consequence of an outbreak of psychic phenomena in his household, a kind of poltergeist invasion. The sermons are presented in cryptic words attributed to the second-century Gnostic teacher Basilides, and at first sight, their relevance to the contemporary world is not obvious. On closer examination, though, not only do the sermons directly speak to that world but they also address questions that were troubling other famous minds in just these years.[34]

Basilides preaches to the legions of flocking ghosts, ghosts that were so numerous in Europe in the year of Verdun. Basilides-Jung tells his hearers that they have misunderstood the fundamental nature of reality, and especially the absolute reality of the pleroma, the divine fullness, which contains within itself all opposites, and which is at once everything and nothing, black and white. But although ultimate reality may contain and reconcile all opposites, mere humans cannot and do not, and they err fatally when they do not realize this fact. When humans strive for the good and beautiful, they cannot fail to attain the evil and ugly, which are necessary components of full reality. Misunderstanding this, they wrongly accept external realities as if they represent absolute truth and fall into the trap of accepting worldly ideologies, succumbing to savage fanaticism.

Put into worldly terms, those Europeans who in 1914 launched a crusade for righteousness, peace, and justice were unconsciously grasping for evil, violence, and injustice, and by 1916 that paradox looked like a solid piece of political analysis. Rather than basing themselves in external realities, wise people should look within, to integrate competing forces and passions and reject the dualism of good and evil—or as we might say, of the Allies and the Central Powers. Truth was found not in dualities, but in one reality that stood above both God and the devil, and incorporated both.

Occult Science: Rudolf Steiner

IN HIS DAY, BY far the best-known member of this group of spiritual entrepreneurs was Rudolf Steiner (1861–1925), a multifaceted genius active in many fields—medicine, education, theater, and agriculture, apart from philosophy and mystical religion. He exercised remarkable political influence, giving an aura of sanctity to the German war effort even beyond what it had already received from the Protestant preachers.[35]

Steiner's world grew out of the larger Theosophical movement, which gained a European presence quite as significant as that in England or America. Like other thinkers of the time, Steiner integrated his Asian-based and occult insights into a version of alternative mystical Christianity. His personal version of Theosophy grew into a breakaway sect that in 1912 he formalized under the title of anthroposophy, "human wisdom." He then created a spiritual and intellectual headquarters at Dornach, near Basel in Switzerland, a European study center that attracted high-profile disciples from across the continent.[36]

Steiner enjoyed prophetic status among many influential Germans, including some of the Reich's political and military leaders. Most significant was the von Moltke family, which was central to the making of modern Germany. One Helmuth von Moltke was the key leader of the German army that routed Austria-Hungary in 1866 and France in 1870. His nephew, Helmuth the Younger, was chief of the general staff in the years before 1914 and made the critical decisions about German strategy at the outbreak of war. Later von Moltkes distinguished themselves as active opponents of the Hitler regime.[37] In the years leading up to the Great War, this family was utterly immersed in the occult, and the younger Helmuth moved in a circle deeply interested in freemasonry, transcendentalism, Theosophy, and spiritualism. From 1903, the family became close to

Steiner, who served as Helmuth's guru. When the German armies came within an inch of defeating France in 1914, their commander was apparently meditating on verses and mantras that Steiner had supplied him, which used words thoroughly familiar from contemporary German war theology:

Victorious will be the power
Which by the fate of the times
Is predestined for that people
Who protected by the spirit
Will for mankind's salvation
In Europe's heart
Wrest light from the battle.[38]

For Steiner—and presumably for the von Moltkes—the war was absolutely predestined through Europe's karma. The eastern and western Allied nations both represented opposing cosmic forces that he termed Ahrimanic (materialistic and technological) and Luciferian (fantastic and speculative). Despite their fearsome names, neither was diabolical nor evil in its own right, but they represented profoundly unbalanced views of reality that must be reconciled or balanced through a mediator, a Christ figure, which would be Germany and Austria-Hungary.[39] As for Jung, the goal was to transcend the illusions of division. Von Moltke himself believed in the inevitability of a war that would lay the foundations for the Parousia, Christ's Second Coming. No less than his Lutheran contemporaries, Steiner preached Germany's messianic role in Europe.

Helmuth von Moltke's interest in European affairs was not dampened by his death in 1916—or at least this is suggested by the continuing communications Steiner claimed to pass on from the other world. Like the contemporary British officer Raymond Lodge, von Moltke's influence only grew after death. For practical purposes, it does not matter whether the deceased general was in fact speaking from beyond the grave but rather that such words were circulating as his. Through Steiner, the deceased von Moltke offered many revelations about his past and that of the world, and presented sensational new understandings of the war and its cosmic significance. In May 1917, for example, he warned,

> We were the last ones to conduct wars in the old spirit. Now Ahriman is fighting a desperate battle in the ether and the battle on earth is only a shadow image of the Ahrimanic battle. It can only come to an end when the Germans have found themselves. They will find the way up and the way down. They will have to discover a new Olympus and a new underworld. The Zeppelin is a mockery of Olympus, the submarine the fear of this underworld.

However bizarre such historical mysticism might appear, these supposed revelations commanded the attention of an amazingly wide audience at the highest reaches of the German establishment.[40]

Faith and Race

ALTHOUGH STEINER'S VISION WAS usually progressive, esoteric theologies also appealed to militarist and reactionary circles, and by no means just in Germany. By the end of the war, the effective military ruler of the German Empire was Erich Ludendorff, who utterly condemned Steiner's influence but who himself delved into racial mysticism and neo-paganism. His wife became a prominent advocate of racial (*völkisch*) paganism. In 1918, Ludendorff commanded the German army's last mighty offensive, a gambler's throw against the British and French, which bore the code name Michael. Beyond his appearance in Revelation, the archangel Michael had a medieval reputation as Germany's special angelic protector—almost a war god—and he had been the subject of countless patriotic/mystical representations over the previous century.[41]

In other countries, too, highly placed military leaders had esoteric sympathies. The only tsarist general who won any major successes for Russia in the war was Aleksei Brusilov, who later joined the Bolshevik cause. But Brusilov was a firm believer in spiritualism, accepting the maxim "There is no death," and he often attended séances. He was also interested in Theosophy and married a niece of Helena Blavatsky.[42] In Britain, one of Ludendorff's most creative military foes was the boldly innovative theorist J. F. C. Fuller, who pioneered modern methods of armored and mechanized warfare. He organized the key tank attacks that contributed to victory in 1918, and his "Plan 1919" sketched a proposed Allied offensive that uncannily foreshadowed the Blitzkrieg campaigns of the Second World War. His ideas were formative influences on later German generals like Manfred Rommel and Heinz Guderian. But his spiritual notions were no more orthodox than those of his German contemporaries. Fuller was a disciple of grandstanding English occult leader Aleister Crowley, who in 1904 had proclaimed himself the visionary hero of a messianic New Aeon. Fuller actually published a hero-worshipping tract on Crowley, whom he termed "the Star in the West." Although fear of scandal made him distance himself from the master, Fuller continued to publish on occult themes throughout his life, including Kabbalah and yoga.[43]

Such mystical themes were not necessarily linked to patriotic or nationalistic ideologies, but in practice they did have a considerable overlap with political approaches, and specifically with racial theories. Even those Theosophists who extolled the brotherhood of humanity also used the racial terminology of the day, speaking freely of Aryans and Aryanism. Steiner himself was a strong enemy of radical nationalism (and he suffered for it in the vitriolic atmosphere of postwar Germany), but the occult synthesis appealed to the radical Right, who welcomed the supernatural justification it provided to exalting the nation and the race. Some groups revived Germanic paganism, complete with the worship of the ancient gods. Others looked to a distinctively German version of Christianity that they found in Richard Wagner, especially the treatment of the Holy Grail theme in *Parsifal*. Grail names and references appear regularly in the correspondence of the mystically inclined in these years: Steiner's emissary to his well-heeled German disciples was a woman who took the name Kundry, from the character in *Parsifal*.

The years immediately before the war witnessed an upsurge of societies and study groups devoted to the spiritual aspects of racial theory, and in this subculture we find the prehistory of Germany's Nazi movement. Fundamental to all these groups was the concept of purity of race (*Volk*) and blood, of blood and soil (*Blut und Boden*). In Vienna, Guido von List incorporated *völkisch* ideas and Germanic pagan theories, and at the summer solstice in 1911, he formed a mystical secret society called the High Armanen Order. In 1915, Lanz von Liebenfels adapted the older Theosophy and anthroposophy to his own peculiar ariosophy, "Aryan wisdom." In 1912, Theodor Fritsch founded the Reichshammerbund. It was from Theosophy and esoteric Buddhism that these groups appropriated the Indian swastika, which in its origins had no such connotations of hatred and violence. Naturally enough, in the context of the time, von List and von Liebenfels viewed the Great War as an epic struggle of the German race, a cosmic confrontation with the forces of darkness. By 1918, members of various self-described Aryan sects merged into the Thule Society, which would overlap closely with emerging Nazism.[44]

In the United States, too, ideas of cosmic and racial conflict merged. The America that entered the war in 1917 needed no instruction in doctrines of sacrifice and blood, honor and redemption. Quite apart from the events of the war itself, the years between 1915 and 1920 saw a vicious spike in racial conflict, marked by lynching, ethnic violence, and an extraordinary blood-soaked rhetoric of

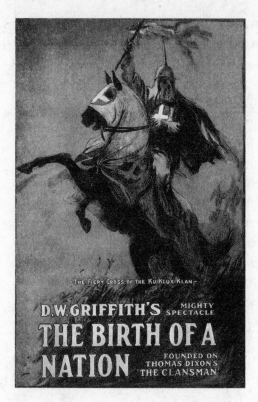

D. W. Griffith's 1915 film *The Birth of a Nation* suggests how Americans linked a sense of racial patriotism to ideas of knightly chivalry.

white supremacy. Some groups were prepared to defend these values to the death. In 1915, D. W. Griffith's *Birth of a Nation* depicted the rescue of the white South after federally imposed Reconstruction—or the act of redemption, as it was often described. The film led directly to the re-formation of the Ku Klux Klan. The new Klan used an array of symbols and uniforms, together with a framework of hierarchies and initiations that fitted well with Europe's contemporary occult sects. Underlying the pageantry was a ferocious commitment to defending racial and national honor by means of savage violence, in defense of their Aryan birthright. Blood must be shed for blood, and blood was the path to salvation—personal, communal, and national.

We can argue about the long-term significance of such esoteric groups, and conspiracy theorists through the years have certainly exaggerated the role of German sects like the Thule Society in shaping Hitler's vision. At most, they provided a style and rhetoric, rather than political substance. But they illustrate once again the racial and political dimensions of cosmic visions of the war.

BELIEVERS OF MANY KINDS expected the struggle of 1914 to be qualitatively different from any previous conflict in history and likely to initiate an apocalyptic era. To achieve such a goal, they were willing to see the civilized world suffer a massive act of blood atonement and sacrificial death. Where they were wrong, of course, was in the speed of the imminent judgment, which was still not in sight at the end of 1916. In the new year, though, the war entered a more intense and still more violent phase. The year 1917 would usher in new prophecies: it would be marked by the fall of kings and by battles in the Holy Land itself.

CHAPTER SIX

Armageddon
Dreams of Apocalypse in the War's Savage Last Year

Four years had War, Pestilence, and Death held sway until the nations of the Old World were torn asunder and lay bleeding, crying out to a just God to free them from the forces of evil.

—INTERTITLE IN THE FILM *The Four Horsemen of the Apocalypse*

EVERY SO OFTEN IN history a single work of art so transforms ways of looking at the world that it inaugurates a new era of perception. Wartime Russia produced one such radical piece in Kazimir Malevich's painting *Black Square,* exhibited in Moscow in 1915 and intended as the founding work of a new school that the artist modestly called "suprematism." The title perfectly describes the painting, which entirely consists of a large black square on a white background, a logical conclusion of years of revolt against representational art.

Although Malevich claimed to scorn politics and glorified only abstract form, he was sufficiently invested in the war to become a propaganda artist in 1914, turning out strident anti-German posters. This makes it more probable, then, that we can legitimately

This U.S. lithograph presents the British capture of Jerusalem alongside the victory of Judas Maccabeus in 165 BC, suggesting the messianic implications of the event. The strongly Zionist President Woodrow Wilson is depicted above.

seek a political commentary in *Black Square,* with all it implied for a world deeply sunk into catastrophic war and a Russia dominated by a failing social order. According to taste, the painting represented the gravestone of the old world, marking its extinction; or else the nothingness mapped the ground zero from which a wholly new order could build, untrammeled by any recollections of the past. Either way, the world stood at *Stunde Null,* "zero hour." Adding to the painting's shock value was its exhibition placement high in a corner of the room, the space that in a religious Orthodox household would be occupied by a cherished icon. It was as if spectators were invited to pray before this image of Nothingness. Malevich recalled the reaction of stunned critics and observers, who lamented, "Everything which we loved is lost! We are in a desert." As *Black Square* proclaimed, a world was ending, and a world was beginning.[1]

Malevich himself had an ambiguous attitude toward religion: although interested in Theosophy, like any good Russian intellectual of his day, he was usually more intrigued by technology, by aircraft rather than angels. But for anyone hoping for the world's end in any spiritual sense, the war offered abundant signs and portents, and never more so than in the year 1917.

A New War

ON JUNE 6, 1917, British general Sir Herbert Plumer told his subordinates that while their actions on the following day might not change history, they would certainly change geography. They did. For almost a year the British had been tunneling under German lines at Messines, near Ypres, to plant some 455 tons of high explosives. On the morning of June 7, nineteen mines were detonated, in the largest planned explosion in human history before the arrival of nuclear weapons, producing a bang that could be heard across much of southern England. Ten thousand Germans died instantly, collapsing a critical sector of their battlefront. Awed observers searched for biblical images to comprehend a sight so terrible. One aptly quoted Psalm 35: "Let a sudden destruction come upon him unawares."[2]

The Messines explosion failed to produce a war-winning victory, as Allied forces were soon (literally) bogged down once more on the western front. But the attack does indicate the colossal scale of the combat at this front, so that even such an immense loss of life seemed almost casual. It also suggests the application of advanced technologies of destruction.

Incredible as it would have seemed in 1914, the war was escalating still further, in its sophistication and its destructive potential. Whether on the ground, over it, or under it, the world of war

The war involved a strange combination of the most modern weaponry with tried-and-true older methods. U.S. forces experimented with gas masks to defend both themselves and their horses.

seemed to have evolved a century in just three years. In retrospect, the aircraft above the battlefields look almost comically fragile, but at the time, the nimble fighters and lumbering bombers were intoxicating symbols of cutting-edge modernity. So were tanks, which now played a central role in warfare, and flamethrowers. Both sides deployed the most sophisticated science of the day as a means to destroy their enemies. New techniques of sound detection allowed observers to locate enemy guns at a distance, while gas warfare evolved into new and more destructive forms. Over the whole scene, though, was the single dominant fact of artillery warfare, which now reached enormous proportions. Unlike earlier battles, where huge masses of shells failed to destroy enemy lines, both sides now learned precise targeting. French and British forces mastered the art of the creeping barrage, concentrating their fire just ahead of an advancing body of troops, who depended on highly accurate targeting to avoid disastrous friendly-fire incidents. And by 1917 the vast majority of shells were actually exploding as they should, a radical change from the conditions of previous years.[3]

Nor did military tactics stand still in the trenches. By 1917, several armies were developing aggressive new tactics for raiding and seizing enemy trenches, using highly trained and well armed elite shock forces. Such storm warfare was a specialty of the Canadian and Australian armies as well as the Germans, with their vaunted *Stosstruppen*. At long last, these storm troops had the potential to destabilize the agonizingly static warfare of the previous years. Yet for all the ferment of innovation, nothing could change the basic fact that neither side could gain victory without horrendous human losses.

At first sight, matters seemed to be going very well for the Allies, who secured a massive boost that spring when the United States joined them in war: millions of fresh American soldiers would shortly be arriving on the western front. At the time, though, the American factor was nothing like as decisive as it might appear. American mobilization was so agonizingly slow that no major intervention could be expected on the western front until the spring of 1918 at the earliest. American strength could be expected to be decisive in the campaigns of 1918 and presumably 1919, but by that point, the Allied cause might be too badly ruined to benefit from their aid.[4]

Just as the United States was entering the war, the Allies were encountering new disasters. In April 1917, the French launched an offensive under their new commander in chief, Robert Nivelle, who believed that a determined series of coordinated assaults could end the entire war within forty-eight hours. The campaign staggered on for weeks, leaving hundreds of thousands of casualties. So large was the cost, so futile the offensive, and so reckless the conduct of French commanders that thousands of French soldiers began collective resistance to official authority. They refused their officers' orders to return to the front in a massive act of mutiny that to some

degree affected 40 percent of infantry formations, ranging from isolated acts of protest to systematic defiance. Desertions mounted. By
the time the Messines mine detonated in June, the Allies faced the
serious possibility of a French collapse and a humiliating end to the
whole war.[5]

The British meanwhile prepared yet another offensive in Flanders. This campaign, the third battle of Ypres, focused on the town
of Passchendaele, which the linguistically challenged British pro-
nounced "Passion-dale," inevitably suggesting Christ's death on
the cross. And "crucifixion" was a fair description of what actually
ensued. The attack began on July 31, but the campaign dragged on
until November, when Canadian forces took what was left of Passchendaele. The whole campaign cost at least half a million casualties on both sides and achieved a gain in land of just five miles. By
one estimate, the gain could be measured at the rate of two inches
per fatality. Harry Patch recalled the battle as "mud, mud, and more
mud mixed together with blood."[6]

The outcome of Passchendaele is contentious. While the British
regard the battle as the nadir of their own generals' callous military
incompetence, German records suggest that the Flanders campaign
brought their own forces to the brink of ruin. General Hermann
von Kuhl described these battles as "the greatest martyrdom of
the World War." For Ludendorff, what had been the superlative
German army was being transformed into what he called a "militia." But both sides would wholeheartedly agree on the intolerable
scale of human destruction.[7]

Russia

THE ALLIES ALSO FACED the imminent danger that other members of the coalition might collapse or withdraw from the war. In
October, Germans and Austrians inflicted a crippling defeat on the

Italians, and Romania actually was forced out of the war that December.[8] Infinitely more serious was the danger to Russia, a principal member of the Entente coalition, whose withdrawal would decisively break the stalemate in Germany's favor. In March 1917, a revolution in Russia forced the tsar's abdication and installed a provisional government. As tsarist Russia had been notorious worldwide for its systematic repression, theocratic rule, and racial persecution, the news thrilled socialists and liberals worldwide, stirring spontaneous celebrations in working-class areas in the British Empire as well as the United States. The collapse of an ancient monarchy sent religious believers racing to their Bibles to find exactly how this toppling of thrones meshed with prophecies in the book of Daniel and elsewhere.

As the year progressed, it became increasingly obvious that the revolution had not created a stable Russian regime that could satisfy the demands of the starving cities and the desperate countryside. Radicals clamored for an immediate end to hostilities, and German authorities were happy to help destabilize a key enemy. Under German auspices, Vladimir Lenin returned to Russia with the goal of leading a Communist revolution. That July, hundreds of thousands of leftists demonstrated in Petrograd (the former Saint Petersburg) as conservatives threatened a military coup. The provisional government kept an unhappy and fragmented Russian army in the field against Germany, but its promises proved increasingly hard to keep. In November, the Bolsheviks launched their own putsch, ensuring that Russia would shortly withdraw from the war.[9]

In military terms, the revolution was a catastrophe for the Western Allies, who would soon have to face the united might of the German armies, immensely strengthened by the millions of soldiers formerly committed to the now-defunct eastern front. But the revolution also fitted well with contemporary expectations of a sweeping global transformation. For radicals, the Bolsheviks augured a new millennium of justice. Conservatives were horrified by the menacing antireligious tone of the Bolshevik message and the prospect of the persecution of the churches.

Fátima

RUSSIAN EVENTS WERE REFLECTED in the continuing popularity of visions and heavenly revelations. Most received only local notice, but a handful achieved global fame. One of the greatest series of apparitions began in May 1917, in the village of Fátima in Portugal, a country that had long succeeded in maintaining its neutrality in the war but which was intimately bound to Great Britain by commercial and sentimental ties. The country declared war on Germany in 1916, and by the following spring, Portuguese forces were in combat on the western front. Eight thousand eventually fell in combat. To put that figure in context, if a country the size of the contemporary United States suffered such casualties, that would be equivalent to losing four hundred thousand American dead.

Alarm about the war thus reached even the remote corners of one of Europe's least developed regions. The Russian revolutions also resonated in a nation that, in its political divisions, closely resembled much of Latin Europe. Portuguese politics focused on the struggle between a pious Catholic establishment and a strong phalanx of highly secular liberals, who loathed the church's superstitions and placed their faith in science, education, and freemasonry. Russian news excited the nation's socialists and liberals, while alarming conservatives and believers.[10]

Those political alignments provide the background for what otherwise seems like a simple story of over-excited piety. In Fátima, a group of shepherd children claimed to have seen an apparition of the Virgin Mary. (The vision was originally announced by the "Angel of Peace," whom learned observers immediately identified as the archangel Michael.) Their story gained fame as the visions

Expectant believers await the promised miracle at Fátima,
October 13, 1917

were repeated each month through the summer, with the promise of some undisclosed glory to occur on the sixth visitation, in October. Both sides in Portuguese national affairs, pious and secular, became deeply interested in the reported visions and avidly awaited the Virgin's promised return. Faithful Catholics looked for a miracle, while liberals relished an unprecedented opportunity to debunk clerical deception and peasant gullibility.[11]

On the day of the expected miracle, October 13, tens of thousands gathered to worship or mock. And then, in one of the more puzzling examples of crowd psychology, a vast crowd with a sizable contingent of anticlericals and anti-Catholics described a miraculous vision of the sun dancing in the heavens. Reportedly, the clouds cleared to reveal the sun displaying a curious and alarming color, before that sun began to behave very oddly:

It began to revolve vertiginously on its axis, like the most magnificent fire-wheel that could be imagined, taking on all the colors of the rainbow and sending forth multicolored flashes

of light, producing the most astounding effect. This sublime
and incomparable spectacle, which was repeated three distinct
times, lasted for about ten minutes. The immense multitude,
overcome by the evidence of such a tremendous prodigy, threw
themselves on their knees.

The sun zigzagged toward the world in what onlookers reasonably assumed to mark the end of the world. If the heavens had
wanted to illustrate the Woman Clothed with the Sun, as foretold
in Revelation, could they have offered a more precise fulfillment
of prophecy?[12]

What happened that day has inspired a good deal of serious scientific debate, and researchers have advanced plausible explanations,
perhaps involving dust clouds. If not an actual miracle, though, then
it is odd that a meteorological freak (to take an obvious example)
should have occurred on such a heavily advertised date. The date
was all the more important, coming so shortly before the sensational
Bolshevik seizure of power in Russia: the actual coup took place
on November 7 and 8, although the difference of calendars meant
that this was commemorated as the October Revolution. The Portuguese event offered rich material for anyone looking for a cosmic
sign, and it reverberated through the coming century.

The German Messiah

EDUCATED PROTESTANTS LOOKED ASKANCE at such end-time
expectations, with all the medieval trappings of miracle. Instead,
they had their own assemblage of messianic signs, which likewise
came to the fore in the dreadful autumn of 1917. In a masterpiece
of publishing good fortune, it was in this year that Cyrus Scofield
published the second and more comprehensive edition of his reference Bible, a clear manifesto of premillennial theology. Looking at

the world situation, who could doubt the relevance of such a text?

Germany's churches had overwhelmingly supported the country's entry into war and provided strong ideological support regardless of denomination or faction. By 1917, though, cracks were showing in the once-solid interfaith alliance. One sensitive issue was the declaration of unrestricted submarine warfare, which apart from its practical dangers (namely, bringing the United States into the war) raised grievous ethical issues about targeting civilians. Catholics and more liberal Protestants also became sympathetic to calls for peace negotiations, even if that would result in something short of unqualified triumph. Demands for future annexations proved particularly divisive. The liberal *Die Christliche Welt* raised increasingly daring questions about the empire's true war aims, and respected theologians like Otto Baumgarten wrote against annexations. Ernst Troeltsch himself came to favor a compromise peace. Critically, so did the Catholic Center Party.[13]

In July 1917, the Reichstag passed a peace resolution rejecting any "lust of conquest" and calling for "a peace of understanding and a lasting reconciliation of peoples." "Any violations of territory, and political, economic, and financial persecutions are incompatible with such a peace." Hence, Germany would not claim annexations or indemnities and would submit disputes to international arbitration. Although the resolution was hedged around with pledges about fighting to the end if an honorable settlement were not reached, this was a major departure from the old united front. The peace resolution marked the beginning of a political alliance between Social Democrats and the more liberal churches that became the basis of the coalition that dominated Germany through the Weimar Republic of the 1920s. In August, the pope presented his own plan for a comprehensive peace settlement. As we have seen, he envisaged not just stopping the war but decisively restructuring European societies away from militarism.[14]

Other Christians, though, especially Lutherans, remained firmly

committed to the full agenda of August 1914, and they were appalled
at such apparent weakness. Militarists found their ultimate symbol in
Martin Luther himself, who in this era achieved a messianic reputation. German churches had long venerated Luther, but adulation
reached new heights with the rise of intense nationalism following
the creation of the new empire in 1871. In this age, too, some of
Germany's greatest scholars undertook what has become known as
the "Luther Renaissance." One was historian Karl Holl, a direct link
from the brilliant Tübingen school of biblical criticism in the previous
century. Holl's pupils at the University of Berlin included Emanuel
Hirsch, who also studied under von Harnack. Among Hirsch's other
achievements, he was a pioneering advocate of the work of Søren
Kierkegaard, but he was best known as the intellectual genius of
the new Luther movement. Both Holl and Hirsch would become
standard-bearers of an emerging church-based extreme Right.[15]

By 1914, Luther had become the centerpiece of a religious-
nationalist vision in which his Reformation marked almost a re-
founding of Christianity itself. Luther, in this vision, became the
German savior, who offered a special revelation to and for the
German people. When combined with the Lutheran vision of the
state as an entity that fulfilled its historical destiny by relentlessly
pursuing its own interests, Luther became a wonderful figurehead
for aggressive nationalism at its most ruthless. For patriotic Germans, Luther's hymn "Ein feste Burg ist unser Gott" (A mighty
fortress is our God) became a second national anthem.[16]

Lutheran theologians became strident voices for expansionist
militarism. One of the most celebrated was Reinhold Seeberg, an
intellectual superstar whose *Fundamental Truths of the Christian Religion*
made its mark on Anglo-American theology. In 1915, he organized
the so-called *Intellektuelleneingabe,* the "petition of the intellectuals."
This was yet another scholars' manifesto but this time demanding far-
reaching territorial annexations in both eastern and western Europe
as Germany's right and proper war aims. He was assuredly not pre-

pared to relax his position in the controversies of 1917, and he did not stand alone. During 1917, hard-liners like Holl were appalled at the moderation of other church leaders over matters like the submarine campaign, and they aligned themselves with the superpatriotic Rightist groups. Holl himself joined the pro-war and pro-annexation German Fatherland Party (Deutsche Vaterlandspartei).[17]

Luther also had an anniversary approaching. His most famous single act was the posting of his Ninety-Five Theses at Wittenberg on October 31, 1517, a date that Protestants commonly commemorated as Reformation Day. Inevitably, the four hundredth anniversary of so momentous an occasion was going to be treated specially, but in the context of domestic and international politics at this time, the Luther celebration, *Reformationsfeier,* became a messianic hymning of the German spirit. Through the year, the Reformation pioneer was celebrated by cultural events and lectures, culminating in a weeklong festival centered on Wittenberg. By the time the event began, the slaughter at the third battle of Ypres was ending its third month, and German forces were under deadly pressure.[18]

Going far beyond the expected formal gathering of church leaders and academics, the occasion gave the opportunity for an outpouring of superpatriotic speeches, of nationalism at its most high-flown, with a current of anti-Semitism. Preachers celebrated the exalted spirit of August 1914, that time when earth had been so close to heaven, and the world of holy struggle and sacrifice that it had initiated. Speakers praised the German army, which was well represented in bands, choirs, and parades, and they proudly noted news of victories in Italy and Galicia. Throughout, the emphasis was on German Christian youth and the mighty new Germany they would build. Pastor Theodor Knolle published his sermon under the title *Luther Unser Mitkämpfer*—Luther, our comrade in arms, our fellow warrior. (The event naturally caused serious tensions with German Catholics, who were otherwise thoroughly devoted to the national cause.)[19]

The Wittenberg event became a paean to last-ditch resistance. Speakers recalled as uniquely German symbols the memories of Wittenberg, but also of Worms, where Luther famously confronted the emperor, declaring "Here I stand: I can do no other." For participants, that was the Savior's message that modern-day Germans should take to heart when hearing the slightest talk of compromise, whether it stemmed from a pope or an American president. The German Evangelical League used the event as an excuse to restate some of Luther's harsher and more authoritarian sayings (which are never too hard to locate). They rejected any American-derived exaltation of democratic government as a good or necessary component of human happiness. Read thus, Luther was urging the imperial Germany of 1918 to fight to the last.[20]

For all the tributes to Luther as Savior or Messiah, no German presumably expected him to return to earth in the clouds as many still expected the coming of Christ. But we can still legitimately speak of the vision of Luther in religious terms, as the human symbol of a nation with a divine mission. For religious nationalists, not only did Germany have its own Christ, Germany *was* its own Christ.

Jerusalem and the Prophet

IF GERMANY HAD LUTHER, the Anglo-American world found a still more unlikely messianic figure in the brilliant but quite secular British general Edmund Allenby, the man who conquered Jerusalem in December 1917. Although the Palestine campaign was marginal to the outcome of the war as a whole, its symbolic significance was incalculable. From early Christian times, the city of Jerusalem had been central to Christian apocalyptic, no less than to Jewish hopes and dreams. Revelation itself culminated with a vision of Christ ruling a new Jerusalem. And now, finally, Christian control of the city became a realistic possibility.

In 1914, Palestine was part of a shrinking Ottoman Empire, which dreaded being swallowed up by aggressive European nations. In a last-ditch bid for survival, the empire joined the Central Powers in 1914 and actually survived early campaigns with some success. Heavy British commitments elsewhere made it difficult for them to concentrate on the frontier that separated their own sphere of influence in Egypt from Ottoman Palestine.[21]

The war entered a new phase in June 1917 when Allenby took command in the Middle East theater. He brought with him a passion for bold new tactics, including fast-moving mobile warfare, based on light cavalry units. He also destabilized enemy positions by using proxy forces in their rear, namely the Arab rebels under the command of the legendary T. E. Lawrence. Over the following months, Allenby launched a series of aggressive offensives, which retrod steps familiar to any reader of the Bible. While the British had stumbled in two battles of Gaza that spring, Allenby now fought a third and victorious engagement at that ancient city of the Philistines. He followed with an attack on Beersheba on October 31. So confident were the British of imminent victory that on November 2, they were able to issue the Balfour Declaration, proclaiming British sympathy for the establishment of a Jewish national home in the soon-to-be-conquered Palestine. Gaining ground quickly, Allenby beat his declared deadline of taking Jerusalem by Christmas. After Ottoman forces evacuated the city, Allenby occupied Jerusalem on December 9.

Throughout these years, biblical place names were daily in the world's headlines. The British took Jericho in February 1918, followed by a campaign in the Jordan Valley, culminating with the capture of Damascus on October 1. British soldiers recalled, "We used the Bibles as guide-books to Palestine." Allenby's forces then moved toward a decisive battle that finally occurred in late September 1918 at Megiddo. In military terms alone, Megiddo was a stunning victory—a blitzkrieg, in effect, in which Allenby deployed highly mobile ground forces working closely with effective air power. But Megiddo was also the setting for the biblical battle of Armageddon, the setting for a thrilling moment in the book of Revelation that precedes the fall of Babylon. Allenby himself referred to "the Field of Armageddon" in his dispatches, and editors around the world happily followed his usage. When the general received a peerage, he was inevitably known as Allenby of Armageddon.[22]

The biblical quality of this campaign raised grave difficulties for the British government. While it was natural to think in terms of a new crusade, such language would be extraordinarily damaging for the vast portions of Britain's worldwide empire in which Muslims abounded, particularly in India, where anti-imperial sentiment was rife. Much like the United States following the September 11 attacks, British authorities tried strenuously to suppress talk of crusade or any suggestion that the war was directed against Muslims, and they highlighted the heroic Arab and other Muslim forces who had joined them in their struggle against Ottoman tyranny.[23] Unlike the modern United States, moreover, the British were armed with sweeping powers of news censorship.

Allenby himself played his role very carefully indeed. Conscious of his worldwide media audience, especially in the United States, he stage-managed his entry into the city to preserve the delicate balance between the glory of conquest and the humility of the Christian general. Remarkably for the time, and doubly so for a career cavalry general, he even entered not on horseback but on foot, as a sign of humility intended to contrast with the kaiser's self-aggrandizing visit to the city in 1898. Allenby took every opportunity to show his awareness of the city's ancient roots and its sacred position for multiple faiths.

Unfortunately for British authorities, the symbolism of Jerusalem was so compelling that they could at best exercise some damage control over the crusading rhetoric. The story was doubly attractive for English speakers, for whom the story of Richard Coeur de Lion

General Allenby enters Jerusalem on foot, to show his
respect for the Holy City

and the Third Crusade was a mainstay of popular culture, which
Sir Walter Scott had integrated into the legend of Robin Hood.
When the city fell, the English magazine *Punch* featured a cartoon
of Richard gazing down on Jerusalem, saying, "At last my dream
comes true!" In the Catholic world, all Rome's churches greeted
the capture by singing "Te Deums."[24]

As little as he wanted the title, popular acclaim made Allenby
the ultimate Crusader, the subject of a growing corpus of neo-
medieval mythology. When his secretary, Raymond Savage, published Allenby's biography in 1925, he had to confront a rash of
pious legends: that Allenby entered Jerusalem with a Bible in one
hand and a crucifix in the other, that he made his staff kneel in
prayer with him before battle or made them join Bible study every
night; and of course, this saintly Allenby was often seen carrying
his Bible into battle. On entering Jerusalem, he reputedly exulted,
"Today the wars of the crusaders are completed." All the tales were
false, or at least wildly padded, but they were essential in imagining the warlord of what believers worldwide stubbornly insisted on
calling a crusade.[25]

Although Savage debunked the myths of the Bible-toting commander, he himself harked back to the original Crusades at every opportunity. At every stage of his history, older ghosts intruded:

> Thus the army stood on the spot where the people of Israel made their solemn vows and elected Saul to rule over them, and where Richard Coeur de Lion afterward offered his prayer as he approached the crest to view Jerusalem: "Lord God, I pray that I may never see thy holy city if I may not rescue it from the hands of thine enemies." . . . Resurgent when Saladin conquered Galilee, the Crescent had dominated the cradle of Christianity in unbroken sway for its destined span from that sanguinary October to October, 1917, exactly seven hundred and thirty years.

Similar themes dominated the wave of books that celebrated the victories, with such titles as *Khaki Crusaders* (1919), *The Modern Crusaders* (1920), and *The Last Crusade* (1920) as well as the propaganda film *The New Crusaders*.[26]

Of its nature, a crusade is a religious war, but many observers were still more explicit in placing a prophetic mantle on Allenby's shoulders, especially when this act was so closely associated with a promised return of the Jews to their homeland. At sunset on December 9, 1917, there began the Jewish festival of Hanukkah, which commemorates the miraculous deliverance of the Jewish people. The event is obviously significant to Jews, but also to Christians. Hanukkah, oddly, is the only Jewish feast apart from Passover that is explicitly mentioned in the Christian Gospels and the only one directly associated with the life of Jesus. A contemporary American image depicted the two Hanukkah heroes in parallel: Judas Maccabeus entering Jerusalem in 165 BC and Allenby in 1917. Over Allenby's head stood a text from Isaiah 59: "And there will come for Zion a Redeemer." Saint Paul quotes the verse in Romans as a prefiguring of Christ.[27]

The year 1917 also marked a neat four hundred years since the great Ottoman victories over the Egyptian Mamluk dynasty, which had effectively established Turkish power over the Levant—and, critically, had given the Ottomans the city of Jerusalem. In interpreting this chronology, evangelical Christians turned to the medieval Jewish Kabbalist Rabbi Judah Ben Samuel, who reputedly prophesied not only the establishment of Ottoman power but that they would retain their hold over Jerusalem for eight Jubilees, that is, four hundred years. Even for Muslims, Allenby's story supposedly carried special weight. Savage reported that "many of the Arab rulers" who witnessed the entry into Jerusalem recalled a prophecy concerning "God, the Prophet—*Allah Nabi* [Allenby]!" Another commonplace of the time noted that in Arabic script, the name Allenby was close to *al-Nabi,* "the Prophet." [28]

After centuries of immersion in biblical stories and prophecies, of intimate familiarity with names like Megiddo and Damascus, suddenly these names were in the headlines and even on the cinema screens. It was hard to avoid thinking of Jesus's own words: today, this scripture is fulfilled in your hearing.

Plague

AND THEN TO A world already thoroughly smitten with war, death, and famine there came a plague of unprecedented scale. In 1918, as the final battles of the war began, there appeared a virulent new strain of influenza that swept the world, killing millions—far more, in fact, than the actual combat of the war itself. Its biblical quality was neatly captured in Katherine Anne Porter's classic tale of the disease as it struck Denver, Colorado. Her story bore the suitably Revelation-themed title *Pale Horse, Pale Rider.*

The pandemic struck in two distinct waves. The first appeared in the United States in March 1918, when millions of troops were

In a nightmarish image, American police wear masks to reduce the danger
of infection during the 1918 influenza epidemic. The image suggests parallels
with the common use of gas masks by soldiers at the front line.

billeted together in close quarters that proved an ideal incubator for
the new illness. Transatlantic troopships proved particularly effective for this purpose. By June, the sickness had reached India and
Australia. In the first phase, the old and weak were especially likely
to perish, but a second and still more lethal form of influenza arrived
in August, and this claimed the young and strong. Mortality was at
its highest in the closing months of 1918.[29]

Raw statistics only hint at the scale of destruction. At the time,
Western observers focused on the devastation in their own countries—600,000 dead in the United States, 400,000 in France, 250,000
in Britain—but the global consequences were far larger. In all, the
Great War itself killed perhaps 10 million in four years. In just one
year, from mid-1918 through mid-1919, the Spanish flu pandemic
killed at least 50 million, and some estimates put the death toll at
twice that. And this occurred at a time when global population was
around 1.8 billion, little over a quarter of what it is today. If the
estimate of 100 million is correct, that would account for almost
10 percent of the world's young adults at that time. A third of the
world's population was affected to some degree.

To put the disaster in context, the most notorious epidemic of our own time is AIDS, which claimed some 25 million lives between 1981 and 2011. The influenza epidemic killed far more in four months than has AIDS in its career thus far, and it had a much greater impact on the social fabric.

The Last Year

THE PLAGUE OF 1918 swept a world anticipating battles on a cosmic scale. Any thoughtful observer knew that two key facts would determine the outcome of the European war, namely the collapse of Russia and the imminent arrival of U.S. military forces. Putting those two together made it certain that the Germans would launch a massive offensive on the western front in the spring of 1918, with the goal of knocking out the Allies before U.S. forces could become serious players in the conflict. The lethal combination of "Yanks and tanks" had to be preempted. Given the balance of military power at the time, that also meant that the main blow—Operation Michael—would be directed against the British.

When the attack finally came, on March 21, it fully lived up to expectations, with seventy German divisions smashing into Allied positions, mainly the British Fifth Army, which was still recovering from Passchendaele. On the first day alone, the Germans fired three million shells, a third of them chemical. Overhead, fleets of hundreds of fighter aircraft battled each other. By the end of that day, British and Germans together had suffered almost eighty thousand casualties, including nineteen thousand dead, while twenty thousand British soldiers surrendered to the advancing Germans. This was among the worst days for casualties in the entire war.[30]

A sober military account, though, gives only a limited sense of the mood of the time. Ernst Jünger's memoir of Michael is Wagnerian in its mood, a picture of speed, dynamism, and exhilara-

A British machine gun unit

tion that fully qualifies as a mystical experience. Even for such a long-serving veteran, the experience of overwhelming triumph—however brief—was life changing:

> The incredible massing of forces in the hour of destiny, to
> fight for a distant future, and the violence it so surprisingly,
> stunningly unleashed, had taken me for the first time into
> the depths of something that was more than mere personal
> experience.

On the home front, German newspapers spoke of a revival of the spirit of 1914.[31]

Initially, the Germans triumphed along the line. After years of inching forward along the trenches, suddenly the attacking forces were sweeping across France, gaining up to forty miles in a month. Making the Allied retreat still more bitter was the knowledge that the land being lost in days was the same terrain gained at horrendous price in earlier offensives, including the old Somme battlefields. A second great attack—Operation Georgette—began on April 9, with the aim of seizing the Channel ports. Two days later, Field Marshal Douglas Haig issued his famous statement warning British forces that they stood with their backs to the wall. Of these "extreme days," Vera Brittain reported, "Nothing had ever equaled them before—not the Somme, not Arras, not Passchendaele—for into our minds had crept for the first time the secret, incredible fear that we might lose the war." In May, the French bore the brunt of the assault, and Paris itself seemed likely to fall. German soldiers were astonished to see the fanatical attacks that British aircraft of the newly formed RAF launched against their advancing columns. British planes flew in lower and faster than they ever had in the past, giving pilots next to no time to pull up in order to evade antiaircraft fire. These were virtual suicide attacks. The Germans understood fully: both sides knew this was the final battle for control of the continent and, without exaggeration, for the fate of the world.[32]

In these weeks, it looked as though the Germans would accomplish exactly what they eventually did in 1940. They would potentially force Allied armies to evacuate the continent from some small port—Dunkirk, perhaps? France, Italy, and Russia would all be knocked out of the Entente alliance. In that case, the British, Canadians, and Americans would begin a new phase of the war in which they would regroup for a D-day invasion, to be launched in 1920 or 1921.[33]

But the Germans failed in their objectives. Their last push in mid-July was contained, leaving the Allies to plan their riposte. Even better, from the Allied point of view, German advances had given them a much larger front to defend, while the ruthless attacks by Germany's elite shock troops had badly reduced the number of prime fighters available to them. On March 21 alone the Germans lost almost eleven thousand killed. The German army survived by padding the ranks with older and inferior troops, who lacked the all-or-nothing spirit of that spring.[34]

The spring offensives also showed both sides the enormous

A British SE5a fighter, 1918, one of the world's most advanced military
technologies at the time

imbalance in logistics and supplies. When the Germans occupied
British bunkers, they were astonished at the wealth of food and
drink they saw all around them. British prisoners in German hands,
meanwhile, were delighted to see how badly stocked their captors
were and how deficient their mechanical equipment. Watching a
film like *All Quiet on the Western Front,* based on the author's personal experience on the German lines, anyone familiar with the
Allied side of the war is startled by the near starvation the German
forces expected on a routine basis. Already American and British
manufacturing and transportation had decisively won the logistic
war, and the disparities were growing apace. Even at the flood tide
of German victories that spring, the imbalance of supplies contributed directly to slowing the advance, as men wandered off on loot-
ing expeditions, seizing food, wine, and clothing in quantities they
had not seen in years.[35]

In July, French and American forces began a sweeping counter-
offensive in the second Battle of the Marne. The British also began

their great offensive. During the previous year they had experimented with new offensive tactics, especially at the Battle of Cambrai, which showed how Allied forces could use tanks and artillery to penetrate German defenses. The Hundred Days campaign that began in August involved British, French, American, Canadian, and Australian forces, among contributions from many smaller nations.[36]

Although not well known by a single familiar name, such as Waterloo and Gettysburg, the Hundred Days deserve to be remembered among the most important battles in human history. In a series of devastating blows, the Allies dismantled the already weakened German forces on the western front. The British described one battle in particular, at Amiens that August, as "the day we won the war." (Ludendorff called it "the black day of the German army.") By late September, the British were reoccupying the lands for which they had fought so hard in the previous year's Passchendaele campaign but now measuring their daily progress in miles rather than yards. Allied armies stormed the Hindenburg line, and U.S. forces took the initiative in the Meuse-Argonne. Of some fifty thousand U.S. battle casualties, the great majority perished during or after that September.[37]

In all, the Hundred Days battles inflicted over two million casualties on the various fighting forces, but the Germans suffered much worse than their enemies. German morale plummeted, strikes became commonplace, and outright mutiny threatened the imperial fleet. Army discipline disintegrated. By this stage, seven hundred thousand German soldiers and sailors had deserted.

At the start of October, the German high command warned that the war could no longer be continued, as the armed forces faced imminent annihilation. They called for an immediate armistice, to prevent the country falling into total chaos and Red revolution. Meanwhile, Germany's Allies were slipping away one by one: in the final months of the war, Bulgaria, the Ottoman Empire, and Austria-Hungary all made their separate peace with the Allies. In

November, finally, the kaiser abdicated, leaving the way clear for an armistice on the 11th. The ancient Habsburg dominion also crumbled, as the Austro-Hungarian Empire fragmented into several new nation-states.

IF NOT ACTUAL ARMAGEDDON, the Central Powers were reduced to something like the political vacuum imagined in Malevich's *Black Square*. When Hitler learned of the kaiser's abdication, he recalled, "Again, everything went black before my eyes." But millions in the Allied nations could join in a shared complaint: everything they loved was indeed lost.

Worlds were ending.

CHAPTER SEVEN

The Sleep of Religion
Europe's Crisis and the Rise of Secular Messiahs

Here lies blood; and let it lie
Speechless still and never cry.
—JOHN CLEVELAND, 1641

I knew that the old world was finished.
—JOHN COLLIER, 1919

JUST AS THE WAR began with Machen's tale of risen bowmen, so it ended with the reburial of a new generation of military ghosts. The war's most innovative film appeared three years after *Intolerance,* and it grew directly from battlefield experience. During the final battles of 1918, director Abel Gance was making his *J'Accuse* near the Saint-Mihiel front, using as extras some two thousand serving French soldiers; most would actually be killed before the armistice that November. The film ends with a searing adaptation of the Christian Last Judgment, and it also echoes the popular wartime French myth of "Debout les Morts." In this legendary sequence, which made Gance the most celebrated European director of the

A patriotic angel defends Germans from Bolshevism, with its attendant evils of war, hunger, and unemployment, in this 1918 poster by Walter Schnackenberg.

age, legions of dead French soldiers rise from their graves and march back to their home villages, to ask friends and relatives if they had been worthy of all the war's sacrifices. In *J'Accuse,* at least, the risen dead are satisfied with the answers they receive and return to the sleep of the grave.[1]

Through the war years, apocalyptic and millenarian messages had constantly bombarded Western publics, proclaiming a time of judgment when the supernatural was pouring through into secular reality. It is difficult to hear those messages so constantly without absorbing them, but at the end of 1918, Western nations faced two extremely difficult and perhaps unanswerable questions. What does a nation do after it has lost a war that it identified as holy? And just as intractable, what does a country do after it has won such a conflict? Europe and the Middle East were deluged in sacrificial blood, yet old injustices remained stubbornly in place, in a new world of hunger and poverty. As early as 1920, a sweeping history of the just-completed conflict bore the title of *The First World War,* with the pointed implication that others were yet to come. Awareness of present and future woes could not fail to affect attitudes to faith, to religion, and to the churches and preachers who had urged nations on to the war that killed ten million. In the words of Czechoslovak statesman Tomáš Masaryk, the new Europe was "a laboratory built on a graveyard."[2]

The good news for the churches was that the war did not kill religion. Some faiths, some religious ideas, continued to flourish for decades afterward, and we cannot draw a direct and inevitable causal line from the war years to later European secularization. Yet religion could not remain unaffected, or untainted. The most dangerous consequence was not that religious and apocalyptic ideas might vanish, rather that they would metastasize into new and sinister forms. As they watched Europe's new nightmares unfold in the 1920s and 1930s, with the continental drift toward Fascism, Nazism, and racial extermination, perceptive religious leaders should have heard countless echoes from their own rhetoric of the holy war and holy nation. Ghosts marched.

The Survival of the Churches

IF THE CHURCHES' PASSIONATE support for the war had caused a catastrophic decline in their popularity and driven a continent-wide secularization, that might seem a suitable punishment, not to mention an appropriate moral lesson. It would have been a war to end faith. Of course events did not proceed in that way, or at least not immediately. For one thing, it would be decades before the view of the war as a monument to human stupidity would gain the ortho-

European State Borders Before and After World War I

dox status it possesses today. Despite the huge losses, few on either side questioned the need for the war to have been fought.[3]

Looking at a map of Europe before and after the war illustrates a historic change in the political dimensions of faith. In 1914, something like Christendom was clearly the accepted political-religious order in much of Europe, especially that vast area of the continent dominated by the three holy empires of Russia, Germany, and Austria-Hungary. By 1918, that order was dying or dead, and social crisis was most acute in the states that were once included in those realms. In the words of Anglican cleric Dean Inge, "The three great European empires are, at the time of writing, in a state of septic dissolution." But the story was not one of simple decline: churches not only kept their prestige and political power in many nations but, at least in the short term, some actually enhanced their standing.[4]

The Catholic Church especially seemed to have done well, to the point that, fairly or otherwise, a popular German saying declared, "Luther lost the war!" Michael Burleigh has suggested that "a sort of geo-strategic audit" would show significant gains for the Catholic Church. After all, the once-rival Russian church was collapsing, while Muslims no longer held the holy places of Palestine. Germany's new republic ended the traditionally close link between the monarchy and the Protestant churches. "Internationally the Church could say it had stood for peace, while no French or Italian nationalists could claim that the patriotic fervor of the clergy was wanting."[5] Far from being compromised or discredited, clergy retained their prestige and many won high praise for their wartime role as chaplains. (In France, they had fought as frontline soldiers.) Across the Allied nations, for Protestants and Catholics alike, Cardinal Mercier won glory for his role as Belgium's national leader during the crisis of occupation. In his day, he commanded a reputation for holiness and heroism much like that of the Dalai Lama or Desmond Tutu in more recent times.

In the immediate aftermath of the war, moreover, parts of Europe still notionally remained within the scope of Christendom, in that many states defined themselves as Christian and gave preferential or even exclusive status to a particular church. Such establishment continued to be the situation in Great Britain as well as most of Europe's smaller nations, and across Scandinavia and much of eastern Europe. Christian leaders wielded real political influence and did so through the 1940s. Catholic political parties became a potent force after the war, as the church combated rising new secular movements. Throughout Europe, too, clergy became ever more visible as the nations' experts in ritual observance. Across the denominational spectrum, churches acquired a critical social role as the custodians of the vast new ceremonial enterprise that developed around the commemoration of the war dead, with the frequent need for dedications and annual services.[6]

So confident were they in their standing within their own societies that churches could afford to make bold steps toward coop-
eration with rival believers. In 1925, the senior bishop of Sweden's
national Lutheran church brought together church leaders from
England, Germany, and France, as a step toward reconciliation.
That move marked a critical stage in the ecumenical movement and
the founding of the World Council of Churches.

The institutional strength of the churches was based on the continuing loyalty of ordinary believers, which at least at first seems to
have been little affected by the war. Spiritual concerns were very
much in evidence at the front, and the war actively encouraged fundamental rethinking about issues of life and death. Among ordinary
Christian believers, levels of belief and practice remained historically
high through the 1920s, consistently so in Catholic countries but also
in Protestant lands like England. As Jonathan Ebel has suggested in
an American context, looking at the war's effects on participants, we
should think less of disenchantment so much as *re*-enchantment, a
renewed interest in spirituality, and a quest for certainty.[7]

In the United States, too, churches won important ideological
victories from the war. For decades, Protestant churches had made
the regulation or suppression of alcohol a core of their social program, but it was the war that made complete prohibition feasible,
and by the draconian solution of a full-scale constitutional amend-
ment. Although we usually think of Prohibition as a defining feature of 1920s America, the political debate that permitted the legal
change was entirely a product of the war, and the key congressional
votes occurred before the end of 1917. Whatever the religious basis
of its advocates, the argument that proved overwhelming was that
alcohol weakened a nation girding itself for war, and patriotic duty
demanded its suppression. The result was to proclaim the triumph
of white Protestant values over those of the Catholics and Jews who
were now such a visible presence in American cities. The patriotic
argument about moral rigorism also led to the shuttering of the

open vice areas that had prevailed before the war, and again the victory of a puritanical Protestant ethic.[8]

In the postwar decade, America experienced a series of culture wars. These culminated in the spectacular of the Scopes Trial in 1925, when a Tennessee teacher was tried for violating a fundamentalist-inspired state law against teaching evolution. Although John Scopes was convicted, the dreadful national publicity did much to discredit fundamentalist and antievolutionist thought. But despite this setback, religious adherence remained very high, and so did interest in some of the core evangelical causes, including dispensationalism and Christian Zionism. Defeated in 1925, evangelical churches nevertheless continued to build institutions and organizational structures that would provide a firm foundation for social and political activism later in the century. They clung to the prophetic and premillenarian teachings that had been so widely popularized by the experience of war.[9]

Moving Backward

OUTSIDE THE CHURCHES, TOO, spiritual enthusiasm remained unchecked. The efflorescence of esoteric and mystical sects continued after 1918, in both Europe and North America. As Thomas Hardy lamented in 1922,

> At present, when belief in witches of Endor is displacing the Darwinian theory and "the truth that shall make you free," men's minds appear . . . to be moving backwards rather than on.

Spiritualism flourished. In the 1920s, a spiritualist photographer became famous for the photographs she took during the annual commemoration of the war dead at London's Cenotaph. Each year, mainstream newspapers gave front-page prominence to these images, which appeared to show the faces of countless dead souls clustered over the monument. Not until 1924 was her blatant fraud exposed. Some well-known activists made a startling transition from secular politics to passionate faith, whether occult or apocalyptic. By the 1920s, celebrated British feminist leader Christabel Pankhurst had become an outspoken advocate of Christ's imminent Second Coming.[10]

Meanwhile, self-styled prophets attracted significant followings, and some organized sects. The most important of the new messiahs was the Theosophical movement's Jiddu Krishnamurti, a young Indian boy whom the group's leaders had identified as the prophet of a glorious new mystical era. Krishnamurti attracted wild hopes through the 1920s before he formally rejected godhood. In 1922, Russian writer Ilya Ehrenburg satirized the obsessions and superstitions of contemporary Europe in his novel *The Extraordinary Adventures of Julio Jurenito and His Disciples*. The book described the career of an amoral anarchistic messiah, an Antichrist for the modern world.[11]

Through the decade we also see the continuation and the thorough mainstreaming of the apocalyptic fascination from the war years. The cinema was crucial to this process. The film industry benefited enormously from the war years, as civilians had flocked to theaters for entertainment, while governments supported the industry for propaganda purposes. In 1917, Ludendorff's general staff had sponsored the creation of UFA (Universum Film AG), which became the nation's largest film producer and a major driving force in German cinema through the twentieth century. Mystical and esoteric ideas were in vogue among the communities making the movies that represented the leading edge of cultural experimentation, in Germany itself but also in the film world then emerging in Hollywood. When notorious British occultist Aleister Crowley visited Los Angeles in 1918, he was lionized by fans from the filmmaking world, whom he scorned as "the swarming maggots of near-occultists."[12]

Through these channels, the general public had a constant diet of supernatural themes. This intense cultural work helped ensure that spiritual and apocalyptic interpretations of the recent war remained in the popular consciousness long after the conclusion of hostilities. The fact that films were silent meant that such productions could reach a global audience to a degree that was impossible in later years, as language barriers scarcely existed.

One of the most successful films of the silent era was the 1921 production of *The Four Horsemen of the Apocalypse,* based on Blasco Ibañez's novel. (In cinematic history, the film is best recalled for making a megastar out of Rudolph Valentino.) The film would not have been made if not for the enthusiasm of screenwriter June Mathis, a devout believer in the occult who was enthralled by its apocalyptic and uncanny themes. The cinematic version not only retained the novel's heavy reliance on Revelation but also used this as the essential framework of the war narrative. Throughout, the film interpreted the war in terms of "the breaking of the Seven Seals of Prophecy," "the age of fulfillment," and "the angel of prophecy." The four horsemen themselves appear literally and repeatedly, riding through the heavens over the battlefields. Even the Beast appears on screen, as a fire-breathing behemoth unleashed on the world in 1914. This mystical blockbuster earned over four million dollars at the box office, a huge sum at the time.

In Europe, esoteric obsessions bore fruit with a wave of occult-related and supernatural films during and immediately after the war, films about diabolism, ritual magic, and witchcraft. Germany's legendary expressionist cinema of the Weimar years was commonly the work of occult-minded filmmakers and writers whose long-standing esoteric interests were further enhanced by wartime military service. The vampire classic *Nosferatu* was the work of German military veterans who hoped to popularize esoteric and hermetic ideas through a series of mass-market productions: director F. W. Murnau was a wartime fighter pilot. Murnau's films commonly deploy apocalyptic images, and his *Faust* begins with a vision of the four horsemen. Both *Nosferatu* and *Faust* depict catastrophic urban plagues that would immediately have suggested for contemporary audiences the wartime influenza epidemic. *The Golem* was based on a 1915 bestseller by the fiercely antiwar Austrian author Gustav Meyrink, a passionate devotee of Theosophy and the occult. Not surprisingly, the film offered a knowledgeable depiction of Kabbalistic-derived ritual magic.[13]

The most influential filmmaker of these years was Fritz Lang, whose strongly Catholic interests combined with his attraction to mythological themes; he had also seen heavy military duty in the Austrian service and been repeatedly wounded. Throughout the postwar years his films return to themes of apocalyptic warfare and destruction, usually accompanied by plague and spiritual corruption, all of which inevitably recall the wartime rhetoric of cosmic confrontation. His two-part 1924 epic *Die Nibelungen* brought Wagnerian images of the world's end to a global audience.

But Lang also drank deeply from Christian sources. His 1927 work *Metropolis* is commonly regarded as one of the classics of cinema, and at the time it was probably the most expensive film ever made. Only in light of recent restoration work, though, can we see how explicitly it draws on apocalyptic themes in its prophetic depiction of modern society. Partly, *Metropolis* reflects the ideas of Oswald Spengler, whose sensationally popular book *The Decline of the West* appeared in 1918. Spengler presented nightmare forecasts of the vast megalopolis, ruled by the superrich, with politics reduced to demagoguery and Caesarism, and religion marked by strange oriental cults. Lang borrowed that model but added

The evil genius Rotwang and his robot, the pseudo-Maria, from *Metropolis*. In the background we see a satanic inverted pentagram.

explicit references to the Bible, and particularly Revelation. In the future world of *Metropolis,* the ruling classes dwell in their own Tower of Babel, while the industrial working class is literally enslaved to Moloch. The plot depicts the contest between two female figures who respectively recall the Woman Clothed with the Sun and the Whore of Babylon—the former is named Maria, while her evil counterpart is associated with a satanic inverted pentacle. The film directly quotes Revelation's account of the Beast and the Whore. Repeatedly, we see the visions of cosmic destruction awaiting the futuristic city.[14]

Through the 1920s, mainstream churches across the West regularly expressed their alarm and unhappiness about the proliferation of cults and esoteric movements, and the popularity of alternative spiritual ideas. We might argue, though, that the very popularity of such movements speaks to the vast and continuing interest in religion and the continuing belief that the recent conflict had had its religious dimensions.

Russia's Martyrdom

POLITICAL CHANGES, THOUGH, THREATENED to stifle the power of religion, even to snuff it out altogether. For millions of believers, the comfortable old order of church and state was replaced by a kind of anti-Christendom.

By far the greatest shock was the Russian Revolution. Within just a decade of the Bolshevik putsch, one of the world's great churches was uprooted and most of its leaders were dead or in exile. This experience was at once an appalling lesson for other Christians around the world and an enticing example for would-be revolutionaries. The Russian disaster shaped the world's religious politics for a generation.

The Russian church neither died nor faded away gently, but was violently killed. At the start of the war, the church was flourishing institutionally, with its intimate ties to government and an infrastructure that supported over a hundred thousand priests and deacons and another hundred thousand monks and nuns. Beyond its size, as we have seen, it was also flourishing spiritually, and at least initially the war strengthened faith, as church and monastic institutions supported the war effort, and pilgrimage sites recorded record numbers of visitors. But political changes proved lethal. The Great War placed impossible burdens upon an already fragile state mechanism, and demonstrated the sheer inability of either government or army to handle modern warfare. In the ensuing chaos, the Bolsheviks did a much better job than the church in seizing on millenarian hopes and nightmares, and channeled them into social revolution. Even so, when the old regime collapsed in early 1917, it was by no means obvious that Christians faced imminent catastrophe, and the radical upsurge led many Orthodox believers to seek dramatic reforms within the church itself. The church even restored its patriarchate.[15]

Initially, the church hoped to continue within an Orthodox Russia governed by a democratic state, with most of the old religious order and privileges intact, but the Bolshevik seizure of power that November utterly changed the rules of the political game. Ideologically, the Bolsheviks insisted on total control of all organs of power, and they opposed the existence of any rival body that could potentially challenge Party power. The Party at all levels was pathologically opposed to religion and religious institutions. In February 1918, the regime issued a decree of separation, cutting the links between the church and the educational system. The church was denied the right to hold property, and all church land was nationalized.[16]

When historians recall the Bolshevik Revolution and its aftermath, they rarely stress the religious and spiritual substance of the conflict, of what became a full-scale religious civil war. We might even speak of an anti-crusade, a term that neatly catches the religious fervor of the revolutionaries and their desire to recreate the world anew; in his account of millennial movements through history, Richard Landes aptly writes of the "Bolshevik Apocalypse." The socialist anthem of these years, the Internationale, reads like an adaptation of Revelation. As its lyrics proclaim, this is the eruption of the end times, the final struggle; the foundations of the world are about to change; let's make a clean slate of the past. The revolution found an early monument in Alexander Blok's eerie January 1918 poem "The Twelve," one of the triumphs of modern Russian literature. Ostensibly a description of twelve boozy, loud-mouthed Red Guard paramilitaries swaggering through a Petrograd street, thugs and blasphemers, we are shocked to find that "in front of the blood-drenched flag walks Jesus Christ," the spiritual head of these twelve new apostles. Blok knew his apocalyptic all too well: a disciple of Soloviev, he had delved deeply into both Theosophy and Revelation.[17]

Already in 1918 the Bolsheviks began a ferocious persecution that diminished in the mid-1920s only when the most prominent targets had been eliminated. The church suffered dreadfully during the civil war that raged until 1922, killing millions and producing an age of mass Christian martyrdom at least as bad as that inflicted by the Ottoman Turks a few years before. Bolshevik forces seized clergy as hostages to be used as bargaining chips against rival forces or to ensure the good behavior of restive regions, and they executed them as needed in a policy the regime itself described as "terrorism." Communist authorities incited mob violence, as the Bolsheviks organized their followers into militant antireligious groups.[18]

Much as in the Western European Reformation centuries before, violence resulted from official attempts to seize church buildings and land, and particularly to confiscate liturgical vessels and icons. The Bolsheviks targeted the monasteries they condemned as "powerful screws in the exploiting machine." As early as January 1918, Bolshevik leader Alexandra Kollontai ordered the seizure of the historic Alexander Nevsky monastery in Petrograd in order to house war invalids. Clergy and lay believers protested, singing hymns and psalms and carrying icons, only to be met with gunfire. Kollontai boasted of her role in the resulting massacre, proclaiming herself the "female Antichrist." By 1920, two-thirds of the nation's monasteries had been dissolved, and in some notorious cases, the buildings were transformed into prisons and concentration camps. The great Solovetsky Monastery complex on the White Sea became a labor camp and indeed the prototype of the infamous gulag system.[19]

Russia's martyrology reached daunting proportions. Metropolitan Vladimir of Kiev perished in 1918, shot outside the Monastery of the Caves. Another victim was Bishop Hermogenes of Tobolsk, who in his earlier career had been dean of the Tbilisi seminary in Georgia, from which he had expelled the young Josef Stalin: the bishop was drowned in a Siberian river. Archbishop Andronicus of Perm was killed the following year, followed by most of his clergy. In 1920, Bishop Joachim of Nizhny Novgorod was crucified upside down from the iconostasis in his cathedral. In 1922, a firing squad executed the powerful Benjamin, metropolitan of Petrograd / Saint

Petersburg. The repression was indiscriminate, paying no attention to the victims' records as critics of tsarist injustice and anti-Semitism. In the new order, though, none of those reforming credentials made the slightest difference.[20]

Persecution claimed many lives at lower levels of the church. In 1924, Aleksandr Valentinov published a horrific account of persecutions and pogroms in the *Black Book* (also known as *The Assault of Heaven*). From Archangel, we hear how

> a priest of the name of Shangin was killed and his body was cut into pieces; in Petchora the archpriest Surtzev was beaten for several days on end, then he was shot and his body was thrown into the river. In the same place, an old priest, Rasputin [no relation to the mystic] was tied to a telegraph stay and shot, his body was given to the dogs.[21]

Some of these stories were true, some fabricated or exaggerated, yet studies of individual dioceses and regions confirm the mass killing of priests and believers. Local Red officials hunted down priests as enthusiastically as their aristocratic predecessors had pursued wolves and wild boar.

The government exploited the church's internal divisions, and in the process, they helped turn the official persecution into a full-blown spiritual crisis. By the late 1920s the surviving church had fractured in three directions—some to the radical left, some mainstream Orthodox, while stubborn traditional believers began their own underground networks. These last became a catacomb church, with its own clandestine churches and even secret monasteries. Between 1927 and 1940, active Orthodox churches all but vanished from the Russian Republic, as their numbers fell from thirty thousand to just five hundred. The absolute nature of the Bolshevik triumph was symbolized in 1931 by the dynamiting of Moscow's cherished Cathedral of Christ the Savior.[22]

Russia: Uprooting Faith

THE CRUSHING OF THE institutional church coincided with a struggle against popular faith. Throughout the religious conflicts in the post-1917 decade, Bolshevik policies repeatedly faced mass protests from believers, who in the early days could muster crowds in the tens of thousands. Furious crowds mobilized to prevent the despoliation of cathedrals and monasteries. Seeing a real threat to state authority, Bolsheviks directed their attention to attacking the spiritual centers of power, namely saints' relics and shrines. The government ordered "corpses and mummies" to be seized and transferred to museums, leading local Communists to begin a quite literal digging up of Russia's religious past. This campaign featured stage-managed investigations and exposés of alleged relics, showing many to be bogus and actually containing piles of junk or animal bones rather than the venerated remains of holy figures.[23]

Although the church's surviving clergy were anxious to avoid further provocations to the regime, some dissidents openly denounced the Red regime as either the Antichrist or his servants. Just how thoroughly ordinary believers understood the persecution in cosmic terms is indicated by the abundant stories of apparitions and miracles, presumably evidence of God's support for his threatened followers. Across the new Soviet Union, the 1920s were a great age for miracle tales—for mysterious glowing icons, bleeding crucifixes, or mystical lights seen over churches, and in major cities as well as the countryside. As in ancient times, tales of reported miracles were commonly given the most hostile settings, so that miraculous icons were seen in the homes of dedicated Red atheists or even Jews, who were duly converted by the experience. In Ukraine, a religious upsurge in 1923–24 began when a Bolshevik fired at a wooden figure of Christ, which promptly issued real blood, and the Virgin appeared to comfort her son. Her tears gave rise to a miraculous healing spring. Other apparitions followed, provoking pilgrims to gather en masse—at least in the tens of thousands—to await the possible Day of Judgment. They erected several thousand wooden crosses. Nationwide, Communist officials faced an escalating war of apparitions as the end of one legend was promptly followed by the birth of another. As a Soviet official despairingly admitted, "Religion is like a nail—the harder you hit it, the deeper it goes in." [24]

Ultimately, Russian popular faith would be destroyed only by crushing the communities in which it flourished, which meant, above all, the vast peasant population. Only in the 1930s was rural faith crushed by collectivization and by the savage official campaigns against the better-off peasants, the so-called kulaks. In both movements, the state employed the standard tactics of terrorism, but now augmented by the use of deadly famines. Millions died, and the deeply rooted world of rural Orthodoxy was devastated beyond repair.

The Communist nation that emerged on the graveyard of Christian Russia established its legitimacy by forming its own pseudo-religious cult that borrowed cynically from the Orthodox past. Party ideology was founded on initiations and rites of passages, on secular martyrs and saints, on a ritual cycle of the year—and on the veneration of the great deity on earth, Josef Stalin. [25]

The Great Disappointment

MOST FRIGHTENING FOR BELIEVERS was the possibility that Russian-style developments could affect the whole of Europe. Leftist revolutions and mass protests swept the continent in 1919, creating short-lived Communist states in Hungary and Bavaria, while radical labor movements threatened state power in Italy and even Britain, terrifying the old respectable classes. [26]

For all its exalted hopes, the Red Year of 1919 produced no new Russias, and a broad international reaction increasingly drew on

Italy's Fascist examples. As the Red tide withdrew, Fascist movements and authoritarian military regimes became commonplace across Europe. But here, too, religious themes were much in evidence. This varied according to the traditions of individual nations, but the holy war tradition left a powerful inheritance, which was further strengthened by the postwar anti-Communist reaction. And although most of the new esoteric sects and cults were avowedly nonpolitical, they contributed to the mood of messianic expectation and popularized mystical ideas of race, giving a pseudo-religious dimension to the emerging reactionary and nationalist mood of the new decade.[27]

Rightist veteran movements exploited the wartime rhetoric of yesterday's dead comrades rising to join the battles of today. From a media legend ("The Bowmen," "Debout les Morts!") the image of the ghost legion was transformed into a fundamental component of Rightist rhetoric. In 1929, the Nazi Party's new anthem, the Horst Wessel Lied, proclaimed, "Comrades shot by the Red Front and reactionaries / March in spirit within our ranks."

Throughout the interwar years, the boundaries between political extremism and religious zeal would be hard to discern. Even in the United States, the Ku Klux Klan commanded several million followers by the mid-1920s and pledged to resist non-Protestant immigration and the advances of Roman Catholicism. In its paramilitary structure, its taste for uniforms and mystic symbols and its cult of violence, the Klan clearly should be counted in the ranks of the Fascist and ultranationalist movements then so much the vogue in Europe, but the American model was explicit in its religious grounding. Protestant clergy were prominent among its local leaders, and the movement's anthem was the revivalist hymn "The Old Rugged Cross."[28]

Germany: To the Unconquered

WHILE SOME CHURCHES WERE effectively destroyed, others survived, but at the cost of making deadly compromises with the emerging political order. The political dangers were starkly obvious in Germany.

Germany's Armageddon began a year later than Russia's. In November 1918, the country suffered a grievous defeat as the armed forces collapsed. Conservatives and nationalists sought solace in the myths that accumulated around that year and the growing belief that German forces would have remained unconquered had they not been betrayed by the domestic "stab in the back," the *Dolchstoss*. What else could explain the extreme (apparent) suddenness of this failure? Germans had after all come close to victory in the spring of 1918, and propaganda through that summer had resolutely failed to acknowledge either the Allied recovery or the near disintegration of the German military. In reality, the main mystery about the war's outcome was not why Germany lost in 1918 but why it had managed to continue fighting as long as it did. For patriotic activists, though, the events of October and November 1918 were a dreadful surprise, a mystery that was variously blamed on socialists, leftists, pacifists, and—increasingly—Jews. In the Nazi era, "the traitors of 1918" became a familiar cliché. As Herbert Marcuse observed in 1943, "The system of National Socialism has been devised for the very purpose of making a repetition of 1918 impossible." [29]

For religious thinkers too, especially for Protestants, 1918 was a nightmare inversion of the hopes of August 1914, and that ignominious reversal demanded explanation. Perhaps a whole generation of Protestant thinkers and preachers had been absolutely wrong and misguided in everything they had believed and taught, but a darker alternative view was possible. Church leaders might have been correct in their basic analysis, but they had not factored in the machinations of sinister outside forces.[30]

Just as they had led the nationalist cause in 1914, German Protestant clergy offered some of the clearest statements of national despair and betrayal four years later. One of Germany's legendary Protestant preachers, Bruno Doehring, was a pioneering advocate of the stab-in-the-back mythology. As he declared in 1918, God had not abandoned his people, rather our *Volk* had abandoned him, as sinister elites "treacherously desecrated the altar of the fatherland." Although he did not single out Jews for blame, other Rightists would soon do so. Theologian Reinhold Seeberg composed an epitaph for a war monument that is at once a perfect example of Latin at its most precise and concise and a chilling manifesto for the generation of 1940. Seeberg addressed the graduates of the University of Berlin killed in the war as *Invictis Victi Victuri*—to the unconquered, from the conquered, who will themselves conquer.[31]

Recalling 1914, preachers framed the national crisis in religious terms. Witnessing the new democratic republic, Hermann Lahusen lamented,

> **Prussia is gone. Germany is gone, utopians rule us. The Kaiser lies sick in bed. And God? And divine justice? We are living through Golgotha.**

When Gerhard Tolzien sought to understand why the Allies were inexplicably winning, he returned to the familiar theme of the descent of the spirit, but in the form of a satanic parody of Pentecost: "Another spirit has come upon us. An evil spirit that rolls like a cloud of gas through the homeland right up to the front." Among the Catholic hierarchy, Cardinal von Faulhaber denounced the republic as founded upon betrayal.[32]

The new German republic was nothing like as radical or as Red as its Far Right critics feared. The new constitution of 1919 separated church and state and proclaimed full religious liberty, but churches retained most of their prewar privileges, although with a more decentralized structure. Many of the outspoken wartime nationalists made their peace with the republic, yet with reservations. Von Harnack and Troeltsch both accepted the republic, as did liberals like Paul Martin Rade, and the movement that followed his newspaper *Die Christliche Welt*. But other Protestant clergy contributed powerfully to the reactionary ideology that flourished in the interwar years. Far from just going along passively with an increasingly resentful and vengeful national mood, religious thinkers emerged as visible ideological leaders of the new nationalism.

Germany: Luther's Vision

INSURGENT NATIONALISM FOUND A focus in the revived interest in Martin Luther, which was invigorated by the commemorations of 1917. Granted, historical figures regularly undergo periods of revival and reevaluation, but the so-called Luther Renaissance had immediate political ramifications in the Germany of the 1920s, with its intoxicating messianic vision of the nation and its *Volk*. Based particularly at the University of Erlangen, the Luther revival was the work of such influential theologians and public intellectuals as Karl Holl, Werner Elert, and Paul Althaus, all pivotal thinkers of the Christian Far Right.[33]

Two themes from the Lutheran tradition proved highly useful in this era. One was the exaltation of the state that could be drawn, fairly or otherwise, from Luther's teachings. Luther had praised Christian kingdoms and states as a driving force in his desired church reforms, invaluable opponents against the international Papal church. He found support for this in texts like Romans 13, in which Paul urged Christians to submit to the established powers, which are of God. In a modern context, this theory could be used to justify Christian faith in a state that could advance the kingdom of God, rising above selfish individualism. Given the messianic status now commonly accorded to Luther himself, it was easy to transfer that kind of exalted expectation to the future leader of such a state, someone who might fulfill the disappointed hopes once placed in Kaiser Wilhelm. Selectively quoted, Luther was a splendid patron saint for a totalitarian regime.[34]

Still more sensitive was the proper Christian attitude toward Jews. Luther himself denounced the Jews of his day in language so ugly that the Nazis had no need to distort his writings in order to recycle them for their own ends. He had explicitly called for Jews to be subject to forced labor in special institutions. More generally, his whole theology was founded on a conflict between the old Hebrew law and the liberating gospel of Christ, a theory that assuredly did not imply rejecting the Old Testament or the prophets. But selectively quoted, Luther could also be used for a more fundamental critique of historic Christianity, with its roots in the Hebrew Bible.

Again, the Luther commemoration of 1917 emerges as a key ideological turning point. From the late nineteenth century, a number of cranky pastors and scholars had mounted fringe campaigns to purge Christianity of its Jewish roots, even to the point of removing the Old Testament from the Christian Bible. The 1917 festivities offered these activists an ideal opportunity to present their views to a national audience, and they offered a new set of Ninety-Five Theses intended to free Christianity of its "unnatural connection" with Judaism, to create a *Deutschchristentum* on "pure Protestant foundations." Just as racial science had conclusively shown the deadly dangers of mixing Germanic and non-Germanic blood, they argued, so cultural intermingling was no less pernicious. In their demeaning portrayal of Judaism, these critics harked back to the ancient Christian heresy of Marcion, who posited a deadly rivalry between the dark, near-satanic Jewish deity and the dazzling God of Light who was proclaimed by his son, Jesus. They followed Marcion in arguing that the church must reject its Jewish origins and acknowledge the mission of Jesus as a wholly new venture. Jesus himself was certainly an Aryan, not a Jew.[35]

Over the next decade, *völkisch* militants organized as a political and religious movement aimed at an *Entjudung* (de-Judification) of the church. In 1921, Pastor Friedrich Andersen popularized his views in the book *The German Savior,* published by the Munich firm Deutscher Volksverlag, a centerpiece of that city's extreme Right. Andersen's text was surrounded by advertisements for other books by Nazi or proto-Nazi authors, including Hitler's early mentor Anton Drexler. For Andersen, Marcion was perhaps the greatest of the church fathers, superior even to Saint Augustine.[36]

Better-known theologians, including Erich Vogelsang and Reinhold Seeberg, also favored this vision of an Aryan Jesus. Even von Harnack contributed to the debate. Personally, he rejected racial or biological anti-Semitism and could never understand why this racial theme so obsessed his ultra-Right correspondents. He favored assimilating Jews, who should be persuaded to abandon their obsolete faith for the truth of Christianity. In 1921, though, he published his great study of Marcion. Von Harnack endorsed Marcion's radical propositions and called for the modern German church to exclude the Old Testament from its canon. As he proclaimed,

> To reject the Old Testament in the second century was an error the Church rightly resisted; to maintain it in the sixteenth century was a destiny the Reformation could not yet escape; but still to preserve it in the nineteenth century as one of the canonical documents of Protestantism is the result of religious and ecclesiastical paralysis.[37]

Racial attitudes gathered strength in the churches through the 1920s. In 1930, Alfred Rosenberg's book *The Myth of the Twentieth Century* sought to give a spiritual foundation to Nazism. Rosen-

berg declared firmly that Jesus was not a Jew. Jesus's noble teachings had been corrupted, first by the Jewish Paul, and later by the
cynical churches, especially by Roman Catholicism. By 1931, the
völkisch movements coalesced into a new pressure group of Deutsche
Christen—German Christians—who struggled for control of individual Protestant churches. By 1933, with powerful state support,
the racist movement had taken control of several churches in the
Nazi cause and placed its head as Reichsbischof, the senior cleric
overseeing the nation's united Protestant churches. In the event,
the German Christians never achieved the total reorganization they
sought, mainly because the Nazi leadership discarded them once
they had served their purpose.[38]

Quite apart from the sectarian (and disreputable) world of the
German Christians, similarly pernicious ideas established themselves in the German Lutheran mainstream. Responding to Hitler's
seizure of power, distinguished Erlangen theologian Paul Althaus
crowed, "Our Protestant churches have greeted the turning point
of 1933 as a gift and miracle of God." The Nazi Revolution was
an Easter moment, a time of resurrection and grace, "a new day of
life." Christians were "bound by God's will to the promotion of
National Socialism." The totalitarian state was fully justified if it
truly embodied the Volk. At Göttingen, Emanuel Hirsch compared
Hitler to Christ and saw the Nazi takeover as a "sunrise of divine
goodness after endless dark years of wrath and misery." Tübingen's
Gerhard Kittel, a renowned scholar of the New Testament and its
Jewish context, heartily espoused the rhetoric of the Volk, with all
its "blood and soil and history," and lauded the Führer. All three
men fully supported the Nazi goals of at least segregating Jews
from German life and removing believers of Jewish origin from
the churches.[39]

The churches' attitudes to reviving nationalism were anything
but predictable, and some Protestant leaders who had lauded Germany's power in the Great War era were appalled by the racial el-

ements of Nazism, as well as its pagan worship of the state and military might. From many examples, we might single out Martin Niemöller, a lethally effective U-boat commander in the Great War who resigned his commission because he could not accept the legitimacy of the Weimar Republic. As a Lutheran pastor in the 1920s he preached national revival, and he initially welcomed Hitler's seizure of power. He also accepted Jewish bloodguilt for the death of Christ. He was nobody's liberal. Even so, the regime's attempt to exclude non-Aryan Christians from the churches pushed him into total opposition. Worldwide, Pastor Niemöller, who only barely escaped execution, became a powerful symbol of anti-Nazi resistance.[40]

Some older historians attempted to place much of the blame for Nazism on Luther's legacy and even to draw a straight line "from Luther to Hitler." Any such attempt is unfair both to Luther and to most Lutherans, intellectual leaders as well as ordinary believers. But at least some theologians and scholars were prepared to follow the extremist line to its logical conclusions.

Catholics: With Burning Concern

FOR THE WORLD'S CATHOLICS, too, the war's outcome transformed political attitudes. As for Germans, the central question was the relationship between religious institutions and secular power, what we might call the fundamental crisis of Christendom generated by the experience of war. The Russian cataclysm produced a powerful sense of imminent threat that sometimes made church leaders willing to compromise with unsavory and dangerous movements. Memories of 1917 shaped Catholic political attitudes—and much of Catholic culture—through much of the century.

Across Europe, Catholic clergy were aghast to see how a seemingly powerful and popular church could be destroyed so rapidly and totally by the actions of a ruthless regime with no compunction about inflicting violence and terror. If the Russian church could evaporate, then no other body was safe. At least through the 1960s we cannot understand the politics of the Vatican, and of individual European churches, except in this context. Of course anti-Communism dominated Catholic thought: Rationally, how could it have done otherwise? If Kiev and Saint Petersburg could suffer hecatombs of priests and faithful yesterday, why should not Cologne, Paris, or Rome tomorrow? All future political actions must be founded on the absolute need to prevent another persecuting state like the Soviet Union.[41]

For Catholics "1917" carried other dreadful memories, in recalling the revolution that had swept away the power of Mexico's Catholic Church and the aggressively anticlerical Querétaro constitution passed in that year. Although the most draconian clauses were not enforced immediately, they were fully implemented during the 1920s, leading to a persecution of the church and a brutal civil war that killed tens of thousands. As in Russia, this all occurred within a country traditionally regarded as a church bastion. Papal fears grew still more intense with the rise of new persecutions in Spain after 1936. By the 1930s, Pope Pius XI was denouncing the "Terrible Triangle" of anti-Christian persecution and mass murder, in the Soviet Union, Mexico, and (now) Spain.[42]

The Red nightmare drove Catholic leaders to several possible responses. Some clergy supported hard-line anti-Communist positions and reactionary parties, including anti-Semitic groups who saw the roots of Bolshevism in Jewish conspiracies. Other thinkers sought to understand the nature of Communism's appeal and ensure that the church's ideological message could compete with it effectively. This was the driving force of the ambitious Social Catholicism of the 1930s, which placed clergy at the forefront of movements for labor rights and social justice. Most urgently, the Communist threat placed an enormous premium on settling outstanding disputes with secular states, which, whatever their other flaws, posed nothing like so immediate a danger to the church's survival. Hence, the Vatican settled its long-standing conflicts with secular republican France in 1924 and Fascist Italy in 1929, in each case specifying the proper scope of church and state power. The church gradually learned to live with separation and official secularism.

Inevitably, the church used spiritual resources to buttress its secular defense, placing ever-greater stress on the veneration of the Virgin Mary, as revealed through visions such as Fátima. Fátima after all placed Mary in the forefront of the struggle against Communism, with the hope of Russia's ultimate conversion. One memory of 1917 became the antidote to other legacies of that year. Through the most perilous years of the Cold War, the church positioned Mary as the ultimate resort against Communist advances, a trend that culminated with the declaration of the dogma of the Virgin's Assumption in 1950. Although the church never officially declared that Communism or any particular Soviet leader constituted the Antichrist, the doctrine flourished in unofficial church culture through the 1950s, with a special focus on the diabolical figure of Stalin.[43]

Only by recalling the power of these Russian memories can we appreciate the very delicate path the Vatican, and individual hierarchies, had to tread when dealing with the German Nazi regime that took power in 1933. The Vatican's role in these matters is a painfully controversial topic, which has inspired a sizable mythology, but on occasion the church placed itself in considerable danger. In 1937, famously, the Vatican issued the encyclical *Mit Brennender Sorge* (*With Burning Concern*), which frankly denounced many aspects of Nazi teaching, and presented the Nazi worship of the state as outright idolatry. Through the war years, moreover, the political actions of Pope Pius XII were honorable and often heroic, as demonstrated by the loathing in which the Nazis held him. But overall, the Catholic response to Hitler was equivocal. At least initially, the German hierarchy favored the Hitler who restored order and made the country a bastion against Bolshevism, and only gradually did some clergy become alarmed at the regime's totalitarian and racist policies. Moreover, even if the Vatican rescued many individual Jews and denounced tyranny, why did Pius not speak out prophetically against the mass persecutions of Jews and the Holocaust that was already rumored?

Yet Russian developments had taught Pius so painfully just what a danger the church itself faced from persecution from a totalitarian regime, whether or not the perpetrators were Communist or Nazi. And indeed, Nazi leaders freely discussed such a policy of eradication, making dechristianization a real prospect once victory was achieved. The fact that the Nazis never had the opportunity to implement their plans does not mean that the dangers were anything but real, and the Vatican had to be keenly aware of the risks. The Russian experience was an open wound.[44]

WITHOUT UNDERSTANDING THE GREAT War, and especially its religious dimension, we can make no sense of the era of dictatorships and the ensuing Second World War. But quite apart from its strictly political dimensions, the 1914–18 conflict transformed the ways in which many Christians believed, and particularly their relationship to the secular state and culture. If the war led some believers to support toxic regimes, it also drove others to oppose repression and militarism and develop a sweeping critique of the churches' alliance with secular states. Although initially confined to academic circles, those ideas gradually became popularized—so commonplace and familiar, in fact, that it almost seems difficult to believe that churches could ever have held any other positions.

CHAPTER EIGHT

The Ruins of Christendom
Reconstructing Christian Faith at the End of the Age

So it is with all the advances of the Kingdom of Heaven. They are hindered less by the world than by a Christianity that has bound itself to this world.
—LEONHARD RAGAZ

IN OCTOBER 1914, GERMANY'S leading theologians put their names to the controversial manifesto that presented their nation's cause to the world of learning and culture. Among its horrified readers was Karl Barth, then a young pastor in neutral Switzerland. Reading the signatories of that document,

> I discovered almost all of my theological teachers whom I had greatly venerated. In despair over what this indicated about the signs of the time, I suddenly realized that I could not any longer follow either their ethics and dogmatics or their understanding of the Bible and of history. For me at least, nineteenth century theology no longer held any future.[1]

For Barth and like-minded critics, questions naturally presented themselves: When those great Christian scholars signed those pro-

Karl Barth:
the scholar as
revolutionary

paganda statements, how did they differentiate themselves from any other superpatriotic bourgeois of the time? How exactly did the kingdom of God that they preached relate to worldly states, to empires and kingdoms? The theologies that emerged from the ensuing debates shaped Christian responses to war and the state through the end of the century and beyond.[2]

If Christianity itself did not perish, Christendom was mortally wounded. However healthy the churches seemed in the 1920s, some visionaries recognized the need for a sweeping reassessment of Christian faith. The best-known prophet of a radical new orthodoxy was Barth himself, who urged Christians to accept separation from the world's values, rejecting the unquestioning demands of modernity and the calls of state worship. Quite apart from the revolutions shaking Protestant thought, similar ideas were in these same years shaping Catholic thinkers as well. And as we will see, other faiths too would be transformed by this radical quest to rediscover sources of divine authority.

Against Christendom

HOWEVER DEEPLY ROOTED THE state alliance was in Christian thought, the circumstances of 1914 presented a stark challenge to mainstream assumptions. Some Christians opposed the war, while others went much further in challenging the ideal of Christendom itself. For some, the manifesto marked the breaking point. Overnight, the radical nationalism of the German clergy compromised that nation's prestige around the Protestant world—in belligerent Britain, but also in still-neutral America. Even in the German-speaking lands, German *Kriegstheologie* found important critics. One influential figure was the courageous Christoph Blumhardt, the son of a charismatic evangelist and himself a Lutheran pastor with a distinguished record as a revivalist, exorcist, and faith healer. Since the 1890s, Blumhardt had developed an innovative Christian Socialism aimed at establishing God's kingdom on earth through the pursuit of justice and peace, and he opposed war as a catastrophic obstacle to such hopes.[3]

Blumhardt found disciples, particularly in Switzerland. One leading Swiss voice in the war debates was pastor Leonhard Ragaz, whose faith led him to support socialist and pro-labor causes. Like Blumhardt, he struggled against the pro-war rhetoric of German Protestants. Responding to Far Right German theologian Gottfried Traub, Ragaz complained:

> You always know some way to explain the message of Jesus as conditioned by contemporary historical circumstance and to empty it of its uniqueness and force. . . . You defend the war, you know how to melt the 42 centimetre canon with the Cross of Christ, and to equate the *furore teutonicus* [the fanatical courage of the German armed forces] with the Holy Spirit. You are enthusiasts for *Realpolitik* more than the

politicians, and enthusiasts for the war more than the soldiers.
. . . You can always come up with a formula which imparts
a religious justification for whatever the world deems it good
to do. For this reason you are more dangerous than the pure
representatives of this world.[4]

Karl Barth himself, then twenty-eight, was serving a parish in
the small industrial town of Safenwil, halfway between Basel and
Zurich, and barely twenty miles from the German border. Responding to the German churches' attitudes to war in 1914, he went
far beyond merely criticizing particular individuals. As the war progressed, he developed a whole theory of authority within Christianity that demanded a reimagining of long-orthodox beliefs about the
church's relationship to secular culture, ideas that would constitute
an intellectual and spiritual revolution. Modern theologian Richard
Burnett remarks, "Barth's break with liberalism in the summer of
1915 is the most important event that has occurred in theology in
over two hundred years." Barth is often called the greatest Christian
theologian of the twentieth century, possibly since Thomas Aqui-
nas, and his thinking is inseparable from the crisis of the Great War.[5]

Barth had grown up in German liberal Protestantism, which
represented the finest flower of modern intellectual life. Then came
1914 and the manifesto. As Barth wrote, "It was like the Twilight
of the Gods when I saw the reaction of Harnack, Herrmann, Rade,
Eucken and company to the new situation." The inclusion of Paul
Martin Rade in Barth's list deserves notice, because Rade was anything but a wild militarist. An exponent of the Social Gospel, Rade
edited the liberal paper *Die Christliche Welt,* which during the war
published some daring gestures toward peace and reconciliation. In
1914, though, the fact that even Rade's paper assumed the justice of
Germany's cause appalled Barth quite as much as the shrieking of
the warmongers.[6]

We should not take Barth's much-quoted statement at face

value, not least because he misdates the manifesto by two months and probably conflates two similar statements endorsed by prominent thinkers. He was after all recalling these events at a long distance, and he may or may not have experienced a single star-shell moment of revelation, a "dark day" (*Dies ater*), as opposed to a series of lesser shocks and reevaluations. But whatever the exact process, Barth's theological assumptions lay in ruins.[7]

Seeking alternatives to liberal Protestantism, he discovered the work of Blumhardt and his Swiss disciples, but he went beyond their socialism. He read authors like Dostoevsky and Kierkegaard, who affirmed a Christianity rooted not in reason or the standards of this world but rather in what the world saw as absurdity. He also developed his own distinctive ideas, based on a radical separation between God, the absolutely holy, and a world that could, with all the best intentions, never rise unassisted beyond its sins and failures. Barth began a rereading of the Bible, in a manner quite different from the scholarly detachment of the academics:

> A new world projects itself into our old ordinary world. We may reject it. We may say, "It is nothing; this is imagination, madness, this God." But we may not deny nor prevent our being led by Bible "history" far out beyond what is elsewhere called history—into a new world, into the world of God.

While not rejecting scholarly criticism, Barth sought "to look beyond history into the Spirit of the Bible, which is the Eternal Spirit."[8]

As he spoke to local audiences of pastors and scholars, reports began to spread about this daring intellectual from a tiny parish, and of his startling views. In November 1915, he spoke in Basel on the theme of "Wartime and the Kingdom of God," where he presented the fundamental message: the world remains the world, but God is God—"Gott ist Gott und Welt bleibt Welt." He went even further in characterizing the world as ruled by the devil, so that any attempt to change it would be worthless and doomed to failure. Christians must rather await the coming of the kingdom of God. As the war degenerated into ever worse carnage, Barth's stance became more overtly millenarian, placing his hopes in a direct divine intervention.[9]

In the summer of 1916, Barth began his intense two-year study of Paul's Letter to the Romans, one of the most daring texts within the New Testament and the most influential single scripture in shaping the thought of the early Protestant reformers. Central to the Epistle is the idea of justification, of making righteous, through faith in Jesus Christ. This justification is a supreme act of grace, that is, of God's undeserved and inexplicable free gift. Paul says that without this grace, human beings can achieve or become nothing good, and he describes at length the all-encompassing sins and delusions in which the unredeemed world wallows. "[They] changed the truth of God into a lie, and worshipped and served the creature more than the Creator."[10]

Such warnings of idolatry made excellent sense in the Europe of 1916, and especially in understanding the churches' reactions to the times. As Calvin had noted centuries before, every human being is a great maker of idols, of illusory creatures to worship, and the contemporary world offered plenty of such monstrous creatures— empires and nations, progress and culture, peace and victory. All, though, were empty phantoms at best, seductive demons at worst. The development of Barth's thought echoes that of Jung, who was writing just thirty miles away at this time and who had just produced *The Seven Sermons to the Dead*. Like Jung, Barth portrayed a world fallen into illusion and self-deception, and a world prepared to annihilate a whole continent in the name of the false gods it erected. Barth too demanded that Christians reject the world's deceptive dualities, its false claims to allegiance.

By 1919, Barth published the first edition of his commentary on Romans, initially with a small publisher and a print run of just a thousand copies. But it was the second edition, published in 1922, that "burst like a bombshell on the playground of the European theologians."[11] The book was a frontal attack on the liberal conventions that had shaped mainstream theology since the Enlightenment. Exactly as von Harnack was publishing his book on Marcion, urging that the churches remove the Old Testament from their canon, Barth called on readers to reenter the world of the whole Bible, both Testaments, with the humility of pilgrims. His work also drew conclusions diametrically opposed to those of the nationalistic Luther Renaissance then gripping German Protestantism.[12]

Wholly Other

BARTH'S WRITINGS RESTED ON some straightforward and quite revolutionary assumptions. He rejected liberal theology, *Kulturprotestantismus,* which taught that the Christian message rang true only when it made sense to the feelings and conscience of advanced modern Christians. The problem with this approach was that human beings—no matter how educated or how senior in church hierarchies—were extraordinarily gullible when it came to differentiating between the will of God and their own self-interest, the prejudices of themselves, their class, and their nation. The familiar Christian distinction between the church and the world all but ceased to exist, and where any conflict emerged between the two, the world (the culture) always triumphed. For Barth, reliance on individual feeling was a path to destruction. Christians should be alarmed when mainstream culture starts finding the faith unthreatening, or even begins to think that Christianity makes sense.

Barth's work turned the liberal assumption on its head. Instead of the world judging God, perhaps God was the absolute standard by which the world should be judged, and found utterly wanting. Barth reevaluated Christianity according to fundamental principles that would have been quite familiar to Calvin or Luther. Just assume, Barth began, that God is absolute and holy in a way that nothing human or worldly ever can be, or can even conceive. You can't speak about God by speaking about man in a loud voice. Think of God in whatever way you like, using the best critical tools of your age, following the advice of the wisest and holiest, and you will still reach the same conclusion: God is *ganz Andere,* "wholly other."

Even at their best, according to their noblest unaided efforts, human beings must fall short of this absolute standard, and they are deluded if they believe they can rise higher than that. Yet they do make that assumption, and the ruin they make of their efforts can be seen in the deeply flawed and destructive arrangements of the present world. The only solution is to acknowledge that God's reality matters in a way the sinful world never can. The Epistle to the Romans was

> a revelation of the unknown God; God chooses to come to man, not man to God. Even after the revelation man cannot know God, for he is ever the unknown God. In manifesting himself to man he is farther away than before.

God's ways trumped anything that humanity could offer: "One drop of eternity is of greater weight than a vast ocean of finite things." [13]

Barth's ideas would become known as "neoorthodoxy," although that conservative-sounding term fails to capture the startling nature of the underlying thought (Barth himself hated the term). This was no mere return to fundamentalism. The neoorthodox were open to scholarly approaches to the Bible and rejected notions of inerrancy, the theory that the biblical text is free of error. But on occasion, particularly during the horrible years when the Swiss almost literally lived within the sound of the cannon, Barth's reactions sounded as if they came from a more primitive age, a prophetic time.

Between the Times

OFTEN IDEAS THAT MIGHT seem daring or even revolutionary to theologians and philosophers make little mark on the wider
public. In the case of Barth and his circle, though, his influence
went far beyond the academy, or the churches, and had sweeping
political implications into the 1960s and beyond.

In the immediate aftermath of war and defeat, a traumatized
German-speaking academic world was open to radical views, and
Barth's work appeared at the same time as others equally critical of
the limitations of human reason. The attack on simplistic reason and
materialism was a powerful cultural and artistic force in the early
twentieth century, one that in many instances led to an exaltation
of the irrational, the unconscious, and the intuitive, even the anti-
rational. The shocks of war ensured that these same currents would
transform theology.

Barth's first book reached the reading public shortly after that
of Rudolf Otto, and the two were often linked as the thinkers who
set the theological agenda for the new decade. Otto's wartime book
Das Heilige (*The Holy,* 1917) traced human religious experience to
the overwhelming sense of inexpressible awe that results from encounters with something otherworldly—what Otto termed the
numinous. Religious experience grew out of this perception of *mysterium tremendum,* a mystery before which one trembles. Although
Barth and Otto followed quite different scholarly paths, they agreed
that humans could have very limited success in trying to comprehend a "wholly other" that was infinitely far beyond their rational
capacities. The full subtitle of Otto's book can be translated as *On
the Irrational in the Idea of the Divine and Its Relation to the Rational.*[14]

The language of awe, mystery, terror, and incomprehension
resonated at a time when the experience of war had shown how remarkably little civilization had to offer in terms of comprehending

absolute realities. Another pioneer of German thought in the 1920s was Martin Heidegger, a near contemporary of Barth's. Heidegger left the Catholic Church in late 1918 and largely abandoned religious faith, but he likewise scorned the potential of abstract reason to comprehend absolute realities. Also eye-opening for readers in the immediate aftermath of war was the writing of Søren Kierkegaard, which now became widely available in German. Already seventy years before, Kierkegaard had drawn a stark distinction between the act of faith and the political and ecclesiastical structures founded upon it.[15]

Barth became the center of a deeply influential theological school that included some of the greatest thinkers of the day, among them Rudolf Bultmann and Emil Brunner, who collaborated on the journal *Zwischen den Zeiten* (*Between the Times*). Barth himself spent much of the rest of his career writing his *Church Dogmatics,* a forty-year project that became the basis of much theological endeavor in the Protestant world.[16] Even those who challenged neoorthodoxy were deeply affected by Barth's work and his wartime insights. We see his influence in such important thinkers as Paul Tillich and Reinhold Niebuhr, who were so central to American theological thought later in the century.

Paul Tillich himself well illustrates the role of the Great War in breaking the hold of nineteenth-century idealism. Born in 1886, he was a contemporary of Barth but, unlike him, was a German subject and accordingly served in the imperial forces. He saw frontline service as an army chaplain and won the Iron Cross, but the horrors of Verdun constituted a life-changing epiphany. Like Barth, he saw the war as the collapse of older hopes and aspirations, writing that

the World War in my own experience was the catastrophe of idealistic thinking in general. . . . If a reunion of theology and philosophy should again become possible, it could be achieved only in such a way as would do justice to this experience of the abyss of our existence.

At the end of the war, he found new hope through an exalted work of Christian art, as Botticelli's Renaissance painting of the Madonna with angels filled him with a transforming ecstasy, a sense of revelation. He began to explore the themes of history and culture that would dominate his career. In 1933, he left Germany for the United States.[17]

Neoorthodoxy played a special role in Germany itself. The rise of Nazi power gave acute expression to the issues that had driven Barth during the First World War. At the time of the Nazi takeover in 1933 Barth was a professor in Germany, teaching theology at Bonn, and he witnessed the churches' response to political catastrophe with a sense of shock. The racist German Christian movement seemed set to become a robust force in the nation's religious life, while the mainstream Evangelical church accepted Nazi doctrines of racial exclusion. If Christians, both Protestant and Catholic, had not supported the Nazis in overwhelming numbers, then the regime could never have achieved the success it did or lasted as long as it did in the face of devastating military defeats. Barth saw the German Christians as the logical conclusion of the liberal Protestantism that placed such faith in the prevailing culture.[18]

Barth's ideas gave Christians an ideological basis for resistance to the regime. In 1934, he was a prime mover in the famous Barmen Declaration, in which a devoted minority of Protestant thinkers rejected the church's subordination to the state and to all secular powers. Barmen also marked the creation of the so-called Confessing Church, which tried to maintain Christian integrity in opposition to dictatorial and racist actions. Its best-known leader was Dietrich Bonhoeffer, who was also a pupil of von Harnack and whose dissertation adviser was Reinhold Seeberg. Often, though, Bonhoeffer echoes Barth's insights from the previous war, especially in his analysis of the aggressive German state. For Bonhoeffer, Hitler was the Antichrist, or at least a servant of the Antichrist, and in 1944, he became involved with the plot to assassinate the Nazi leader.[19]

In his heroic death, Bonhoeffer justly became the martyr of neoorthodoxy and its whole critique of a Christianity yoked to a state or a culture. That questioning became a commonplace of post-1945 liberalism, initially among Protestants, who dedicated themselves to political activism against racial injustice and inequality in North America or southern Africa. From the 1960s, though, similar questions fueled a powerful movement of liberation theology among Roman Catholics, particularly in Latin America.

Back to the Sources

BY MID-CENTURY, THE THEOLOGICAL ferment originating in the German-speaking Protestant churches had spread worldwide, to the point that academic scholars were attracting mass-media attention: Barth, Niebuhr, and Tillich all appeared on covers of *Time* magazine. But for other Christians, too, the Great War cast a very long shadow and subverted long-standing ideas of the proper relationship between church and state. It forced believers to return to their own roots in terms of reasserting the value of spiritual authority, whether that meant the Bible, for Protestants, or the practices of the most ancient church, for Catholics and Orthodox. Across the spectrum, we see a far-reaching effort at what French thinkers termed *ressourcement,* the return to the sources of thought and belief.

The Great War made the modern Catholic Church. If the war left the church open to reactionary politics, it also drove Catholic leaders to newer and more positive visions that would maintain their influence through the present day. Without their direct experience of war, we can scarcely understand the attitudes of some of the most significant Catholic thinkers of the century. This was especially true in France, which did not exempt clergy from military conscription. If we look at France's most influential thinkers of the era, Henri-Marie de Lubac was severely wounded at Verdun, where lay philosopher Étienne Gilson also served (across the lines from Tillich). Mystical genius Pierre Teilhard de Chardin was a highly decorated frontline veteran, who described his war experience as a "meeting with the Absolute." Jacques Maritain served briefly in the French forces before being invalided out. All had many friends who fought and perished in those years or suffered from occupation. Although later theologian Yves Congar was only ten when the war broke out, his diaries record the agonizing years in which German forces occupied his home, and which daily brought home to him the war's effects on civilians. In various ways, each of these—de Lubac, Gilson, de Chardin, Maritain, Congar—formed Catholic thought for decades to come.[20]

Each of these thinkers, moreover, enjoyed long lives. Together, they shaped what some termed *nouvelle théologie,* "new theology," a term initially used scornfully in the sense of a faddish innovation. More accurately, though, their theology was anything but new in its emphasis on *ressourcement,* a return to the strange world of the Bible and the early fathers and free of the trappings of political compromise.

These Catholic thinkers also strove to limit the ambitions of the state and its claims upon the souls of individual believers. At the time, the best known of these thinkers was Maritain, whose theories were founded on liberal humanism and a revived theory of natural rights. For Maritain, secular states could only demand the loyalty of Christians when they acknowledged the whole complex spiritual side of humanity. Among other achievements, he played a central role in drafting the Universal Declaration of Human Rights of 1948, and his concept of the "dignity of the human person" became integral to Catholic political thought. In one of his best-known books, *Integral Humanism* (1936), Maritain explored the prospects for a new Christendom, but one that would operate very differently from older models and be based on an acceptance of pluralism. This was a Christendom that decisively rejected militarism, tyranny, and even nationalism, in any traditional sense, and extolled social justice.[21]

In the long term, the most important of the group was de Lubac. After the war, his extensive writings urged the church to ground itself in the ancient teachings of the church fathers, while becoming profoundly sensitive to the concerns of ordinary lay believers in a world constantly endangered by violence and injustice. However glorious its supernatural claims, the church was part of history, which meant that it could not be divorced from political and cultural realities. While never directly challenging the hierarchy, he retained a thorough distrust of unjust authority and became a prominent resister in the Second World War.

De Lubac repeatedly faced censure for his daring views, but his ideas guided the Second Vatican Council of 1963–65, which transformed the Catholic Church. The Council was called by the epochal Pope John XXIII, yet another Great War veteran who served as a military chaplain and stretcher-bearer through the horrific Italian campaigns. (Congar would also live long enough to serve as a key thinker in the conciliar era). Arguably, that revolutionary Council deserves to be regarded as the most momentous single event in the history of Christianity during the mid-twentieth century. Among other achievements, the Council resoundingly declared that the church was not just the hierarchy or the clergy but rather the whole people of God. It also emphasized biblical authority in a way that departed far from the Catholic practice of several centuries and urged all the faithful to turn to their Bibles.

In 1991, de Lubac died vindicated, as a revered cardinal of the church. He outlived the Soviet Union that had played a dominant role in Catholic thinking for so long. He did not, though, live to see the accession of Pope Francis I in 2013, a Jesuit like himself, and a man who echoed his own thought so closely. In his powerful warnings about the church's over-close alliance with the world, about "spiritual worldliness," Pope Francis explicitly and repeatedly quoted de Lubac. In the first homily that he gave following his election, Francis also quoted Léon Bloy, whom we have already encountered proclaiming the imminent apocalypse in 1916. The Verdun generation still exercised its influence in a new century.[22]

Making Europe

THESE NEW VISIONS OF Christianity also had a direct, and surprising, impact on practical politics, and particularly after the Second World War. By the early 1950s, Europeans were in despair about the prospects for ever restoring peace and prosperity to their continent, and reasonable observers warned of a new dark age. Communist dictatorship prevailed across the Iron Curtain, and Western Europe's independence often seemed tenuous. The best and most successful political alternative was the work of Christian Democratic politicians who envisioned a united Europe, democratic and anti-Communist, and founded on Catholic social principles. The new union would rise above the nationalistic claims inherent in the familiar dream of church-state alliances.

All these activists owed their worldviews to their First World War experiences. Germany's Konrad Adenauer served as mayor of Cologne in the hungry years of 1917–18, successfully navigating the city through the time of despair and chaos. His great allies in the cause of European unification were Robert Schuman and Alcide De Gasperi, who both found their national identities changed by post-1918 border shifts, which suddenly made Schuman French and De Gasperi Italian. This experience gave them a strong sense of just how temporary and malleable Europe's current political boundaries could be.[23]

Their political outlook was profoundly rooted in religious attitudes. All were faithfully Catholic, and Schuman is currently under consideration for beatification and potential sainthood. A devotee of Maritain, he was deeply influenced by his vision of integrating Christian values into a democratic Europe. In their European

vision, they were pursuing ideas that had been regularly proposed
by successive popes from Benedict XV, who had so earnestly denounced the divisions of the Great War. Since the 1930s, popes
had been contemplating a United States of Europe. The European
movement that actually emerged in the 1950s—the ancestor of today's European Union—inevitably had a strong Catholic and Christian ideology at its core. More specifically, its Catholic leaders were
inspired by the Marian devotional upsurge that followed the 1950
proclamation of the Assumption. Coincidentally or not, the crucial
diplomatic agreement that serves as the charter for the modern European Union is the 1957 Treaty of Rome.[24]

That emphasis is commemorated in the flag that we see today
as the symbol of the European Union, twelve gold stars on a blue
field. When the Council of Europe designed a new flag, it chose
an assemblage that in the context of the time frankly evoked the
image of the Virgin Mary, the woman crowned with twelve stars
and depicted in blue garb. The flag's designer has explicitly credited
the passage in the book of Revelation as his source for the image,
which was formally adopted on December 8, 1955, the feast of the
Immaculate Conception. All that is omitted in the eventual product
is the Virgin herself, in a natural bow to Europe's Protestants and
its other faiths. For a Catholic generation whose consciousness was
formed in 1916 and 1917, how could they envision a united Europe
except in Marian and apocalyptic terms? Not surprisingly, given its
secular coloring, the modern-day EU strives to dismiss the Marian
connection as an embarrassing myth, but the iconographic evidence
leaves no doubt of the original intention.[25]

Europe's Christianity survived the Great War, but in ways that
would have startled and often horrified the church leaders of the
previous centuries. The war sparked a religious and cultural revolution within the faith.

THE GREAT WAR WAS predominantly both a European and a Christian event. Although the war involved non-Christian states such as Japan and the Ottoman Empire, not to mention imperial possessions such as India, by far the largest roles were taken by countries that were Christian in their religious and cultural tradition, and European in their geographical setting or ethnic makeup. Naturally enough, then, the war left its deepest imprint on Christian churches and Christian thought in Europe itself. But in its global scale, the war could not fail to affect Christians in the wider non-Euro-American world, and all the other faiths with which Christians had been in contact for so long.

Canadian enlistment poster: the British Empire links Jewish emancipation to the Allied cause. The three men photographed—Herbert Samuel, Rufus Isaacs (Viscount Reading), and Edwin Montagu—were all prominent Anglo-Jewish leaders.

CHAPTER NINE

A New Zion

The Crisis of European Judaism
and the Vision of a New World

When there is a great war in the world, the power of Messiah is aroused.
—RABBI ABRAHAM ISAAC KOOK

FOR JEWS, AS FOR Christians, the most important trends of
the twentieth century can be traced precisely to the Great War
era. In twentieth-century Jewish history, two events stand out as
among the most important in the whole development of the Jewish
people. One is the Holocaust, the culmination of fanatical anti-
Semitism. The other is the establishment of the state of Israel, with
all that meant for the revival of Jewish culture and the renewal of
the Hebrew language. Together, these phenomena redrew the map
of the Jewish world. In 1900, Europe was home to over 80 percent of the world's Jews; today, over 80 percent are located in just
two countries, Israel and the United States. Although the origins of
these changes long predated 1914, the war hugely accelerated trends
that were already in progress.

At first sight, we seem to be dealing with long-term historical
trends dating back well into the nineteenth century. Modern West-

ern anti-Semitism dates from the late 1870s, and France's Drey-fus affair placed Jewish issues on European political agendas in the 1890s. During the same years, Russia formalized aggressive anti-Semitism with a new wave of discriminatory laws, expulsions, and ethnic relocations. The consequence was Jewish emigration from eastern Europe, which in turn provoked swelling anti-Semitism in Western countries. Growing tensions led to pressure for a Jewish national homeland and new support for the Zionist movement. Al-ready by the 1890s Hebrew revivalists were raising their children in modern Hebrew. In 1909, pioneers founded the nucleus of what would become the first Hebrew-speaking city in modern times, Tel Aviv, and the first kibbutz dates from 1910.[1]

But the fact that ideas were on the political agenda did not mean they would inevitably achieve the importance they did, and in both cases—anti-Semitism and Zionism—the Great War created passions and pressures that inspired new activism. Jews slotted easily enough into the apocalyptic visions of these years, whether as the heralds of the messianic age or as diabolic agents. The outcome of war did much to determine which of these two options dominated postwar discourse. In victorious America and Britain, Christian enthusiasts continued to support the Zionist dream. In defeated Germany, anti-Semitism reached new heights, as it did for some years in crippled Russia. The religious politics of the 1920s and 1930s flowed natu-rally from the First World War.

Minorities and the War

POLITICALLY, THE SURGE OF nationalist and patriotic senti-ment in 1914 encouraged minorities of all shades to believe that they might end any remnants of exclusion or prejudice. Some minority groups became stridently patriotic, and there is no reason to doubt the genuineness of the response. In the United States, the most con-

Main Centers of Jewish Population in 1914

troversial religious group at the start of the century was the Mormons, to the point that the U.S. Congress debated for years before finally agreeing that a duly elected Mormon senator might take his seat. The war fundamentally changed that hostile atmosphere, as Mormons showed themselves resolutely patriotic and delivered impressively high recruitment rates to the forces. Old prejudices faded.[2]

Europe's Jews hoped for a similarly benevolent outcome, particularly as the world's Jewish population in 1914 was heavily concentrated in the warring nations. By far the largest share was in such eastern territories as Poland, Lithuania, Galicia, Ukraine, and Byelorussia. This concentration of populations was the result of a series of catastrophes in the fourteenth century, the mass killings and ethnic purges that drove Jews out of Western Europe in the years around the Black Death. Jews moved east to seek security in Polish and Lithuanian lands. As these older states declined, Europe's Jews fell increasingly under Russian power, and the Russian Pale of Settlement continued as the undisputed Jewish heartland. The other largest population was found across the border, in Austro-Hungarian realms. By 1914, then, the twin empires, Romanov and Habsburg, together ruled eight million Jews, who lived on the front lines in the approaching death struggle between the competing states.[3]

Influential communities also existed elsewhere, in other nations utterly committed to the war effort. Germany was home to six hundred thousand Jews, Romania to three hundred thousand, France to two hundred thousand, Great Britain to two hundred fifty thousand. The great new presence on the Jewish world map was the United States, the destination for so many eastern European migrants. Between 1900 and 1914, a hundred thousand Jews arrived in the United States each year, overwhelmingly from the Russian and Austro-Hungarian Empires, and from Romania. When the country entered the war in 1917, its Jewish population was almost two million.[4]

In their hundreds of thousands, Jews served in the respective armed forces, chiefly because every combatant power imposed compulsory military service. Perhaps half a million Jews served in Russian uniforms, a hundred thousand in Germany, and forty thousand in Britain. Inevitably, given the prejudices of the time, Jews were often blamed for shirking and cowardice, for profiteering and black-market activities. Generally, though, these soldiers served and suffered like every other part of the population, although accurate figures are hard to come by. Reportedly, German Jews lost twelve thousand men in active service, British Jews ten thousand. Some individuals earned high distinctions for valor. Several British Jews won the Victoria Cross, a decoration awarded very sparingly. Thirty-five thousand German Jews received decorations.[5]

Jews were also prominent in the war leadership of the combatant nations. In the opening years of the war, Britain's Liberal cabinet included two Jews, Herbert Samuel and Edwin Montagu, both major players in national affairs. Among scientists struggling to win the war, the British valued Zionist pioneer Chaim Weizmann for chemical innovations that allowed the manufacture of enough explosives to meet the insatiable demands of the artillery in Flanders. Fritz Haber, one of the world's greatest chemists, devoted himself to pioneering modern techniques of chemical warfare in the German cause. Haber's chlorine confronted Weizmann's shells. Although Haber was officially Lutheran, his Jewish identity would later lead to his exile from Nazi persecution. In practical terms, by far the most important Jewish figure in wartime Germany was corporate magnate Walther Rathenau, whose father had founded the electrical giant AEG. During the war, Rathenau kept German industry functioning through the worst of the Allied blockade.[6]

Jews conspicuously shared in the national sacrifice, and throughout Western Europe, at least, Jewish thinkers hoped this fact would secure them a new role in peacetime. (Russian Jews had fewer grounds for optimism.) German Jews in particular placed great confidence in the *Burgfrieden,* the patriotic national compact in which race and religion all merged into common Germanness. Of course, there were isolated dissidents and active pacifists, but overwhelmingly German Jews of all shades—Orthodox, liberal, Zionist—served their country, and religious leaders warned against any kind of resistance or dereliction of duty.[7]

The New Maccabees

SOME INTELLECTUALS WERE FEROCIOUSLY nationalistic. To the horror of his leftist friends, even Martin Buber succumbed and compared the German war effort with the Maccabean struggle against oppression. Equally devoted to the imperial cause was

Joseph Wohlgemuth, a teacher in the Orthodox Rabbinical Seminary and the editor of the Orthodox flagship magazine *Jeschurun*. In 1915, Wohlgemuth hymned Germany's cause in language instantly recognizable from contemporary Lutheran sermons. The German people, he said, played a historic role as God's people at a time of world crisis and divine judgment: the emperor himself was legendary for his piety and his friendship to Jewish causes.[8]

If not exactly declaring a Jewish holy war, plenty of Jewish thinkers were happy to accept the sanctity of the broader German cause. In 1914, philosopher Hermann Cohen published a widely hailed pamphlet on *Deutschtum und Judentum,* "Germanism and Judaism," in which he lauded the German identity that he identified with its Protestant and Old Testament roots. For Cohen, the German spirit *was* the Jewish spirit, and a victorious war would bring that truth to light. The nascent Zionist movement shared this enthusiasm for what seemed like a natural German-Jewish alliance: German would presumably be the language of the future Israel. By serving in the German army, a Jew was assisting the national ally, Turkey, and thus promoting the well-being of Palestinian Jews.[9]

One notorious superpatriot in this era was nationalist poet Ernst Lissauer, who condemned England for interfering in what he felt should have been a straightforward clash between Germany, France, and Russia. Lissauer actually coined the slogan "Gott strafe England!," which became a commonplace patriotic greeting and toast. In 1914, Lissauer composed a "Hate Song Against England," which was venomous even in an age of ruthless propaganda:

> We will never forego our hate,
> We have all but a single hate,
> We love as one, we hate as one,
> We have one foe and one alone—
> ENGLAND![10]

The "Hate Song" remained popular throughout both world wars. Yet despite receiving high praise from the court and the army, the song's fanatical sentiments made it controversial among the Far Right, and anti-Semites rejected it as un-German. Surely, they protested, Lissauer's monomaniacal attack on an enemy nation must have stemmed from his warped grounding in the Hebrew tradition. Real Germans knew nothing of such implacable hatred against any nation or race.

The Russian Ogre

FOR JEWISH COMMENTATORS ON the war, Germany had one supreme advantage, namely that it was not Russia. However much anti-Semitism might surface in Germany, German Jews were in a superbly better position than their counterparts in the Russian realms, where anti-Semitism was codified in law, and where anti-Jewish hatred might at any moment erupt into a riot or show trial. The very word "pogrom" was a pernicious Russian contribution to human culture, which gained currency in English in the 1880s. Despite the efforts of individual prelates, anti-Semitism was deeply ingrained in the Orthodox Church, which exercised such influence at court. Some clergy supported the Black Hundreds, the anti-Semitic gangs that were the ancestor of all Europe's twentieth-century Fascist paramilitary groups.[11]

Anti-Semitic ideologies were also growing apace within Russia. Growing political tensions in the late nineteenth century drove reactionaries to blame Jews for the unrest, commonly with the assumption that subversives were motivated by a diabolical hostility toward Holy Orthodox Russia. While many Jews were gaining emancipation across Europe in these years and seeking full political rights, anti-Jewish campaigns were reviving some of the grimmest atrocity stories of the Middle Ages, including the blood libel—the

legend that Jews sacrificed Christian children as a required part of
their faith. However archaic in form, the story resonated wonderfully with blood-centered themes of the age, including the popular
cult of blood sacrifice for the good of the nation, and racial purity.
Blood-libel stories surfaced in the Ottoman Empire in the mid-
nineteenth century and somewhat later in Austria-Hungary, but it
was especially on Russian soil that these tales found their most hospitable setting. In 1903, a deadly pogrom in Kishinev (in present-
day Moldova) was fueled by charges that Jews had killed a Christian
boy to use his blood for Passover matzo. Similar accusations led
to the sensational 1913 trial of Menachem Mendel Beilis in Kiev,
which gave European liberals still further proof of the repressive and
superstitious nature of the tsarist regime. It also convinced many
thousands of Russian Jews of the urgent need to emigrate.[12]

The situation in Russia was by no means wholly bleak, and
many Jews had established solid positions for themselves in a large
and complex empire with many local variations and distinctions.
But future prospects did not look promising. Russia's reputation
for intolerance was actually growing in the years before the war, as
the regime offered frightening plans to return to the Pale of Settlement those Jews who had migrated to other regions—in effect a
far-reaching ethnic cleansing of Jewish professionals and intellectuals.[13] In contrast to these horrors, Germany represented modernity,
emancipation, and civilization. It was a country well worth fighting for.

Pour la Patrie

IN OTHER COUNTRIES, TOO, the war inspired an era of good
feelings, when, at least officially, any form of bigotry against fellow
citizens was simply unpatriotic. The nation was all. British and
French Jews commended themselves wholly to the war effort, al-

though with more qualms than their German counterparts, and we rarely hear anything like the same holy war rhetoric or naked triumphalism. For one thing, Jews in London or Paris loathed Russia as an oppressive autocracy, although the fact that the tsar was a crucial military ally meant that they had to remain discreet. French and British Jews were also likely to have German family ties. Nevertheless, Jews were vigorously patriotic. The slogan of England's Jewish community, quoted frequently in newspapers and on banners on public buildings, was "England has been all she could be to Jews, Jews will be all they can be to England." [14]

In France, even the old anti-Dreyfusard and anti-Semitic Maurice Barrès published his tribute to the diverse "spiritual families" that made up the nation: traditionalists/Catholics, socialists, Protestants, and, yes, Jews. Barrès and other pamphleteers recounted inspiring stories about Jewish patriotism and devotion. One tale in particular circulated widely among devout Catholics and was a common theme in propaganda imagery. Reportedly, a dying soldier mistook a rabbi for a Catholic priest and begged for his spiritual aid. The rabbi comforted him, to the point of offering him a cross. Shortly afterward, the rabbi himself was struck and died in the arms of a Catholic priest. In the words of Pierre Drieu La Rochelle—later to be a forthright anti-Semite and Nazi collaborationist—"The Jews gave of their best for the fatherlands in that war." [15]

In the United States, too, the war marked new heights of official acceptance for Jews, who were well represented in the armed services. Although the project began long before the outbreak of war, it was a happy accident that in 1917 a new biblical translation gave English-speaking Jews a solid version of the Tanakh, and one that in tone and cadence often echoed the Protestant King James version. This was a significant step in cultural integration, contributing to the growing trend to see American Jews not as aliens but as part of a spectrum of faith that famously comprehended "Protestant, Catholic, and Jew." [16]

Return to Zion

ESPECIALLY IN THE ANGLO-AMERICAN world, wartime good feelings added a new element to an existing pro-Jewish current, a philo-Semitism that resonated with evangelical Protestants. Yes, this sympathy coexisted with widespread anti-Semitic rhetoric, but on occasion pro-Jewish attitudes could have far-reaching political effects. Without that sentiment, we would not see the other great trend in Jewish history in this era, namely the success of Zionism.[17]

However inevitable the Zionist triumph seems in retrospect, it certainly was not so at the time. While early Zionists hoped to settle in Palestine, that prospect seemed difficult when the land was under firm Ottoman control, and for several years Jewish activists cast around for another territory for settlement, perhaps outside the Middle East. Even Theodor Herzl himself was prepared to be flexible, at least on an interim basis. Candidate territories were suggested in East Africa, Mesopotamia, eastern Libya, and even Argentina. In 1903, the Kishinev massacre galvanized Jews to seek a new refuge, and this movement coalesced into the Jewish Territorial Organization, ITO, which attracted influential supporters. The fact that these alternative settlements eventually came to nothing does not mean that they were not seriously proposed. If world events had developed differently, they might have become more plausible contenders.

The Ottoman entry into war fundamentally changed Zionist expectations, as that empire's lands were likely to be in play after peace was restored. The war made Zionism practically feasible. Already in 1915 Herbert Samuel was proposing a British protectorate in Palestine, and Allenby's "crusade" in 1917–18 vastly expanded British options. Zionists made well-publicized efforts to show their support for the British imperial cause, including the formation of distinctive military units within the British army, culminating with a Jewish regiment in 1917. Appropriately, the Jewish Legion participated in the great victory at Megiddo. Legion veterans would long remain prominent in Zionist affairs and in the culture and politics of the later Israeli state.[18]

But the Jewish homeland was still not a given. The British especially were happily promising the then-Ottoman lands (including Palestine) to various parties, including to the family of Hussein, the sharif of Mecca. In 1915, moreover, British diplomat Mark Sykes negotiated secretly with his French counterpart, François Georges-Picot, to divide up the region between their two nations, placing Palestine under international control. Those previous promises were still in the background when Sykes led British negotiations with the Zionists through 1917. Different outcomes were still in play.[19]

Eventual Zionist success also makes it difficult to recall just how many powerful Jewish voices bitterly opposed their ambitions, on the grounds that a homeland in Palestine or elsewhere might ruin Jewish hopes of acceptance into any and all Western societies. To claim that Jews outside Palestine were homeless made nonsense of two centuries of integration and emancipation. Zionism, in this view, was founded on the anti-Semitic tenet that Jews and non-Jews could not coexist. Because Walther Rathenau believed in total Jewish assimilation into German society, he mocked Zionism or separatism as eccentricities. American patricians like financiers Jacob Schiff and Otto Kahn likewise loathed Zionism because it ran flat contrary to their hopes for assimilation. The movement might also set an insidious trap for Jews: Might a future Western state declare that its Jewish residents were citizens of a hypothetical Israel and thus not entitled to the rights and privileges they previously enjoyed within Europe?

In May 1917, some of the most prominent figures in British Jewish life denounced Zionism in a declaration published in the London *Times*:

> Emancipated Jews in this country regard themselves primarily
> as a religious community. . . . They hold Judaism to be a
> religious system, with which their political status has no
> concern, and they maintain that, as citizens of the countries in
> which they live, they are fully and sincerely identified with the
> national spirit and interests of those countries. It follows that
> the establishment of a Jewish nationality in Palestine, founded
> on this theory of Jewish homelessness, must have the effect
> throughout the world of stamping the Jews as strangers in their
> native lands.

The signatories included Claude Montefiore, from one of the most storied Anglo-Jewish families, and cabinet member Edwin Montagu. Montagu considered Zionism "a mischievous political creed, untenable by any patriotic citizen of the United Kingdom."[20] Critics further worried about the prospect of a Zionist state institutionalizing racial supremacy:

> The proposal to invest the Jewish settlers in Palestine with
> certain special rights in excess of those enjoyed by the rest of
> the population . . . would prove a veritable calamity for the
> whole Jewish people.

Montagu was appalled by the idea of a special Jewish role in the proposed state, where citizenship would be determined by a religious test of the kind that Jews elsewhere regarded as intolerable discrimination. "Turks and other Mahommedans [sic] in Palestine will be regarded as foreigners, just in the same way as Jews will hereafter be treated as foreigners in every country but Palestine." The *Times* letter detonated a furious debate among Britain's Jewish elite, leading to the forced resignation of the head of the Anglo-Jewish Association. But still the Palestine homeland idea remained controversial.[21]

The Cause of Christ

BRITISH SYMPATHY FOR ZIONIST aspirations was a complex affair, which owed much to Realpolitik and self-interest. Having a friendly Jewish client state in Palestine would be a wonderful way for Britain to ensure control over the Suez Canal, the pathway to India and the Asian possessions. A pro-Zionist policy made great sense in the immediate context of the war. It would win and maintain American support, at a time when Jews were becoming a significant electoral bloc in U.S. cities. And the British were alarmed at reports that the Germans might themselves establish a Jewish homeland on the soil of their Ottoman ally.[22]

But for many Anglo-American Christians, Zionism did not need to be grounded in such cynical calculations. Unwittingly, Zionist pioneers were raising multiple flags for Christian audiences on both sides of the Atlantic, for both friends and enemies. For many Christians, the prospect of a Jewish return to a new Israel fitted precisely into the end-time speculations that were becoming so popular in just these years.[23]

One turning point occurred in the 1870s, with the wars that exposed the terminally weak condition of the Ottoman Empire and the likelihood that the whole Middle East might soon be liberated from "Moslem tyranny." The prospect of a Jewish return to Zion generated such popular books as *Jesus Is Coming* (1878) by American evangelical William Blackstone, who favored the Jewish restoration as a means of winning mass conversions to Christianity. Blackstone was influenced by such evangelical superstars as Dwight Moody and Cyrus Scofield, and the return idea was a core component of Scofield's eschatological scheme. Also long popular was Henry Grattan Guinness's 1879 tract *The Approaching End of the Age.* Apparently with prophetically inspired near-accuracy, Grattan Guinness pinpointed 1919 as the year when European nations would restore the

Jews to Palestine. At that point, he proclaimed, "the last warning bell will have rung . . . then the mystery of God will be all but finished, and the manifestation of Christ immediate."[24] By 1917, these prophecies were being presented regularly in evangelical newspapers like the *Christian Herald*.

Another spokesman for the Christian Zionist cause was Sir Andrew Wingate, a distinguished imperial civil servant who believed that history was moving swiftly toward "the resurrection of the Jews as a nation." His huge 1918 tract on *Palestine, Mesopotamia, and the Jews* explained how "the British Empire [was] chosen to give the Gospel to the nations, and deliverance to the Jews." Naturally, the frontispiece depicted Allenby's entry into Jerusalem, that contemporary messianic sign. Wingate's role gains added significance from his relationship to the later military genius Orde Wingate, his nephew, a principal architect of what became the Israeli armed forces.[25]

Whatever Jews thought they were doing, some Christians at least knew they were advancing the earthly rule of Christ. Blackstone himself became a pioneer of active Zionist politics. From the 1890s, he came to support a homeland that would give Jews a refuge from persecution, and as Jews rather than as prospective Christians. In 1891, Blackstone collected hundreds of influential American signatures for a memorial designed to implement this plan. American Jewish leader Louis Brandeis actually called Blackstone "the Father of Zionism." Zionism in these years enjoyed a real vogue among Anglo-American thinkers. It provided the theme of M. P. Shiel's popular 1901 fantasy novel *Lord of the Sea,* in which a modern-day messiah leads his people triumphantly back to a restored Israel: the messianic Jewish state duly leads human progress in the new century.[26]

The British political leadership of the time was no stranger to these hopes. By 1917, the British government had strong representation from Wales and Scotland, areas sympathetic to the aspirations of small nations—and also strongholds of radical Protestant sentiment. The prime minister was Welsh Baptist David Lloyd George, whose biblical upbringing led him to claim that he knew the geography of Palestine better than that of England. By 1917, seven of nine gentile members of the cabinet were evangelical by personal conviction, or else stemmed from families in that tradition. Although evangelical ideas customarily marked Liberal party supporters, the Conservative foreign secretary, A. J. Balfour, was sympathetic. A committed religious thinker, Balfour in 1914 delivered the prestigious Gifford Lectures at Glasgow; evangelical C. S. Lewis would later describe the resulting book, *Theism and Humanism,* as a critical influence on his own religious development (Balfour also had a long-standing interest in psychic phenomena).[27]

Religious ideologies played their part in securing U.S. support for the British move, and above all that meant the president, Woodrow Wilson, a devout Presbyterian and the son of a clergyman. Louis Brandeis was well aware of the need to enlist Christian support for Zionism, and in 1916, he persuaded William Blackstone to create a new memorial that would appeal to Protestants and evangelicals. This powerful constituency had ready access to Wilson, who was receptive to the message. But like his British counterparts, Wilson was already sympathetic to pro-Jewish causes, which he linked with American ideals. Privately, he confessed to a rabbi his joy "that I, the son of the manse, should be able to help restore the Holy Land to its people."[28]

Seen in this light, the 1917 declaration looks less like a sudden ideological departure than a logical fulfillment of long-familiar trends. Dated November 2, the letter stated British support for "the establishment in Palestine of a national home for the Jewish people, and will use their best endeavours to facilitate the achievement of this object." Responding to the concerns raised by Jewish anti-Zionists during the previous months, the letter also warned that "nothing shall be done which may prejudice the civil and religious rights of existing non-Jewish communities in Palestine, or the rights and political status enjoyed by Jews in any other country."[29] But even with qualifications, it was the imperial support for the Zionist enterprise that made the headlines. Jews celebrated in Britain and America as well as in Russian cities. This Russian element was potentially important at a time when the situation in that country was so unstable, and when the Allies were trying desperately to retain the support of any new regime. News of Balfour's letter coincided closely with the Bolshevik coup d'état a few days afterward.

Christians of all shades were likewise delighted. One prominent American minister of the time was A. B. Simpson, founder of the Christian Missionary Alliance and a fervent believer in dispensationalism and prophecy. Simpson wept with joy as he read the Balfour Declaration to his congregation.[30]

The Visible Sign of the End

SOME JEWS ALSO SHARED end-times hopes and fears, in a way that seems remarkable given the normal historical emphasis on the secular character of Zionism. Zionist leaders tended to be highly Western in their outlook, with a strong commitment to liberal or socialist ideologies. As they watched the great changes in progress in the world, though, other Jews returned to older religious and apocalyptic beliefs. When eastern Europe's Jewish communities faced massacre and expulsion in the war years, they automatically turned to spiritual texts that explained cosmic catastrophe and promised the coming of a messianic age.[31] Often these speculations remained at a strictly local level, but occasionally we find visible thinkers and scholars exploring similar ideas. At the time, these mystics exercised little influence on mainstream Jewish thought, either in Europe or in the emerging settlement in Palestine, but from a modern-day perspective, we see just how influential their ideas would be.

Such pessimistic views ran contrary to the strict nationalist consensus of the time. Even so, a few brave souls operated in inner exile within the combatant nations themselves. In August 1916, for instance, young German intellectual Gershom Scholem commemorated the anniversary of the war's outbreak in bitter terms:

> Today in heaven a mighty Kaddish will be said for Europe.
> But rather than a prayer of renewal, it would be a prayer
> of condemnation: Calling out from Zion, God lifts up his
> voice against the seducers in Berlin and the wretches in Saint
> Petersburg.[32]

For Jews, as for non-Jews, the most daring activity took place on the neutral ground of Switzerland. One resident of Switzerland at this time was the neoorthodox rabbi Isaac Breuer. Like Scholem, he had to explain the cosmic evils in progress around him, which appeared to make nonsense of any claims that a just God ruled the world. In seeking a solution to his dilemma, Breuer adopted a kind of dualism. Turning to the Kabbalah, he used the idea that in order to create the world, God had withdrawn from his creation, in the mighty act of *tzimtzum*. To oversimplify, the space vacated by the divine presence was colonized by forces of great power that were ultimately illusory. If they were not exactly satanic, then they represented a kind of dark God or non-God, the *Sitra Ahra,* or "Other Side." This war, with all its evils, was a war of *Sitra Ahra,* and it reduced human beings to bestial status; so also did the modern state, which battened upon the powers granted to it by the enthusiasm for war. The only refuge from the struggle was in the creation of a Jewish state, but something quite different from what the secular Zionists wanted. Breuer wanted a messianic Torah-based state for what was clearly a new phase of cosmic history.[33]

In terms of his lasting significance, an even greater thinker was Rav Abraham Isaac Kook, a leader of the Orthodox Jewish settlers in Palestine, who in 1916 became rabbi of an East London synagogue. In later life, he became the Ashkenazic chief rabbi of Palestine and his family are still today revered figures for Israel's Orthodox and ultra-Orthodox. In 1914, the outbreak of war left him stranded in Switzerland, at Saint Gallen, where he undertook some significant writing. In his famous work *Orot HaKodesh* (*The Lights of Holiness*), he placed the war firmly in an eschatological framework that would not have surprised Christian thinkers. "The present world war," he wrote, "is possessed of an awesome, deep and great expectation attached to the changes of time, and the visible sign of the End in the settlement of the land of Israel." Like the Christian dispensationalists, Kook believed that the war and the coming return to Zion portended the end of the existing world order:

> The blood that was shed in the land will be atoned only by the blood of those who shed it, and the atonement must come: Total dismantling of all the foundations of contemporary civilization, with all of their falsity and deception, with all their poison and venom. The entire civilization that rings false must be effaced from the world and in its stead will arise a kingdom of a holy elite.

The war's horrors arose from human self-deception and sinfulness, and a stark inability to understand the limits of human wisdom:

> The spiritual fabric that in its present state could not prevent, despite all its glorious wisdom, wholesale slaughter and such fearful world destruction, has proven itself invalid from its inception . . . and all its progress is not but false counsel and evil entrapment. . . . Therefore, the entire contemporary civilization is doomed and on its ruins will be established a world order of truth and God-consciousness.[34]

Long before the Holocaust, the experience of the Great War created an intimate mystical link between apocalyptic violence, the return to Zion, and the hope for messianic liberation. Rav Kook's views were institutionalized through the rabbinic seminary he founded in Jerusalem in 1924, Mercaz HaRav, whose alumni have long been prominent in the religious-Zionist cause. The rabbi's son, Zvi Yehuda Kook, applied his father's apocalyptic insights directly to modern politics, claiming that the secular Zionists who founded Israel had unwittingly created the conditions for the imminent establishment of the messianic kingdom. In pursuit of this goal, religious Jews had a special duty to occupy the whole of the land, through what has become a highly active and controversial settler movement.[35] Whatever its secular origins, the modern state of Israel has witnessed the enormous growth of religious-oriented sects, Orthodox and ultra-Orthodox, with a fervent commitment to these apocalyptic and messianic doctrines.

However varied their dreams and expectations, Jews took advantage of the Balfour policy to begin a mass settlement of Palestine. In 1860, the land had perhaps seven thousand Jews, rising to sixty thousand by 1914, but the growth was then dramatic. Between 1919 and 1930, one hundred twenty thousand Jews arrived, with the peak immigration in 1925. The Jewish share of the population grew from perhaps 5 percent in 1880 to 16 percent in 1931, and that was before the Nazi seizure of power in Germany. By 1948, the Jewish population was six hundred fifty thousand.[36]

The postwar influx also transformed relationships between the Jews and the majority Arab population. Already in 1920, attacks on Jewish settlements led to rioting that Westerners described with the grimly familiar word "pogrom." When Jewish leaders felt that the British could not or preferred not to protect them, they began creating their own autonomous defense organizations, including what became the Haganah resistance. The origins of modern Israel—and of the modern Palestinian national movement—date to the years immediately following Balfour's Declaration.[37]

Zion's Nightmares

THE ZIONIST DREAM FUELED the anti–Semitic nightmare. Jews featured in apocalyptic nightmares as well as utopian fantasies, and both genres flourished in the pre–Great War world. Through the Middle Ages, Jews had regularly played a central role in apocalyptic expectations, when the Antichrist was portrayed in Jewish terms. Suitably modernized, that theme revived forcefully during the freshly redefined Jewish question at the turn of the twentieth century, as the new Zionist movement gave an identifiable shape to ancient fears of Jewish conspiracy.

At the end of the nineteenth century, anti-Jewish militants composed the notorious forged text that became known as *The Protocols of the Elders of Zion*. This was purportedly the record of a secret conclave of Jewish leaders who described the sinister means they would use to conquer and exploit the gentile world. Besides its political aspects, the work originally had a religious and apocalyptic coloring. In 1905, *The Protocols* appeared for the first time in a full printed edition, in a mystical tract by Russian Sergei Nilus on the coming of the Antichrist. Nilus's reputation as an Orthodox spiritual writer popularized notions of the Antichrist in a Jewish context, and gave reactionary believers a framework with which to understand the rising forces of socialism and Bolshevism.[38]

Mystically oriented conspiracy themes percolated for decades in Russia before eventually circulating through the West as a direct consequence of the 1917 revolution. These ideas found a Western market readily prepared to accept them, especially in Germany and Austria-Hungary. Although the outbreak of war dulled overt anti-Semitic agitation in the Central Power nations, familiar themes survived, if in sublimated forms.

Through the first two years of war, while Germans were celebrating the national coalition of faiths, German media were rife with stories of the deadly national enemy, the greedy usurious villains who founded an empire on lies, the vampires who sucked German blood. In fact, propagandists were referring to the English, but the language sounds exactly like *The Protocols,* not to mention the standard anti-Jewish rhetoric of the Nazi era. Clerical leaders knew that Jesus would share their denunciations of the English as "pharisees and hypocrites!" Johann Rump used another Jewish-tinged insult when he termed England "this Judas among the nations": Judas had sold Christ for silver. Pastor Gerhard Tolzien saw England as "a Moloch that will devour everything, a vampire that will suck tribute from all the veins of the earth." [39]

The rhetoric was already present, ready and waiting to be directed against an appropriate target. Of necessity, messianic nations must have satanic foes.

Counting Jews

AS VICTORY SEEMED EVER more remote and national sufferings became acute, embittered populations turned to scapegoats, and Jews returned to center stage as Germany's deadliest foe. The spirit of 1914 was predicated on the idea of a divinely inspired nation sweeping inexorably toward an easy victory, but by 1916, optimism was in short supply. Quite mainstream political figures were suggesting the need for a compromise peace. In response, Far Right groups demanded victory and annexations. Nationalist groups proliferated, most impressively the extremist Deutsche Vaterlandspartei, as well as smaller sects like the Pan-German League and the Reichs-hammerbund. A patriotic coalition blamed subversive forces—Jews above all—for Germany's failings. [40]

During 1916, overt anti-Semitic propaganda returned in force. Patriotic media saw Jewish manipulation behind the Allied war effort, particularly in the form of the freemasonry that supposedly dominated those countries. In the case of France, such a charge was easy enough to make, as Masons genuinely were very powerful in the republican and anticlerical cause, although very few were Jews. In his account of media attitudes at the time, novelist Arnold Zweig was barely resorting to parody when he had an officer—formerly the editor of a Far Right newspaper—ask:

> And what about the Jewish press propaganda in favor of the enemy, hey? All the Jew journalists daily dipped their pens in poison and wrote against German Michael, and most of all the press, Jew Lord Northcliffe, whose pestilential papers had flooded the world with lying stories of atrocities, especially in Belgium. . . . And the Americans too had half a dozen such, with Hearst at their head. They cropped up everywhere, these Semitic scribblers. . . . So long as [the Jews] enjoyed equal rights with their racial superiors, Germany would never prosper, in spite of all her heroic deeds.[41]

Neither media tycoon, Northcliffe nor Hearst, was in fact Jewish.

We have already encountered the post-1918 stab-in-the-back legend, but versions of this myth were circulating long before the German collapse, and indeed at times when the country's armed forces were plausibly within reach of victory. Hunger, above all, was the most powerful engine driving hatred and paranoia, and it was rather a stab-in-the-belly myth that prompted anti-Jewish agitation. As the Allied blockade hit hard from 1916, the Central Powers suffered serious unrest in the form of riots and strikes. As in any famine, the hungry were quick to assume that the well-off and better connected were somehow monopolizing food, that they were either hoarding supplies or singularly lucky in black-market dealings. As the truly wealthy and aristocratic lived in comfortably remote settings, urban discontent focused instead on professional and upper-middle-class families who lived locally, and who were often Jewish.[42]

Popular resentment also focused on allegations that Jews were not pulling their weight in the German war effort. According to popular folklore, Jews were not serving in the military in anything like their proper numbers, and even if they were in uniform, they were not fighting at the front. Letters of protest poured into the war ministry. In October 1916, the German war minister announced that the army would begin to tally Jewish representation in the front lines, through a Judenzählung, or "Jewish census." The most damaging aspect of this inquiry was not any data that it might conceivably hope to find but the fact that the government was publicly proclaiming its recognition of a problem, that Jews were shirkers and manipulators. This impression could not be combated by any number of official statements that anti-Semitism played no role in the decision.[43]

Actually, the census might have been useful if it had been undertaken and reported fairly, as it would have shown just how false the current charges were: 80 percent of Jewish soldiers were indeed at the front. As it was, the fact of counting was publicized, but the results were never made available, leaving ordinary citizens with a generalized impression that a terrible problem must exist. Perhaps the absence of promised official data meant that the results were so embarrassing they must have been suppressed by high-placed conspirators. In 1919, Reichshammerbund leader Alfred Roth presented a highly slanted version of the investigation in his book *The Jews in the Army,* which became holy writ for the anti-Semitic Right.[44]

Later German experience should not lead us to exaggerate the significance of the Judenzählung affair. Of itself, it did not mark any notable escalation in anti-Jewish activism and certainly did not make inevitable the disasters of the 1930s. German Jews were still vastly better situated than their Russian counterparts. But as contemporary Jewish intellectuals realized, the incident was remarkable for its time and place. The panic over Jewish shirkers took place not in some benighted province of Russia or the Ottoman Empire, where it could be blamed on backwoods religious hatreds, but in a country that loudly claimed to be the heart of Western civilization, science, and culture. Jewish emancipation in Germany was very advanced, and the affair came just two years after the Pentecost moment when German nationality supposedly overwhelmed all lesser divisions of faith, ideology, or ethnicity. For Jews, it should have been the best of all possible times. Yet even in these circumstances the government was willing to perpetrate something that could not fail to smear Jews as Jews. Anti-Semitic campaigns were all the uglier when seen in an international context. However commonplace anti-Semitism might have been in everyday life in Britain, France, or the United States, it was inconceivable that those governments would have done anything comparable at this time at any official level.

Jews found this affair traumatic, and its effects were lasting. When the census was announced, philosopher Franz Rosenzweig complained bitterly:

> We are Germans, this you can safely say about our political affiliation, as long as this State which "counts" so wonderfully still recognizes us among its citizens. . . . The people, however, (in contrast to the State) do not count us among themselves.

Among many who found this a life-changing moment was Arnold Zweig, who had volunteered for the German army in 1914 and who saw distinguished service in France, Hungary, and Serbia. At this stage, he was a secular Jew who was painfully aware of the anti-Semitism he saw around him, in the army and in the national media, but this did not affect his deep loyalty to the empire and its cause. But then news of the census arrived as he was fighting at Verdun, risking his life in some of the most savage battles in human history. Zweig felt betrayed, and disgusted. In his furious short story "Judenzählung Before Verdun," Zweig imagined the angel Azrael, Master of the Dead, blowing his horn to summon all the Jews who have died in the German army so they could be properly counted. The angel's goal is to determine how many Jews have dodged their proper duty by getting themselves inconsiderately killed in action.[45]

This transforming event focused his concerns about his position as a German Jew. As he wrote to Martin Buber the following year, "If there was no anti-Semitism in the army, the unbearable call to duty would be almost easy. . . . I now regard myself personally as a captured civilian and a stateless foreigner." Posted to German army headquarters in Lithuania, he encountered eastern Jews and became acutely conscious of a war that set Jews against fellow Jews. Besides discovering his Jewish identity, he also moved toward outright pacifism. By the 1930s, his novels on the war made him a world-famous voice in the antiwar cause.[46]

The year 1917 also brought the Luther commemorations, which Far Right activists used to demand that any vestiges of Jewish influence be purged from a resurrected German Christianity. From that perspective, Jews should form no part of German religion, any more than of its political life. Perhaps after all, *Judentum* could not coexist with *Deutschtum,* and Germany was not quite as different from Russia as had always been assumed. Together with the Luther celebration and the famine protests, the census debacle also raised a still more nagging question: If military setbacks could provoke such a reaction against Jews, who were accused only of hindering an ultimate German victory, what would happen if the nation were to suffer a crushing defeat?[47]

Even those German Jews utterly committed to assimilation now had to rethink the degree of their assimilation, and the result was a fundamental reevaluation of Jewish identity. The Zionist cause was one obvious beneficiary: the 1917 Reformationsfeier coincided almost to the day with the release of the Balfour Declaration. But some intellectuals focused more on cultural roots, including aspects of Judaism that had been discarded in the headlong rush toward emancipation.

German rejection promoted a new degree of ethnic and religious solidarity with those large Jewish communities who lived in more benighted countries, especially in the Russian and Polish Pale. Since the late nineteenth century, German Jews had been troubled and often disgusted by the primitive living conditions of the Ostjuden in the eastern shtetl, whose powerful sense of community and tradition was admired chiefly by romantic-minded intellectuals. Even before the war, Martin Buber had popularized the rich Hasidic cultures of the east, and Buber now became prominent in what we might call a Jewish *ressourcement,* a revival of older values. With Franz Rosenzweig, he undertook a retranslation of the Hebrew Bible to give German Jews a more reliable text and one less reliant on prevailing Lutheran norms. In 1920, Arnold Zweig collaborated with artist Hermann Struck to produce *The Face of East European Jewry,* a collection of portraits, with commentary, designed to humanize those easterners whom German Jews sometimes regarded as almost an inferior race.[48]

Also in 1919, Gershom Scholem began his doctoral work on what was then considered the radically unfashionable if not actively embarrassing topic of Kabbalistic mysticism, with all its messianic and apocalyptic dimensions, all its irrationalism. Fighting what he termed the censorship of the Jewish past (and overcoming intense resistance from his family and friends), Scholem initiated the modern study of this vast portion of Judaism's heritage.[49]

The Lost World

THE GERMAN CRISIS COINCIDED with cataclysmic changes in the Jewish worlds of Russia and eastern Europe. For centuries, Jewish cultural and religious life had been focused in that region, but the war and its aftermath ruined those traditional Jewish societies, much as it crippled the Orthodox Christian church in those regions.

The resulting Russian crisis spilled over into Western Europe and further drove anti-Semitic agitation. Jews in 1914 had seen Russia as the worst of all possible worlds and Germany, probably, as the best. After 1918, Russian ways and Russian ills flooded into Germany.

The frontline combat of the war itself began the process, as the major campaigns of the eastern front mainly took place within the principal Jewish region, the Pale. Different states worried about the loyalty of minority races within their territories, who might be tempted to ally with invaders, and they removed or suppressed them accordingly. This concern was acute for the Russian Empire, which was fighting to defend a western frontier that was home to several million Jews who had little reason to love tsarist authority. In the winter of 1914–15, the Habsburg territory of Galicia was the scene of intense combat and an oppressive Russian occupation, which proved a disaster for the million or so Jews of the region. Russian forces, already deeply imbued with anti-Jewish hatred, now found new excuses for violence in the rampant conspiracy theories accusing Jews of favoring the Germans. Months of pogrom, massacre, and rape ensued, while Polish Catholic civilians undertook their own vigilante attacks on Jewish neighbors. Taking the occupied lands together with atrocities on the Russian side of the border, tsarist forces killed some two hundred thousand Jews in these campaigns. To borrow Timothy Snyder's phrase about eastern Europe's later killing grounds, we witness in these years the birth of the "bloodlands."[50]

However harsh the German and Austrian forces who later reoccupied the area might have been, they seemed like liberators to the surviving Jews, and the Germans made Russian savagery a centerpiece of their propaganda on the eastern front. The assumption that minorities were prone to sedition became a self-fulfilling prophecy. As Germans and Austrians occupied large swaths of the contested regions in 1915 and 1916, the Russians acted to forestall any danger that Jews might rise to join the invaders. Six hundred thousand were deported from the region, with little consideration about humane resettlement elsewhere. In the words of a book written in the 1940s, all civilians stood in deep peril in this region, "but the Jews, already proscribed by the Russians and Poles, met with a concentrated orgy of hatred, bloodlust, and vindictive opportunity that threatened to wipe them out in one vast holocaust." American Jews compared the new horrors with recent Turkish atrocities against the Armenians.[51]

Worse was to come after the formal end of hostilities in the Great War itself, with the eruption of still bloodier combats across the former Russian lands. The putsch that we usually dignify with the name of the Russian Revolution itself claimed few lives, but it provoked a civil war that lasted from 1918 through 1923, which involved the armed forces of several other nations, including the United States. Overall deaths ran into the millions. Ultra-reactionaries and anti-Semites were well represented in the White military units who challenged the Red regime and who used the slogan "Strike at the Jews and save Russia!" The resulting anti-Jewish violence was far worse than events of the tsarist years. At the turn of the century, even the most internationally notorious pogroms normally claimed dozens of lives, but the carnage of the civil war dwarfed these outbreaks. Perhaps a hundred thousand Jews perished in these years, and by no means all at White hands; some Red units shared in the atrocities.[52]

When the war ended, the Communists established their rule as part of the new Soviet state. Jews were prominently represented in the Bolshevik leadership at all levels—most notably, with military commander Leon Trotsky—and for a few brief years in the 1920s, it looked as if the revolution might mark a Jewish cultural renaissance. Yiddish cultural organizations flourished, as did those avant-garde modernist movements in which Jews were so well represented. But the regime had no sympathy for any manifestations of religion, Christian or otherwise, and cultural freedom was suppressed once the state secured its hold on the country. Even in the '20s, synagogues and yeshivas were as likely to be confiscated as were churches and monasteries, and die-hard clergy of any and all faiths could be imprisoned or killed. Deep-rooted Hasidic communities were now scattered, as the movement lost such once-famous names as Lubavitch and Breslov. For all its other flaws, the regime created by Lenin and Stalin never targeted Jews for mass killings on racial lines, but religious life was hard to sustain, particularly as the Soviet Union moved into the intolerance and paranoia of the mid-1930s. The state prohibited members of the Communist Party from circumcising their sons, which forced anyone hoping for any position or influence in the new regime to choose between faith and ideology. As traditional religion disintegrated, Jews in the Soviet Union—and in much of eastern Europe—searched for new ideologies, often Marxist or socialist, with a strong secularist bent.[53]

Surviving Jewish believers had to make a simple but perilous decision, either to flee the Soviet state entirely or to try to survive and await easier times. Many rabbis and students did in fact go underground within the Soviet Union, despite the risks, and thousands died in the purges of the 1930s. Many of those who survived the Soviet onslaught succumbed to the Nazi massacres soon afterward. By 1945, to use the Nazi phrase, the old Pale region was virtually Jew-free.

Poisoning Europe

THE COLLAPSE OF THE Russian Empire vastly aggravated ethnic hatreds far beyond the frontiers of the newly proclaimed Soviet Union. In the short term, the Bolshevik example inspired revolutionary upheavals across a continent still bleeding from the war. Although the radical ideas were not new, the successes of Lenin and Trotsky gave a shining example for Europe's new Communist movements. Yet the crisis also left a bitter racial inheritance, as conservatives focused on the Jewish origins of radical leaders like Germany's Rosa Luxemburg and Hungary's merciless Béla Kun (born Kohn). To the horror of reactionaries, Jews were also prominent in the new Social Democratic regimes that emerged to replace the old empires. One Jew designed the constitution of the Weimar Republic, which found an able leader in another Jew, Walther Rathenau. But the German republic was born in disastrous circumstances of defeat and economic ruin. Jews became associated not just with Red revolution but with national weakness and state failure, symbolized by the collapse of the German currency in 1922–23.[54]

It was a short step to believing that Jews were actively trying to destroy Europe's once-great Christian states, presumably with the goal of establishing absolutist Jewish-Bolshevik tyrannies, as outlined in *The Protocols*. Once that idea was firmly established, true believers could reinterpret Jewish activity in the Great War, and claim that Jews had consistently worked to promote national defeat in 1918. Although it rarely pays to challenge conspiracy theories with hard fact, we should in decency remember that without Rathenau's organizational genius, the German Empire could not even have kept fighting into 1918. If he really was pursuing a Jewish conspiracy to undermine Germany, he was playing a very devious game indeed. Yet such considerations did not prevent a Far Right gang from assassinating him in 1922, in a devastating blow against the new republic. (The fact they struck at the summer solstice indicates the growing power of esoteric and neo-pagan ideas among ultranationalists.)

Some of Germany's wartime leaders now overtly preached toxic anti-Semitism barely distinguishable from that of the later Nazis. As early as 1918, the kaiser told his war council that Germany was fighting a sinister alliance led by international Jewry and the Freemasons. After his loss of power and exile, he became ever vocal about Jewish-Masonic-British conspiracies, which he linked to the schemes of the Antichrist, although he had the decency to condemn Nazi pogroms against Jews. In 1923, Ludendorff actually joined Hitler in his ludicrous Munich putsch. In 1927, the general published his tract *Destruction of Freemasonry Through Revelation of their Secrets,* which presented masonry as a front organization for the global Jewish conspiracy. Masons and Jews were responsible for chaos, subversion, and armed revolution through history, as they strove to create the Jewish world government. The five-pointed star symbol of Bolshevik Russia marked the movement's progress toward its true goal: the triumph of the six-pointed Star of David. (Although Ludendorff made a tactical alliance with Hitler, he had no sympathy for him as a national leader. He denounced Hindenburg's decision to make Hitler chancellor in 1933, warning that the demagogue would lead Germany into the abyss).[55]

Communist advances also had terrible effects on Romania's thriving Jewish population. After 1918, conservatives feared subversion from Russian and Hungarian Communists, whom they linked to Jewish conspiracies. This supposed menace stirred both religious and biological anti-Semitism and gave the impetus for a particularly vicious Fascist movement, the Iron Guard, also known as the Legion of the Archangel Michael. In the 1940s, native Romanian militias slaughtered Jews so enthusiastically that their German allies needed only to watch admiringly: three hundred thousand Jews perished.[56]

If Europe's revolutions were in some sense a Russian export, then so was the anti-Semitic framework used to interpret these movements. Of course, anti-Jewish theories were deeply entrenched across the West long before 1914, but the aftermath of the Russian Revolution vastly strengthened their views. The émigrés who flocked to Berlin and Paris carried with them the pernicious heritage of conspiratorial anti-Semitism, an ideology that (they believed) had been dreadfully confirmed by the events of the Revolution. From this perspective, the Russian Revolution was not a social upheaval but a Jewish religious war against a great Christian realm, a gigantic blood sacrifice. Through the 1920s, anti-Soviet propaganda posters were not just brutally anti-Semitic but they explicitly presented

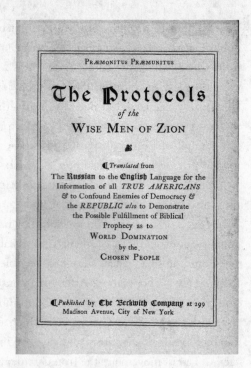

PRÆMONITUS PRÆMUNITUS

The Protocols
of the
WISE MEN OF ZION

❦

❡ *Translated* from
The **Russian** to the **English** Language for the
Information of all *TRUE AMERICANS*
& to Confound Enemies of Democracy &
the *REPUBLIC also* to Demonstrate
the Possible Fulfillment of Biblical
Prophecy as to
WORLD DOMINATION
by the
CHOSEN PEOPLE

❡ *Published* by **The Beckwith Company** at 299
Madison Avenue, City of New York

The title page of the second U.S. edition of *The Protocols of the Elders of Zion* (1920). The Latin motto *Praemonitus Praemunitus* means "forewarned is forearmed."

the Jewish religion as a satanic construct. Jewish Communist leaders like Trotsky were portrayed as priests immolating Holy Mother Russia and her Christian children. The iniquitous blood libel now became a primary means of interpreting Communist ideology.[57]

We can map the spread of ultra-Right Russian émigrés by the appearance of *The Protocols* in Western nations. By 1920, the work was creating a sensation throughout the West, and serious mainstream media were debating whether the West had prevented a German grab for world power only to succumb to a Jewish takeover. Russian exiles were the conduit by which *The Protocols* reached magnate Henry Ford. Ford used the newspaper the *Dearborn Independent* to publish the texts, which thus reached a mass audience in both North America and Germany itself. Soon, the forgery had spread worldwide, with an Arabic translation by the late 1920s. The text has been termed the "warrant for genocide."[58]

Historians hate the word "inevitable." From the standpoint of the mid-1920s, it was not inevitable that the democratic German republic was doomed, or even if it was, that it would necessarily be replaced by a Far Right movement as opposed to a Communist successor. Nor would an ultra-Right Germany under different leadership necessarily have pursued Hitler's exterminationist policy. Historians argue fiercely about the roots of the Holocaust and whether the mass killings represented a very long-term Nazi plan or an ad hoc response to rapidly changing military pressures and opportunities on the eastern front. Was the Holocaust policy set in stone from as early as 1933 or only from 1941?

The Great War did not inevitably, of itself, lead to the destruction of Jewish Europe. But it made that outcome possible and conceivable in a way that would have amazed all but the most extreme fringe theorists of 1914. The war changed everything.

THE WAR'S IMPACT ON Jews aroused the interest, sympathetic or otherwise, of many Western Christians. Even educated observers, though, paid far less attention to religious changes occurring in other parts of the world, changes that from a Eurocentric view seemed marginal to world affairs and could be easily dismissed in terms of primitive fanaticism. Looking back, those overseas conflicts deserve our attention at least as much as the diplomatic niceties then transfixing the newspapers of Europe and the United States.

Soldiers from Cameroon in the service of the German Empire

CHAPTER TEN

Those from Below
The Spiritual Liberation of the World's Subject Peoples

The War of the Color Line will outdo in savage inhumanity
any war this world has yet seen. For colored folk have
much to remember and they will not forget.
—W. E. B. DuBois, 1915

In 1897, John Chilembwe traveled from his native Nyasaland, the modern nation of Malawi, to the United States, where he was inspired by such towering figures as Booker T. Washington. For a thoughtful African appalled at colonial exploitation, these visions of black liberation and self-determination were intoxicating, and they continued to develop after he returned to his homeland as an ordained Baptist minister. The outbreak of war made the grievances still more acute. For the British Empire, war meant greater exploitation of colonial territories, more taxes, demands for labor, and pressure to join the armed forces. In January 1915, Chilembwe led an open revolt in Nyasaland after the model of John Brown, to "strike a blow and die, for our blood will surely mean something at last." Two hundred rebels attacked local plantations, killing several whites. Colonial authorities responded savagely, killing Chilembwe and many supporters. But the failed rising left a long aftermath in terms of nationalist and Africanist sentiment, so that Chilembwe today is Malawi's greatest national hero. More broadly, the rising marks a critical stage in the growth of native Christianity in black Africa, where the faith was only beginning to emerge from its paternalistic and missionary roots.[1]

While the great powers were making exalted claims for their own divine missions, so the world's underdogs were also seeking their own place in history and framing their claims in supernatural or spiritual terms. Throughout the war years anticolonial and imperial movements proliferated around the world, often with the vigorous encouragement of rival powers and intelligence agencies. In many cases, as in the Chilembwe rising, these protests against global white supremacy would take religious forms, and some would leave an inheritance until the present day, chiefly for the emerging worlds of Christianity and Islam. Many of the transforming events that reshaped religion in this era must be understood as part of this worldwide millenarian upsurge.

The World War

ALTHOUGH MODERN HISTORICAL MEMORY focuses strictly on the trenches of the western front, the Great War was a worldwide conflict, with savagery unleashed across Africa, Asia, and Oceania: it was a war of jungles, oceans, and steppes, as much as of Flanders fields. The western front became a world front.

In 1914, most of the great powers were empires holding authority over widely separated regions beyond Europe; colonies and imperial territories were an essential status symbol. That meant that no international conflict could involve just the nation-states alone, or that its consequences could be confined to Europe. When France declared war, it did so on behalf of not just its metropolitan core in Europe but every Pacific island and African colony it had grabbed over the previous century. When France went to war, so did Senegal, Madagascar, and dozens of other occupied territories, just as Fiji, Newfoundland, and a host of other colonial possessions followed Britain. Neighboring lands in Africa or Asia suddenly found themselves at war with each other, although local residents had no great awareness of the Balkan rivalries that detonated the larger conflict. When the Ottoman Turks entered the war on Germany's side in 1914, this automatically spread the war across the Middle East. Even the Pacific became a war zone, as the Japanese were faithful allies of Great Britain. In the fall of 1914, Japanese forces seized the Chinese port of Qingdao from the Germans following a bloody siege, and the Japanese navy protected British Columbia from German raiders and submarines. By 1917, even China and Brazil joined the Allied coalition. In the South Atlantic, British ships sank a German squadron off the Falkland Islands.

Aside from direct combat in distant territories, the war's effects were felt in distant regions through the enlistment of millions of colonial subjects as soldiers or laborers. In many cases, these colonial forces were transported to the areas of greatest military need, in Western Europe. The war came to them, and they came to the war. Both French and British armies made extensive use of Asian and African colonial soldiers on the western front, in addition to Chinese laborers. Over a million Indian soldiers served in the British ranks, fighting in Iraq and East Africa as well as the western front and Ottoman Turkey; seventy-five thousand died. The French used some six hundred thousand colonial soldiers, drawn from North and West Africa, from Madagascar and Vietnam, and over seventy thousand perished. The most famous units were the Senegalese tirailleurs from West Africa; two hundred thousand fought in the war, and thirty thousand died. When the Germans launched their first gas attack on the western front in 1915, Algerian divisions in the French army bore the brunt of the assault.[2]

British Indian troops charging German positions
at Neuve-Chapelle, 1915

Just as in the Second World War, this exposure to a vastly wider world could not fail to stir the consciousness of colonial subjects, whose expanded political awareness would be evident in the anti-colonial movements of the immediate postwar years. The insatiable demands of combatant powers for food and natural resources revolutionized economies around the world, massively expanding global contacts and communication.

Quite apart from combat losses, the war spread disease to the far corners of the empire, and the influenza epidemic became a global plague. The war created ideal conditions for infection, bringing masses of people together in unprecedented ways. In many cases, these were members of remote communities that hitherto had little regular contact with the wider world. India alone might have lost twenty million people, or 5 percent of its total population, and in particular areas the death count reached 20 percent. (Making matters still worse, the next two years were marked by widespread crop failures and famine.) Over a million perished in the Dutch East Indies.[3]

Europe's Extremity

ARNOLD ZWEIG'S GREAT CYCLE of novels about the war bore the overall title The Great War of the White Men. The outbreak of war created a powerful mood of expectation around the world, a sense that the global order—the white man's hegemony—was crumbling. Partly, this unsettling new mood was an outgrowth of imperial war propaganda. News and images of warfare spread worldwide in a period of weeks or days, and movies and photographs were rapidly available in the most remote corners of the sprawling world empires. If England, France, Germany, and the United States were constantly deploying the language of holy war and apocalypse, it is scarcely surprising that their dependents and subjects absorbed these ideas and applied them to their own situation. Stories of miracles and apparitions achieved a global circulation, as the juggernaut power of modern media, communication, and propaganda brought these enthralling images to unprecedented audiences across the globe.

But these imperial subjects often had their own lively traditions of anti-colonial and anti-imperial thought, which drew on local cultural and religious sources. When the needs of war provoked unrest and destabilization in the colonies, militant nationalists happily supplied their own solutions to the growing crisis, all the more efficiently when the colonial powers had the bulk of their armed forces trapped in the stalemate in Flanders and northern France. For centuries, Irish nationalists had understood the rich potential of exploiting an international crisis to advance their own ends. As the adage went, England's extremity is Ireland's opportunity. Now dissenters and dissidents around the world would apply that principle against their own masters. It was in 1915 that Mexico's epic revolutionary struggle acquired its best-known literary memorial with Mariano Azuela's novel *Los de Abajo* (*The Underdogs*)—a title that neatly summarizes the intermingled sense of class and racial protest so common in this age.[4]

Often, too, anti-imperial forces cooperated with each other; they shared ideas and tactics, and again, European empires themselves must take the responsibility for this situation. Since the late 1860s, the world had entered a frantic new era of globalization, in which the new technologies of steamships, railroads, and the telegraph vastly expanded trade and communications. (The Suez Canal opened in 1869.) The new century brought radio, the internal combustion engine, and aircraft. The empires vastly enhanced contacts between different regions of the world, and they removed obstacles to travel, trade, and the dissemination of news. Startling transcontinental linkages among dissident populations now became possible.[5]

Revolutionary movements appeared around the imperial worlds. As 1915 began, white South African Boer hard-liners were in the last stages of their stubborn revolt against the British imperial system, while native peoples in Madagascar rose against the French. By the year's end, heavy-handed imperial rule, oppression, and conscription policies in West Africa generated a revolutionary rising, the Volta-Bani War, across the vast territory of French West Africa, in what is now Burkina Faso and Mali. This revolt turned into a major yearlong conflict, in which insurgents fielded armies twenty thousand strong, an outcome far beyond Chilembwe's wildest dreams. Worse for the Allied cause, given the global situation, the region's Islamic minority played a critical role in sparking and leading the movement, giving the French a taste of full-scale jihad warfare.[6]

Even in the United States, surging racial tensions raised concerns of violence and insurrection. The war years coincided with a vicious spike in racial conflict, marked by lynching and ethnic violence; as we have seen, the reformed Ku Klux Klan dates from 1915. The savage character of this era is suggested by an event that occurred in Waco, Texas, in May 1916, when a young black man named Jesse Washington was accused of the rape and murder of a propertied white woman and was lynched by a crowd. Such events happened dozens of times each year across the country in this era. But the Waco Horror (as it became known) went far beyond even the normal scale of atrocity. Washington was publicly displayed before a crowd of fifteen thousand local residents, who cheered as he was castrated, tortured, and progressively dismembered. He was then burned alive over a period of an hour. So proud were local citizens of the act that they marketed postcards showing Washington's charred and mutilated remains. Across the nation, the incident shocked many who had grown complacent about the fact of lynching, and the affair gave a powerful boost to the nascent NAACP. Sociologist Orlando Patterson has argued that these ritualistic acts should be regarded as a modern form of human sacrifice. Hundreds of African Americans were massacred in a 1917 pogrom in East Saint Louis.[7]

But might the underdog yet turn? Controversial documents that surfaced in 1915 appeared to offer plans for a general racial revolution against white supremacy throughout the American Southwest. According to the alleged Plan of San Diego, the oppressed races would form a Liberation Army of Races and the People, comprising Mexicans, Mexican Americans, African Americans, Native Americans, and Japanese. This polyglot Liberation Army would launch a race war against Anglos in Texas, California, Colorado, Arizona, and New Mexico, killing all white males over the age of sixteen. Anglo Texans took these rumors seriously enough to launch a fierce repression that killed several hundred Latinos suspected of radical sympathies. In 1916, moreover, Jamaican Marcus Garvey settled in the United States where he became the best-known face of black nationalism and pan-African radicalism. His message appealed mightily to African Americans alarmed at race violence and inspired by millenarian hopes. Briefly, at the decade's end, Garvey commanded a national mass movement.[8]

Fifth Columns

SOME OF THESE INSURGENCIES and protest movements were local and spontaneous in nature, but often they were sponsored or assisted by one or another of the great powers as part of their larger war strategy. Both the Allies and the Central Powers waged clandestine warfare to disrupt and destabilize their enemies, deploying whatever methods came to hand. In July 1916, German agents struck at the then-neutral United States, hoping to prevent war supplies reaching the Allies. They blew up an ammunition depot at Black Tom Island in New York Harbor, a fearsome series of blasts equivalent to an earthquake registering 5.5 on the Richter scale. The attack inflicted $20 million of damage in the currency of the time, perhaps half a billion dollars in modern terms.[9]

Combatants worked systematically to provoke unrest among the subjects of their enemies, cynically using whatever causes and grievances might be effective in a given case. Naturally, they used modern media and propaganda where possible, encouraging defeatism and subversion in enemy states: German intelligence clandestinely owned some French media outlets and regularly bought the friendship of others. In Russia, they secretly sponsored the Bolshevik *Pravda*. Although the term "fifth column" is an anachronism, dating from the Spanish war of the 1930s, the concept was very familiar to intelligence agencies and policy makers decades before. All major powers worked diligently to establish sympathetic factions within the territories of their opponents, factions that would ideally rise in armed revolt at the appropriate time.[10]

Such a strategy was natural, given the multiethnic and multinational nature of most of the leading powers and the range of issues that could stir revolt. Russia and Austria-Hungary were both huge polyglot empires comprising many subject peoples who wanted independence. In the Habsburg realms, ethnic Germans and Hungarians combined—the two traditionally dominant races—made up considerably less than half of the population, and the empire was known, somewhat unfairly, as the *Völkerkerker,* the prison house of nations. Within the Russian Empire, similarly, Slavs made up just 75 percent of the population in 1914, and Great Russians—the dominant race—were actually a minority. Britain and France were more homogeneous in their metropolitan territories, but their colonial empires were a quite different matter. In global terms, people of English stock made up a tiny proportion of the vast population of the subjects of the British Empire. The potential for external mischief making was limitless.

Again, the Irish offer a natural case study. Even before the war, Irish nationalists had sought German aid and weaponry to assist a rising against England, and from 1914 German intelligence worked hard to build these linkages. Irish nationalist militant Roger Casement spent 1915 in Germany seeking to develop Irish armed forces to fight against the British. His plans would culminate in the Easter Rising of 1916. The Germans were just as happy to arm the Protestant Unionists who were the deadly foes of the mainly Catholic separatists. (The Germans used both Irish and Indian networks to organize the Black Tom attack.)

To varying degrees, all the powers used similar tactics. They carried out propaganda among subject peoples, created and sponsored rebel and guerrilla forces among them, supplied them with weapons and advisers, and in some cases used exiled activists as the core of regular military units. Writing in 1919, evangelical author A. J. MacDonald remarked that

> German machinations . . . were given time to hatch trouble in British Columbia, California, Japan, the Dutch East Indies, Siam and China. Attempts were made to seduce the Indian troops at Hong Kong, Singapore, Penang and Rangoon, with serious results at Singapore. Insurrection and dacoitry

[banditry], fomented by German agents from these foreign
bases, broke out in Bengal, the Punjab, Burma and on the
North West frontier during the latter part of 1914 and the
early part of 1915.[11]

The Germans could have offered a similar list of what the Allies
were perpetrating in their spheres of influence around the globe. It
sometimes seems as if you could not throw a stone from the coasts
of Europe or the Middle East in 1915 without hitting a dinghy carrying a clandestine agent escorting arms supplies and gold to some
rebel army awaiting the signal to rise in bloody revolt.

Modern readers might be skeptical of such accounts, asking reasonably whether colonized people actually needed foreign spies to
drive them to resistance, in Ireland or elsewhere. Blaming unrest on
external agitators is a classic way of delegitimizing authentic popular movements, and the Chilembwe affair shows that serious popular insurrections could occur without any participation by sinister
outside forces. Yet the major powers did their best to exploit what
grievances did exist. The British really did sponsor proxy revolutionary movements among the Arabs, and the Germans among the
Irish and Indians. The Russians played on revolutionary sentiments
among the Czechs and Slovaks, against their Austro-Hungarian
masters, and supported Armenian separatists seeking freedom from
the Ottoman Empire.

My Enemy's Enemy

COVERT AGITATION STIRRED RESENTMENT among colonized
peoples who sometimes espoused ideologies that were equally hostile to both sides in the global conflict. Imperial agents, though,
cared little about the long-term effects of their dabbling, provided
that the insurrections they incited damaged their immediate en-

emies. The Germans were happy to support Lenin's Bolshevik movement when they realized that, of all Russia's competing factions, the Reds were the ones most likely to take the country out of war should they ever seize power. The kaiser's government paid little heed to the chance that Lenin's heirs might become a deadly danger to future German governments. And the empires had still less regard for possible future perils when they looked to Africa or Asia. Modern Americans might draw parallels with the U.S. support of anti-Soviet Islamists and mujahideen in the Afghanistan of the 1980s. In the First World War era, too, the immediate demands of war had effects that reverberated long after the peace treaties were signed.

Then, as later, imperial manipulation aroused hopes of freedom and self-determination among Muslim peoples, although such expectations easily took religious or reactionary forms. As the Allies sought ways of undermining the Ottoman Empire, it was natural to ally with discontented subject peoples, a strategy that various predecessor empires had used regularly in the region at least since biblical times. At the start of the war, the French were already plotting with Lebanese and Syrian secessionists, who would be brutally suppressed when their conspiracy was exposed. Their British allies engineered a revolt of the tribes of the Arabian Peninsula, under the leadership of the sharif of Mecca.[12]

Covert interventions could have unintended consequences for those subject peoples who agreed to work for rival powers, and who laid themselves open to (justified) charges of treason and subversion. Sometimes nations confined themselves to punishing agitators and overt rebel leaders: the British executed Sir Roger Casement and most of the leaders of the Easter Rising. In some cases, though, regimes with an absolutist tradition struck indiscriminately at whole populations, punishing guilty and innocent alike. We have already seen how the Russians deported hundreds of thousands of Jews from frontline regions, where their mixed loyalties were supposed to make them dangerous to the war effort. When the Ottoman Turks in 1915 faced a simultaneous assault by Russian and British invaders, the regime made the appalling decision to eliminate its sizable Armenian Christian population, which the Russians had so long courted.

Clandestine politics also encouraged conspiratorial attitudes. These gave credence to existing suspicions of ethnic and religious minorities, fueling hatred and bigotry, and these curses affected the West as much as the colonial territories. After years of mutual covert interference in the affairs of foreign states, it is scarcely surprising that so many Germans were ready to believe charges of a stab in the back, *Dolchstoss,* in 1918. This is just what the Germans themselves had helped inflict on the Russians the previous year. Nor need there have been much surprise when *The Protocols of the Elders of Zion* surfaced in the West in 1919–20, with its descriptions of secret revolutionary councils and clandestine propaganda. In the context of the age, such subversive efforts were the standard operating procedure of real world politics. The *Protocols,* like the *Dolchstoss,* were certainly fictitious, but recent events had made them plausible enough for many informed people to believe them.[13]

Wars of Religion

IN SOME INSTANCES, SUCH as the U.S. border wars, religion played a strictly marginal role in conflicts defined by race and ethnicity. W. E. B. DuBois imagined the "War of the Color Line," and white racial theorist Lothrop Stoddard categorized these movements as part of a "rising tide of color against White world supremacy." Commonly, though, the insurgencies of these years had a strongly religious cast, and so did the divisions they incited. Warring powers themselves contributed to stirring religious zeal, and to fostering later conflicts. In doing this, they rarely had any religious or sectar-

The stab in the back, the *Dolchstoss*, as portrayed
in a 1919 Austrian postcard

ian motives, but the long-term consequences could be dreadful.[14]

Often the risings and revolutions of this era were explicitly religious in their inspiration, as troubled populations looked to leaders who could frame their sufferings in cosmic terms. Chilembwe eloquently presented the Baptist tradition of apocalyptic; Islamic rebels in South Asia or North Africa easily found Quranic passages to justify jihad against oppressive infidel rulers. On other occasions, though, the rebellions of these years followed no specific faith or creed but fitted into a more broadly religious or millenarian model.

The mobilization of subject peoples brought religious beliefs and ideologies more centrally into the political realm, because ethnic minorities were so often defined by distinctive religious beliefs that set them against the creed of the ruling powers. Even when elites might have become secular, ordinary people tended to maintain their faiths against those of their rulers, whether in Ireland, India, or Armenia, and religious identifications became all the stronger in times of crisis and conflict. As the Jewish experience reminds us, early proclamations of religious and racial unity soon gave way to real tensions under the stresses of war, to struggles between denominations as well as between faiths. Across Europe, Protestants and Catholics sometimes saw the world conflict in denominational terms, and the British Empire repeatedly had to strive to retain the loyalty of Catholic populations. In Ireland, Canada, and Australia, Catholic churches led popular campaigns against British demands for a military draft. In extreme cases, religious suspicions and hatreds escalated to open violence, as when Turkish or Syrian Muslims struck back at local Christians they regarded as infidel plotters against Islam.

In their various ways, then, the diverse conflicts and revolutionary movements drove both religious activism and religious conflict. And as in Europe, disappointed millenarian hopes shaped the postwar world.

The Second Mutiny

ALTHOUGH THE TIDE OF unrest affected so many different parts of the world, one outbreak in particular demands attention in terms of posing a direct threat to a combatant power, and because of its long-term religious significance. It also amply illustrates the transnational character of activism in these years.

This insurgency was the mutiny of Indian troops at the British base of Singapore. The crisis grew out of nationalist resentment of British rule of India, which in its wealth and population was by far the world's most important imperial possession, the kind of prize to which all other powers aspired. In the fevered atmosphere of 1915, India also produced the most potentially dangerous nationalist agitation. And the rebellion would also have lasting consequences in shaping the later history of world religions, both Islam and Hinduism.

In the early twentieth century, India had a vigorous nationalist movement with strong factions backing violent or terrorist action. Because of Britain's effective counter-subversive operations within

India itself, radicals established international networks and sought foreign allies. Like Chilembwe, some found North American inspiration. In 1913, Punjabi migrants to North America formed the revolutionary Ghadar (Revolt) movement, which allied with the domestic radicals of the IWW, the Industrial Workers of the World. Together, IWW and Ghadar sent volunteers to help the Mexican Revolution. Ghadar militants carried out propaganda among Indian soldiers—sepoys—stationed outside the motherland. With high hopes of these activities, the Germans enlisted Indian revolutionaries into a German-based Berlin committee. Through the German connection, the Indians allied with radical Irish nationalists, who had ample experience in anti-imperial conspiracy, and the groups collaborated in arms trafficking.[15]

By the start of 1915, activists were plotting an Indian rising that would, like the great mutiny of 1857, be based within the armed forces. Various plots for risings coalesced into a scheme for a widespread military insurrection in February. Ideally, rebellious soldiers (mainly Sikhs) would raise the nationalist flag in several centers at once—first in the Punjab, then in Delhi, Lahore, and Bengal, and in the great imperial base of Singapore. British intelligence managed to detect and suppress most of these stirrings, leading to a grand treason trial at Lahore in 1915.[16]

Religious grievances—specifically Muslim fears and resentments—made the Singapore garrison a special case. In the context of the time, Hindu and Sikh agitation received most of the attention when British authorities responded to Indian nationalism, while Muslims stood somewhat apart. Nationalists played down these differences: Ghadar itself was aggressively secular, operating under the slogan "No pundits [Hindu scholars] or mullahs do we need."[17] Western contemporaries used the term "Hindu" as more or less synonymous with "Indian." When the United States joined the war in 1917, American authorities prosecuted Ghadar militants for what they termed the "Hindu-German conspiracy." In the wider political context, though, Muslims could play a pivotal role in nationalist organization during the Great War, all the more so when Muslims made up a third of Britain's Indian army. Although most Indian Muslims still asserted their loyalty to Britain, many were nervous about the prospect of being shipped to a battlefront where they could find themselves killing fellow Muslims, and nationalists did all they could to exploit that unrest.

From late 1914, Muslim activists carried out a lengthy campaign of persuasion among Singapore's Indian units, who were mainly Pathans (Pashtuns) from India's northwest regions, areas that are still far from tranquil even today. Sepoys were urged to think first of solidarity with fellow believers and obedience to the caliph; British authorities identified the local Singapore imam as a key propagandist for militant Islamist teachings. This propaganda bore fruit with a spectacular mutiny the following February. Eight hundred rebel soldiers wandered the streets killing dozens of whites at random, but they also freed German prisoners of war, whom they viewed as potential allies. The rising was suppressed by various loyalist and Allied forces, including Japanese, French, and Russian naval contingents. Several hundred perished, including forty-eight mutineers executed by British authorities.[18]

At the time, no serious observer would have treated stirrings in the distant corners of the empire with anything like the importance of the titanic conflicts on the western front. For one thing, governments at the time were anxious to suppress news of insurrections for fear of inspiring imitators, and the Singapore rising was substantially hushed up. Other risings similarly failed to register with media or the public. Despite its massive scale, even the Volta-Bani War in French Africa was ignored by nonspecialists until recent times. The Arab Revolt attracted Western devotees because it was recorded by Lawrence of Arabia, a swashbuckling English hero with a magnificent gift for self-publicity. Yet these events did leave a substantial inheritance, and Singapore in particular marks a critical stage in the growing self-confidence of Muslim activists within the wider Indian independence movement.

MOST WESTERN OBSERVERS VIEWED affairs in Africa and Asia as colorful irrelevancies, and that was particularly true in matters of religion. Except for a handful of specialized academics, why should anyone care about the fate of Christianity outside its natural home in Europe and North America, or pay the slightest heed to the historical dead end that was Islam? A century later, such disregard looks very blinkered. So much of the religious history of the subsequent era does in fact focus on those twin facts: Islam, and Christianity outside the Euro-American sphere. So much of that story, in fact, is a continuation and sequel of the turmoil that began in 1914. Those from below would not always remain in the humble places that the empires assigned them.

The cover of the 1918 book *Ravished Armenia,* the powerful
exposé of the Armenian genocide

CHAPTER ELEVEN

Genocide
The Destruction of the
Oldest Christian World

Who, after all, speaks today of the annihilation of the Armenians?
—ADOLF HITLER

WHEN SOCIETIES COMMEMORATE THE great events of
their past, they usually focus on historical moments that were at the
time violent, frightening, or chaotic, rather than spells of peace and
prosperity. Well-behaved eras seldom make history. And indeed the
Great War years have been highly productive of stirring and memo-
rable moments, moments that demand to be recalled as historical
turning points. The history of the Middle East offers an overabun-
dance of key years, any of which can usefully serve as the end or
beginning of pivotal periods: 1915, the Armenian massacres; 1916,
both the Arab Revolt and the martyrdom of nationalist leaders in
Syria and Lebanon; 1917, the Balfour Declaration; 1919, the beginning of Turkey's national liberation movement; 1919–20, the peace
settlement that substantially drew the region's map as we know it
today; 1920, the Great Iraqi Revolution; and 1922–23, the expulsion
of Asia Minor's Greek populations. This era cursed with anniversa-

ries fundamentally changed the religious picture of the Middle East, and thereby of the wider world.

In a sense, these events actually created what we today call the Middle East. Modern observers recognize the existence of a region known by that term, which is largely defined by its Islamic faith. The western boundary of this large territory roughly follows the line of Turkey's European territories, which stretch a little west of Istanbul. This division is not entirely neat, as Christians are still scattered across the Middle East, Israel is predominantly Jewish, and ancient Muslim communities survive in the Balkans. Generally, though, traveling east from Istanbul means entering another culture, another history, and another civilization, and that Islamic dominance remains obvious as far east as Pakistan. In common perceptions, the Middle East is a Muslim East.

For most of the past millennium, though, that division would have seemed absurd. From the sixteenth century through the twentieth, even when the Middle East and the Balkans were under the control of Ottoman Turkey, much of that larger region was very diverse in faith as well as ethnicity. Instead of today's fairly homogeneous Middle East, we would do better to think of a religiously complex region extending from the Danube to the Euphrates, from Belgrade to Baghdad. Much of what we now call the Middle East was no more solidly Muslim than Europe—with all its Jews and Muslims—was monolithically Christian.[1]

The separation of religions and cultures was a long-drawn-out process, and even in 1900, any thought of a total religious purge on either side would have been unthinkable. The decisive historical change came only in 1915, with the systematic massacres that Ottoman authorities perpetrated on their Christian subjects. Apart from actual killing, millions of civilians—Christian and Muslim—were subject to forced population transfers during and immediately after the war. This "great simplification" created the world we know today, in which a mainly Muslim Middle East stands against a Europe defined by its Christian heritage—and a Christianity that scarcely acknowledges its lost Middle Eastern dimension. Religious polarization also forced surviving Christians to rethink their survival in the new political order, inspiring movements and ideologies that would prevail through the twentieth century.

The Oldest Christian World

FAR FROM BEING MARGINAL newcomers, the Christian peoples of the Ottoman Empire were the descendants of the most ancient churches, including residents of many places mentioned in the New Testament. These surviving communities were still numerous at the start of the last century. If we take the Middle East to include all the land from Egypt to Persia, including Anatolia and the Arabian Peninsula, then Christians represented 11 percent of the total population. By far the largest contingents were the Armenians and the Greek Orthodox, which remained numerous within the Ottoman Empire itself. Christians still constituted 20 percent of the population of Asia Minor. Even in Constantinople itself, Christians made up half the population—at least four hundred thousand people—compared to 44 percent Muslim and 5 percent Jews.[2]

Other ancient centers were equally diverse. In the thriving commercial metropolis of Smyrna, which already had a church mentioned in the New Testament book of Revelation, Greek Christians made up over half the population of three hundred thousand in 1909, not counting Armenians and Western Catholics. The Turks called it the city of the *giaour,* the infidels. The Orthodox metropolitan, Chrysostomos, ruled in splendor that harked back to Byzantine times. Other Christian centers remained, deep in the empire's interior. On the Black Sea, the ancient port of Trebizond was still half Christian. It had

50,000 inhabitants, among whom are 12,000 Greeks, 10,000
Armenians, some Jews, and a few hundred Catholics. . . .
Trebizond has a citadel, at least forty mosques, ten Greek
churches, some of which have preserved ancient paintings,
several Armenian churches, etc.[3]

Still more evocative was Diyarbakir, a large city in what is today
southeastern Turkey, near the Syrian border. In recent years, the
city has often appeared in the headlines because of armed conflict
between its Kurdish population and Turkish authorities, although
religion plays no part in the struggle: both Turks and Kurds are
overwhelmingly Muslim, and the modern city has virtually no minority faiths. Yet for centuries Diyarbakir was one of the most prestigious centers of the Christian world. Under the name of Amida,
the city was the seat of a patriarch of the Syriac-speaking Jacobite
church, which traced its origins to the apostles. In 1909, the *Catholic
Encyclopedia* recorded that the city

has about 35,000 inhabitants, of whom are 20,000 are
Mussulmans (Arabians, Turks, Kurds, etc.), 2,300 Catholics
(Chaldeans, Armenians, Syrians, Melchites, Latins), 8,500
Gregorian Armenians, 900 Protestant Armenians, 950 Jacobite
Syrians, 900 Orthodox Greeks, and 300 Jews.

Diyarbakir boasted "an Armenian Catholic bishop, a Syrian Catholic bishop, a Syrian Jacobite bishop, a Chaldean Catholic archbishop,
and a Greek Orthodox metropolitan under the jurisdiction of the
Patriarch of Antioch."[4] So many bishops in one middling city.

In terms of ethnicity rather than faith, Diyarbakir was about
one-third Armenian, a proportion much smaller than it had been
before a wave of anti-Christian massacres in 1894–95. But Diyarbakir's Armenians and other Christians persisted. Like other minorities in the prewar world—like the Jews of Byelorussia or Ukraine—

they clung to the stubborn belief that persecutions and pogroms might come and go, but realistically, no regime could ever eliminate a whole people.[5]

Crisis of Empire

HISTORICALLY, SUCH A FAITH in continuity might have been reasonable, but these were exceptional times. The 1915 genocide was not a random outbreak of primitive religious hatred or anti-Christian bigotry but a direct response to the dynamics of warfare. The policy represented a life-or-death decision by Ottoman authorities, who were terrified that Christian minorities would give European powers a plausible excuse to subject, dismantle, and colonize their land. And while this fact does not for a moment justify the violence, we should recognize the Turks were reading European ambitions with deadly accuracy.[6]

From the fourteenth century, the Ottomans had built a vast empire based in Asia Minor, but its power extended much further afield. At its height in 1600, Ottoman power stretched over the whole Levant and the Black Sea region as well as Egypt, North Africa, and southeastern Europe, including much of Hungary. Ottoman power began to crumble at the end of the eighteenth century, with the French invasion of Egypt and the Russian expansion around the Black Sea and into the Caucasus. Imperial powers snapped up outlying regions of the empire: the French took Algeria in the 1830s and Tunisia in 1881, and the British controlled Egypt by 1882. Meanwhile, Christian subject peoples like the Greeks and Bulgarians rose to assert their independence. By 1880, the question was not whether but when the Ottoman regime would collapse, and exactly who would be the beneficiaries. It survived as long as it did only because of the ferocious rivalries between the European Christian powers. While the Russians wanted to organize an amicable partition of Ottoman lands, rival powers like the British and French dreaded the expansion of tsarist power into the Mediterranean world. Further raising tensions, Western powers began to care deeply about the promising oil discoveries that were making news in Ottoman-ruled Mesopotamia and Arabia (and in neighboring Persia). One key date in the region's history came in 1911, when the British government declared its intention to move from coal to oil as the main source of power for its navy.[7]

European powers hoped to use Christian minorities within the Ottoman world as the basis for expanding their hegemony. The French regarded greater Syria as part of their natural sphere of influence, the Greeks wanted to dominate the whole Aegean Sea, and the Russians looked to both the empire's Greek Orthodox subjects and the sizable Armenian population. It took little guesswork to determine how the powers would redraw the map, each claiming its own prize. Greater Greece would border on French, British, and Italian zones, while an Armenian state stretching from the Caucasus to the Mediterranean might or might not decide to retain an identity separate from the Russian Empire. Perhaps Armenia in turn would border a Christian state of Assyria in what is now northern Iraq. The whole Ottoman Empire could be absorbed under European control just as thoroughly as the once-thriving Mughal realm in India had fallen under British dominance. Conceivably, as in Algeria, European rule could lead directly to the mass settlement of white Christian immigrants, leaving Muslims as dispossessed strangers in their own countries.

Land and Faith

THE OTTOMAN RESPONSE TOOK both religious and secular forms. As the empire opened up to liberal and westernizing policies in the later nineteenth century, reactionaries struggled to defend older ideas of Islamic supremacy. At least from the 1850s we see the beginnings of a vicious cycle. The more Europeans framed their ambitions in the form of claims to protect Christian minorities, the more hostile local Muslims became to these minorities, and the greater the likelihood of persecution. In turn, this violence gave new justifications to ambitious European powers, as new forms of communication and media brought local acts of violence to a global audience. In 1894–95, Sultan Abdul Hamid ordered mass killings of Armenians that claimed a hundred thousand lives, in what in retrospect looks like a dress rehearsal for the later genocide. American papers described the slaughter as a holocaust.[8]

By the early twentieth century, wars and revolutions in the Balkans further reduced Ottoman power, and an officers' coup in 1908 tried to save the empire by means of radical modernization. Initially, Christian subjects welcomed the revolution that overthrew the nightmarish Abdul Hamid, but the political situation was growing ever darker. In terms of modern geography, the Ottoman Empire of 1914 was de facto reduced to the modern nations of Turkey, Syria, Lebanon, Iraq, Israel/Palestine, and much of Saudi Arabia. When the Young Turk coalition returned to power in a coup in 1913, its ideology had moved from liberal westernization to a hard-edged Turkish nationalism aimed at defending the nation and the race.[9]

Adding to the potential for religious tension was the long record of mutual religious violence over the previous century. Ottoman forces had certainly persecuted Christians, but Christian nations had their own record of religious purges. As Christian powers had encroached on former Ottoman lands, those transfers of power were followed by ethnic and religious purges as old, established Muslim communities were expelled to seek refuge within Ottoman lands. This fate befell Circassian Muslims from the Caucasus region in the 1860s, Bulgarians in the 1870s, and other Balkan populations in 1912–13. By the time of the First World War, the Ottoman Empire

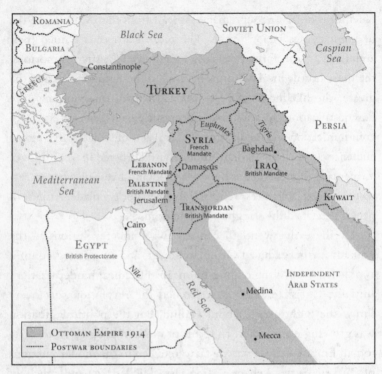

The Ottoman Empire Before and After World War I

included plenty of recent exiles with acute grievances against Christians, ready to defend their faith and their empire against further losses.[10]

This dark inheritance influenced the highest echelons of Ottoman government, which had always found its bureaucrats and military leaders among Islamicized Balkan and Greek populations. Now, though, those Balkan-derived officials were agonizingly aware that their own communities had recently been deported or persecuted, or faced imminent threats. Of the triumvirate that led the empire in 1914, Interior Minister Talaat Pasha stemmed from a family in what is now Bulgaria, War Minister Enver Pasha was of part-Albanian descent, and Navy Minister Djemal Pasha was born on an Aegean island that passed into Greek hands in 1912. Even if they wished to, they could never go home. Later dictator Mustafa Kemal Atatürk was born in what became the Greek city of Thessaloníki. Exiles and expatriates often become the most ferocious superpatriots.

International alignments were also shifting perilously. For a century, the empire's survival had depended on a delicate balance of power between the British and Russians, but the rise of Germany now brought those long-standing foes together in a common cause. When war broke out in 1914, Britain, France, and Russia stood united, and they were joined by other nations with a demonstrated hunger for Ottoman lands: Italy joined the alliance in 1915 and Greece two years afterward. This solidarity made it likely that any postwar settlement would be followed by a massive redistribution of Ottoman lands. That prospect became a certainty when, in October 1914, the empire decided to enter the war as an ally of Germany and Austria-Hungary. The fate of the Ottoman Empire would now be wholly decided by the outcome of the European war. If Germany lost the war, or indeed if it gained anything short of a decisive victory, the Ottoman state was finished. Six hundred years of Ottoman history would end.[11]

The Turks at War

WHEN WAR BROKE OUT, Russian forces advanced from the Caucasus into territories heavily populated by Armenians. The Russians presented themselves as liberators of oppressed Christians and mobilized Armenian military units within their own armed forces. By the end of 1914, the Russians had inflicted heavy defeats on the Turks, culminating in the slaughter at Sarikamish the following January, when poorly fed and equipped Turkish units collapsed. A Turkish force of a hundred twenty thousand was reduced to forty thousand effective survivors, leaving at least fifty thousand either killed in action or dead from disease. The defeats raised the prospect

Russian forces await action against the Turks at Sarikamish
in the Caucasus, 1914

that 1915 would witness a triumphant Russian offensive. Although
the course of the war exposed catastrophic flaws in Ottoman gener-
alship and logistics, the imperial command blamed their disasters on
Armenian duplicity and subversion.[12]

The British, with their long-standing interests in both the
Middle East and the Indian Ocean, also had the means to strike. By
the spring of 1915, the British government was appalled at its heavy
losses on the western front and sought means to undermine Germany through its weaker allies. One scheme, advocated by Winston Churchill, involved a large naval and amphibious assault on the
Dardanelles, which would place Allied forces within striking distance of Constantinople and, ideally, force the Turks to seek peace.[13]

If the idea of attacking Germany's flanks was reasonable, the
choice of target area was baffling. Military historians still wonder
just why the British selected the heavily defended Dardanelles rather

A British 60-pounder gun in action against Turkish forces at Cape Helles
during the Gallipoli campaign of 1915

than Alexandretta, in an area that would have brought them within
easy striking distance of friendly Christian communities. The problem with the Dardanelles soon became apparent. Naval bombardments began in February 1915, but the strength of Turkish resistance
demanded a landing by ground forces at Gallipoli, which followed
on April 25. Over the coming months, far from leading an easy
march on Constantinople, Allied forces became bogged down in a
brutal stalemate that closely reproduced the trench warfare on the
western front. When the Allies were forced to evacuate in early
1916, they left behind forty thousand dead.[14]

Even this failure, though, paled beside the British effort in Mesopotamia. In the summer of 1915, the British began an invasion that
by November brought Allied forces close to Baghdad. Soon, British
forces were trapped and forced to surrender in one of their empire's
great humiliations.[15] Far from collapsing, the Ottoman Empire—
strengthened by skilled German commanders and advisers—proved
stubborn.

The Great Crime

THESE ALLIED BLUNDERS, AND the Turkish recovery, were nowhere on the horizon in the spring of 1915, when the Turks were well aware of the clear and present dangers their empire was facing. Persecutions of suspect minorities began shortly after the disaster of Sarikamish. Initially, the government purged Armenians serving in the army—some forty thousand strong—and drafted them into forced labor battalions. This policy usually amounted to capital punishment as victims were worked to death or starved. Armenian civilians assembled for forced labor were also killed, and massacres occurred in local areas. Arms searches supplied excuses for violence, as soldiers, police, and vigilantes freely raided Armenian homes, often using torture. When Armenians organized armed resistance in the city of Van that April, Turkish authorities portrayed the rising as the opening phase of a broader Armenian insurrection.[16]

On April 24, the day before the British landings at Gallipoli, the regime arrested two hundred fifty key Armenian cultural and intellectual leaders in an act that today is commemorated as marking the formal start of the genocide. Turkish authorities passed draconian laws to expropriate and confiscate their property, as a prelude to physical removal. In May, the Parliament passed what became known as the Tehcir (Deportation) Law, sanctioning removals.

Officially, Turkish authorities were launching a policy of relocation. They transported Armenians from militarily sensitive regions to more secure territories further afield, in northern Syria, with the desert province of Deir ez-Zor as the destination usually cited. As Armenian men had been drafted for labor, these movements affected mainly women, children, and the elderly. These deportations were forced marches, in which little provision was made to feed or care for civilians, who were removed from their homes without enough notice to pack food or belongings. In the words of U.S. Ambassador Henry Morgenthau:

> For the better part of six months, from April to October, 1915, practically all the highways in Asia Minor were crowded with these unearthly bands of exiles. They could be seen winding in and out of every valley and climbing up the sides of nearly every mountain—moving on and on, they scarcely knew whither, except that every road led to death. Village after village and town after town was evacuated of its Armenian population, under the distressing circumstances already detailed. In these six months, as far as can be ascertained, about 1,200,000 people started on this journey to the Syrian desert.

Many thousands of Armenian civilians died en route, and thousands more when they reached camps unprepared to feed or aid them.[17]

Along the way, Armenians were subject to casual violence, mass rape, and sexual assault, in lands notorious for robbers and bandits. According to Western observers, this humiliating maltreatment was part of a deliberate Turkish policy, by which military leaders in charge of the refugees would deliberately notify local tribes of the imminent arrival of thousands of unprotected women and girls. Rape has always been part of warfare, a predictable consequence of removing social restraints, but it had a special role in a society founded on principles of personal and family honor. Apart from gaining sexual advantage, perpetrators were also in effect destroying both those women and their families—and, by implication, shaming their religion and their race.

For contemporary observers, there was no doubt that the mass deaths were deliberately intended and not simply the result of logistic failure or the breakdown of an overstretched government. The Turkish regime had decided to exterminate a race, or as Morgenthau wrote at the time—prefiguring later Nazi terminology—to solve the Armenian problem. They

> knew that the great majority would never reach their
> destination and that those who did would either die of thirst
> and starvation, or be murdered by the wild Mohammedan
> desert tribes. . . . When the Turkish authorities gave the orders
> for these deportations, they were merely giving the death
> warrant to a whole race.[18]

Through the spring and summer of 1915, Turkish forces and irregulars massacred Armenian communities, killing thousands by mass burnings and drownings. Armenian populations were cleared from the empire's eastern regions in June and July. Cilicia was cleansed during July and August and the southeastern lands by September. In 1916, the purges moved to northern Syria and Mesopotamia. Much of the killing was the work of chetes, organized killing squads drawn from military police units bolstered by convicts and local militias. In some places, paramilitary units operated in harmony with criminal gangs. Muslim exile communities like the Circassians provided many of the most lethal police and paramilitary units.

Diyarbakir itself, ancient Amida, was a particular killing center. In July, the German consul at Mosul protested the savagery being carried out in the area under the local governor, Reshid Bey, who

> is raging like a crazed bloodhound against the Christians of his
> vilayet [province]. Recently he has let gendarmes sent from
> Diyarbakir slaughter like sheep 700 Christians from Mardin
> (mostly Armenian) including the Armenian bishop in the
> night in a place outside the town. Reshid Bey is continuing his
> bloody work against the innocent and their number is today
> over two thousand.

Armenians hanged in a public square

In Mardin—once a venerable Christian monastic center—"a great part of the Armenian Catholics, Jacobites, Chaldeans, and Syriac Catholics have met the same horrible end as those in Diyarbakir."[19] Although the massacre produced many monsters, Reshid Bey is one of the few individuals who is widely recalled for a sadism that went beyond even the demands of the regime. Van's governor, Djevdet Bey, had horseshoes nailed to the feet of Armenian men, who were then forced to march through the streets.

Trebizond was likewise "cleansed." The coastal location that made the city so prosperous also placed it on the front lines on any conflict with the Russians, who would actually occupy it in 1916. By that point, though, the city had been radically transformed. During 1915, it became another assembly point for the killing of thousands of Armenian Christians. As Lord Bryce records,

> They hunted out all the Christians, gathered them together,
> and drove a great crowd of them down the streets of Trebizond,
> past the fortress, to the edge of the sea. There they were all
> put on board sailing boats, carried out some distance on the

Black Sea, and there thrown overboard and drowned. Nearly
the whole Armenian population of from 8,000 to 10,000 were
destroyed—some in this way, some by slaughter, some by being
sent to death elsewhere.[20]

Turkish doctors used exemplary modern means of typhus injections
and poison gas to annihilate others. Within a decade, Christian Trebizond was no more. Today, a city that was once half Christian has over
two hundred thousand residents but virtually no Christians or Jews.

The total number of Armenian dead is not known. In 1915, the
convenient figure of one million victims had already gained canoni-
cal status in western media, although this was probably somewhat
too high for that stage in the campaign. If we take the whole period
of violence from 1914 through the end of the Turkish War of Independence in 1923, then Armenian fatalities ran to perhaps 1.5 million out of a prewar population of around 2.5 million.

Apart from the human cost, the cultural losses were incalculable. In 1915, U.S. Consul Leslie Davis witnessed the destruction
as he rode across formerly Armenian territories of eastern Anatolia:

Everywhere it was a scene of desolation and destruction,
the houses were crumbling to pieces and even the Christian
churches, which had been erected at great expense and with
much sacrifice, had been pulled down. . . . The Mohammedans
in their fanaticism seemed determined not only to exterminate
the Christian population but to remove all traces of their
religion and even to destroy the products of civilization.[21]

A War of Religion?

THE REFERENCE TO MOHAMMEDANS raises thorny questions of motivation, as to exactly why the Ottoman authorities acted as they did. In the modern world, plenty of anti-Islamic websites report the massacres as a textbook example of Muslim extremism. After all, the sultan had proclaimed a jihad when the empire entered the war in 1914, which would apply to domestic traitors seeking to ally with infidel Russians or British. The campaign was not based on ethnic grounds in the sense that Turks murdered Armenians, as many of the executioners were not Turkish in any sense of blood, and as we will see, the victims included several other nationalities. The regime targeted Christians *as Christians*. (Jews were also deported from sensitive areas in Palestine but were subject to nothing like the same genocidal fury.)

Yet the Islamic religious link is anything but straightforward. The empire at this time was under a secular-minded government that preached reform and modernization, and found some of its deadliest enemies in the entrenched Islamic religious elites. Lord Bryce, who exposed the massacres so thoroughly, explicitly denied that Islam in itself justified or inspired the killings, and he cites many instances in which Muslims sheltered Armenian neighbors, in Trebizond and elsewhere. Indeed, what the Ottoman regime did to its minorities was not too different from strictly contemporary actions by various European Christian regimes, including tsarist Russia, Austria-Hungary, and Bulgaria, except that the Ottomans were far more efficient. From a comparative point of view, we might rather blame anti-Christian violence less on religious zeal than on the cynical calculations of a radical modernizing state like that of the later Bolsheviks.[22]

Actually, the two kinds of motivation, religious and secular, were not mutually exclusive, and the fact that Turkish leaders were driven by Realpolitik and clear political goals does not mean that we can rule out religion as a factor driving the violence. The fact that France in 1914 was a vehemently secular state did not prevent millions of its citizens believing their nation was engaged in a crusade for the survival of the Catholic faith. In the Ottoman experience, moreover, the two forces, religious and secular, were so inextricably linked that the one contributed to the other. The atrocities of 1915 differed in scale but not in character from earlier massacres undertaken by the sultan's regime in 1894–95, and again during a political and religious reaction in 1909, and on both those occasions, the violence was explicitly religious and Islamic in character. These hatreds and fears remained latent, ready to manifest themselves when the occasion arose, and the secularized ruling elites were able to exploit these passions. By the time the war broke out, the real threat to national survival sharply intensified popular fears and concerns, as did the immediate pressures of conscription and military violence, social disruption and economic collapse.

The persecutions of 1915 might have begun with secular needs and the demands of military security, but once under way, the mobs and militias drew so freely on Islamic slogans and symbols that we are rather dealing with a popular religious or even apocalyptic movement. Muslim preachers stirred actions against Christians, particularly during Friday prayers, and incensed crowds gathered at mosques. Mobs used the war cry "Allahu Akbar!" and sought the forced conversions of Armenian Christians; they also destroyed or appropriated Christian buildings and institutions. In its combination of millenarianism and scapegoating, this anti–Christian violence recalls the response to other catastrophes through history, including the slaughter of Jews in medieval Europe.

Witnessing this upsurge, a contemporary observer might have predicted that the religious upsurge might have led to the creation of a postwar Turkish state that was fanatically Islamic, which did not occur. The regime of Kemal Atatürk proved a nightmare for

Muslims in its strict secularism, and Kemal himself actually declared that the wartime junta should have faced trial for its crimes against the Armenians. But that government could only have won power, and preached its ultranationalist ideology, in a nation that had been ethnically and religiously purged. Ironically, religious violence and fanaticism laid a foundation for extreme secularism.

Root and Branch

ALTHOUGH ARMENIANS SUFFERED BY far the heaviest toll, persecution also reduced or removed other Christian groups, and again we see a combination of motives, secular and religious. Lord Bryce claimed that the Turkish government seemed to be pursuing a "plan for exterminating Christianity, root and branch." Whether or not Turkish policies constituted genocide, at the least they indicated an absolute disregard for human life that was characteristic of official attitudes to the empire's non-Muslim subjects. When in 1920 the Allies imposed a peace settlement on the Ottomans, they spoke aptly of "the terrorist regime which has existed in Turkey since November 1, 1914." The Syriac churches—Assyrians and Chaldeans—remember their own holocaust in 1915, which gained little international attention because it was so closely bound up with the larger Armenian event. Nevertheless, deaths ran into the hundreds of thousands, eliminating perhaps two-thirds of the Chaldean/Assyrian peoples.[23]

Throughout the empire, the regime penalized Christian communities who lived in strategic areas. And what could be a more logical target for an Allied amphibious assault than western Syria, the region that later became Lebanon, home to so many Maronite Christians? In 1915, a new governor established military courts that imprisoned or exiled thousands and executed communal leaders. The regime ruthlessly plundered Lebanon to supply its war effort, requisitioning food and pack animals and cutting the forests to the point of ruin. Although the campaign was not solely directed against Christians, they were hit hardest by the ensuing famine, which killed a hundred thousand in 1916–17. Lebanon suffered worse than any Ottoman region apart from Armenia itself, and perhaps three hundred thousand died in the whole region of Greater Syria. Relief did not come until the British invasion of 1918.

The Greek Catastrophe

IN TERMS OF THEIR historic importance to the Ottoman Empire, the Greeks were the most important single Christian community, and they represented a conspicuously foreign and European element that might be expected to favor outside enemies. From 1915, Ottoman authorities deported thousands of Greeks from western provinces and drafted some into forced labor brigades, but with nothing like the systematic violence directed against Armenians.

The worst problems did not begin until after the formal end of hostilities, when the Allies gathered to dismember the Ottoman realms on the lines they had agreed during the war. The most ambitious and predatory state was Greece, which launched a historic bid to restore the old Byzantine Empire in a Greater Greece, a "Greece of the two continents and of the five seas." The Greek prime minister explicitly declared his intentions to expel the Ottomans from all predominantly Greek regions, which would mean annexing even larger portions of Anatolia. Greek forces occupied Smyrna in 1919, although the occupation encountered fierce resistance.[24]

In 1920, the Allied nations signed what was intended as a final peace treaty with the Ottomans, a counterpart to the recent Versailles pact with Germany. This Treaty of Sèvres provided for an elaborate partition of the former empire, under which different territories were placed under varying degrees of direct or informal subjection to the victorious powers, chiefly Britain and France. In Asia Minor itself, much of the land would come under the power of France, Italy, Greece, and a newly independent Armenia, while all that remained to an independent Turkey was a heartland in northern and central Anatolia centered on Ankara. While this settlement looked like a fulfillment of the worst Turkish nightmares of the previous century, the greed of the conquerors made it unenforceable. Apart from the Greeks, the Italians demanded more than they were offered, to the point of nearly provoking a war with the other Allies.

Meanwhile, Turkish forces were reorganizing in the Anatolian interior, under Kemal's skillful leadership in what has become known as the Turkish War of Independence. Although the Turks fought French, Italians, and Armenians (and nearly faced another full-scale war with the British), the Greeks stood out as the primary danger.

As the violence progressed over an agonizing three years, ethnic and religious communities were easily identifiable, making it possible to seek out and eliminate a particular group, whether Muslim or Christian. No side had a monopoly on atrocities and pogroms, but the Turks behaved ruthlessly. Greek villages were burned, with a special focus on churches and monasteries, and populations massacred and enslaved. In 1922, the Turks captured the key Greek center of Smyrna, showing no mercy to the conquered. A Turkish mob seized the Greek Orthodox archbishop Chrysostomos, who was murdered under appalling circumstances, stabbed and mutilated with his eyes gouged and his ears and nose cut off. (He was later proclaimed a martyr and saint.) Shortly afterward, the whole city was destroyed in a cataclysmic fire. Tens of thousands of Greeks and Armenians perished in the Smyrna massacres and fire, and some sources give far higher figures. By 1923, the Treaty of Lausanne recognized a state of Turkey in roughly its modern borders, with the various occupations now ended.[25]

The Turkish wars for survival effectively ended the Christian

presence in the region. After the Turkish victory, the new regime
won the privilege of deciding the fate of surviving communities
who were now hated strangers in a new nation. This problem was
of course not peculiar to the region. As the old empires fragmented,
new and newly restructured states founded their existence on ideas
of nationalism and self-determination, which could be deeply troubling for populations who could not be fitted into the new realities. Between 1918 and 1920, for instance, lengthy struggles between
Germans, Poles, and the new Baltic states led to proposals for mass
population exchanges. But transfer policies had their greatest impact
in the former Turkish lands. Between 1923 and 1925, Greece and
Turkey arranged for the exchange of 1.3 million Greek refugees
for 400,000 Turks then resident in Greece (some Turkish enclaves
survived).[26]

Although the exchange is discussed in terms of ethnicity, in
practice this was a religious exchange. When choosing the candidates
for expulsion, Greece, for instance, would automatically identify
Muslim families on the basis of faith, even when those particular
"Turks" spoke only Greek and their ancestors might have lived in
Greece for centuries. Greece was to be an Orthodox Christian country, and Turkey Muslim—although the policies of the new regime
would define the practice of Islam in harshly secular terms. Today,
Turkey is a nation of seventy-five million people with only minus-
cule religious minorities. The oldest Christian world perished.

Commemoration

LIKE THE JEWISH HOLOCAUST, the Armenian Genocide had
an enduring political and cultural significance. Despite Hitler's dis-
missive question, the Armenian experience certainly did remain in
the public consciousness, in the West as well as the Middle East, and
it had a lasting relevance for both Christians and Jews. For Western

Christians, the atrocities reinforced and popularized the brutal stereotype of Islam as a religion of bestial violence and uncontrolled sexuality.[27]

Armenians themselves determined never to let the crime pass into oblivion. After the war's end, militant death squads assassinated many former Ottoman leaders and collaborators, including junta leader Djemal Pasha, as part of Operation Nemesis. One of these actions would have a powerful aftermath, when in Berlin in 1921 an Armenian killed Talaat Pasha, reputed mastermind of the genocide. The assassin's supporters turned his subsequent trial into a new exposé of the genocide, and he succeeded so powerfully in stating their case that the German court freed the Armenian on the basis of the horrors he had undergone.[28]

The atrocities were discussed in bestselling books, including a purported memoir, published in 1918 under the title *Ravished Armenia: The Story of Aurora Mardiganian, the Christian Girl Who Survived the Great Massacres.*[29] *Ravished Armenia* (*Auction of Souls*) became a sensational, and horrific, film in 1919. (The film survives today only in partial form.) Supporting its claims to documentary accuracy, the film featured Aurora herself in the lead role, while Henry Morgenthau also played his own character. Despite the general authenticity of the acts depicted, the film was so shocking that today it would be counted as exploitation, if not as torture porn. One controversial scene showed a row of crosses bearing nude women whom the Turkish persecutors had crucified, in a parody of the death of Christ—a tribute to the crucifixion themes so prevalent in recent wartime propaganda. Another scene depicted Christian women being flogged for refusing to enter the harem. Stressing the pervasive theme of sexual violence, the original poster for the film advertised "a film that will make the blood of American women boil."

Naturally, the Armenian experience had a powerful effect on minorities of all kinds in the turbulent interwar years, and Jews

Crucified Armenian women, from the 1919 film *Ravished Armenia*
(Auction of Souls)

in particular drew ominous lessons about what a sufficiently determined state mechanism could perpetrate. Polish Jewish lawyer
Raphael Lemkin was fascinated by the trial following the killing
of Talaat Pasha. Why, he wondered, did courts try a man for a
single murder while no institutions existed to punish the murderers
of millions? In the absence of international institutions to combat
such massacres, he noted, surviving victims were forced to resort
to vigilante justice. Lemkin developed the concept of "crimes of
barbarity," an offense against international law that demanded to be
punished by a special court or tribunal. He subsequently developed
this into the modern definition of "genocide," a word he coined in
1943.[30]

Armenian memories became founding texts for the Jewish
state. Austrian-Jewish author Franz Werfel powerfully raised global
awareness of the atrocities with his bestselling 1933 novel *The Forty
Days of Musa Dagh,* which hymns the heroic resistance of Armenian fighters during the massacres.[31] The Nazis promptly banned
the book in Germany, citing what they claimed were its false and

inflammatory statements about the genocide. But *Forty Days* survived to stir Jewish militancy during the Nazi years, when it forced activists to consider the possibility of armed resistance; the book found a passionate readership in European ghettos. When in 1942 German forces threatened to break through British lines to invade Palestine, Zionists planned what they called a new Musa Dagh, a fortress on Mount Carmel, where they would fight until the last. Memories of Musa Dagh inspired the earliest fighters of the state of Israel long before the emerging state developed its own native mythology based on the ancient fortress of Masada. Armenian activism also influenced Israeli responses to the country's deadliest enemies, whether Holocaust perpetrators or terrorists. Both were subjected to assassination and covert warfare campaigns that were drawn exactly from Operation Nemesis.

Awakenings

ALTHOUGH MIDDLE EASTERN CHRISTIANS survived in numbers, those communities could never forget the years of massacre, which profoundly shaped their later actions. In fact, we cannot understand the modern history of the Middle East without acknowledging distinctively Christian politics. Right up to the present day, distant echoes of the bloody events during and immediately after the Great War reverberate through the politics of the Arab nations.

After the war, Christians faced a dilemma we have repeatedly encountered, namely that a generally livable old order had collapsed, and it was not clear which of several strategies might serve best in the puzzling world that was emerging from the wreckage of the old empires. The war created a new political order in the Middle East and ignited new forces of Arab nationalism and Islamic revival. As Christians included the better educated and more prosperous groups, they naturally played a major political role, but they had to strike a delicate balance. While Arab Christians were politically active, they were nervous about the rise of Islamic movements, all the more so when Muslim birth rates were so much higher than their own. As the Christian minority shrank in size and influence, they faced an increasing likelihood of persecution by a Muslim majority and conceivably something like a repetition of 1915. So how could they create a strong and independent Arab world without awakening the Islamic giant? How could Christian Arabs avoid another Turkey, another Armenia?

One option was secession, to create a distinctive Christian state, almost a reservation or refuge under imperial protection. In 1920, the French created something like this in the new statelet of Lebanon, although other similar attempts failed bloodily; the ancient Nestorian community was defeated in its effort to create an Assyrian realm on Iraqi territory. More commonly, though, Christians tried to find a way out of the dilemma by seeking to lead a wider community that defined itself as Arab rather than simply Christian or Muslim. Christians thus responded to the new political environment by espousing movements that could gain mass popular appeal while remaining strictly secular and religiously neutral. Although this was in no sense a cynical strategy, it simply made practical sense for Christians to lead their societies in secular, progressive directions.

Christians promoted both nationalism and secularism, founding or leading many of the movements that proved so thorny for the European empires that sought to dominate the region, especially the British and French. Christians were among the founders and most visible militants of the region's once-thriving leftist, socialist, and Communist groups. Others became enthusiastic patriots for secular nationalist causes, including pan-Arabism. The pioneering theorist of modern Arab nationalism was Damascus-born Orthodox Christian Constantin Zureiq. Another Orthodox son of Damascus was Michel Aflaq, cofounder of the Ba'ath (Renaissance)

Party that played such a pivotal role in the modern history of both
Iraq and Syria. The pioneering history of modern Arab nationalism,
and a manifesto for that cause, was *The Arab Awakening* (1938), by
Lebanese-born George Antonius—another Orthodox Christian.[32]
The history of Arab politics in the twentieth century is a saga of
thinkers and leaders with such solidly Christian names as George,
Michael, and Anthony. Coptic Christians supported Egypt's nationalist and secular Wafd (Delegation) Party, which emerged at the end
of the war.

By the 1950s, such Christian-founded movements were offering idealistic followers a heady mixture of socialism, secularism,
and nationalism that was all the more tempting as Arab thinkers
struggled to come to terms with humiliating defeats at the hands of
Israel. Palestinian Christians like George Habash and Nayef Hawat-
meh emerged as the most stubborn and resourceful foes of the Zionist state, and the most effective guerrilla commanders. Although
the religious content was rarely noted in the West, the Palestinian
guerrilla struggle before the 1980s was commonly directed by leaders from staunchly Christian families.[33]

Although nationalist and Ba'athist movements appealed to Muslims as well as Christians, they were most popular with those minority groups who stood to lose everything from an assertion of
power by mainstream Sunni Islam—they appealed to Christians but
also to controversial Muslim groups like Syria's Alawites and Druze.
Syrian and Iraqi Ba'ath regimes suppressed Islamist movements with
a brutality that is difficult to understand except as the response of
threatened minorities who desperately feared for their own fates
should they ever lose their grip on state power. Even Saddam Hussein's Sunni clique took its secularism very seriously.

But for all their efforts to lead the Arab world, Christians have
steadily lost ground, most spectacularly in the past quarter century.
Since the late 1980s, secular regimes and movements in the Middle
East have suffered repeated blows, which have cumulatively been

disastrous for Christian populations. Rapid demographic change combined with a global Islamist revival to fuel the success of potent movements such as Hamas and the Muslim Brotherhood, which eclipsed older secularism. Meanwhile, Saddam's lunatic invasion of Kuwait in 1990 set the stage for the destruction of his regime and the expulsion or exile of most Iraqi Christians. As we approach the horrible centennial of 1915, Syria's minority populations commonly express their fears that they too might suffer a comparable fate. Christians and other minorities have suffered grievously during the civil war that has raged in that country since 2011. In Egypt similarly, recent political and religious upheavals have even raised doubts about the continued survival of Egypt's Copts.

AN OBSERVER OF THE Christian world in the early 1920s would see much to provoke grief and foreboding. Beyond the Middle East, churches were being uprooted in the new Soviet Union and actively suppressed in Mexico. Worse, the vogue for the Soviet model meant that future Communist successes elsewhere were likely to be accompanied by persecutions and the harsh suppression of all religion. Yet while Christianity faced the prospect of a new age of martyrdom in its historic homes, in some newer places—above all, in black Africa—the war had allowed churches to expand mightily. Old congregations and shrines perished as new ones were born thousands of miles distant. If Smyrna and Diyarbakir represented some of the most ancient centers of Christianity, momentous events were also taking place at the faith's newest frontiers.

Only a callous observer could ever claim that Christianity's new gains compensated for the horrible losses in Russia and the Middle East, but beyond question, in these very same years a religious world was being turned upside down.

CHAPTER TWELVE

African Prophets
How New Churches and New Hopes Arose Outside Europe

Ethiopia shall soon stretch out her hands unto God.

—PSALM 68:31

WHEN THE INFLUENZA EPIDEMIC shattered native communities across Africa, people sought Christian leaders to explain God's wrath. As so often in European history, many believers felt that they had received special prophetic gifts and God's power was poured forth regardless of familiar restrictions of race, class, or political power. One such prophet, in South Africa's Eastern Cape, was a middle-aged Xhosa woman, Nontetha Nkwenkwe. While suffering from influenza, she had a dream revelation in which Jesus told her of the dreadful ills besetting the earth, those sins that had provoked God to visit the world with the deadly sickness. On recovery, Nontetha began her prophetic mission to insist that everyone follow strict puritanical rules. Her millenarian followers, the true Israelites, gathered at a holy village to await the apocalypse. Her dream ended in disaster when police stormed the settlement, killing hundreds,

Isaiah Shembe, Zulu prophet. His Nazareth Baptist Church today claims some four million members.

while Nontetha herself spent the remaining years of her life in a mental hospital.[1]

In this instance, a prophetic mission ended in worldly catastrophe, but Africa in these very years produced hundreds if not thousands of Nontethas, commonly responding to the same wave of disasters and plagues that inspired her. The idea of an imminent cosmic catastrophe was nothing new in many African cultures, and neither were bizarre millenarian sects. What was new—here and in much of black Africa—was that these visions were now framed in specifically Christian terms, rather than in the language of the older primal faiths. Christianity was clearly making its presence felt. Unlike Nontetha, though, some of these contemporaries went on to found lasting congregations and churches that would transform Africa.

The Rise of Africa

OVER THE PAST CENTURY, the rise of African Christianity has been one of the most impressive stories in global religion. Although numbers alone do not necessarily give much sense of the quality of religious change, they do offer some context. If numbers are not everything, nor are they nothing, and the statistics for religious change in twentieth-century Africa portray a transformation on a quantitative scale unparalleled in history. According to the World Christian Database, Christians were a small presence on the African continent in 1900, with some ten million believers, or less than 10 percent of the total population. By 2000, that number had grown to 360 million, or around 46 percent, and the estimated total today is close to half a billion. By 2050 Africa should have by far the largest number of Christians in any region, one billion souls, representing a third of the world's Christian population. Some of the world's largest Christian populations will be found in such countries as Nigeria, DR Congo, Uganda, and Ethiopia.[2]

In part, that epochal change is a demographic story, as Africans simply make up a far larger share of the world's population than they did in earlier eras. Fertility rates declined sharply in more economically developed nations while remaining high in Africa, resulting in a radical shift in the distribution of global population. In 1900, Europeans outnumbered Africans by three to one, but by 2050, those proportions will be neatly reversed. Even if the Christian share of Africa's people had remained constant, there would be a great many more African Christians. But the religious change was far more than that, involving as it did many millions of conversions. During the twentieth century, some 40 percent of Africans transferred their loyalties from traditional and animist faiths to Christianity. To find a historical parallel for Christian mass conversions on this scale, we would have to look to Europe in the ninth or tenth centuries. In this process, the Great War era marks the decisive transition. This was a time of religious revolution, the effervescent period in which a mission-based Christian church broke racial and social bounds to become a mainstream faith, an African creed. This was the moment at which Christianity "went native" in Africa, the decisive break-through that would give the faith mass appeal.[3]

When they deigned to look at the African Christian movements of these years, at prophets like Nontetha or John Chilembwe, or the Congo's Simon Kimbangu, white observers saw hysteria and primitive savagery, with only the most tenuous connections to the historic faith. What could a self-styled prophet in an African village possibly have to do with a European intellectual like Barth or von Harnack? But Africans faced questions similar to those agitating Euro-Americans. Africans knew Christianity was a faith intimately tied up with a particular political and cultural structure, but in their case Christendom was part of the whole imperial order, making it difficult to separate the two. Under the stress of the war years, ac-tivists wrenched the religious message free of its trappings, seeking to discover the core teachings of the faith. As in Europe, Africa's prophets found a new basis for Christian belief in a radical rediscov-ery of the scriptures, a quest for the original biblical teachings, and in the African case that usually meant a charismatic emphasis on the continuing gifts of the Spirit. This was an age of prophecies, of an-gelic visions, of dreams of a New Pentecost. Africa, in other words, had surprisingly much in common with contemporary Europe, the tormented Dark Continent to its north.

Africa's Faith

IN 1914, VIRTUALLY THE whole of Africa was notionally under European rule, with the exception of the kingdom of Ethiopia,

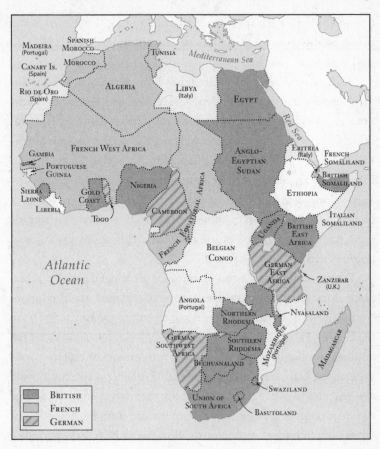

Africa 1914

which had impressively trounced an Italian invasion in 1896. Yet formal imperial rule was a relatively new fact, often dating back no further than a single generation, and it had not necessarily transformed ordinary life. Up to this point, the European impact on religion was quite limited. Across black Africa, substantial majorities still followed traditional or primal religions, and those older practices continued to affect the lives of converts to Islam or Christianity. Of the two, Islam had made by far the greater influence, with a West African presence dating back to the Middle Ages. Probably one-third of all Africans followed Islam, and local believers had a strong predilection for Sufi styles of worship and belief that blended well with local cultures.[4]

Africa's new colonial rulers tended to favor local Muslims as their administrators and soldiers. Old established Romantic traditions encouraged Europeans to think of African Muslims in terms of noble warriors, which fitted well with idealized images of feudalism and the Middle Ages reinforced by Sir Walter Scott's novels. In contrast, Europeans despised pagans or animists as primitive savages, enmired in the heart of darkness. Nor did they have much respect for local Christian converts—ironically, given that spreading Christianity was one of the notional justifications the colonial powers cited for their presence.

From the 1870s, Christian missions developed rapidly across black Africa, although different powers regarded their religious commitment with varying degrees of seriousness. Most active were the British, French, and Germans, although all constantly faced the familiar conflict between the goals of mission and of empire. Conversion to Christianity might be desirable in some ways, but it could also encourage native believers to think themselves entitled to some role in deciding their political or economic futures. Accordingly, white church leaders were slow to allow native believers to advance as clergy and church leaders, leaving the churches definitively as white bastions in a black world.

White churches imposed a Christianity framed entirely within their own worldview, with no place whatsoever for native beliefs and customs. Catholic or Protestant, colonial churches rejected prospective converts who practiced polygamy or the veneration of ancestors, or who still respected the near-universal beliefs in the power of witchcraft. At best, converts could join a European church in theory while resorting to native priests and practitioners for the really important rituals that shaped their lives. This was anything but a recipe for success. In 1900, Africa had just four million Catholics and Protestants combined, including believers of all races, counting white colonists and settlers as well as native converts. (The figure excludes the Orthodox Christians of Ethiopia and Egypt.) By 1914 the new mission churches were a fringe phenomenon, perilously linked to imperial power and white supremacy.

This formula was so unattractive it seems hard to credit that some black Africans found Christianity appealing, even liberating, but they did. By the 1880s Uganda's new Christians were so convinced by the new faith that hundreds were willing to lay down their lives for the cause in an act of mass martyrdom. Christianity exercised a seductive grassroots appeal to many thousands of ordinary people, usually younger individuals or those with less stake in the rituals and orthodoxies of traditional communities than their elders, people not so tightly attached to traditional tribal and village cultures. The most likely converts were those younger and more enterprising souls drawn from their villages to the new colonial centers of trade and activity, the towns, ports, and trading posts, where they encountered new ideas and learned the languages of the colonial powers.

As African people became Christian, they encountered intoxicating ideas, and in the strange new world of the Bible they encountered themes and messages quite different from those offered by the missionaries of the staid colonial churches. They found that large sections of the Bible described societies and cultures very much like those they knew, ancient worlds that practiced nomadism and polygamy, where practices very much like those of contemporary African primal worship were common. They found the greatest men and women of the Bible described not as sober clergy but as inspired prophets and healers. In evangelical Christianity, too, they found a focus on ideas of blood and atonement that meshed well with the sacrificial rites of traditional culture; as in the United States, the emerging religious culture was suffused with blood talk.

From the end of the nineteenth century, native believers began seceding from the mission churches to found their own distinctively

African Christian communities, based on the teachings of charismatic prophets and using local styles of worship. After the Ethiopian defeat of Italian aggression in 1896, some claimed the "Ethiopian" name to boast an identity that was at once Christian and African. American influences were also at work. Some important denominations in South Africa used the "Zionist" title, not from ancient Jerusalem but from the example of a charismatic church based in Zion City, Illinois.[5] Tiny at first, these African Independent Churches (AICs) began to spread, particularly in South Africa. Already on the eve of the Great War, these independent churches were poised for growth, and across the continent we find very similar stories of young converts believing they had been visited by prophecy.

The story of William Wadé Harris likewise suggests just how widespread these visions of an African Christianity had become on the eve of war and just how far they might travel. While in prison for sedition against the Liberian regime, Harris received an angelic visitation that gave him his prophetic powers and a mission to convert the people of Africa. Upon his release, this black Elijah began a triumphant evangelistic campaign throughout the Ivory Coast. What made him so different from so many of his predecessors— and the white preachers who were struggling to draw in a handful of followers—was that he presented the faith in completely Africanized form. He was a black African, as were the women with whom he traveled—presumably his wives. All wore African clothing and carried traditional symbols of authority, but the message he preached was absolutely rooted in a fiery Bible-based Christianity. He treated the traditional pagan faith not with the scorn of a British or German cleric but with the deadly seriousness that might have characterized an ancient apostle. Rather than ignoring the pagan spirits, he proved Christ's all-conquering power by gathering and burning the people's idols and fetishes. By some accounts, he won a hundred thousand converts in just a few months in 1913–14, before French authorities expelled this sensational interloper.[6]

Initially, Harris's influence was strictly localized, but his career showed just how hungry ordinary people were for a message of salvation, of spiritual liberation. That hunger would become still more acute in the catastrophic decade after 1915, when prophets like Harris became a standard feature of African religious life.

Africa at War

AT LEAST FROM THE 1870s, colonial incursions were disrupting traditional societies across the continent, and the changes they introduced created opportunities for new religious beliefs to spread more rapidly than ever could have been achieved by deliberate missionary work. Oppressive demands for labor and supplies wrecked traditional social hierarchies and cultural networks, most sensationally in the Belgian Congo. Even before 1914, European-style wars ignited social transformations, devastating whole regions while creating major new markets for food and labor. Hundreds of thousands of ordinary people were uprooted to fight, or else conscripted to transport goods, to overcome the continent's near-total lack of modern communications. At the turn of the century, the Anglo-Boer War transformed South Africa. Germany meanwhile carried out genocidal conflicts against native subjects in its territories of Southwest Africa (present-day Namibia) and German East Africa (Tanganyika-Rwanda-Burundi).[7]

But these localized precedents paled before the Great War itself. The war dramatically accelerated the social transformation of the previous generation, squeezing a lifetime of tumultuous change into just four years. In 1914, the Germans occupied four huge African territories: apart from Southwest and East Africa, they also held Cameroon and Togo in the west. All, however, were very vulnerable, given Allied naval strength, and most of the German colonies were occupied by mid-1915. The main obstacle in this process was East Africa, where German commander Paul von Lettow-Vorbeck fought a brilliant guerrilla war that tied up British and Allied forces through the end of 1918—given his sparse resources, one of the greatest military achievements of modern times. The conflict sprawled across vast areas of East and Central Africa into what would become the territories of several modern nations; Tanganyika alone covered a far larger area than France and the Low Countries combined. The Allies deployed a million men, several hundred thousand of whom—mainly natives—lost their lives. British and Germans fought naval battles on Lake Tanganyika. Millions of ordinary Africans were drawn into the service of one of the various colonial powers, whether British, French, German, or Belgian (and Lettow-Vorbeck even raided Portuguese territories). Moreover, both British and French also used African soldiers and laborers in the European theater. This huge commitment occurred at a time when Africa's population was only a tenth of what it is today.[8]

Then, in 1918, the great plague began. As we have seen, the second and much deadlier phase of the flu epidemic appeared in multiple sites in August of 1918, initially in ports used for transporting military personnel and supplies. One was the British base at Freetown in Sierra Leone, which meant that the virus now had a foothold in West Africa. Those same ports and trading towns that had done such an impressive job in disseminating new religious ideas were now the transmission points for the lethal influenza. Faith and flu followed the same well-trodden routes. Influenza was soon raging across the continent, from Nigeria in the west to Ethiopia and Somalia in the east. Four or five million Africans perished.

Disastrously for the prestige of the colonial empires, even the most advanced European medicine and science could make little headway against the disease: Africans died like Europeans or Americans. Administrators were alarmed to find ordinary Africans actually blaming whites for spreading the disease, and rejecting their medicines—reasonably enough, as the quinine and aspirin freely handed out by white doctors were quite useless in the circumstances. Coming at a time when Africans were deeply unhappy about the demands of war, the influenza disaster boosted nationalist and anti-imperial sentiment, and discredited theories of white supremacy.

Praying People

THE EPIDEMIC OPENED THE door to new religious messages, at a time when the wartime withdrawal of missions meant that Europeans lost the ability to watch over the seeds they had sown. Across the continent, independent and prophetic Christian movements boomed. This was an era of mass movements, healings, religious risings, nationalist Christian restructuring, Marian visions. And these outbreaks occurred across vast swaths of the continent, with strikingly similar manifestations thousands of miles apart, in utterly different cultural and ethnic settings. We are tempted to speak of an outpouring of the Spirit across Africa, an African Pentecost. Scholar Allan Anderson speaks of an African reformation.[9]

When historians look at the growth of these new African churches, it's easy to miss the critical significance of the war years. Some of the key movements predated 1914, while many of the most influential new churches claim later foundation dates in the mid-1920s or beyond. But a closer look at the careers of the church founders makes it clear just how decisive were the years of war and, specifically, the epidemic.

One product of the upsurge of faith was the Nigerian Aladura movement, the name taken from a Yoruba word meaning "owners of prayer," or "praying people." The term Aladura refers to what has now become a very diverse group of independent churches— the Cherubim and Seraphim, the Church of the Lord (Aladura), the Celestial Church of Christ—all united by their belief in healing and living prophecy. All, moreover, can be traced to a wave of enthusiastic prayer and healing groups founded in 1918.[10]

At the time, the lands that would become Nigeria were a British possession, in which the Muslims of the north held a strong cultural dominance. Christians were a relatively new presence, accounting for barely 1 percent of the population in 1900. Christianity spread over the following years, under the auspices of mission churches like the Anglicans and Methodists. During the war, though, some adventurous converts wanted to push beyond the religious practices they were taught. In 1915, Anglican evangelist Garrick Sokari Braide undertook a mission in the Niger Delta, where, like Harris before him, he urged followers to burn their fetishes. He also claimed exalted status as the Prophet Elijah II. British authorities jailed him for alleged sedition, but not before he created in the Christ Army Church the first of a wave of so-called spiritual churches, which used African customs and liturgies, African styles of prayer. Also at about 1915, Orimolade Tunolase ("Moses") began his special mission in western Nigeria, under angelic inspiration. To his disciples, he was Baba Aladura, Praying Father, and his mission evolved into the Cherubim and Seraphim Church.[11]

It was in 1918 that, based on a dream revelation, an Anglican mission in southwestern Nigeria created a prayer group, Egbe Aladura. This gave its name to the flamboyant movement that spread across the colony, buoyed by stories of healings and even resurrections. After many changes of name, the founding group evolved into Christ Apostolic Church, which in turn became the source of many offshoots and breakaways, usually after some member had claimed a prophetic revelation. New spiritual churches continued to emerge within this tradition into the 1950s and beyond.[12]

Although these churches appeal to very different social groups and cultural traditions, some groups are already well on the way to becoming new global denominations, active in many countries. Today, they use the latest technology to spread their messages, and some churches regularly list members in dozens of countries. The most successful is the Redeemed Christian Church of God (RCCG), which seeks to evangelize North America and Europe as well as Africa. Like other AICs, it has over time moved away from close identification with its African roots or any particular ethnicity or tribe and has become more like a dynamic Pentecostal denomination. Today, RCCG congregations are found in a dozen African nations and across much of Western Europe, and the church has a vibrant presence in North America. But this globalization represents just a new phase in the organic evolution of a movement that has never fully lost its origins in a period of trauma and catastrophe. They are heirs of 1918.[13]

Prophets and Healers

NOT JUST IN NIGERIA, the crises of these years generated a prophetic response. The Gold Coast (Ghana) was hard hit by the influenza epidemic, losing at least a hundred thousand dead. It was amidst this chaos that Joseph Jehu-Appiah ("Jemisemiham") received his divine mission from an apparition of three angels, who ordained him as king. His practices of healing and speaking in tongues led to his ejection from the Methodist Church and to the foundation of a new Musama Disco Christo Church (MDCC), which continues today. Like many independent African churches, the MDCC takes the whole of the Bible very seriously, both Old and New Testaments, but Jehu-Appiah's followers went so far as to recreate the ritual law of the ancient Hebrews. The church has a holy city with a temple, and only on one day of the year may a priest enter the holy of holies. However eccentric it may appear, the MDCC exactly resembled its independent contemporaries in trying to restore true biblical faith. As for the Aladura, God was speaking again as in biblical times, and his African children listened attentively.[14]

In South Africa, too, the war gave a new visibility to independent preachers and prophets. Around 1911, the Zulu prophet Shembe took his prophetic name Isaiah and founded the Nazareth Baptist Church, and from 1916, he began declaring a series of revelations. That church today claims several million members. Another founding father was Engenas Lekganyane, who in 1917 won fame for prophesying British victory over Germany. Shortly afterward, another revelation led him to found the influential Zion Christian Church (ZCC). That church has since grown into a multimillion-strong denomination that wields vast power in modern-day South Africa. In East Africa, it was in 1916 that Alfayo Mango received the spirit baptism that placed him at the forefront of the Roho (Spirit) revival.[15]

But the outpouring of prophecy was not confined to the British realms. The bloodiest manifestation of European colonialism was the Belgian rule in the vast territory of the Congo, where Catholic missions strove to lessen the worst atrocities of power. In 1915, though, at exactly the time of the Chilembwe revolt, the young Simon Kimbangu joined a Baptist mission, where he taught and preached. For him, too, the years of epidemic stirred a sense of living through a spiritual crisis, in which he personally found a special prophetic role. According to his growing band of followers, he healed the sick and raised the dead, the minimum requirements for winning spiritual leadership at this moment in African Christianity. He began a new mission as Christ's emissary on earth, with an ardent commitment to liberate God's oppressed African people, and he established his New Jerusalem at N'Kamba. Sympathizers saw him as no less than the Holy Spirit incarnate on the African continent, the inaugurator of a New Pentecost. Panicked Belgian authorities were less friendly. They arrested Kimbangu, who remained in jail from 1921 until his death in 1951, but his church survived decades of official persecution, and it survives today with anything from four to six million followers. Like the Aladura churches, they have a strong presence in the old colonial nations, and Kimbanguists are well represented in France, Belgium, and Britain.[16]

Into the Mainstream

THE STORIES OF HARRIS (expelled), Nontetha (committed), and Kimbangu (jailed) suggest how nervous colonial authorities were about the prophetic revival they witnessed so uncomprehendingly. Particularly given the experience of John Chilembwe, administrators feared that religious revivalism might provide an excuse or cover for nationalist or antiwhite agitation. This concern was not unreasonable given the religious forms that political activism had often taken in peasant and preliterate society, while on a practical basis a church offered a safe setting to discuss sedition free from the prying eyes of white police officers. Early Euro-American accounts of the new churches focus heavily on this theme of nationalist activism. In 1920, Lothrop Stoddard discussed Chilembwe and the recent Ethiopian churches as chilling manifestations of a global "colored" counterblast against white supremacy.[17] Although not so willing to dismiss the spiritual content of the incandescent native revivals, white churches were equally hostile to what they saw as their primitive and superstitious character.

Most of the new African churches claimed to be strictly nonpolitical and more specifically nonviolent, necessarily as they wanted to avoid suppression by the colonial regimes. Generally, these protestations were quite genuine, and in only a few cases did churches provide a base for militant revolutionary propaganda. Even if pastors disliked white rule, the balance of political power before the 1950s was such that any organized insurrection would be suicidal. But, although they rejected political action, the new independents were striking a major blow for autonomy within the imperial framework. Just in asserting their independent status, they were seceding from white Christianity and colonial power. And once they claimed their own spiritual space, they could pursue the ancient question of the relationship of faith to culture, of determining which portions of historic Christianity are essential to faith and which represent later accretions reflecting centuries of European dominance. The question continues to trouble churches today, in mainstream churches as well as independent sects.

Over the past century, the independent churches have attracted an enormous amount of scholarly attention, sometimes from authors fascinated by these startlingly different practices that seem to lie on the distant fringes of Christianity. As I have suggested, their apparent weirdness is deceptive, as much of what the AICs do actually falls well within the earliest Christian traditions. But in themselves, these churches are not the heart of Africa's Christian story. For all their heroic growth, so much of that expansion would actually be the work of more mainline denominations that would be immediately recognizable to Americans or Europeans—Catholics, Anglicans, Methodists, and Pentecostals. In recent years, the older AICs have faced a choice: whether to harmonize their particular styles with those global denominations or to keep separate and risk stagnation. Some at least, like the RCCG, have taken the former course and have boomed accordingly. Even once-ostracized sects like the Kimbanguists have moved toward the center and actually joined the World Council of Churches.

But even if the AICs were to vanish altogether, which they show no signs of doing, their inheritance remains powerful, and with it, the long-term impact of those Great War–era pioneers. Over time, virtually all the surging churches have become thoroughly African at every level, and they too have followed the original independents in trying to explore the cultural implications of that fact. Methodists, Presbyterians, and Anglicans must struggle to come to terms with the realities of African spirituality, facing exactly the questions that the independents raised a century ago. What is the relationship between the new Christian revelation and older pagan religions? How should Christians regard ancestors, fetishes, or (an acute and widespread dilemma) the belief in witchcraft? How should they respond to the near-universal demand that churches offer spiritual forms of healing? Since the 1960s, African Catholics have been at the forefront of these debates and have struggled to incorporate African cultural forms into their liturgies. For all these mainstream churches, the African focus on charismatic gifts means a reevaluation of ideas of the Spirit, that neglected subfield of theology that bears the daunting title of pneumatology.

If at present these ideas seem far removed from the concerns of Euro-American believers, that situation will change as Global South churches play an ever-greater role in the Christian drama worldwide. When the newer churches write their history, they will give pride of place to those critical years after 1915, when believers tried to make sense of a world plunged into destructive insanity.

Abdülmecid II (1868–1944), the last caliph of Islam

CHAPTER THIRTEEN

Without a Caliph

The Muslim Quest for a Godly Political Order

This war was sent by God to give Muslims their freedom.
—FROM A GERMAN PROPAGANDA LEAFLET

ABDÜLMECID II WAS A cultured European aristocrat. Like most of his class, he held senior military rank, but he never took it too seriously. He was first and foremost an artist, and by no means a dabbler or dilettante. His paintings of Ottoman Turkish themes—including the harem—were sufficiently accomplished to be exhibited in Vienna in 1918. When not painting, his other chief passions in life included collecting butterflies and avoiding political entanglements. Being exiled from his homeland in 1924 must have seemed to him an incalculable blessing rather than a punishment. Butterflies would occupy his twenty remaining years. Always succeeding in remaining on the fringes of great historical events, he died in Paris on the day before the city's liberation from Nazi occupation. And so died His Imperial Majesty, the Commander of the Faithful on Earth, the Caliph of the Faithful, and the Servant of Medina and

Mecca, the last man (to date) to bear that auspicious title. Abdülmecid, the last caliph, was buried in Medina.[1]

It is not easy to frame Abdülmecid in any religious context, still less to imagine him leading a jihad against anyone. If he had not existed, Vladimir Nabokov would have had to invent him. Yet his historical symbolism is immense. He was the last representative of a sequence of caliphs that began with the immediate successors to the Prophet Muhammad himself, and even if the office was often more shadow than substance, it provided a focus of loyalty for the world's Muslims. The First World War, though, destroyed the Ottoman Empire and its sultanate, and in 1924, the caliphate itself was abolished. Those events largely shaped Islamic history over the twentieth century.

The war created the Islamic world as we know it today. The collapse of the Ottoman Empire sent tremors through Muslim regions thousands of miles from Constantinople, destroying the last surviving political structures that had provided any barrier between ordinary Muslims and the overweening power of European empires. The resulting postwar search for new sources of authority led to the creation or revival of virtually all the Islamic movements that we know in the modern world.

For decades, Muslims had debated how to confront modernity, as represented by Western science and liberalism and the competing forces of European imperialism and secular nationalism. These challenges now became hugely more pressing following the experience of occupation, defeat, and internal rebellion, and the catastrophe that overtook Ottoman lands. The postwar situation threatened to reduce virtually all the world's Muslims to the status of either colonial subjects or minorities within newly independent nations dominated by other faiths. Would Islam even survive the twentieth century, except in the most remote and impoverished corners of a white- (and Christian-)controlled imperial world?

Within a few years of the end of the war, we can already see the outlines of all the debates and movements that would shape the Islamic world up to the present day. The new Turkey represented one survival strategy, espousing nationalism and secularism to the point of sidelining religion altogether. Such a solution would maintain the independence of traditionally Muslim societies, if not their values or faith. Elsewhere, Muslims joined Christians or Hindus in broad anti-imperial fronts struggling to create new secular-oriented nations. The war also created the modern political order in the Middle East, marking the birth of a distinctively Arab state system for the first time in half a millennium. Although this development did not necessarily have religious consequences in its own right, the emerging states provided an arena for competing ideologies—secularism and pan-Arabism, but also dynamic Islamist movements.

Although the emerging Islamic nations would not achieve full independence until after a second world war had crippled the colonial powers irretrievably, they had their cultural and spiritual roots in the years immediately following the war of 1914–18. The apparently fatal political crisis facing the Islamic world laid the foundation for vigorous new growth and self-assertiveness. The war made all things possible, and the world is still dealing with the consequences.

An Islamic World

AS A POLITICAL FORCE, Islam in 1914 was inconceivably weaker than it is today. There were perhaps 240 million Muslims in the world, so that Christians outnumbered Muslims by two and a half to one, compared to a modern ratio closer to one and a half. The number of Muslims alive in 1914 was not much larger than the modern Muslim population of just the nation of Indonesia.

These believers had little political clout. With the exception of a few isolated kingdoms operating under the protection of one or another European power, there were just three independent Muslim states in the world, namely the Ottoman Empire, Persia, and Afghanistan. All survived only because the European nations tolerated them in order to prevent destabilizing the balance of power. The three countries combined had populations of only around forty million, of whom perhaps thirty-five million were Muslim. At this stage, moreover, none of these powers had anything like the economic might that would come from the later growth of oil wealth.

The largest concentrations of Muslims lived under European hegemony or direct occupation. By far the largest "Muslim power" was the British Empire, which ruled some seventy-five million Muslims in the Indian subcontinent, plus thirty million elsewhere in Africa and Asia. Another great Asian center of the faith was the Dutch East Indies, the area that today we know as Indonesia, which in 1914 was home to perhaps forty million Muslims. The French likewise ruled far more Muslims than did any of the three explicitly Islamic states, while Russians, Italians, and Spaniards all dominated sizable Muslim populations. European expansion was still proceeding apace in the early twentieth century as imperial powers completed their conquest of North Africa.

Not only were Muslims politically weak but at least in the early stages of European conquest they showed little sense of global unity. Muslims were certainly not passive in the face of European domination. In the century after 1830, every European imperial power had to face insurgencies and jihads in its possessions, so that much of European military history and lore was formed in conflict with Muslim populations. But rarely was there any sense of a coordinated Islamic struggle against Europe, Christendom, or "the West."

Partly that lack of unity reflected problems of communications and transport, but Islam also existed in such diverse manifestations that it was difficult to find common cause. Across the imperial territories, the Islam that prevailed was usually dominated by broad-thinking Sufi orders that formed easy accommodations with neighboring religions, to the extent that it would barely be recognizable by strict modern believers. Most of the world's Muslims lived so comfortably beside Hindus, animists, and Buddhists that Islam in many lands came close to dissolving into a kind of syncretism.

This was especially true in the lands of South and Southeast Asia, where the great mass of the world's Muslims actually lived. Before the twentieth century, India's Muslims represented nothing like the sharply defined ethnic-religious category that we know in modern times, and ordinary people easily divided their devotion between the shrines of Hindu gods and Sufi sheikhs and saints. Although European observers were not always the most accurate guides, British travelers in India not unreasonably assumed that the Islamic symbols and practices they saw everywhere were just components of the broader portrait of Indianness, so that the Qur'an was as much an Indian scripture as the Hindu Bhagavad Gita. In the Dutch East Indies, Islam enjoyed a languid syncretistic relationship with both Hinduism and Chinese religions.

Wholly lacking in political power, "Islam" in any historically recognizable sense scarcely existed in the imperial-ruled lands. Rigid fundamentalists and purists did exist—Arabia's Wahhabis date from the late eighteenth century and the North African Senussis from the 1830s—but such radical voices only slowly gained influence on a wider scale.

Coping with Modernity

THE SAME EMPIRES THAT subjected and often exploited Muslims also made an indispensable contribution to reviving Islamic power and self-confidence. Although European rule over Dar al-Islam had been growing steadily since the eighteenth century, that power became unavoidably intrusive from the 1850s. In India, the mutiny of 1857 swept away the deep-rooted rule of the Mughal dynasty, and by mid-century, Persia too came under the shared hegemony of

Britain and Russia. For the Ottoman Empire, the 1870s marked the crucial transition, with the near collapse of the Ottoman position in the Balkans and Caucasus. From that point on, Europeans inexorably absorbed Ottoman lands, as Westerners pushed to establish Christian missions and schools throughout Islamic territories.

Contact with non-Muslim powers forced Muslims to confront their own relative weakness and redefine their religious identity. The empires made their greatest contribution to reforming Islam by effectively shrinking the globe, making it easier for ideas to spread to every corner of the Muslim world in a matter of weeks and months rather than decades and centuries. Not until the British and Dutch navies sank the pirate fleets could Muslims from distant reaches of the world regularly make their pilgrimage to Mecca and discover there the faith in what appeared to be its stark, primitive austerity. When a pilgrim—a hajji—returned home, his enormous prestige gave him special authority to critique long-standing religious compromises and assert the importance of Arabic as the authentic vehicle for divine truth. Other adventurous believers traveled to explore the very different corners of the Islamic world, so that we find Javanese Muslims studying in Cairo. In any of the great Muslim cities with the slightest pretensions to modernity, a traveler could find newspapers and periodicals published in Calcutta, Cairo, and Constantinople. Imperial centers like London and Paris provided meeting places for Muslim scholars from around the world. For the first time, we can really speak of a transnational Muslim public opinion.

Intellectually, the two greatest centers of the Muslim world were in Egypt and India, both heavily exposed to the latest forms of Western modernity. For some thinkers, reform meant adjusting familiar assumptions to compete in the harsh new world defined by Europe. From the 1870s, Indian Muslims developed a powerful modernizing movement centered on the college of Aligarh, which offered scientific education in the Western mode. Others, though, sought a solution in a return to the days of the Prophet, and a revival of fundamental religious values and structures, ideally enforced by a pure Islamic state. In 1866, a new fundamentalist movement created the seminary at Deoband, an enormously influential base that still exercises its power today: the Afghan Taliban claim roots in Deoband. Others joined the Ahl al-Hadith, the People of the Tradition, determined to differentiate themselves from Sufi accretions to the faith. In the populous Dutch East Indies, modern Islamic politics date from 1912, when the progressive Muhammadiyah movement was formed to resist syncretism and Western culture, and Sarekat Islam organized on more explicitly political grounds. Both would enjoy huge influence, to the point that Muhammadiyah today claims some twenty-five million members.[2]

In Persia, too, imperial domination stirred local Shia Muslim leaders to fervent activism. As the shah made ever more humiliating concessions to foreigners, the senior clergy became the authentic voices of national feeling. The clergy after all had a powerful institutional network in the forms of mosques and religious schools, and especially the great spiritual center of Najaf in what is now Iraq. As in later periods of Iranian history, any secular ruler had to face the prospect of serious rivalry from a powerful *marja* (ayatollah), and in 1905, Shia clergy were prominent supporters of a constitutional revolution. Although that movement failed, clerical opposition would trouble subsequent regimes in both Iran and Iraq right up to the present day.[3]

The Caliph's Banner

BY THE END OF the nineteenth century, several key reformers urged global Islamic unity and sweeping modernization. The most important was Sayyid Jamāl ad-Dīn, known from his origin as al-Afghani, who is the ultimate source of much modern Islamist thought and activism. From the 1860s through the 1890s, al-Afghani roamed freely across South Asia, the Middle East, North Africa, and even Europe. In American terms, he was a Johnny Appleseed character, wandering the world sowing reformist ideas. He urged Muslims to unite and use the latest technology to resist the Europeans before they reduced the whole Middle East to the subservient condition of India. Curiously, he and his followers resembled their Western progressive counterparts in using freemasonry as a vehicle for spiritual reform, and al-Afghani headed Egypt's Masonic lodges. The influence of al-Afghani's many disciples and pupils survives today: they adopted the title of Salafi, claiming that they were returning to the pure principles of the early faith, although not in a simplistic or mechanical way. They urgently wanted to revive Islamic *dawa* (preaching, or missionary efforts) both to convert non-Muslims and to draw weaker Muslims into purer versions of faith.[4]

Muslim activists were returning to a fundamental Islamic idea, namely the unity of the worldwide brotherhood that constituted the *umma,* which should properly be subject to the one true caliph, namely the Ottoman sultan. The incumbent from 1876 through 1909 was the ruthless Abdul Hamid II, whose involvement in the mass murder of Christians in the 1890s has justly given him a dreadful historical reputation. Although distantly related to his cultured successor, Abdülmecid, he seems to come from a different millennium. But in his vision of global Islamic unity as a last throw against total European dominance, Abdul Hamid deserves some credit as a forerunner of many later movements.[5]

This emphasis on the caliph's power was not wholly new, in that revival movements around the world had long declared their loyalty to the sultan, even sending contingents to fight in his wars. Under Abdul Hamid, though, the Ottoman regime cultivated this transnational loyalty as a means of counterbalancing pressures from rapacious Christian empires. The sultan took up al-Afghani's ideas and co-opted his movement. Pan-Islamic ideas even appeared in the Dutch East Indies, where local Muslims traditionally knew the caliph only as a legendary figure who was easily confused with the sharif of Mecca. Ottoman consuls in Batavia (Jakarta) and Singapore began spreading global awareness. Around the world, we see stirrings of solidarity with the Ottoman cause in the Balkan conflicts that immediately preceded the Great War. In 1913, an Indian Muslim leader warned of the pressing need to unite against Western aggression, in the Balkans and elsewhere, which he interpreted as a new crusade:

> The King of Greece orders a new crusade. From the London
> Chancelleries rise calls to Christian fanaticism, and Saint
> Petersburg already speaks of the planting of the cross on the
> dome of Santa Sophia. Today they speak thus; to-morrow
> they will thus speak of Jerusalem and the Mosque of Omar.
> Brothers! Be ye of one mind, that it is the duty of every true
> believer to hasten beneath the Khalifa's banner and to sacrifice
> his life for the safety of the faith.[6]

Besides this active sympathy for the Ottoman regime was the shared sense that the caliphate existed and always would exist. Whatever else had changed during the disasters that had befallen the world of Islam, the caliphate remained as a spiritual center of faith.

Already before 1914, then, Islamic activism was stirring, and Westerners worried about the prospects for future militancy. In 1899, Winston Churchill expressed his deep concern about the "militant and proselytizing faith" of Islam. But short of reversing the process of globalization, it was far from obvious how to respond to the new political faces of Islam. Then, as now, Western countries faced the dilemma of working with active Muslim movements without promoting Islamic radicalism. The Russians found themselves unwittingly sponsoring real or supposed Muslim reformers who were covertly involved in pan-Islamic (or pan-Turkic) movements connected to the Ottoman Empire.

Fears of global Islamism were very much in the air by 1914. In that year, the American magazine *Forum* published an influential piece by Achmed Abdullah, allegedly an Afghan Muslim. Abdullah's origins were in fact more complex, as his father was a Romanov, a Russian kinsman of the tsar, and he himself enjoyed a successful career as a novelist and screenwriter who trafficked freely in oriental stereotypes: his film credits included *The Thief of Bagdad* (1924). None of those wrinkles, though, prevented him being treated as an authentic voice of an insurgent Islamic world on the verge of a historic political breakthrough. He warned Westerners of the consequences, that their racist arrogance would incite

> a coming struggle between Asia, all Asia, against Europe and America. You are heaping up material for a Jihad, a Pan-Islam, a Pan-Asia Holy War, a gigantic day of reckoning, an invasion of a new Attila and Tamerlane who will use rifles and bullets, instead of lances and spears. You are deaf to the voice of reason and fairness, and so you must be taught with the whirring swish of the sword when it is red.[7]

Also in 1914, novelist G. K. Chesterton published his novel *The Flying Inn,* describing the Islamic occupation of England. Already Muslims featured as demonic figures in popular Christian apocalyptic.

Yet for all the warning signs, all the threatening prophecies, Islamist prospects were in reality severely limited, not least because radical hopes were focused on a ramshackle Ottoman Empire and its sultan. Only when the war had exorcised that ghost could Muslims reconstruct a global political vision.

The Impact of War

EVEN IF ISLAM WAS not a serious political force, it could still cause difficulties for the imperial powers. The main Allied nations— Britain, France, and Russia—all ruled major Islamic populations, and the Germans hoped to stir discontent against these rivals. (The Dutch remained neutral.) The prospect of holy warfare became vastly more likely when Ottoman Turkey entered the war on the German side. In November 1914, the sultan's regime formally sanctified the war when the Shaykh ul-Islam issued a fatwa placing all Muslims under a personal duty to fight enemies of the faith. The sultan confirmed the jihad in a proclamation some days later, and a manifesto to this effect was to be distributed throughout the Muslim world. The Germans were happy to support this propaganda effort, circulating leaflets in local tongues declaring, "The time has come to free ourselves from infidel rule." An Egyptian nationalist assured his German readers that "in cities and villages, from sage to simple peasant, all are convinced in the kaiser's love for Islam and friendship for its caliph, and they are hoping and praying for Germany's victory." An American diplomat groaningly described the German attempt to incite a Muslim revolt as "Deutschland über Allah."[8]

In fact, Muslims generally did not rise to overthrow infidel rule, and most Muslim soldiers and civil servants continued to serve their imperial masters faithfully. While they accepted religious authority, Muslims also took very seriously the oaths and obligations they had made when accepting imperial service.

But the jihad proclamation was heard, and the resulting conflicts lasted for years. John Buchan's popular wartime novel *Green-mantle* (1916) describes German plots to spark an anti-Allied jihad across the Islamic East, and does so quite plausibly given Buchan's role as a well-connected Allied propagandist. As a character warns,

The Shaykh ul-Islam in Constantinople proclaims a jihad, urging all Muslims
to come to the aid of the Ottoman Empire against the infidel
Allied powers, November 1914.

the British had been wrong to assume that talk of holy war would
be dismissed as the work of cranks and lunatics. In reality,

> the Syrian army is as fanatical as the hordes of the Mahdi. The
> Senussi have taken a hand in the game. The Persian Muslims
> are threatening trouble. There is a dry wind blowing through
> the east, and the parched grasses wait the spark. And the wind
> is blowing towards the Indian border. . . . It looks as if Islam
> had a bigger hand in the thing than we thought.[9]

Lothrop Stoddard recalled how, in 1914 and 1915,

> Egypt broke into a tumult smothered only by overwhelming
> British reinforcements, Tripoli burst into a flame of insurrection
> that drove the Italians headlong to the coast, Persia was pre-
> vented from joining Turkey only by prompt Russian inter-
> vention, and the Indian Northwest Frontier was the scene of

fighting that required the presence of a quarter of a million Anglo-Indian troops. The British Government has officially admitted that during 1915 the Allies' Asiatic and African possessions stood within a hand's breadth of a cataclysmic insurrection.[10]

The Turks stirred trouble on the northwestern borders of British India, sending a joint Ottoman-German military mission to the emir of Afghanistan. Actual warfare broke out elsewhere on the traditional frontier battlegrounds, where 1915 brought tribal risings by Pashtun peoples in Waziristan. Indian Muslim soldiers also took the lead in the Singapore mutiny. The Turks promoted armed revolts among the Senussis, followers of a rigorist Sufi order who challenged British and Italian power across a vast swath of the lands that now form part of Libya, Egypt, and the Sudan. By 1916, yet another member of the distinguished Wingate clan (related to the English Zionist) led British forces to victory over the Senussis.[11]

The New Order

THE ALLIES, TOO, STIRRED subject peoples against their masters, and with even greater success. The British focused their efforts on the Arab peoples, who were restive under Ottoman rule. Notionally, the sultan in Constantinople ruled both the eastern and the western coastal parts of Arabia, leaving the heartland to traditional anarchy, but local chieftains exercised much independence. Particularly vital was the western portion of the peninsula, the Hejaz, in which stood the two holy cities of Mecca and Medina. These were controlled by the deeply rooted Hashemite family whose head held the title of sharif (noble). In 1915, the British plotted with the current sharif, Hussein bin Ali, who did launch a revolt in the following year.

The revolt did not have a straightforward religious message, as it was a movement of Muslims directed against a Muslim regime, indeed against the caliphate. Historians remember it as the Arab Revolt, an ethnic or nationalist insurgency, and the famous historian George Antonius used 1916 as the starting point for his classic account of the Arab Awakening. As an Arab Christian, though, Antonius had powerful reasons for wanting to stress the movement's nationalist character rather than any religious motivation: his political agenda was firmly based on ethnicity rather than faith.[12] Yet even at this stage nationalism certainly had its religious element, as rebellious Arabs were asserting their claim to be the faithful standard-bearers of Islam and the Arabic Qur'an, a role that had been usurped by the Ottoman regime. However authentic its Islam might be, the Ottoman dynasty was ethnically Turkish, and its officials were disproportionately Balkan or Caucasian in origin. The sharif's family, in contrast, hoped to establish a kingdom that was distinctively Arab as well as Muslim.

More controversially, the British also allied with the rival dynasty of Abdul Aziz Ibn Saud, who was based in Riyadh and who followed the strict Wahhabi tradition. Ibn Saud operated in close alliance with the Ikhwan (Brothers), a fanatical Islamist military order who served as his shock troops. What made the Ikhwan so fearsome was that they ignored familiar Islamic restraints on the conduct of war, treating even non-Wahhabi Muslims as infidels suitable for only plunder and enslavement. Through the first quarter of the century, they were responsible for tens of thousands of deaths, almost entirely of fellow Muslims. Given Ibn Saud's reputation as a virtual bandit chieftain, the British were dubious about drawing him in as an ally. In the circumstances of the time, though, the need to bring down the Ottomans outweighed any concerns about making friends with unsavory connections. And after all, what danger could Wahhabi Islam ever pose to the all-powerful West? In 1915, the Treaty of Darin declared the Saudi state a British protectorate and ally.[13]

The Arab Revolt is familiar to Westerners through the saga of T. E. Lawrence, a leading organizer of the movement: his followers fondly called him Emir Dynamite. With the support of British money and weaponry, the insurrection not only survived but also maintained steady pressure on Ottoman supply routes and railroads, and seized control of large territories before the region could be occupied by British and French forces. By September 1918, Arab rebel forces linked up with British imperial armies in Damascus.[14]

No less famous than the glorious revolt is the story of postwar Allied betrayal. Hussein bin Ali had hoped to bring the whole of Arabia and the Levant into an Arab kingdom, but the British and French had already planned a partition into their own spheres. The Balfour Declaration of 1917 complicated matters still further. By the mid-1920s, the British had created new kingdoms of Iraq and Transjordan and given them respectively to Hussein's sons Faisal and Abdullah—although they remained under strong imperial control. A new nation of Syria was created under French domination, with the Christian region of Lebanon marked out as a separate statelet. Imperial needs strangled any hopes of a new Arab nationalism or any true independence. Growing Western demand for oil added immensely to imperial interest in the region.[15]

Nor could faithful Muslims find much sign of independent religious authority in the new political order, or any obvious successor to the spiritual supremacy claimed by the Ottoman sultans. Of the states that succeeded the old Ottoman realm, only Turkey could claim any true national independence. Under Kemal Atatürk, though, this new Turkish republic was anything but a bastion of Islam, or a friend to the caliphate. In 1922, a British battleship took the last sultan, Mehmet VI, into dignified exile. Although the sultanate was then abolished, Mehmet's aesthetically inclined cousin Abdülmecid briefly held the title of caliph until the new republican Turkey formally abolished that institution as well in 1924, sending the last incumbent off to Paris. The nation then proclaimed official secularism and embarked on an ambitious program to remove vestiges of religion in public life. Proving the regime's determination in religious matters, in 1925 Turkish forces suppressed an Islamist revolt led by a Sufi order.[16]

It was not immediately obvious that the caliphate as such was finished, rather than merely transferred to some new claimant. In 1923, Sharif Hussein staked his claim for the caliphate, plausibly enough given his control of the holy cities and his heroic role in fighting for Arab independence. By 1925, though, the rival dynasty of Ibn Saud had defeated and expelled Hussein's family. Further attempts to restore the office likewise came to nothing, including aspirations by Ibn Saud himself and by Muhammad Amin al-Husayni, Jerusalem's grand mufti. By 1931, the caliphate was a dead letter. By Western calendars, the institution fell only a year short of marking its 1,300th anniversary.[17]

In Persia, too, a political order intimately associated with Islamic power collapsed in these years. The last ruler of the old Qajar dynasty, Ahmad Shah, was still a minor in 1914, and the country was wholly dominated by Britain and Russia. Persia became a theater of prolonged combat during the war, which pitted Russian and British forces against the Ottomans, and Russian and Armenian armies took Tehran in 1915. Persia as a state scarcely existed. By 1921, the country fell under a military regime, leaving Ahmad Shah to join the ranks of the other deposed royals then seeking villas in the more pleasant corners of Latin Europe. In 1925, dictator Reza Khan proclaimed himself shah and his land an empire, which it remained until 1979. What shortly became the nation of Iran also espoused modernization, though less sweepingly than Turkey.[18]

The Arc of Crisis

WHAT MIGHT HAVE MARKED a fatal moment in the further decline of Islam actually was a moment of critical activism, as a revival that had been emerging over the past half century suddenly reached a new maturity. However impressed Westerners were with Turkey's experiment in modernization and secularism, other developments within the Islamic world would carry much greater weight in the long run. The decade following the peace was marked by world-wide anti-imperial resentment and nationalist mobilization. In the Islamic context, the empires had expanded their power over even more new territories at a time when the metropolitan states were weakened by the effects of war and subsequent economic strains. This volatile combination allowed local revolts and agitation to gain traction in a way that would have been impossible before 1914.

Not only did anticolonial risings rage across large sections of the Islamic world in the immediate postwar years but many drew their inspiration explicitly from religious teachings, and the accumulated force of such movements in the early 1920s was stunning. If we want to visualize interreligious struggle in these years, we should imagine a European biplane dropping bombs or gas on a Muslim village, and the aircraft might bear the colors of any one of half a dozen nations. Suddenly, an armed and transnational pan-Islamism seemed like a realistic prospect.

Just to give an idea of the scale of the movements, between 1919 and 1925 Britain's newly founded Royal Air Force saw action against Muslim rebels and enemy regimes in Somalia, Afghanistan, Waziristan, and Iraq. In 1919, Britain was engaged in yet another of its wars in Afghanistan, officially the third full-scale conflict to date. This particular struggle had an even greater significance because that country then remained the last truly independent Muslim regime. Although the British held their position, Afghan forces made deep inroads into traditional centers of colonial power. Through the mid-1920s, the British Raj remained in regular con-flict with the Muslim tribal peoples of Waziristan and the northwest frontier, using aircraft to raid and intimidate dissidents. At the same time, other British units took the field in another familiar theater of Muslim activism: Somaliland. For decades the region had been largely controlled by the Islamist forces of Mohammed Abdullah Hassan, whom the British named the Mad Mullah. Finally, in a war in 1920, the British crushed his dervish state.[19]

Most of the revolts of these years grew directly out of wartime agitation. In Mesopotamia (later Iraq), the Shia people used the war as an opportunity to eject Ottoman officials. In 1917, though, the region fell under British power, and unrest continued. By 1920, the British were meeting growing resistance from both Sunni and Shia populations, as former Ottoman officers buttressed the opposition. (Throughout the various Islamic revolts, we often see the role of such battle-hardened Ottoman veterans, whose postwar military achievements at least matched anything they had accomplished during formal hostilities.) Leading Shia clergy and ayatollahs then issued fatwas proclaiming the illegitimacy of British rule and calling for rebellion. Wide-ranging revolts across the very diverse territory became something close to a national insurrection in 1920, which the British defeated only by deploying the latest technology of air power and gas weaponry. After the revolt, the British ruled the mandate through their old ally Faisal, who received the kingship in 1921. Here, as elsewhere, even where rebellions failed they forced the imperial powers to rule their territories through local middlemen rather than directly, giving Muslim communities some limited autonomy. Still, older religious grievances and tensions never went away.[20]

Also in 1920, the British faced signs of resistance in their new possession of Palestine, although initially nothing close to the scale of the Iraqi rising. The main activist they had to deal with was al-Husayni, another veteran of the Ottoman military who was now a strong Arab nationalist. In 1920, he incited frightening mob attacks against Jerusalem's Jews. The following year, he became the grand mufti of Jerusalem, and increasingly he combined nationalist resistance to Jewish settlement with a pan-Islamic ideology, and a demonstrated willingness to use conspiracy and armed violence in pursuit of both causes. Through the 1940s al-Husayni was the most visible face both of the Palestinian Arab cause and of transnational political Islamism.[21]

A Clash of Civilizations

THE WAR HAD A long aftermath in North Africa, where imperial advances met resistance from the widespread Senussi order. Before the war, the Senussis had already fought the French, and in 1915, under Turkish urging, they began a guerrilla jihad against the British and Italians. After the war, the pacification of Libya was a primary goal of the Italian government, particularly after Mussolini seized power in 1922. Over the next decade, the imperial invaders launched a heavy-handed campaign against the Senussi resistance, killing thousands of civilians and imprisoning many others in concentration camps. From the Arab side, at least, there was no doubt that this was a religious struggle: the resistance leader was Omar al-Mukhtar, a pious Senussi sheikh whom the Italians executed.[22]

The massive imbalance between forces made most of the anticolonial struggles doomed ventures, at least in the short term. In one case, though, asymmetric warfare actually produced a sweeping Muslim victory. French and Spanish forces had occupied Morocco and Northwest Africa at the start of the century, but they encountered resistance from the sturdily independent Berber tribes, particularly those in the mountainous Rif region. Resistance focused on a tribal leader and religious figure called Abd el-Krim, a *qadi* (judge) with Salafi leanings, and in 1916 he was imprisoned for an alleged conspiracy with the Germans. During a dazzlingly effective guerrilla war in 1921, Abd el-Krim's forces crushed Spanish military power in Morocco, killing several thousand European soldiers and leaving him the head of a short-lived Rif Republic.

Abd el-Krim negotiates with magnate Horacio Echevarrieta to
arrange for the return of prisoners taken following the collapse
of Spanish military power.

In 1925, French and Spanish forces responded with an invasion
on a Great War scale, with several hundred thousand troops supported by tanks, aircraft, and mustard gas. Although Abd el-Krim
was defeated, he did live long enough to see Arab nationalist forces
drive the French out of North Africa in the 1960s. The Moroccan
war also had a profound effect on interwar Europe, creating the
Spanish army that would overthrow that nation's government in the
1930s. The extreme savagery of Spain's subsequent civil war owed
much to the importation of habits of colonial warfare that prevailed
in North Africa.[23]

The Russians too faced their Islamist challenges. In fact, the
seventy years of Soviet history possess a neat symmetry. As we know
today, the regime was crippled by its Afghan war of the 1980s, but
the Soviet Union was also born in a struggle against jihad, in Lenin's
time. Following the collapse of tsarist rule, Muslim peoples of the
Russian-ruled Caucasus began an insurrection intended to create
a state based on the strictest interpretation of sharia law. Proclaiming the goals of the rising, one leader threatened to hang all those
who wrote from left to right. The movement reached its height in
1920 in the regions of Daghestan and Chechnya, both areas that
have seen ferocious violence in modern times. Even more than in

The Rif War was marked by extreme brutality. Here, elite Spanish legionaries display gruesome trophies taken during the war against Abd el-Krim's forces.

North Africa, the war had a militantly religious tone throughout. The rebels mobilized large armies of murids, fanatical Sufi devotees, who maintained a staunch resistance into the mid-1920s. The victorious Soviets waged a continuing war against their Islamic rivals, whom they characterized as zikristi—those Sufis who recited the traditional prayer, the dhikr.[24]

But the Caucasus only represented one front in the Russian encounter with jihad. In 1916, tsarist demands for conscription provoked resistance in Muslim Turkistan, which, after the revolution, evolved into the widespread Basmachi Revolt, the *Basmachestvo*. Although the word implies criminal banditry, the movement combined Islamist and populist sentiments, making it an authentic popular national movement. (It also received British support, as part of the Western effort to destabilize Bolshevism.) The Basmachis fielded tens of thousands of guerrillas, fighting on behalf of an autonomous sharia state and operating across most of Soviet Central Asia. The Bolsheviks did not control the region fully until the mid-1920s, and some rebels fought into the next decade. Once again, we find former Ottoman officers heading the revolt, including Enver

Pasha, one of the junta who led the empire during the Great War. Enver traveled to Central Asia in order to draw the area into a pan-Turkic movement against the Christian West, but for all the nationalist and ethnic rhetoric, the last Ottoman general died in the faith of his empire's Islamic founders. Reputedly, Enver suffered the perfect martyr's death in 1922, clutching his Qur'an as he fell in combat with godless Bolsheviks in distant Tajikistan.[25]

The wider jihadi threat even led the Soviets into a foreign intervention, in the Gilan region of northern Iran. During the war years, Germans and Turks had sponsored a "jungle" (*jengelis*) resistance movement here, under the leadership of a Shia mullah, and by 1918 the insurgency had spread through the Caspian Sea region. Soviet naval and army units joined the Persian government in suppressing the movement in 1920–21.[26]

The Soviets were not the only power to face a severe challenge from the Sufi orders. Similar groups led militant resistance to the new secular state of Turkey, culminating in 1925 in a revolt among the Kurds. As part of their counterinsurgency campaign, the Turks used aircraft to bomb rebel villages, proving how decisively they had joined the progressive world of civilized Europe. Ironically, the rebel leaders were executed in Diyarbakir, which had also been the killing ground for Christians just a decade earlier. Turkey then suppressed the orders, which had so long been at the heart of Ottoman cultural life.[27]

No less surprising than the scale of the uprisings is how they have been treated in later memory, and how for so long their religious element was neglected. Even Europeans recognized that these movements produced heroic figures, whom they imagined as romantic bandits. In 1921, Rudolph Valentino's film *The Sheik* had been a worldwide sensation, and however improbably, the 1925 U.S. operetta *The Desert Song* was a romantic fantasy about the Rif rebels, who in this version owed their success to the leadership of a dissident Frenchman called the Red Shadow.

Later generations treated these movements more seriously, but they too erred in judging the movements according to the standards of the day, so that rebel leaders became nationalists of secular or even proto-Marxist bent. (The Soviets treated their own Muslim insurgents as thugs and bandits, pure and simple.) Politically, even Abd el-Krim became a red shadow, as accounts of his campaigns became holy writ for the leftist guerrilla thinkers of later eras, including Ho Chi Minh and Che Guevara, while he inspired the nationalist Algerian rebels of the 1950s. Egyptians and Libyans venerate a secularized Omar al-Mukhtar, who gives his name to streets in Gaza and elsewhere, and the Mad Mullah is Somalia's national hero. Iraqis commemorate their 1920 rebellion as the Great Iraqi Revolution, a purely nationalist movement that supposedly transcended ethnic and religious divisions.

Missing in most such commemorations, at least until recently, was the primarily Islamic motivation of these risings, which were so regularly led by Islamic judges and preachers and authorized by religious sheikhs, teachers, and ayatollahs. Frequently the rebels also organized in religious brotherhoods, following one or another of the Sufi traditions: they were bands of brothers. If the modern world faced a series of simultaneous wars like this, we would have no hesitation in speaking grimly of a global jihad, with a scope and appeal far beyond anything ever achieved by al-Qaeda. Few would deny claims of a worldwide clash of civilizations, and of faiths.

Back to God

IN TERMS OF THE fate of modern Islam, the most important conflict of these years occurred in the Arabian Peninsula, where removing Ottoman imperial authority created wholly new political opportunities. When most modern Westerners look at the region, they automatically think of the largest portion under the name of Saudi Arabia, as if this is an ancient name for the territory. Yet far from being lost in the mist of Oriental antiquity, the state of that name is a strictly modern invention, proclaimed as recently as 1932. In practice, modern Arabia—with all the Saudi impact on global religious alignments, as much as economics—is strictly a twentieth-century product.[28]

Arabia at the start of the twentieth century contained several competing tribes and statelets that operated with considerable independence. This balance of power could be sustained only as long as external forces did not try to take advantage of the perpetual internal conflicts for their own purposes, and that changed as the Ottomans drifted into hostility with the British Empire. When the British allied with the sharif, Ottoman power and restraints were quickly removed from the territory. The Saudis took advantage of wartime chaos to expand their power, under the leadership of Ibn Saud and his Ikhwan warriors.[29]

In 1924, Ibn Saud captured Mecca, which had been in the hands of the rival clan of the sharif since the thirteenth century. At first, foreign Muslims were nervous about the transition of power, given Ibn Saud's barbarous reputation. The new rulers made no secret of their loathing for the veneration that had grown up around the ancient tombs and shrines associated with Muhammad's family, and in the name of returning to the austere purity of the faith, the Saudi state began an iconoclastic rampage. Understandably, Muslims worldwide were deeply concerned about participating in the annual pilgrimage to Mecca, but the first hajj under Saudi control involved nothing worse than the usual chaos. The regime soon achieved a remarkable stability, given its origins. Even the pious credentials of the new state could not deter its still more extreme elements among the Ikhwan, who raided freely across the new borders of Iraq and Transjordan. Between 1927 and 1929, the Brothers launched a full-scale revolt against the Saudi regime, which the dynasty suppressed with the aid of British air power.

An era of consolidation followed. By 1927, Ibn Saud had united the Kingdom of Nejd and Hejaz, and in 1932, he was proclaimed king of the new Saudi Arabia, putting a faithful Wahhabi dynasty in charge of a vast state (twice as large as Texas and California combined) with enormous economic potential. By the late 1930s, the breathtaking scale of the kingdom's oil reserves was beginning to become apparent. Even at this date, of course, Saudi Arabia was a marginal player in world affairs, and not until the 1970s would the kingdom gain its role as both a global energy powerhouse and a base for militant Islamist politics. But the foundations were laid during and right after the Great War.

Brothers

ALTHOUGH ARMED DISSIDENCE STILL smoldered in some regions, by the end of the 1920s, the new political order ruling the Islamic world was achieving stability, with a network of new states. More important in the long run, though, would be the popular organizations and movements that emerged from the war and its immediate aftermath.

Every modern account of Islamic extremism in the world begins with a number of key groups and individuals. Egypt's Muslim Brotherhood produced such influential alumni as Sayyid Qutb. Also critical are Pakistani organizations like the Jamaat-e-Islami, founded by Maulana Syed Abul A'ala Mawdudi. (Especially in the Indian subcontinent, "maulana" is a respectful title for religious dignitaries.) From these groups and thinkers we can trace a direct line to many of the world's most militant and aggressive organizations, the bane of modern-day Western security agencies. But while figures like Mawdudi and Qutb were most active and influential in the 1950s and 1960s, the movements they represented can be traced to the post-1918 spiritual crisis that left the Muslim world with no obvious center or focus of loyalty.[30]

Immediately following 1918, anti-imperial activism focused on nationalism, not necessarily with any religious coloring. Inevitably, given its cultural sophistication and cosmopolitan outlook, Egypt took the lead in these political debates. In the immediate aftermath of the war, Egypt was a center of nationalist militancy that straddled religious boundaries. The dominant anti-British movement was the Wafd Party, which was militantly interreligious and preached the unity of cross and crescent—a necessity in a country with such a large Coptic Christian minority. By the mid-1920s, though, it was clear that the British could not lightly be displaced from such a strategically vital land. Meanwhile, some Islamic thinkers were seeking a quite different direction. Although they were inspired by the patriotic outpouring of 1919, they emphasized a return to the roots of Islam, and a number of small groups emerged, usually rooted in Sufi orders. In 1928, Hassan al-Banna founded the most important such group, the Ikhwan al-Muslimun (Muslim Brotherhood), which aimed to restore the lost caliphate. The Brotherhood drew loosely on the older ideas of al-Afghani and his disciples, but now presented them to a mass popular audience and operated in intimate alliance with mosques and other cultural institutions. This innovative structure allowed the Brotherhood to become an enduring presence in Egyptian life over the coming century, to the point of briefly holding national power in 2012–13.[31]

Globally, the Brotherhood was so significant because of its influence on another figure just reaching political consciousness in these years, Sayyid Qutb (born 1906). Qutb took Islamist ideas to fateful extremes, envisaging a new Islamic state firmly based on a restored caliphate, a theocratic regime that would enforce strict sharia laws. Qutb also revived an older fringe view that narrowed the definition of true Muslims to those believers who accepted the ideology in its purest form, leaving the remainder of self-described Muslims as de facto infidels, kafirs, living in a world of pagan ignorance, *jahiliyyah*. These weaker brethren must be proclaimed and exposed as kafirs through the declaration of *takfir*, a kind of anathema. By these standards, all existing Muslim regimes were in fact nothing of the kind, and it was the absolute duty of true believers to withdraw from them, culturally if not physically, to struggle for a pure society that would bring in the renewed caliphate. Qutb's ideas underlie most modern Islamist extremist movements, including al-Qaeda.[32]

India and the Khilafat

MIDDLE EASTERN EVENTS REVERBERATED in South and Southeast Asia, where even modernizing thinkers could scarcely cope with the idea of a world without a caliph. In the Dutch East Indies, the threat to the caliphate stirred an unprecedented wave of Islamic internationalism in the early 1920s. For the first time, a broad range of Muslim activists, progressive and traditional, demonstrated a new resentment at living under rule that was not just foreign but infidel, and in 1922 all the main Muslim parties and cultural organizations submerged their differences in a sturdy Indies All-Islam Congress. However little East Indian Muslims had ever known or cared about the caliph, suddenly that institution came to symbolize all the cultural glories and religious identity that had been lost at the hands of colonialism.[33]

In the case of the East Indies, where Muslims constituted the vast majority of the population, Islamic activism was increasingly diverted into secular forms, into socialism and Indonesian nationalism. In British India, though, where the caliphate affair inspired an equally strong reaction, it led to a quite different political outcome. In a land where Muslims were definitely in a minority, the new consciousness of Islamic identity demanded a wholly new political assertiveness and separatism, which eventually led to the Muslim state of Pakistan.

Ever since the emergence of Indian nationalism, Hindus, Sikhs, and Muslims shared common anti-imperial sentiments. From the start of the new century, though, Muslims became ever more alarmed at the huge numerical dominance of the Hindus, and they feared for their future in an independent India. Muslim leaders who disliked the humiliations of British imperial rule worried that a future independent India might be deeply inhospitable for non-Hindu minorities, even if their ranks ran into the tens of millions. Some Muslim leaders set aside their qualms sufficiently to throw their lot entirely with the predominantly Hindu Congress movement, while others adopted a pro-British stance—less from love of the Europeans than out of fear of Hindus.[34]

From 1913, a new generation of activists tried to bridge religious rivalries, under the leadership of Muhammad Ali Jinnah, a Muslim who was also a fervent nationalist. This alliance was all the more important following the outbreak of war, when nationalists hoped that India's huge contributions to the imperial cause would persuade the British to grant more autonomy. Meanwhile, Mahatma Gandhi's return to India from South Africa in 1915 presaged a new era of mass political activism in the nationalist cause. In preparation for a new political world, the Indian National Congress and the Muslim League agreed in 1916 to the Lucknow Pact, which carefully (and generously) specified Muslim rights and privileges within a future independent India. The pact allowed Muslims a third of the offices in a new government, considerably more than their share of the population.[35]

The two sides agreed on creating separate electorates, a point that would prove critically important for defining religious loyalties. If a new India elected its leaders on something like the British or U.S. system of "first past the post," then widely diffused electorates would have nothing like the influence to which their numbers entitled them. Ethnic or religious minorities would be poorly represented. In 1909, the British proposed a separate system, under which Muslims voted for separate lists and were guaranteed a certain share of legislative seats, and that system was confirmed after the war. That arrangement seemed fair and rational, but the problem then arose of defining who exactly was a Muslim—no easy matter in villages where religious practices borrowed from multiple traditions. The electoral system could only work if the authorities had accurate census data on religion, which meant insisting that Indians decide whether they were Hindu or Muslim, a distinction that would once have been close to meaningless. From 1919, under the auspices of British bureaucracy, Indians began a process of religious and communal self-identification that made Muslims more explicitly Muslim and Hindus more Hindu. That separation would ultimately lead to savage conflict.

Initially, it looked as if the two faiths had resolved their differences, but then the end of the war brought the collapse of the Ottoman Empire and a startling upsurge of Muslim political identity. British observer Sir Theodore Morison warned his compatriots how India's Muslims were reacting to events in distant Constantinople:

> The Mohammedan world is ablaze with anger from end to end at the partition of Turkey. The outbreaks of violence in centres so far remote as Kabul and Cairo are symptoms only of this widespread resentment. . . . In India itself the whole of the Mohammedan community from Peshawar to Arcot is seething with passion upon this subject. Women inside the Zenanas [women's quarters] are weeping over it. Merchants who usually take no interest in public affairs are leaving their shops and counting-houses to organize remonstrances and petitions; even the medieval theologians of Deoband and the Nadwat ul-Ulama [Organization of Scholars] whose detachment from the modern world is proverbial, are coming from their cloisters to protest against the destruction of Islam.[36]

The immediate consequence was the creation of a powerful Muslim mass movement in India, the Khilafat (Caliphate), which served as a vital platform for Muslim opinion within Indian politics. Initially, the movement urged the British to protect the institution of the caliphate during Turkey's postwar turmoil. Its leader was Maulana Muhammad Ali, who had with his brother Shaukat Ali been interned for pro-Turkish sympathies during the war. In 1919, Muhammad Ali led a delegation to England to press, unsuccessfully, for British support for the caliph. When that failed, despairing Indian Muslims sought various solutions, including actually fleeing infidel rule to seek their fortunes in a sharia country—which in practice left Afghanistan as their only option. However daunting the prospect, some sixty thousand Indians actually made their exodus, their hejira, to Afghanistan around 1920, although most soon abandoned the effort. More practically, other Muslim activists used the Khilafat impulse as a basis for seeking global Muslim unity. Meanwhile, during the 1920s, conservative movements like the Ahl al-Hadith were extending their power into new regions and bases, preparing the foundations for their later expansion.[37]

The Khilafat Movement was born at a time of furious nationalist protest against British rule, and Muslim activists enthusiastically joined with other Indians in pressing for an independent India. Gandhi welcomed these allies, so that in 1923 Muhammad Ali actually became president of the Indian National Congress. Muslim modernizers, though, were alarmed by the traditional Islamist ideas of the Khilafat, particularly when they were linked to Gandhi's populist mass politics. For Muslim nationalists like Jinnah, the combination of tactics and ideology threatened to lead to lethal religious conflicts—as it would, catastrophically, in the 1940s. The violence and ethnic cleansing of India's partition claimed several million lives.

Muslims in fact faced a dilemma common to religious politics of any shade, namely that faith worked well to define communities and their values, but there was always the danger that militants would push religious demands to extremes, raising the potential for confrontation with other groups. Already in the 1920s there were worrying portents of what life might be like in an independent India. In 1921, Malabar Muslims spread rumors that British power had collapsed and that Islamic power was being restored. A dangerous rebellion followed, led by Khilafat militants following a self-styled local caliph. The rebels slaughtered hundreds of Hindus and forcibly converted others, until British forces finally restored order.[38]

By 1924, the Khilafat Movement lost its reason for existence when the new Turkish state formally ended the caliphate and no obvious candidate for the office presented himself. Party members moved to other groups. Some joined the Congress Party, where these Muslims worked with members of other religions to create a nation theoretically pledged to nonsectarian secularism. A few are remembered as distinguished founding fathers of the new Indian nation.

But the Islamist turmoil made its mark, and the vision of Islamic autonomy and self-sufficiency left a mighty heritage for later movements. Above all, the Khilafat agitation gave Muslims a third political option, over and above the simple alternatives of British Raj or total independence. This third course would involve a new separate state, soon to be named Pakistan. The new vision was best outlined by the distinguished Sir Muhammad Iqbal, who had shared in the Khilafat enthusiasm and who now saw Pakistan as the best hope for Muslims. The Pakistan cause also attracted the support of Muhammad Ali, who was deeply disaffected with any talk of an independent India and disturbed by the increasingly overt Hindu tone of the Indian nationalists. Together with Shaukat Ali, he campaigned for the new state, while supporting worldwide Islamic unity.

The Alis reconciled with Jinnah, and with him, they are regarded as the forefathers of the later state of Pakistan. In its early days, the country preached a vision of Islam that was both moderate and modernizing, but the state would always face basic questions of religious identity: If this was in fact a state for Muslims, should it not also be an Islamic state? And what exactly did that mean in the modern world?

Spreading Faith

THE PAKISTAN IDEA OFFERED Indian Muslims one way of living in a post-caliphate world, but other solutions offered themselves. One was to renew efforts to restore the caliphate itself, a stubborn cause that continued to find expression through the decade. As late as 1931 Shaukat Ali was the co-organizer of a World Islamic Congress in Jerusalem, the last gasp of restoration efforts. Other activists emphasized the revival of Muslim spiritual values, a calling of the barely practicing lost sheep of the house of Islam back to fundamental truths. This meant drawing sharp lines between the life and practice of ordinary Muslims in diverse and syncretistic societies like India and leading them back to a starkly defined Islamic practice, part of a global Islamic reformation.

Some of these movements, which sprang from the crisis of the 1920s, are regarded suspiciously today. One such is the Tablighi Jamaat, the Society for Spreading Faith, a worldwide missionary and preaching order that critics cite, fairly or not, as a thin cover for radical Islamist conspiracy. In its origins, it grew out of India's conservative Deobandi movement, which strove to wean ordinary Muslims from alien faiths and to restore the basic teachings of early Islam. In the crisis years of the mid-1920s, one Deobandi believer named Maulana Muhammad Ilyas sent devoted followers around the world to practice *dawa,* preaching or mission, through one-on-one interactions with listeners. Over the years, the Tablighis have won influential followers around the world, including several leaders of Islamic nations like Pakistan and Bangladesh. Claiming tens of millions of ordinary adherents, the Tablighis boast of being the largest single movement within modern Islam. Although notionally nonpolitical and nonpartisan, the simple back-to-basics Islam that the movement preaches has contributed powerfully to the rise of fundamentalist religious activism in South Asia and around the world.[39]

Even more significant as a forerunner of later Islamism was Maulana Mawdudi, the wide-ranging scholar who offered a comprehensive vision of a fundamentalist Islam that could confront the modern world. Although Mawdudi was born in 1903, he was already involved in journalism and political activism before the end of the Great War, and by the start of the 1920s he was participating in the fierce controversies then dividing Muslim thinkers in the age of the Khilafat. In 1941, he founded the Jamaat-e-Islami, the ancestor of all the main Islamist movements in Pakistan and South Asia, including the most notorious terrorist groups (though Mawdudi himself did not advocate such acts). To varying degrees, all these groups—peaceful and otherwise—share his vision of a theo-democracy: a modern state founded on Islamic values and institutions. To Mawdudi belongs the honor of shaping Islamist thought across the usual Sunni-Shia sectarian boundaries: his work profoundly influenced Sayyid Qutb, but also the Ayatollah Ruhollah Khomeini.[40]

Among Shia Muslims, too, the Great War left a lasting heritage. One of the lasting legacies of the conflict was the shift of Shia religious authority from the Mesopotamian Najaf following the Iraqi revolt. The beneficiary was the emerging intellectual center of Qom, in Persia, the nursery of generations of later ayatollahs. Although the school's new heads disdained political activism, they could not fail to see how quickly and easily secular regimes had crumbled over the past decade, leaving clergy as the voices of moral authority and the defenders of ordinary believers. In 1921, the nineteen-year-old Khomeini was already a student at Qom, long before his later elevation to the prestigious rank of ayatollah. Like his counterparts in Egypt, Palestine, and British India, Khomeini grew up seeking a world order founded on a primitive vision of authentically Islamic religious authority.[41]

For Islam, the twentieth century was a period of spectacular growth in numbers and influence. Partly, as for Christianity, this was a demographic story in that Muslims happened to be concentrated in those parts of the world with the highest fertility rates, chiefly in South Asia and black Africa. Today, there are six times as many Muslims as there were a century ago. Moreover, the economic picture has changed massively with the growth of the oil economy. Presumably both these trends would have occurred much as they did whether or not the world wars had occurred and regardless of their outcome.

But in other important ways, the shape of modern Islam owes much to the Great War, and especially to the resulting upsurge of activist movements and the creation of autonomous states. Beyond their political significance, these states have also had a huge impact on the way in which ordinary Muslims around the world have worshipped and believed. Through its vast donations to religious causes and building enterprises, the Saudi state has encouraged a worldwide tilt toward strict Salafi and fundamentalist Islam very different from the once-dominant Sufi models. In combination with South Asian revivalist groups like the Tablighi Jamaat and Egypt's Muslim Brotherhood, Saudi influence has given global Sunni Islam a conservative and traditionalist tone that would have astounded the optimistic modernizers of the pre-1914 era.

All these conservative forces had their origins in the conflict that Europeans called the Great War. In using this term, they had little idea of just how deeply that struggle might affect those who, at the outset, seemed to have so little investment in its outcome.

Conclusion

The kingdom of heaven suffereth violence, and the violent take it by force.
—MATT. 11:12

We all became by hundreds years older.
—ANNA AKHMATOVA

IN EVERY SPHERE OF life, the First World War cast a long shadow across the twentieth century. In religious terms, that influence might seem wholly destructive, and educated Europeans often hark back to that conflict as the origin of the continent's later secularization. In this view, the war left European nations cynical about exalted claims of all kinds, while churches were so utterly compromised as to leave them weakened beyond recognition. Philosopher Theodor Adorno famously declared, "To write poetry after Auschwitz is barbaric," and we might assume that it was just as inconceivable to practice faith after Verdun or the Armenian massacres.[1]

As we have seen, that picture is oversimple, and we have to distinguish between the war's short- and long-term impacts. If we take a long view, through the end of the century, not only did the war not kill religion, it actually revived some faiths—even if the specific forms they took might alarm many Westerners. That is all the more obvious when we shift our focus from Europe to the wider world, where religious life is thriving to a degree that seems absurd to many Europeans. In 1991, French scholar Gilles Kepel commented on the unexpected return of religion to the global stage in a book aptly titled *The Revenge of God*. In that process of divine reassertion, the Great War marked the crucial beginning.[2]

Another War

AT A GLANCE, THE Second World War supports the view that religion—or at least, Christianity—was wrecked beyond recovery by 1918. If the second war was politically and militarily a direct continuation of the first, the two conflicts were starkly different in their religious content. In Europe, even at moments of greatest exaltation, the second war produced no overtly religious manifestations vaguely comparable with those of the first. Yes, people might have resorted to churches in times of crisis, while religious and apocalyptic values underlay the secularized ideals of the totalitarian states. But it is very difficult to find propaganda imagery depicting supernatural intervention on the battlefield of the kind that was so commonplace a generation earlier: angels steered clear of this conflict.[3]

When leaders did refer to God—as even Stalin did in rare and startling instances—the usage was strictly conventional ("God bless our nation!"). Despite some rhetorical references to the divine will in *Mein Kampf,* Hitler never showed himself anything other than a convinced scientific materialist in the best nineteenth-century mode. When Dwight Eisenhower recorded his campaigns as a *Crusade in Europe,* readers knew better than to expect any nod to theology or supernatural motivation. Even Winston Churchill, who proclaimed that the Battle of Britain would determine "the survival of Christian civilization," described his relationship to the church as that of a flying buttress, who faithfully supported the institution from the outside.

With isolated exceptions, the combatant nations of the second war eschewed visions, apparitions, prophecies, and angels, and those stories that were reported attracted nothing like the worldwide fanfare of "The Bowmen." If ghosts and angels proliferated in popular film and novels (as they did, from *Here Comes Mr. Jordan* and *It's a Wonderful Life* on down) it was in works clearly designated as fantastic fiction rather than sensational headline news. To adapt the title of another supernatural-themed film of these years, heaven could wait. The great religious writers of the era, such as C. S. Lewis and Dietrich Bonhoeffer, saw themselves as isolated believers in a world that was secular if not paganized.

Something had changed in the substance of politics, not least in the declining practice of church establishment. But we can also see the effects of the first war and its embarrassing lessons about the prostitution of religious rhetoric. However religious its population might be in terms of practice, U.S. churches rarely deployed anything like the language that was so mocked in Abrams's *Preachers Present Arms*. They had been too well warned. Perhaps when holy war rhetoric reaches a certain extreme, it discredits itself beyond redemption and becomes its own gravedigger.

All Thine

IF HOLY WAR RHETORIC evaporated, religion survived much longer as part of the political story, even in Europe. If religion, and specifically Christianity, was not much in evidence during the Second World War, it staged a massive comeback during the ensuing confrontation with Communism that we call the Cold War. We have already seen how Great War memories influenced the Catholic thinkers who dominated the Second Vatican Council, and also the political leaders at the heart of the new project to build a united Europe.

Those memories remained vividly alive during the papacy of John Paul II, who lived to usher in the new century. Although not born until 1920, his anti-Communist views were inextricably linked with the vision of Fátima and a mystical veneration for the Virgin. She was the subject of his apostolic motto, which proclaimed *Totus Tuus*—"All Thine." His obsession with Fátima grew even greater with the unsuccessful assassination attempt on May 13, 1981, the precise anniversary of the children's original vision in 1917. The coincidence of dates gave John Paul even greater respect for Fátima's secret revelations, in which he claimed to find a description of his own narrow escape. At the Fátima shrine, he left one of the bullets in the crown of the figure of the Virgin.[4] For most people, the perception of following a special destiny might be a psychological curiosity, but John Paul was no ordinary believer, and the events of 1981 encouraged him to still more intense involvement in his ongoing crusade against Communism. The continuing crisis between the Polish Communist regime and the church reached a critical stage some months later when that nation declared martial law—in retrospect, a crucial moment in the collapse of Communism in Eastern Europe.

In other ways, too, shades of the Great War survived in Rome into the present century. When John Paul died in 2005, his successor was Joseph Ratzinger, who chose as his papal name Benedict XVI. In doing so, he was acknowledging the earlier Benedict, the pope of the Great War, whom he termed "that courageous prophet of peace, who guided the Church through turbulent times of war." Under the twenty-first-century Benedict, too, the church continued to advance the cause of sainthood for the last Habsburg emperor, Charles I, who ruled Austria-Hungary from 1916 and who struggled to restore peace.[5]

The Roman Catholic Church long remained a postwar church—but the first war, not the second.

New Christians

BEYOND QUESTION, CHRISTIAN CHURCHES in modern-day Europe have declined precipitously in numbers and stature, or at least in some countries—loyalties remain stronger in eastern parts of the continent. So marked has been this process of secularization, in fact, that Western academics have taken it as an inevitable by-product of modernity. As the world modernizes, as the state grows, they claim, so religion fades away. On a global scale, however, such a process is by no means apparent. Worldwide, modernization and urbanization have been accompanied by a swelling of religious belief and practice, and that rising tide has lifted Christian churches as well as other faiths. In the global picture, secular Europe looks like what sociologist Grace Davie has called the "exceptional case."[6]

The consequence has been a revolutionary shift of Christian numbers outside the traditional heartlands of that religion, and any attempt at writing this history has to come to terms with the Great War and its immediate aftermath. Apart from the geographical nature of the shift, we also see a sweeping change in church structures. While state-linked or state-supported churches accounted for a sizable majority of Christian believers in 1914, today they claim only a tiny share. "Christendom" in anything like its old sense has, in a century, come close to extinction.

In matters of doctrine, too, the typical Christian is a very different animal from her or his counterpart a century ago, as beliefs that would once have been regarded as eccentric or fanatical have gained something like mainstream status. The greatest beneficiaries have been Pentecostal and charismatic movements, which benefited enormously from the apocalyptic atmosphere of the war years. According to a major study by the Pew Foundation, over half a billion Christians today can be categorized as Pentecostal and charismatic, around a quarter of the whole body of the faithful. The faster Christian numbers have grown outside the traditional West, the greater the growth among those Christians holding a special fascination for the Holy Spirit.

Non-charismatic evangelical Protestants have also enjoyed a global boom. In the United States, evangelicals largely withdrew from organized political development through the mid-twentieth century but returned in full force during the 1970s, a decade that marks the beginning of a broad religious awakening. Since that point, evangelical activism has been manifested in groups like the Moral Majority, and various related organizations of the Christian Right. Underlying this activism, though, is a religious interpretation absolutely rooted in the premillenarian theories of the end times popularized during the war years. One of the bestselling religious books in modern times, and a great source for conservative religious activism, is Hal Lindsey's 1970 title *The Late Great Planet Earth,* which largely summarizes and updates the dispensationalism of Cyrus Scofield and his reference Bible. Central to the belief system is the modern Jewish return to Palestine, which supposedly inaugurated the sequence of prophetic warnings and exhortations outlined in the Bible. The Balfour Declaration set a stopwatch that continues to tick toward the moment of judgment and the annihilation of the existing world order. At the end of the century, the dispensationalist package supplied the framework for the Left Behind series by Tim LaHaye and Jerry Jenkins, which sold sixty-five million copies.

Global Faith

NOT JUST AMONG AMERICANS, or among Christians more generally, traditionalist religious movements emerged as major political players from the 1970s onward, whether we are dealing with

Christians, Muslims, Jews, or Hindus. So substantial has been the growth of religious adherents, and their political activism, as to raise real questions about the general narrative of inevitable secularization. Secularization, in fact, looks less like an inevitable component of social development than a transient historical phase that was particularly convincing and widespread during the quarter century or so after the Second World War. During the 1970s, a series of economic crises undermined the postwar political consensus and the broader narrative of secular progress, and created mass support for religious movements that would not long since have been dismissed as irrelevant if not medieval. At the same time, the growing intensity of globalization and the spread of mass media meant the much wider and faster dissemination of ideas and movements than had been conceivable hitherto—and vastly faster than in 1914.

The most sensational of the modern-day religious revivals has been the upsurge of Islam, a religion that today claims the loyalty of perhaps 1.5 billion worldwide. Most alarming for the West, of course, has been not the growth of Islam as such but of militant and revolutionary versions of the faith. Historically, this is a modern phenomenon. Through the mid-twentieth century, the concept of the Muslim world seemed to describe no more than a broad cultural inheritance, scarcely relevant to real-world politics of secular nationalism and socialism. Condescending perceptions changed suddenly with an explosion of Islamic militancy. The post-1975 decade witnessed the Iranian Revolution and the Soviet war in Afghanistan, the assassination of Egypt's President Sadat and the rise of Palestinian Hamas. Even many well-informed Westerners saw these events as erupting from nowhere, or from an imaginary medieval past. To varying degrees, though, all the movements traced their origins to the Great War era. So did the nations of Saudi Arabia and Pakistan, those storm centers of the new Islamic world.

Also in the 1970s, distinctly religious alignments assumed a new

significance in the Jewish state. Buoyed by their surging demograph-
ics, Orthodox and ultra-Orthodox Jews became much more visible
and important in Israeli politics, and they were further strengthened
by the rise of the settler movement. All these groups looked to the
Kook family, the heirs of Rabbi Abraham Isaac, whose apocalyptic
views owed so much to the thought world of 1915 and 1916.[7]

Tectonic Faith

STUDYING THE DENSELY PACKED events of the Great War, it is
often easy to forget just what a shockingly brief span of time they
covered: just four years for formal hostilities, with several more
years of chaos immediately following—but still less than a decade
in all. And yet, as we have seen, the world changed totally in this
time. Although Norman Stone was speaking chiefly of military
and political trends, we readily echo his observation that "in four
years, the world went from 1870 to 1940." In religious terms, we
might prefer to set the dates still wider apart—perhaps from 1850
to 1950.[8]

One catastrophic war fueled very rapid changes in religion, but
the story's implications go far beyond that single historical moment,
offering as they do a template for understanding the phenomenon of
radical religious change, in both past and present, and perhaps even
in the near future. The most unsettling lesson may be the breathtaking speed with which a world can change, the brief moment during
which a seemingly rock-solid order can be swept away. Changes
that seem inevitable to us in retrospect were at the time wholly unexpected. In turn, values and behavior that seem natural and proper
to us today can in just a few years look like fossils from a distant
geological epoch. As John Stuart Mill remarked, "the crotchet [ec-
centricity] of one generation becomes the truth of the next, and the
truism of the one after." The Great War shows how the religious

world we know might indeed be turned upside down within a very short space of time.

In religion, as in politics and culture, we should see the pace of change not as steady, gradual evolution but as what biologists call punctuated equilibrium—long periods of relative stasis and stability interrupted by rare but very fast-moving moments of revolutionary or cataclysmic transformation. These radical innovations then take decades or centuries for the mainstream to absorb fully, until they are in their turn overthrown by a new wave of turmoil. In describing this process, we might adapt a phrase that scholars of religion use to describe societies living in areas highly prone to volcanoes and earthquakes, and whose ritual life revolves around placating and preventing those mighty forces: their religious practice is thus "tectonic faith." Throughout history, we often find changes in faith as sudden shifts akin to those wrenching the earth's tectonic plates.

Repeatedly over the centuries, great wars and natural catastrophes have ignited influential new movements in religion— fundamental shifts in religious consciousness, fervent revivalism and awakenings, and apocalyptic expectation. Of course, not every this-worldly disaster produces a spiritual effect, and rarely does the social trauma initiate something wholly new. Rather, it takes trends that already exist in a given society in embryonic form and provides a sudden and revolutionary impetus toward rapid expansion. Wars, economic crises, and famines in the 1730s ignited the intensely studied transatlantic Christian revival that we call the Great Awakening, and the 1755 Lisbon earthquake drove Europe toward Enlightenment. On occasion, especially at times of plague and pestilence, such crises have spawned wholly new denominations, new religious orders or mystical societies. Such revolutions are the keys to religious history.

Inevitably, these eras of crisis and apparent doom produce endtimes expectations, dreams or nightmares that the present world order will soon be reaching a fiery consummation. These hopes and fears matter so much because often they induce people to pro-voke the end times, to accelerate the process of history, and those dreams can lead directly to revolutions and pogroms. Such eras are commonly prolific in conspiracy paranoia and quests to identify the Antichrist, and esoteric movements abound. Overt violence aside, such sweeping events shape the worldviews of thinkers active at the time, and they cast a shadow decades afterward. We see one such apocalyptic era at the time of the Reformation, around 1520, and another at the height of the French revolutionary expansion throughout Europe, in 1798. The conflict that we so appropriately call the Great War was the latest of this series, and it unfolded on the largest historical canvas.

Might another such realignment occur at some future point, a new moment of tectonic faith, with all that implies for innova-tion and transformation? For the advanced nations, at least, such a prognosis is very unlikely, because any kind of major war would so utterly devastate all participants. But elsewhere, the picture is rather different. War, famine, and calamity are still possible and even likely for much of the world, particularly those regions of the Global South that are already home to the world's most numerous populations of religious believers, of Christians, Muslims, Buddhists, and Hindus, and where those communities are growing steadily. When we trace the southward movement of Christianity, we also see faith becom-ing synonymous with the most volatile and ecologically threatened area of the world. Environmental change poses an added danger. If predictions of climate change have any validity whatever, then the process will have its most acute effects on exactly those regions near the tropics where Christianity and Islam are both growing so rapidly. Could such disasters really come to pass without inspiring new apocalyptic visions, without drawing new battle lines between creeds? Catastrophe might once more precipitate a worldwide reli-gious transformation.

BUT EVEN IF SUCH a time of troubles does occur, we can say confidently that nobody now living will survive to trace its full effects. Not only did the First World War show how calamity can transform the world, but it also suggested just how long it takes for the results to become apparent. Observing a revolution is quite different from comprehending it. Only now, after a century, are we beginning to understand just how utterly that war destroyed one religious world and created another.

Acknowledgments

I'm grateful to many friends and colleagues who have offered support or advice in writing this book, including Tobias Brinkmann, Sophie de Schaepdrijver, Byron Johnson, Jeff Levin, Gregg Roeber, and Catherine Wanner; and to Greg Miller of Malone University.

Thanks to my editor at HarperOne, Roger Freet, and my agent, Elyse Cheney.

I want to acknowledge the superb assistance of Nick Pruitt in tracking down visual resources.

And as so very often in the past, thanks to my wife, Liz Jenkins.

ILLUSTRATION CREDITS

179 Cropped from *Liberty's Victorious Conflict: A Photographic History of the World War* Magazine Circulation, 1918, 18.

182 Courtesy of the U.S. National Archives and Records Administration.

184 By John Warwick Brooke. Courtesy of the Imperial War Museums.

186 Courtesy of the government of the United Kingdom.

190 By Walter Schnackenberg. Courtesy of the Library of Congress.

199 Courtesy of Kino Lorber.

218 Photograph by Maria Netter. Courtesy of Karl Barth Archiv, Basel.

234 From the Smithsonian Institution. Courtesy of the Library of Congress.

266 *The Protocols of the Elders of Zion* (New York: Beckwith Company, 1920).

268 Reprinted from the *New York Times*. Courtesy of the Library of Congress, Serials and Government Publications Division.

272 From *The Great War,* ed. H. W. Wilson (London: Amalgamated Press, 1916).

281 Courtesy of *Arbeiter-Zeitung,* Vienna.

286 Courtesy of the Armenian Genocide Museum-Institute.

296 From the Imperial War Museum collection. Courtesy of Wikimedia Commons.

297 Photograph by Ernest Brooks. Courtesy of the Imperial War Museums.

301 Courtesy of the Armenian Genocide Museum-Institute.

310 Courtesy of the Armenian Genocide Museum-Institute.

316 From B. G. M. Sundkler, *Bantu Prophets in South Africa* (London: International African Institute, 1961).

332 Courtesy of the Library of Congress.

344 Photographer unknown. Image courtesy of the Turkish government.

352 From Fundación Euskomedia.

353 Unknown photographer. From Jacques Roger-Mathieu, *Memoirs of Abd el Krim* (Paris: Librairie des Champs Élysées, 1926). Courtesy of Wikimedia Commons.

NOTES

INTRODUCTION: *From Angels to Armageddon*

1. Arthur Machen, *The Angels of Mons* (London: Simpkin, Marshall, Hamilton, Kemp, 1915), 19–24; David Clarke, *The Angel of Mons* (Hoboken, NJ: Wiley, 2004); and for the battle itself, see Terence Zuber, *The Mons Myth* (London: History Press, 2010).

2. Machen is quoted from Machen, *The Angels of Mons,* 17; Ralph Shirley, *The Angel Warriors at Mons* (London: Newspaper Publicity, 1915); and Harold Begbie, *On the Side of Angels* (London: Hodder and Stoughton, 1915).

3. The fighting dogs are described in Harry Patch and Richard van Emden, *The Last Fighting Tommy* (London: Bloomsbury, 2007), 104–5.

4. J. C. Squire, *The Survival of the Fittest and Other Poems* (London: George Allen and Unwin, 1916).

5. Michael Snape, *God and the British Soldier* (New York: Routledge, 2005); John Fuller, *Troop Morale and Popular Culture in the British and Dominion Armies 1914–1918* (Oxford: Oxford University Press, 1991); Stéphane Audoin-Rouzeau, *Men at War, 1914–1918* (Providence, RI: Berg, 1992); Richard Schweitzer, *The Cross and the Trenches* (Westport, CT: Praeger, 2003); and for Russia, see Karen Petrone, *The Great War in Russian Memory* (Bloomington: Indiana University Press, 2011), 43–44.

6. Salman Rushdie, *Midnight's Children* (New York: Random House: 1980), 47.

7. Stefan Goebel, *The Great War and Medieval Memory* (Cambridge: Cambridge University Press, 2007); Christopher Tyerman, *The Debate on the Crusades* (Manchester, UK: Manchester University Press, 2011); and Jay Rubenstein, *Armies of Heaven* (New York: Basic Books, 2011).

8. "Proclamation of Sultan Mehmed V, November 1914," www.firstworldwar.com /source/mehmed_fetva.htm.

9. Paul Claudel, *La Nuit de Noël de 1914* (Paris: A l'Art Catholique, 1915), 27–28, my translation.

10. McKim is quoted from Ray Hamilton Abrams, *Preachers Present Arms* (New York: Round Table Press, 1933), 55.

11. Lyman Abbott, "To Love Is to Hate," *Outlook* 119 (May 1918): 99–100; Dieffenbach is quoted from Abrams, *Preachers Present Arms,* 67–68; and Alan Seaburg, "Albert Dieffenbach," Dictionary of Unitarian and Universalist Biography, http://www25.uua.org/uuhs/duub/articles/albertdieffenbach.html.

12. Newell Dwight Hillis, *The Blot on the Kaiser's 'Scutcheon* (New York: Fleming H. Revell, 1918), 59.

13. For a debunking of claims about war fever in 1914, see Jeffrey Verhey, *The Spirit of 1914* (Cambridge: Cambridge University Press, 2000); Gerd Krumeich, "'Gott mit Uns': La Grande Guerre Fut-Elle Une Guerre de Religion?" in *1914–1945: L'Ère de la Guerre,* eds. Anne Duménil, Nicolas Beaupré, and Christian Ingrao, vol. 1 (Paris: Noêsis, 2004), 117–30; Catriona Pennell, *A Kingdom United* (Oxford: Oxford University Press, 2012); for war enthusiasm in various countries in 1914, see Lothar Kettenacker and Torsten Riotte, eds., *The Legacies of Two World Wars* (New York: Berghahn Books, 2011); for popular culture and media, see Hubertus F. Jahn, *Patriotic Culture in Russia During World War I* (Ithaca, NY: Cornell University Press, 1995); Michael Hammond, *The Big Show* (Exeter, UK: University of Exeter Press, 2006); and for the process of learning and internalizing official ideologies, see Michael S. Neiberg, *Dance of the Furies* (Cambridge, MA: Belknap Press / Harvard University Press, 2011).

14. Ritzhaupt is quoted from Wilhelm Pressel, *Die Kriegspredigt 1914–1918 in der Evangelischen Kirche Deutschlands* (Göttingen: Vandenhoeck and Ruprecht, 1967), 153, my translation; John A. Moses, "Justifying War as the Will of God," *Colloquium* 31, no. 1 (1999): 3–20; and Günter Brakelmann, "Der Kriegsprotestantismus 1870–1871 und 1914–1918," in *Nationalprotestantische Mentalitäten in Deutschland (1870–1970),* eds. Manfred Gailus and Hartmut Lehmann (Göttingen: Vandenhoeck and Ruprecht, 2005).

15. Dietrich Vorwerk, *Hurra und Halleluja* (Schwerin in Mecklenburg, Germany: F. Bahn, 1914), my translation.

16. Snape, *God and the British Soldier;* Annette Becker, *War and Faith* (New York: Berg, 1998); Adrian Gregory, *The Last Great War* (Cambridge: Cambridge University Press, 2009); and Jonathan H. Ebel, *Faith in the Fight* (Princeton, NJ: Princeton University Press, 2010).

17. For "Debout les Morts!" see Leonard V. Smith, *The Embattled Self* (Ithaca, NY: Cornell University Press, 2007), 72–75.

18. Paul Boyer, *When Time Shall Be No More* (Cambridge, MA: Belknap Press / Harvard University Press, 1992); Bernard McGinn, *Antichrist* (San Francisco: HarperSanFrancisco, 1994); Andrew Cunningham and Ole Peter Grell, *The Four Horsemen of the Apocalypse* (New York: Cambridge University Press, 2000); and Catherine Wessinger, ed., *The Oxford Handbook of Millennialism* (New York: Oxford University Press, 2011).

19. The manifesto is quoted in Frances Carey, ed., *The Apocalypse and the Shape of Things to Come* (Toronto: University of Toronto Press, 1999), 279.

20. Vera Brittain, *Testament of Youth* (New York: Macmillan, 1933), 414–17.

21. Roger Ford, *Eden to Armageddon* (New York: Pegasus Books, 2010); and Scofield is quoted in Boyer, *When Time Shall Be No More,* 102.

22. Michael Burleigh, *Sacred Causes* (New York: HarperPress, 2006), 38–122.

23. *The Cambridge History of Christianity,* ed. Hugh McLeod, vol. 9, *World Christianities c. 1914 – c. 2000* (Cambridge: Cambridge University Press, 2006); and Andrew Preston, *Sword of the Spirit, Shield of Faith* (New York: Knopf, 2012).

24. Hilaire Belloc, *Europe and the Faith* (New York: Paulist Press, 1920); and World Christian Database, www.worldchristiandatabase.org/wcd/.

25. Philip Jenkins, *The Next Christendom,* 3rd ed. (New York: Oxford University Press, 2011).

26. Geoffrey Wheatcroft, "Perfidious Albion," review of *The Balfour Declaration: The Origins of the Arab-Israeli Conflict,* by Jonathan Schneer, *New Statesman,* August 23, 2010, www.newstatesman.com/books/2010/08/arab-palestine-jewish-rights.

27. *The New Cambridge History of Islam,* ed. Francis Robinson, vol. 5, *The Islamic World in the Age of Western Dominance* (Cambridge: Cambridge University Press, 2010).

CHAPTER ONE: *The Great War*

1. The First World War continues to attract a vast scholarly literature. Throughout this book I have used Martin Gilbert, *The First World War* (New York: Henry Holt, 1994); John Keegan, *The First World War* (New York: Vintage Books, 1998); Hew Strachan, *The First World War* (New York: Viking, 2004); Michael S. Neiberg, *Fighting the Great War* (Cambridge, MA: Harvard University Press, 2005); John Horne, ed., *A Companion to World War I* (Malden, MA: Wiley-Blackwell, 2010); Lawrence Sondhaus, *World War I* (Cambridge: Cambridge University Press, 2011); and Max Hastings, *Catastrophe* (London: Collins, 2013). See now Adrian Gregory, *A War of Peoples* (Oxford: Oxford University Press, 2014).

2. Holger H. Herwig, *The Marne, 1914* (New York: Random House, 2009), 148; David Stevenson, *Cataclysm* (New York: Basic Books, 2004), 45; Hastings, *Catastrophe.*

3. For Saint-Cyr, see Herwig, *The Marne, 1914,* 315.

4. Holger H. Herwig, *The First World War* (London: Edward Arnold, 1997); Douglas Mackaman and Michael Mays, eds., *World War I and the Cultures of Modernity* (Jackson: University Press of Mississippi, 2000); Leonard V. Smith, Stéphane Audoin-Rouzeau, and Annette Becker, *France and the Great War, 1914–1918* (Cambridge: Cambridge University Press, 2003); Roger Chickering, *Imperial Germany and the Great War, 1914–1918,* 2nd ed. (Cambridge: Cambridge University Press, 2004); Adrian Gregory, *The Last Great War* (Cambridge: Cambridge University Press, 2009); Jay Winter, ed., *The Legacy of the Great War* (Columbia: University of Missouri Press, 2009); and for the Meuse-Argonne campaign, see Edward G. Lengel, *To Conquer Hell* (London: Aurum Press, 2008). For the legacy of bereavement and widowhood, see Erika Kuhlman, *Of Little Comfort* (New York: New York University Press, 2012).

5. Ina Zweiniger-Bargielowska, Rachel Duffett, and Alain Drouard, eds., *Food and War in Twentieth Century Europe* (Burlington, VT: Ashgate, 2011).

6. Gary Sheffield, *Forgotten Victory* (London: Headline Review, 2001); Jay Winter and Antoine Prost, *The Great War in History* (Cambridge: Cambridge University Press, 2005); and for continuing debates, see Winter, ed., *The Legacy of the Great War.*

7. Geoffrey R. Searle, *A New England?* (Oxford: Clarendon Press, 2004); Brian Bond, *The Unquiet Western Front* (Cambridge: Cambridge University Press, 2008); David Williams, *Media, Memory, and the First World War* (Montreal: McGill-Queen's University Press, 2009); Emma Hanna, *The Great War on the Small Screen* (Edinburgh: Edinburgh University Press, 2009); and Harry Patch is quoted from John Nichols, "Of War, Peace and the Distant Memory of a Christmas Truce," *Nation,* December 24, 2009, www.thenation.com/blog/war-peace-and-distant-memory-christmas-truce#. Randall Stevenson, *Literature and the Great War 1914–1918* (Oxford: Oxford University Press, 2013).

8. Jasper Copping, "Historians Complain Government's WWI Commemoration

Focuses on British Defeats," *Daily Telegraph,* May 5, 2013, www.telegraph.co.uk /history/britain-at-war/10037507/Historians-complain-Governments-WW1 -commemoration-focuses-on-British-defeats.html.

9. For Slavdom and Germandom, see Gilbert, *The First World War,* 8–9; Annika Mombauer, *The Origins of the First World War* (London: Longman, 2002); Hew Strachan, *The Outbreak of the First World War* (New York: Oxford University Press, 2004); David Fromkin, *Europe's Last Summer* (New York: Alfred A. Knopf, 2004); Mark Hewitson, *Germany and the Causes of the First World War* (New York: Berg, 2004); William Mulligan, *The Origins of the First World War* (Cambridge: Cambridge University Press, 2010); Ian F. W. Beckett, *The Making of the First World War* (New Haven, CT: Yale University Press, 2012); and Christopher Clark, *The Sleepwalkers* (New York: HarperCollins, 2013).

10. One popular British bestseller of the 1930s—Dennis Wheatley's *The Devil Rides Out*—offered a cogent case for Russia's guilt in inciting the war (London: Mandarin, 1934). For a modern analysis of Russia's role, see Sean McMeekin, *The Russian Origins of the First World War* (Cambridge, MA: Belknap Press / Harvard University Press, 2011).

11. Fritz Fischer, *Germany's Aims in the First World War* (New York: Norton, 1967).

12. Newell Dwight Hillis, *The Blot on the Kaiser's 'Scutcheon* (New York: Fleming H. Revell, 1918), 57–58; and compare Newell Dwight Hillis, *The Atrocities of Germany* (New York: Liberty Loan Committee, 1917).

13. "He was found transfixed" is from Arthur Ponsonby, *Falsehood in War-Time: Propaganda Lies of the First World War* (London: George Allen and Unwin, 1928); Michael Thomas Isenberg, *War on Film* (Madison, NJ: Fairleigh Dickinson University Press, 1981); Peter Buitenhuis, *The Great War of Words* (Vancouver: University of British Columbia Press, 1987); and Paul Fussell, *The Great War and Modern Memory* (New York: Oxford University Press, 1975), 116.

14. Annette Becker, *Oubliés de la Grande Guerre* (Paris: Noêsis, 1998); John Horne and Alan Kramer, *German Atrocities, 1914* (New Haven, CT: Yale University Press, 2001); Larry Zuckerman, *The Rape of Belgium* (New York: New York University Press, 2004); and Jeff Lipkes, *Rehearsals* (Louvain, Belgium: Louvain University Press, 2007).

15. Matthew Stibbe, ed., *Captivity, Forced Labour, and Forced Migration in Europe During the First World War* (New York: Routledge, 2009); and Annette Becker, *Les Cicatrices Rouges* (Paris: Fayard, 2010).

16. Vejas Gabriel Liulevicius, *War Land on the Eastern Front* (Cambridge: Cambridge University Press, 2000); and for the German exploitation of occupied Romania, see Lisa Mayerhofer, *Zwischen Freund und Feind* (Munich: Martin Meidenbauer, 2010).

17. For expectations of the war, see Niall Ferguson, *The Pity of War* (New York: Basic Books, 1999). Charles Emmerson, *1913* (New York: PublicAffairs, 2013); Margaret MacMillan, *The War That Ended Peace* (London: Profile, 2013).

18. For the experts who really did expect a massive and prolonged confrontation, see Manfred Franz Boemeke and Roger Chickering, eds., *Anticipating Total War* (Cambridge: Cambridge University Press, 1999); and Holger Afflerbach and David Stevenson, eds., *An Improbable War?* (New York: Berghahn Books, 2007).

19. Richard C. Hall, *The Balkan Wars, 1912–1913* (New York: Routledge, 2000). For the weeks leading up to the outbreak of war, see Sean McMeekin, *July 1914* (London: Icon, 2013). Nigel Jones, *Peace and War* (London: Head of Zeus, 2014).

20. Herwig, *The Marne, 1914.*

21. "Captain Cook," *Blackadder Goes Forth,* series 4, episode 1, directed by Richard Boden, aired September 28, 1989, BBC One.

22. Lyn Macdonald, *1915: The Death of Innocence* (London: Penguin, 1997); Winston Groom, *A Storm in Flanders* (New York: Atlantic Monthly Press, 2002); Robin Neillands, *The Death of Glory* (London: John Murray, 2007); and Ross Wilson, *Landscapes of the Western Front* (London: Routledge, 2011).

23. Olivier Lepick, *La Grande Guerre chimique 1914–1918* (Paris: Presses Universitaires de France, 1998); Albert Palazzo, *Seeking Victory on the Western Front* (Lincoln: University of Nebraska, 2000). Mark Adkin, *The Western Front Companion* (London: Aurum, 2013).

24. "It wasn't a case" is from Christopher Hawtree, "Harry Patch," *Guardian,* July 25, 2009, www.theguardian.com/world/2009/jul/25/harry-patch-obituary; the French Jesuit (Paul Dubrulle) is quoted in Alistair Horne, *The Price of Glory* (London: St. Martin's Press, 1963), 177; Henry Allingham is quoted from Henry Allingham, "This Much I Know," *Guardian Observer,* November 8, 2008, www .theguardian.com/lifeandstyle/2008/nov/09/henry-allingham-war-veteran; and for animals in the war, see Richard van Emden, *Tommy's Ark* (London: Bloomsbury, 2011).

25. Harry Patch and Richard van Emden, *The Last Fighting Tommy* (London: Bloomsbury, 2007); "The smell of a half-million unbathed men" is from Herwig, *The Marne, 1914,* 158; Rudolf Binding, *A Fatalist at War* (Boston: Houghton Mifflin, 1929), 65; and the observer at Verdun is quoted from Horne, *The Price of Glory,* 175.

26. Harry Patch is quoted from "From Memory to History," *Economist,* December 17, 2009, www.economist.com/node/15108655; and "the torture and the fatigue" is quoted in Martin Gilbert, *The Somme* (London: John Murray, 2006), 42.

27. Malcolm Brown and Shirley Seaton, *Christmas Truce* (London: Macmillan, 1994); Richard van Emden, *Meeting the Enemy* (London: Bloomsbury, 2013).

28. Peter Hart, *The Somme* (New York: Pegasus, 2008), 421; and for the deteriorating situation of prisoners of war, see Heather Jones, *Violence Against Prisoners of War in the First World War* (New York: Cambridge University Press, 2011).

29. For the Artois attack, see Horne, *The Price of Glory,* 25.

30. John Terraine, *White Heat* (London: Sidgwick and Jackson, 1982); Gordon Corrigan, *Mud, Blood, and Poppycock* (London: Cassell, 2003); and Michel Goya, *La Chair et l'Acier* (Paris: Tallandier, 2004).

31. Norman Stone, *The Eastern Front: 1914–1917* (London: Weidenfeld and Nicolson, 1974).

32. "The Stalingrad of World War I" is from Graydon A. Tunstall, *Blood on the Snow* (Lawrence: University Press of Kansas, 2010), 212; and Timothy C. Dowling, *The Brusilov Offensive* (Bloomington: Indiana University Press, 2008). Hans Magenschab, *Der Große Krieg* (Innsbruck, Austria: Tyrolia, 2013). The classic account of Austria-Hungary's role in the war is Manfried Rauchensteiner, *Der Tod des Doppeladlers* (Vienna: Verlag Styria, 1993).

33. Isabel V. Hull, *Absolute Destruction* (Cambridge: Cambridge University Press, 2005); Alan Kramer, *Dynamic of Destruction* (Oxford: Oxford University Press, 2007); Michael Perraudin and Jürgen Zimmerer, eds., *German Colonialism and National Identity* (London: Taylor and Francis, 2009); and for U.S. parallels, see James R. Arnold, *The Moro War* (New York: Bloomsbury Press, 2011).

34. Kramer, *Dynamic of Destruction,* 132–44; for the linkage between colonial struggles and later anti-Semitism, see Christian S. Davis, *Colonialism, Antisemitism, and Germans of Jewish Descent in Imperial Germany* (Ann Arbor: University of Michigan Press, 2011); and Volker Langbehn and Mohammad Salama, eds., *German Colonialism* (New York: Columbia University Press, 2011).

35. For the "competition" remark, see *Report of the International Commission to Inquire into the Causes and Conduct of the Balkan Wars* (Washington, DC: Carnegie Endowment for International Peace, 1914), 16; Hall, *The Balkan Wars, 1912–1913;* and Andrej Mitrović, *Serbia's Great War, 1914–1918* (London: Hurst, 2007).

36. Roger Chickering and Stig Förster, eds., *Great War, Total War* (Cambridge: Cambridge University Press, 2000).

37. Horne, *The Price of Glory,* 1; Ian Ousby, *The Road to Verdun* (New York: Doubleday, 2002); Robert T. Foley, *German Strategy and the Path to Verdun* (Cambridge: Cambridge University Press, 2005); and Matti Münch, *Verdun* (Munich: Martin Meidenbauer, 2006).

38. Robin Prior and Trevor Wilson, *The Somme* (New Haven, CT: Yale University Press, 2005); Christopher Duffy, *Through German Eyes* (London: Phoenix Press, 2007); Hart, *The Somme;* and William Philpott, *Three Armies on the Somme* (New York: Knopf, 2010).

39. Ernst Jünger, *Storm of Steel* (London: Penguin Classics, 2004), 91–95.

40. "Somme. The whole history" is quoted from Philipp Witkop, ed., *German Students' War Letters* (Philadelphia: Pine Street Books, 2002), 322; and Binding is quoted from Jay W. Baird, *Hitler's War Poets* (Cambridge: Cambridge University Press, 2008), 46.

41. The passage is from J. R. R. Tolkien, *The Two Towers* (London: George Allen and Unwin, 1954); and Martin Gilbert, "What Tolkien Taught Me About the Battle of the Somme," *The Cutting Edge,* August 25, 2008, www.thecuttingedgenews.com /index.php?article=716&pageid=23&pagename=Arts.

42. Kramer, *Dynamic of Destruction,* 152–55, places much of the blame for the German famine on decisions taken by German authorities themselves. Madeleine Zabriskie Doty, *Short Rations* (New York: Century, 1917); C. Paul Vincent, *The Politics of Hunger* (Athens: Ohio University Press, 1985); Jay Winter and Jean-Louis Robert, eds., *Capital Cities at War* (Cambridge: Cambridge University Press, 1997); Belinda Davis, *Home Fires Burning* (Chapel Hill: University of North Carolina Press, 2000); Chickering, *Imperial Germany and the Great War;* Arnd Bauerkämper and Elise Julien, *Durchhalten!* (Göttingen: Vandenhoeck and Ruprecht, 2010); and Gerhard Hirschfeld and Gerd Krumeich, *Deutschland im Ersten Weltkrieg* (Frankfurt am Main, Germany: S. Fischer, 2013).

43. For the practical limitations of the blockade model, see Nicholas A. Lambert, *Planning Armageddon* (Cambridge, MA: Harvard University Press, 2012).

CHAPTER TWO: *God's War*

1. Louis-Ferdinand Céline, *Voyage au Bout de la Nuit* (Brussels: Froissart, 1949), 19, my translation; for the religious aspects of the war, see Michael Snape, "The Great War," in *The Cambridge History of Christianity,* ed. Hugh McLeod, vol. 9, *World Christianities c. 1914 – c. 2000* (Cambridge: Cambridge University Press, 2006), 131–50; Alan Kramer, *Dynamic of Destruction* (Oxford: Oxford University Press, 2007), 175–80, 240–44; and Annette Becker, "Faith, Ideologies, and the 'Cultures

of War,'" in *A Companion to World War I,* ed. John Horne (Malden, MA: Wiley-Blackwell, 2010), 234–47.

2. Theron F. Schlabach and Richard T. Hughes, eds., *Proclaim Peace* (Urbana: University of Illinois Press, 1997); Frances H. Early, *A World Without War* (Syracuse, NY: Syracuse University Press, 1997); Will Ellsworth-Jones, *We Will Not Fight* (London: Aurum Press, 2008); and Adam Hochschild, *To End All Wars* (London: Macmillan, 2011).

3. John F. Pollard, *The Unknown Pope* (London: Geoffrey Chapman, 2000); and Luigi Degli Occhi, *Benedetto XV* (Milan: Casa Editrice R. Caddeo, 1921).

4. "The appalling spectacle" is from Pope Benedict XV, *Ubi Primum,* September 8, 1914; "There is no limit to the measure" is from Pope Benedict XV, *Ad Beatissimi Apostolorum,* November 1, 1914; and the "suicide" reference is from Henry E. G. Rope, *Benedict XV, the Pope of Peace* (London: J. Gifford, 1941), 104–5.

5. Wolfgang Steglich, ed., *Der Friedensappell Papst Benedikts XV. vom 1. August 1917 und die Mittelmächte* (Wiesbaden: Franz Steiner Verlag, 1970).

6. Volker Rolf Berghahn, *Modern Germany* (Cambridge: Cambridge University Press, 1987); and Mary Anne Perkins, *Christendom and European Identity* (New York: Walter de Gruyter, 2004).

7. Michael Burleigh, *Sacred Causes* (New York: HarperPress, 2006); and for Nonconformists, see Alan Wilkinson, *Dissent or Conform?* (London: SCM Press, 1986).

8. For American parallels, see George C. Rable, *God's Almost Chosen Peoples* (Chapel Hill: University of North Carolina Press, 2010).

9. Orlando Figes, *Crimea: The Last Crusade* (London: Allen Lane, 2010).

10. Lydia Mamreov Mountford, "The Kaiser in Jerusalem," *New York Times,* November 27, 1898.

11. *The Cambridge History of Russia,* ed. Dominic Lieven, vol. 2 (New York: Cambridge University Press, 2006), especially the chapter by Gregory L. Freeze, "Russian Orthodoxy."

12. *The Cambridge History of Russia,* ed. Lieven, vol. 2; and Sean McMeekin, *The Russian Origins of the First World War* (Cambridge, MA: Belknap Press / Harvard University Press, 2011). For apocalyptic dreams, see G. T. Zervos, "The Apocalypse of Daniel," in *The Old Testament Pseudepigrapha,* 2 vols., ed. James H. Charlesworth (Garden City, NY: Doubleday, 1983–85), 761–62.

13. "A run on the bank of God" is quoted from Adrian Gregory, *The Last Great War* (Cambridge: Cambridge University Press, 2009), 153. I have drawn repeatedly on Gregory's chapter in this book on "Redemption Through War," 152–86.

14. Arthur F. Winnington-Ingram, *A Day of God* (London: Young Churchman, 1914); Winnington-Ingram is quoted from Becker, "Faith, Ideologies, and the 'Cultures of War,'" 237–38; Burleigh, *Sacred Causes,* 450–51; John A. Moses, "The British and German Churches and the Perception of War, 1908–1914," *War and Society* 5, no. 1 (May 1987): 23–43; and Arlie J. Hoover, *God, Germany, and Britain in the Great War* (New York: Praeger, 1989).

15. Gregory, *The Last Great War,* 168–70; "Intensely silly bishop" is from Adrian Hastings, *A History of English Christianity, 1920–1990,* 3rd ed. (London: SCM, 1991), 45; Diggle is quoted from Albert Marrin, *The Last Crusade* (Durham, NC: Duke University Press, 1974), 141; "Predestined instruments" is quoted from Snape, "The Great War," 136–37; Charles E. Bailey, "The British Protestant Theologians in the First World War," *Harvard Theological Review* 77 (1984): 195–221; and for holy war

ideas in Britain, see Keith Robbins, *England, Ireland, Scotland, Wales* (Oxford: Oxford University Press, 2008), 96–150.

16. David Lloyd George, *The Great Crusade* (New York: George H. Doran, 1918), 23; and Stefan Goebel, *The Great War and Medieval Memory* (Cambridge: Cambridge University Press, 2007).

17. Randall Davidson's sermon is quoted from Michael George and Christine George, *Dover and Folkestone During the Great War* (Havertown, PA: Casemate Publishers, 2009), 73–74; William Temple, *Christianity and War* (Oxford: Oxford University Press, 1914), 3; and for *John Bull,* see Gregory, *The Last Great War,* 183.

18. Hew Strachan, *The Outbreak of the First World War* (New York: Oxford University Press, 2004).

19. Jeffrey Verhey, *The Spirit of 1914* (Cambridge: Cambridge University Press, 2000).

20. "The spirit of God" is quoted from Wilhelm Pressel, *Die Kriegspredigt 1914–1918 in der Evangelischen Kirche Deutschlands* (Göttingen: Vandenhoeck and Ruprecht, 1967), 17, my translation; and for Freybe, see Hoover, *God, Germany, and Britain in the Great War,* 11. The boast about national unity also draws on a famous Pauline passage in Gal. 3:28.

21. Quoted in Jay W. Baird, *Hitler's War Poets* (Cambridge: Cambridge University Press, 2008), 41.

22. Pressel, *Die Kriegspredigt 1914–1918,* 110; Karl Hammer, *Deutsche Kriegstheologie, 1870–1918* (Munich: Kösel-Verlag, 1971); Gerhard Besier, *Die Protestantischen Kirchen Europas im Ersten Weltkrieg* (Göttingen: Vandenhoeck and Ruprecht, 1984); and Matthew Stibbe, *German Anglophobia and the Great War, 1914–1918* (Cambridge: Cambridge University Press, 2006).

23. J. P. Bang, *Hurrah and Hallelujah* (London: Hodder and Stoughton, 1916); compare William Archer, ed., *Gems [sic] of German Thought* (New York: Doubleday, Page, 1917); Dietrich Vorwerk, *Hurra und Halleluja* (Schwerin in Mecklenburg, Germany: F. Bahn, 1914); Hammer, *Deutsche Kriegstheologie;* John A. Moses, "Justifying War as the Will of God," *Colloquium* 31, no. 1 (1999): 17; and John A. Moses, "Bonhoeffer's Germany," in *The Cambridge Companion to Dietrich Bonhoeffer,* ed. John W. de Gruchy (Cambridge: Cambridge University Press, 1999), 7–9.

24. For the "Sword Blessing," see Franz Koehler, *Der Weltkrieg im Lichte der Deutsch-Protestantischen Kriegspredigt* (Tübingen: J. C. B. Mohr / Paul Siebeck, 1915), 54–55; Pressel, *Die Kriegspredigt 1914–1918,* 172–74; Rendtorff is quoted from Frank J. Gordon, "Liberal German Churchmen and the First World War," *German Studies Review* 4, no. 1 (February 1981): 40; Wilhelm Laible, ed., *Deutsche Theologen über den Krieg* (Leipzig, Germany: Dörffling and Franke, 1915); and Karl Hönn, *Der Kampf des Deutschen Geistes im Weltkrieg* (Gotha, Germany: F. A. Perthes, 1915).

25. For the Austro-Hungarian Empire, see Wilhelm Achleitner, *Gott im Krieg* (Vienna: Böhlau, 1997); for Belgium, see Fernand Mayence, *Cardinal Mercier's Story* (New York: George H. Doran, 1920); and Ilse Meseberg-Haubold, *Der Widerstand Kardinal Merciers Gegen die Deutsche Besetzung Belgiens, 1914–1918* (Frankfurt am Main: Peter Lang, 1982).

26. Engelbert Krebs, "On the Meaning of Sacrifice" (Vom Opfersinn) (1914–1915), http://germanhistorydocs.ghi-dc.org/sub_document.cfm?document_id=950; for German Catholics and the war, see Heinrich Missala, *Gott mit Uns* (Munich: Kösel-Verlag, 1968); Johann Klier, *Von der Kriegspredigt zum Friedensappell* (Munich: Kommissionsverlag UNI-Druck, 1991); for Catholic controversialists, see

Georg Pfeilschifter and Goetz Briefs, eds., *German Culture, Catholicism, and the World War* (St. Paul, MN: Wanderer Printing, 1916); and Alfred Baudrillart, *The German War and Catholicism* (Paris: Bloud and Gay, 1915).

27. Katrin Keller and Hans-Dieter Schmid, eds., *Vom Kult zur Kulisse* (Leipzig, Germany: Leipziger Universitätsverlag, 1995); and Gunther Mai, *Das Kyffhäuser-Denkmal 1896–1996* (Cologne: Böhlau, 1997).

28. Adolf von Harnack, *History of Dogma*, 7 vols. (London: Williams and Norgate, 1896–1899); and G. Wayne Glick, *The Reality of Christianity* (New York: Harper, 1967).

29. "Aufruf Deutscher Kirchenmänner und Professoren: An die Evangelischen Christen im Ausland," in Gerhard Besier, *Die Protestantischen Kirchen Europas im Ersten Weltkrieg* (Göttingen: Vandenhoeck and Ruprecht, 1984), 40–45; and for an Allied riposte, see *To the Christian Scholars of Europe and America*, 4th impression (London: Humphrey Milford, Oxford University Press, 1919).

30. The document is translated as the "Manifesto of the Ninety-Three German Intellectuals to the Civilized World," www.fransamaltingvongeusau.com/documents/dl1/h1/1.1.3.pdf; Jürgen von Ungern-Sternberg and Wolfgang von Ungern-Sternberg, *Der Aufruf "An die Kulturwelt!"* (Stuttgart: Steiner, 1996); Johanna Klatt and Robert Lorenz, eds., *Manifeste* (Bielefeld, Germany: Transcript, 2011); and Wolfgang J. Mommsen and Elisabeth Müller-Luckner, eds., *Kultur und Krieg* (Munich: R. Oldenbourg Verlag, 1996).

31. Adolf von Harnack, *Militia Christi* (Darmstadt, Germany: Wissenschaftliche Buchgesellschaft, 1963); and Adolf von Harnack, *Aus der Friedens- und Kriegsarbeit* (Giessen, Germany: Alfred Töpelmann, 1916), 279–361.

32. Julian Jenkins, "War Theology, 1914 and Germany's Sonderweg," *Journal of Religious History* 15 (1989): 292–310. The Kaiser Wilhelm Foundation survives today with undimmed glory as the Max Planck Society.

33. For Troeltsch, see A. Rasmusson, "Church and Nation-State," *Nederduitse Gereformeerde Teologiese Tydskrif* 46 (2005): 511–24; and for liberal German anger at England in the early stages of the war, see Gordon, "Liberal German Churchmen and the First World War," 39–62.

34. Arlie J. Hoover, *The Gospel of Nationalism* (Stuttgart: Franz Steiner Verlag, 1986).

35. Marcel Stoetzler, *The State, the Nation, and the Jews* (Lincoln: University of Nebraska Press, 2008).

36. Gogarten is quoted from Klaus Vondung, *The Apocalypse in Germany*, trans. Stephen D. Ricks (Columbia: University of Missouri Press, 2000), 155; William R. Hutchison and Hartmut Lehmann, eds., *Many Are Chosen* (Minneapolis: Fortress Press, 1994); for Seeberg, see Günter Brakelmann, *Protestantische Kriegstheologie im Ersten Weltkrieg* (Bielefeld, Germany: Luther-Verlag, 1974); and Thomas Kaufmann, "Die Harnacks und die Seebergs," in *Nationalprotestantische Mentalitäten in Deutschland 1870–1970*, eds. Manfred Gailus and Hartmut Lehmann (Göttingen: Vandenhoeck and Ruprecht, 2005), 165–222.

37. Troeltsch is quoted from Rasmusson, "Church and Nation-State," 512; and George L. Mosse, *The Crisis of German Ideology* (New York: Grosset and Dunlap, 1964).

38. Moses, "Bonhoeffer's Germany"; and John A. Moses, "State, War, Revolution, and the German Evangelical Church, 1914–18," *Journal of Religious History* 17, no. 1 (1992): 47–59.

39. "The All-Highest Lord" is from Pressel, *Die Kriegspredigt 1914–1918*, 46, 99–106, my

translation; for Lehmann, see Bang, *Hurrah and Hallelujah,* 74–98; for Ihmels, see Pressel, *Die Kriegspredigt 1914–1918,* 101; and for the "born hero," see Pressel, *Die Kriegspredigt 1914–1918,* 238–43, my translation.

CHAPTER THREE: *Witnesses for Christ*

1. Michael Burleigh, *Earthly Powers* (New York: HarperCollins, 2005).
2. Kay Chadwick, ed., *Catholicism, Politics, and Society in Twentieth-Century France* (Liverpool: Liverpool University Press, 2000); and Frederick Brown, *For the Soul of France* (New York: Alfred A. Knopf, 2010).
3. For Protestant support for the war, see Laurent Gambarotto, *Foi et Patrie* (Geneva: Labor et Fides, 1996); and for Jews, see Chapter 9.
4. Jacques Fontana, *Les Catholiques Français Pendant la Grande Guerre* (Paris: Éditions du Cerf, 1990); and Annette Becker, *War and Faith* (New York: Berg, 1998).
5. Becker, *War and Faith,* 77–79.
6. Péguy's original verses can be found at Les Lettres Volées, www.lettresvolees.fr /degaulle/peguy.html. The translation here is adapted from Alan Kramer, *Dynamic of Destruction* (Oxford: Oxford University Press, 2007).
7. Yann Harlaut, *L'Ange au Sourire de Reims* (Langres, France: D. Guéniot, 2008).
8. Raymond A. Jonas, *The Tragic Tale of Claire Ferchaud and the Great War* (Berkeley: University of California Press, 2005); and Claudia Schlager, "Le Drapeau National au Sacré Coeur," in *Alliierte im Himmel,* ed. Gottfried Korff (Tübingen: Tübinger Vereinigung für Volkskunde, 2006), 201–22.
9. Jonas, *The Tragic Tale of Claire Ferchaud;* and for Saint Martin, see Christopher G. Flood, "Poetry, Drama, Diplomacy," *Journal of European Studies* 18, no. 1 (March 1988): 37–61.
10. David M. Kennedy, *Over Here* (New York: Oxford University Press, 1980); Byron Farwell, *Over There* (New York: Norton, 1999); and Jennifer D. Keene, *Doughboys, the Great War, and the Remaking of America* (Baltimore, MD: Johns Hopkins University Press, 2001).
11. Ray Hamilton Abrams, *Preachers Present Arms* (New York: Round Table Press, 1933); compare Patrick J. Quinn, *The Conning of America* (Amsterdam: Rodopi, 2001); Sydney E. Ahlstrom, *A Religious History of the American People,* updated edition (New Haven, CT: Yale University Press, 2004), 883–90; Alan Axelrod, *Selling the Great War* (New York: Palgrave Macmillan, 2009); Celia Malone Kingsbury, *For Home and Country* (Lincoln: University of Nebraska, 2010); and for English parallels to Abrams's book, see Irene Cooper Willis, *England's Holy War* (New York: A. A. Knopf, 1928). Richard Gamble, "Between God and Caesar," in Stephen J. Stein, ed., *The Cambridge History of Religions in America* (New York: Cambridge University Press, 2012) vol. ii, 634–52.
12. Henry Churchill King is quoted from George Bedborough, *Arms and the Clergy, 1914–1918* (St. Paul, MN: Pioneer Press, 1934), 104; Tweedy is from Elias Hershey Sneath, ed., *Religion and the War* (New Haven, CT: Yale University Press, 1918), 82; and George F. Pentecost, *Fighting for Faith* (New York: George H. Doran, 1918).
13. Quotes are from Abrams, *Preachers Present Arms,* 67–68.
14. For progressive attitudes, see Richard M. Gamble, *The War for Righteousness* (Wilmington, DE: ISI Books, 2003); "a crusade to make" is from Lyman Abbott, *The Twentieth Century Crusade* (New York: Macmillan, 1918), epigraph; and

compare Dale Edward Soden, *The Reverend Mark Matthews* (Seattle: University of Washington Press, 2001).

15. Michael Thomas Isenberg, *War on Film* (Madison, NJ: Fairleigh Dickinson University Press, 1981); and for propaganda themes in American music, see Glenn Watkins, *Proof Through the Night* (Berkeley: University of California Press, 2003).

16. For the process of dehumanization, see Kramer, *Dynamic of Destruction;* and Kingsbury, *For Home and Country*.

17. Pressel, *Die Kriegspredigt 1914–1918,* 127–34; and "Can God find pleasure" is from J. P. Bang, *Hurrah and Hallelujah* (London: Hodder and Stoughton, 1916), 118.

18. "It is England" is from Bang, *Hurrah and Hallelujah,* 47; Tolzien is quoted from Klaus Vondung, *The Apocalypse in Germany,* trans. Stephen D. Ricks (Columbia: University of Missouri Press, 2000), 270; and for Wilhelm, see Matthew Stibbe, *German Anglophobia and the Great War, 1914–1918* (Cambridge: Cambridge University Press, 2006), 175–76.

19. Taft is quoted from Sneath, ed., *Religion and the War,* 23; for England as Mephistopheles, see Arlie J. Hoover, *God, Germany, and Britain in the Great War* (New York: Praeger, 1989), 55–56; Abrams, *Preachers Present Arms,* 55–56; "a struggle between two gospels" is from A. F. Winnington-Ingram, *A Day of God* (London: Wells, Gardner, Darton, 1914), 30; and Fred Bridgham, "Bernhardi and the Ideas of 1914" in *The First World War as a Clash of Cultures,* ed. Fred Bridgham (Woodbridge, UK: Boydell and Brewer, 2006), 187–88.

20. "In utter despair" is quoted from Newell Dwight Hillis, *The Blot on the Kaiser's 'Scutcheon* (New York: Fleming H. Revell, 1918), 57, see 59 for the sterilization passage.

21. Pressel, *Die Kriegspredigt 1914–1918,* 45–46.

22. Adrian Gregory, *The Last Great War* (Cambridge: Cambridge University Press, 2009), 152–86; and Pressel, *Die Kriegspredigt 1914–1918,* 163–68, 233–38.

23. Lloyd George is quoted from *World War I,* eds. Spencer C. Tucker and Priscilla Mary Roberts (Santa Barbara, CA: ABC-CLIO, 2005), 2252.

24. For the carol, see Becker, *War and Faith,* 39; Peter Harrington, "Religious and Spiritual Themes in British Academic Art During the Great War," *First World War Studies* 2, no. 2 (2011): 145–64; Gregory, *The Last Great War,* 156–57; and for the religious content of the Russian war effort, see Karen Petrone, *The Great War in Russian Memory* (Bloomington: Indiana University Press, 2011), 31–74, see 36 for the grave inscriptions.

25. Lyman Abbott, "Lenten Lessons," *Outlook* (April 9, 1919): 598–99; Wright is quoted from Gamble, *War for Righteousness,* 176; Francke is quoted from Sherwood Eddy, *With Our Soldiers in France* (New York: Association Press, 1917), 163–64; and for the Good Friday concept, see Becker, *War and Faith*.

26. René Gaëll, *Les Soutanes sous la Mitraille* (Paris: H. Gautier, 1915), translated as *Priests in the Firing Line,* trans. H. Hamilton Gibbs (New York: Longmans, Green, 1916); compare Maurice Barrès, *Les Diverses Familles Spirituelles de la France* (Paris: Émile Paul Frères, 1917), 25–30; and for Catholic sacrificial ideas in French culture, see Ivan Strenski, *Contesting Sacrifice* (Chicago: University of Chicago Press, 2002).

27. Paul Claudel, *La Nuit de Noël de 1914* (Paris: A l'Art Catholique, 1915), my translation.

28. Tim Pat Coogan, *1916: The Easter Rising* (London: Cassell, 2001); Joost Augusteijn, *Patrick Pearse* (New York: Palgrave Macmillan, 2010); and Fearghal McGarry, *The Rising* (Oxford: Oxford University Press, 2010).

29. Diana Souhami, *Edith Cavell* (London: Quercus, 2010); and Alan G.V. Simmonds, *Britain and World War One* (London: Routledge, 2012).

30. "From German blood" is from Walter Flex, "Das Grosse Abendmahl," in *Vom Grossen Abendmahl* (Munich: Beck, 1918), 5–7, my translation; "The sacrifice of the best" is from George L. Mosse, *Masses and Man* (Detroit: Wayne State University Press, 1987), 265; "To fight, to die" is from George L. Mosse, *Fallen Soldiers* (Oxford: Oxford University Press, 1991), 78; and for the German clergy, see Roger Chickering, *The Great War and Urban Life in Germany* (New York: Cambridge University Press, 2007), 487.

31. Mark Thompson, *The White War* (London: Faber and Faber, 2008), 148.

32. John C. Procter, *The War and Sacrificial Death* (London: World Evangelical Alliance, 1917).

CHAPTER FOUR: *The Ways of God*

1. Max Egremont, *Siegfried Sassoon* (New York: Farrar, Straus, and Giroux, 2006).

2. Quoted by Martin Gilbert, *The Somme* (London: John Murray, 2006), 247.

3. D. S. Cairns, *The Army and Religion* (New York: Association Press, 1920).

4. Hugh McLeod, *Secularisation in Western Europe, 1848–1914* (New York: St. Martin's Press, 2000); and Geoffrey R. Searle, *A New England?* (Oxford: Clarendon Press, 2004).

5. Mark D. Steinberg and Heather J. Coleman, eds., *Sacred Stories* (Bloomington: Indiana University Press, 2007); Jennifer Hedda, *His Kingdom Come* (DeKalb: Northern Illinois University Press, 2008); Wayne Dowler, *Russia in 1913* (DeKalb: Northern Illinois University Press, 2010); and Irina Paert, *Spiritual Elders* (DeKalb: Northern Illinois University Press, 2010).

6. Michael Snape, *God and the British Soldier* (New York: Routledge, 2005), 19–58; Annette Becker, *War and Faith* (New York: Berg, 1998); Adrian Gregory, *The Last Great War* (Cambridge: Cambridge University Press, 2009); the phrase "diffusive Christianity" was coined by Jeffrey Cox in his *The English Churches in a Secular Society* (New York: Oxford University Press, 1982); and Roberto Morozzo Della Rocca, "La Religiosità del Soldato Italiano in Guerra," in *Storia Vissuta del Popolo Cristiano,* ed. J. Delumeau (Turin: Società Editrice Internazionale, 1985), 773–808.

7. Snape, *God and the British Soldier,* 156.

8. Chaplains' memoirs represent a vast subgenre of Great War writing. From many examples, see for instance Frederick B. MacNutt, ed., *The Church in the Furnace* (London: Macmillan, 1917); Celestine N. Bittle, *Soldiering for Cross and Flag* (New York: Bruce, 1929); for scholarly studies, see Roberto Morozzo Della Rocca, *La Fede e la Guerra* (Rome: Ed. Studium, 1980); Nadine-Josette Chaline, ed., *Chrétiens dans la Première Guerre Mondiale* (Paris: Éditions du Cerf, 1993); Duff Crerar, *Padres in No Man's Land* (Montreal: McGill-Queen's University Press, 1995); Richard Budd, *Serving Two Masters* (Lincoln: University of Nebraska Press, 2002); Linda Parker, *The Whole Armour of God* (Solihull, UK: Helion, 2009); Edward Madigan, *Faith Under Fire* (London: Palgrave Macmillan, 2011); and Michael Snape and Edward Madigan, eds., *The Clergy in Khaki* (London: Ashgate, 2013). Bob Holman, *Woodbine Willie* (London: Lion Books, 2013).

9. H. G. Wells, *Mr. Britling Sees It Through* (New York: MacMillan, 1916).

10. Snape, *God and the British Soldier;* John Fuller, *Troop Morale and Popular Culture in the British and Dominion Armies, 1914–1918* (Oxford: Oxford University Press, 1991); Stéphane Audoin-Rouzeau, *Men at War, 1914–1918* (Providence, RI: Berg, 1992); and Richard Schweitzer, *The Cross and the Trenches* (Westport, CT: Praeger, 2003).

11. For tastes in scripture, see Schweitzer, *The Cross and the Trenches,* 32–34; and Snape, *God and the British Soldier,* 235–36.

12. Jonathan H. Ebel, *Faith in the Fight* (Princeton, NJ: Princeton University Press, 2010).

13. Paul Fussell, *The Great War and Modern Memory* (New York: Oxford University Press, 1975), 137–44.

14. "It is like" is from Wilfred Owen, *The Collected Poems of Wilfred Owen,* ed. Cecil Day-Lewis (London: New Directions Publishing, 1965), 160.

15. "Private Harry Patch," *Daily Telegraph,* July 25, 2009, www.telegraph.co.uk/news /obituaries/military-obituaries/army-obituaries/5907316/Private-Harry-Patch .html.

16. Becker, *War and Faith.*

17. Quoted in Fussell, *The Great War and Modern Memory,* 119; Nicholas Saunders, "Crucifix, Calvary, and Cross," *World Archaeology* 35 (2003): 7–21; and Snape, *God and the British Soldier,* 42–45.

18. Teilhard is quoted from Becker, *War and Faith,* 23; for "Christ in Flanders," see http://beck.library.emory.edu/greatwar/poetry/eaton/Eaton040/; and Alistair Horne, *The Price of Glory* (New York: St Martin's Press, 1963), 185.

19. K. J. Gilchrist, *A Morning After War* (New York: Peter Lang, 2005).

20. Walter Flex, *Der Wanderer Zwischen Beiden Welten* (Munich: Beck, 1916).

21. Ebel, *Faith in the Fight;* Fussell, *The Great War and Modern Memory,* 115; and see Alan Seeger, "Maktoob," http://theotherpages.org/poems/books/seeger/seeger6 .html.

22. Hanns Bächtold-Stäubli, *Deutscher Soldatenbrauch und Soldatenglaube* (Strasbourg: K. J. Trübner, 1917); compare Ralph Winkle, "Connaître au Fond l'Âme du Soldat," in *Alliierte im Himmel,* ed. Gottfried Korff (Tübingen: Tübinger Vereinigung für Volkskunde, 2006), 349–70; for the continuing interchange between the front and the soldiers' rural homes, see Benjamin Ziemann, *War Experiences in Rural Germany, 1914–1923,* trans. Alex Skinner (New York: Berg, 2007); and for French frontline superstitions, see Lucien Roure, *Au Pays de l'Occultisme,* 2nd ed. (Paris: G. Beauchesne, 1925).

23. Bächtold-Stäubli, *Deutscher Soldatenbrauch und Soldatenglaube;* and Bruno Grabinski, *Das Übersinnliche im Weltkriege* (Hildesheim, Germany: F. Borgmeyer, 1917).

24. Fussell, *The Great War and Modern Memory,* 131–35; and Tim Cook, "Black-Hearted Traitors, Crucified Martyrs, and the Leaning Virgin," in *Finding Common Ground,* eds. Jennifer D. Keene and Michael S. Neiberg (Leiden, The Netherlands: Brill, 2011), 21–42.

25. "No frontline soldier" is from Fussell, *The Great War and Modern Memory,* 124; "A thousand shall fall" is from Ps. 91:7–11; and Snape, *God and the British Soldier,* 33–38.

26. For the soldier burying the dead, see Philipp Witkop, ed., *German Students' War Letters* (Philadelphia: Pine Street Books, 2002), 42; Becker, *War and Faith;* and Karen Petrone, *The Great War in Russian Memory* (Bloomington: Indiana University Press, 2011), 34–35.

27. Bächtold-Stäubli, *Deutscher Soldatenbrauch und Soldatenglaube.*

28. Neil Tweedie, "I've Never Got Over It," *Daily Telegraph,* July 12, 2007, www .telegraph.co.uk/news/features/3633344/Ive-never-got-over-it.html; and Harry Patch and Richard van Emden, *The Last Fighting Tommy* (London: Bloomsbury, 2007), 94.

29. Arthur E. Copping, *Souls in Khaki* (New York: G. H. Doran, 1917).

30. Vera Brittain, *Testament of Youth* (New York: Macmillan, 1933), 414–17.

31. Leonard V. Smith, *The Embattled Self* (Ithaca, NY: Cornell University Press, 2007), 72–75.

32. "Superstitions of the Fighting Man," in *War Budget,* 1917, www.greatwardifferent .com/Great_War/Superstitions/Superstitions_01.htm.

33. William Harvey Leathem, *The Comrade in White* (New York: Fleming H. Revell, 1916); Peter Harrington, "Religious and Spiritual Themes in British Academic Art During the Great War," *First World War Studies* 2, no. 2 (2011): 145–64; and for a poetic treatment, see Robert Haven Schauffler, "The White Comrade," www .bartleby.com/266/121.html.

34. Hereward Carrington, *Psychical Phenomena and the War* (New York: Dodd, Mead, 1918), 151–52; E. M. Martin, *Dreams in War Time* (Stratford-upon-Avon, UK: Shakespeare Head, 1915); and Rosa Stuart, *Dreams and Visions of the War* (London: C. Arthur Pearson, 1917).

35. Snape, *God and the British Soldier,* 40.

36. Petrone, *The Great War in Russian Memory,* 34–53; and Sofia Fedorchenko, *Ivan Speaks* (Boston: Houghton Mifflin, 1919).

37. Roger Chickering, *The Great War and Urban Life in Germany: Freiburg 1914–1918* (New York: Cambridge University Press, 2007), 486.

38. Susanne Brandt, "Nagelfiguren," in *Matters of Conflict,* ed. Nicholas J. Saunders (New York: Routledge, 2004), 62–67; and for the "nail epidemic," see Gerhard Schneider, "Der Schöne Gedanke ins Groteske Verkehrt?" in *Alliierte im Himmel,* ed. Gottfried Korff, 311–47.

39. "Is German *Kultur*" is from Becker, *War and Faith,* 102; for a sampling of the prophetic literature, see Ralph Shirley, *Prophecies and Omens of the Great War* (London: William Rider and Son, 1914); Sepharial, *The Great Devastation* (London: Foulsham, 1914); W. F. T. Salt, *The Great War—In the Divine Light of Prophecy: Is It Armageddon?* (Bristol, UK: F. Walker, 1915); Friedrich Zurbonsen, *Die Prophezeiungen zum Weltkrieg 1914–1915* (Cologne: Bachem, 1915); T. Troward, *The Years 1914 to 1923 in Bible Prophecy* (London: Stead, Danby, 1915); Willis F. Jordan, *The European War from a Bible Standpoint* (New York: Charles C. Cook, 1915); Sepharial, *Why the War Will End in 1917* (London: R. Hayes, 1916); Allan Heywood Bright, *The Prophetic Literature of the War* (Liverpool: D. Marples, 1916); R. K. Arnaud, *The New Prophecy* (London: Hodder and Stoughton, 1917); Euston Nurse, *Prophecy and the War* (London: Skeffington, 1918); Euston Nurse, *Palestine and the War* (London: Elliott Skeffington, 1918); Theodore Graebner, *Prophecy and the War* (St. Louis, MO: Concordia Publishing House, 1918); George Harold Lancaster, *Prophecy, the War, and the Near East* (London: Marshall Brothers, 1918); and the whole genre is surveyed, and mocked, in Herbert Thurston, *The War and the Prophets* (London: Burns and Oates, 1915).

40. For the French literature, see J. H. Lavaur, *Comment se Réalise en ce Moment Même la Fin de l'Empire Allemand Annoncée Par Plusieurs Prophéties Célèbres* (Paris: Éditions Pratiques et Documentaires, 1914); R. d'Arman, *Les Prédictions sur la Fin de l'Allemagne* (Paris: Éditions et Librairie, 1915); Georges Stoffler, *La Prophétie de*

Sainte Odile et la Fin de la Guerre (Paris: Dorbon Ainé, 1916); Joanny Bricaud, *La Guerre et les Prophéties Célèbres* (Paris: Bibliothèque Chacornac, 1916); and Adéodat Graffont, *La Guerre Actuelle Célébrée en Vers Antiques* (Paris: H. Daragon, 1918).

41. "The transient conditions" is from Wellesley Tudor Pole, "Thoughts About War" in *Theosophical Outlook* (San Francisco) 3, no. 40 (October 5, 1918): 318; and Snape, *God and the British Soldier*, 38–42.

42. The "British compendium" is Carrington, *Psychical Phenomena and the War;* and Arthur Conan Doyle, *The New Revelation* (New York: George H. Doran, 1918).

43. E. H. Jones, *The Road to En-Dor* (London: John Lane, 1920).

44. Oliver Lodge, *Raymond or Life After Death* (New York: G. H. Doran, 1916).

45. "The chief interest" is from MacNutt, ed., *The Church in the Furnace*, 110; compare Wellesley Tudor Pole, *Private Dowding* (New York: Dodd, Mead, 1919); Frederick W. Kendall, *Gone West* (New York: Alfred Knopf, 1919); Rene Kollar, *Searching for Raymond* (Lanham, MD: Lexington Books, 2000); and Georgina Byrne, *Modern Spiritualism and the Church of England, 1850–1939* (Woodbridge, UK: Boydell Press, 2010).

CHAPTER FIVE: *The War of the End of the World*

1. Rev. 18:2.

2. Alan Kramer, *Dynamic of Destruction* (Oxford: Oxford University Press, 2007), 176, 179; and Catherine Wessinger, ed., *The Oxford Handbook of Millennialism* (New York: Oxford University Press, 2011).

3. Bernard McGinn, John James Collins, and Stephen J. Stein, eds., *The Continuum History of Apocalypticism* (New York: Continuum, 2003).

4. James H. Moorhead, *World Without End* (Bloomington: Indiana University Press, 1999).

5. *The Scofield Study Bible* (New York: Oxford University Press, 2003).

6. Paul Boyer, *When Time Shall Be No More* (Cambridge, MA: Belknap Press / Harvard University Press, 1992), 100–1, see 101 for Torrey; and for "the nations of Europe," see Jonathan Kirsch, *A History of the End of the World* (New York: Harper-Collins, 2007), 203.

7. Acts 2:17; and Grant Wacker, *Heaven Below* (Cambridge, MA: Harvard University Press, 2001).

8. Sydney E. Ahlstrom, *A Religious History of the American People,* updated edition (New Haven, CT: Yale University Press, 2004); and Brian Stanley, *The World Missionary Conference, Edinburgh 1910* (Grand Rapids, MI: William B. Eerdmans, 2009).

9. Billy Sunday is quoted from John F. Piper, Jr., *The American Churches in World War I* (Athens: Ohio University Press, 1985), 11; Carver is quoted from Elias Hershey Sneath, ed., *Religion and the War* (New Haven, CT: Yale University Press, 1918), 84–85; James Martin Gray, *A Text-Book on Prophecy* (New York: Fleming H. Revell, 1918); H. C. Morrison, *The World War in Prophecy* (Louisville, KY: Pentecostal, 1917); and Bernard McGinn, *Antichrist* (San Francisco: HarperSanFrancisco, 1994).

10. Charles Taze Russell, *The Finished Mystery* (Brooklyn, NY: International Bible Students Association, 1918); and Philip Jenkins, "Spy Mad," *Pennsylvania History* 63, no. 2 (1996): 204–31.

11. Klaus Vondung, *The Apocalypse in Germany,* trans. Stephen D. Ricks (Columbia: University of Missouri Press, 2000), 154–68, see 63 and 270–1 for Ganghofer.

12. Rev. 12.

13. Sandra L. Zimdars-Swartz, *Encountering Mary* (Princeton, NJ: Princeton University Press, 1991).

14. Léon Bloy, *Au Seuil de l'Apocalypse 1913–1915* (Paris: Mercure de France, 1916).

15. Vicente Blasco Ibañez, *The Four Horsemen of the Apocalypse* (New York: E. P. Dutton, 1918).

16. Irina Paert, *Spiritual Elders* (DeKalb: Northern Illinois University Press, 2010); and Loren Graham and Jean-Michel Kantor, *Naming Infinity* (Cambridge, MA: Belknap Press / Harvard University Press, 2010).

17. Anna Akhmatova is quoted from *Poems of Akhmatova*, ed. Stanley Kunitz, trans. Stanley Kunitz and Max Hayward (New York: Houghton Mifflin Harcourt, 1997), 59; and for the eclipse, see Wayne Dowler, *Russia in 1913* (DeKalb: Northern Illinois University Press, 2010), 127.

18. Soloviev's story can be found at www.goodcatholicbooks.org/antichrist.html. Soloviev's "Antichrist" was not available in English before 1915. The great English Antichrist novel of these years was Robert H. Benson, *Lord of the World* (New York: Dodd, Mead, 1908).

19. For the serpent poster, see Aaron J. Cohen, *Imagining the Unimaginable* (Lincoln: University of Nebraska Press, 2007), 81–82; and for the film *The Antichrist,* see Hubertus F. Jahn, *Patriotic Culture in Russia During World War I* (Ithaca, NY: Cornell University Press, 1995), 166.

20. Wassily Kandinsky, *Concerning the Spiritual in Art* (1912; repr., New York: Wittenborn, 1947); for the war's relationship to modernism, see Vincent Sherry, *The Great War and the Language of Modernism* (New York: Oxford University Press, 2003); Kramer, *Dynamic of Destruction,* 169–70, 195; Philipp Blom, *The Vertigo Years* (New York: Basic Books, 2008); Michael J. K. Walsh, ed., *London, Modernism, and 1914* (Cambridge: Cambridge University Press, 2010); Pericles Lewis, ed., *The Cambridge Companion to European Modernism* (Cambridge: Cambridge University Press, 2010); Eric M. Reisenauer, "A World in Crisis and Transition," *First World War Studies* 2 (2011): 217–32; and Emilio Gentile, *L'Apocalypse de la Modernité* (Paris: Aubier, 2011). Charles Emmerson, *1913* (New York: PublicAffairs, 2013).

21. Vondung, *The Apocalypse in Germany,* 292–307; Frances Carey, "The Apocalyptic Imagination," in *The Apocalypse and the Shape of Things to Come,* ed. Frances Carey (Toronto: University of Toronto Press, 1999): 297–319; and for Meidner's return to Jewish apocalyptic ideas in the war years, see his "Aschaffenburg Journal" (1918) in Ludwig Meidner, *Septemberschrei* (Berlin: Paul Cassirer, 1920).

22. Andrei Bely, *Petersburg,* trans. Robert Maguire and John E. Malmsted (Bloomington: Indiana University Press, 1979), 68–69; and Mark D. Steinberg, *Petersburg Fin de Siècle* (New Haven, CT: Yale University Press, 2011).

23. Carey, *The Apocalypse and the Shape of Things to Come,* 278–82; Mary Ann Caws, *Manifesto* (Lincoln: University of Nebraska Press, 2001), 277.

24. Jane Ashton Sharp, *Russian Modernism Between East and West* (Cambridge: Cambridge University Press, 2006); and for angels as figures in British modernism, see Suzanne Hobson, *Angels of Modernism* (London: Palgrave Macmillan, 2012).

25. Emanuel E. Garcia, "Scriabin's *Mysterium* and the Birth of Genius," (2007), www.componisten.net/downloads/ScriabinMysterium.pdf; for the Russian context, see Maria Carlson, *No Religion Higher than Truth* (Princeton, NJ: Princeton Uni-

versity Press, 1993); and Bernice Glatzer Rosenthal, ed., *The Occult in Russian and Soviet Culture* (Ithaca, NY: Cornell University Press, 1997).

26. Modris Eksteins, *Rites of Spring* (New York: Bantam Books, 1990); Frederick Burwick and Paul Douglass, eds., *The Crisis in Modernism* (New York: Cambridge University Press, 1992); Vincent Sherry, ed., *The Cambridge Companion to the Literature of the First World War* (New York: Cambridge University Press, 2005); and Blom, *The Vertigo Years*.

27. Philip Jenkins, *Mystics and Messiahs* (New York: Oxford University Press, 2000); Jill Galvan, *The Sympathetic Medium* (Ithaca, NY: Cornell University Press, 2010); and for the French experience, see John Warne Monroe, *Laboratories of Faith* (Ithaca, NY: Cornell University Press, 2008).

28. Ray Stannard Baker, *The Spiritual Unrest* (New York: Frederick A. Stokes, 1910), 190–92; and William James, *Writings 1902–1910* (New York: Library of America, 1987), 1238.

29. Joscelyn Godwin, *The Theosophical Enlightenment* (Albany: State University of New York Press, 1994); Joy Dixon, *Divine Feminine* (Baltimore, MD: Johns Hopkins University Press, 2001); Nicholas Goodrick-Clarke and Clare Goodrick-Clarke, *G. R. S. Mead and the Gnostic Quest* (Berkeley: North Atlantic Books, 2005); for the impact of Theosophy on the cultural avant-garde, see for example Ken Monteith, *Yeats and Theosophy* (New York: Routledge, 2008); June O. Leavitt, *The Mystical Life of Franz Kafka* (New York: Oxford University Press, 2012); George Moore, *The Brook Kerith* (London: Macmillan, 1916); and Paul Fussell, *The Great War and Modern Memory* (New York: Oxford University Press, 1975), 118–19.

30. Adele Heller and Lois Rudnick, eds., *1915, The Cultural Moment* (New Brunswick, NJ: Rutgers University Press, 1991); and Jenkins, *Mystics and Messiahs*.

31. Wellesley Tudor Pole, *The Great War* (London: G. Bell, 1915), 76.

32. *Zentralblatt für Okkultismus,* vol. x (1916–17) and vol. xi (1917–18); compare for the German literature A. R. Metapsychicus [pseud.], *Prophetische Stimmen über den Weltkrieg 1914–15,* 2nd ed. (Leipzig, Germany: O. Mutze, 1915); Bruno Grabinski, *Neuere Mystik* (Hildesheim, Germany: F. Borgmeyer, 1916); and Demeter Georgievitz-Weitzer, *Das Übersinnliche und der Weltkrieg* (Freiburg im Breisgau, Germany: Hofmann, 1921).

33. C. G. Jung, *Jung on Synchronicity and the Paranormal* (Abingdon, UK: Psychology Press, 1997), 133–34; and Richard Noll, *The Jung Cult* (Princeton, NJ: Princeton University Press, 1994).

34. Stephan A. Hoeller, *The Gnostic Jung and the Seven Sermons to the Dead* (Wheaton, IL: Theosophical Publishing House, 1982); and the sermons can be found at www .gnosis.org/library/7Sermons.htm.

35. Gary Lachman, *Rudolf Steiner* (New York: Penguin, 2007); and Blom, *The Vertigo Years*.

36. Helmut Zander, *Anthroposophie in Deutschland* (Göttingen: Vandenhoeck and Ruprecht, 2007); and Corinna Treitel, *A Science for the Soul* (Baltimore, MD: Johns Hopkins University Press, 2004).

37. Annika Mombauer, *Helmuth von Moltke and the Origins of the First World War* (Cambridge: Cambridge University Press, 2001).

38. Johannes Tautz, ed., *An Eliza von Moltke und Helmuth von Moltke Gerichtete Briefe, Meditationen und Sprüche von Rudolf Steiner 1904–1915* (Basel, Switzerland: Perseus-

Verlag, 1993); and T. H. Meyer, ed., *Light for the New Millennium* (London: Rudolf Steiner Press, 1997).

39. Rudolf Steiner, *The Influences of Lucifer and Ahriman,* trans. D. S. Osmond (Dornach, Switzerland: Steiner Books, 1993), 34.

40. Meyer, ed., *Light for the New Millennium.*

41. Maja Galle, *Der Erzengel Michael in der Deutschen Kunst des 19. Jahrhunderts* (Munich: Herbert Utz Verlag, 2002); Thomas Fliege, "Mein Deutschland Sei Mein Engel Michael," in *Alliierte im Himmel,* ed. Gottfried Korff (Tübingen: Tübinger Vereinigung für Volkskunde, 2006): 159–99; and for Ludendorff, Steiner, and Moltke, see Erich Ludendorff, *Das Marne-Drama* (Munich: Ludensdorff Verlag, 1934).

42. Karen Petrone, *The Great War in Russian Memory* (Bloomington: Indiana University Press, 2011), 60–67; and Michael Hagemeister, "Russian Cosmism in the 1920s and Today," in *The Occult in Russian and Soviet Culture,* ed. Bernice Glatzer Rosenthal (Ithaca, NY: Cornell University Press), 192.

43. J. F. C. Fuller, *The Star in the West* (New York: Walter Scott, 1907).

44. Nicholas Goodrick-Clarke, *The Occult Roots of Nazism,* new edition (New York: I. B. Tauris, 2004); and Nicholas Goodrick-Clarke, *Black Sun* (New York: New York University Press, 2002).

CHAPTER SIX: *Armageddon*

1. Andréi Nakov, *Malevich* (Farnham, UK: Lund Humphries, 2010); and Aleksandra Shatskikh, *Black Square* (New Haven, CT: Yale University Press, 2012).

2. Richard Schweitzer, *The Cross and the Trenches* (Westport, CT: Praeger, 2003), 33.

3. Tim Travers, *How the War Was Won* (London: Routledge, 1992).

4. Ian F. W. Beckett, ed., *1917: Beyond the Western Front* (Leiden, The Netherlands: Brill, 2009).

5. Leonard V. Smith, *Between Mutiny and Obedience* (Princeton, NJ: Princeton University Press, 1994); and André Loez and Nicolas Mariot, eds., *Obéir-Désobéir* (Paris: Éditions La Découverte, 2008).

6. Lyn MacDonald, *They Called It Passchendaele* (London: Michael Joseph, 1978); and Harry Patch is quoted from "Last First World War Veteran Turns 109," *Daily Telegraph,* June 18, 2007.

7. Robin Pryor and Trevor Wilson, *Passchendaele* (New Haven, CT: Yale University Press, 1996); and von Kuhl is quoted from Martin Gilbert, *The First World War* (New York: Henry Holt, 1994), 365.

8. Mark Thompson, *The White War* (London: Faber and Faber, 2008).

9. W. Bruce Lincoln, *Passage Through Armageddon* (New York: Simon and Schuster, 1986).

10. David Birmingham, *A Concise History of Portugal,* 2nd ed. (Cambridge: Cambridge University Press, 2003); and Jeffrey S. Bennett, *When the Sun Danced* (Charlottesville: University of Virginia Press, 2012).

11. W. T. Walsh, *Our Lady of Fátima* (New York: Image Books, 1954).

12. The quote is from João de Marchi, *The Immaculate Heart* (New York: Farrar, Straus, and Young, 1952).

13. For *Die Christliche Welt,* see James M. Stayer, *Martin Luther, German Saviour* (Montreal: McGill-Queen's University Press, 2000), 26; Frank J. Gordon, "Liberal German Churchmen and the First World War," *German Studies Review* 4, no. 1 (February 1981): 39–62; Otto Baumgarten, *Christentum und Weltkrieg* (Tübingen:

J. C. B. Mohr [Paul Siebeck], 1918); Günter Brakelmann, *Krieg und Gewissen* (Göttingen: Vandenhoeck and Ruprecht, 1991); and for the peace issue in German sermons in these years, see Wilhelm Pressel, *Die Kriegspredigt 1914–1918 in der Evangelischen Kirche Deutschlands* (Göttingen: Vandenhoeck and Ruprecht, 1967), 269–94.

14. Gottfried Mehnert, *Evangelische Kirche und Politik 1917–1919* (Düsseldorf: Droste Verlag, 1959); and Johann Klier, *Von der Kriegspredigt zum Friedensappell* (Munich: Kommissionsverlag UNI-Druck, 1991).

15. Stayer, *Martin Luther, German Saviour;* and for Hirsch, see Robert P. Ericksen, *Theologians Under Hitler* (New Haven, CT: Yale University Press, 1985), 120–97.

16. Pressel, *Die Kriegspredigt 1914–1918,* 24–25, 89–96.

17. Günter Brakelmann, *Protestantische Kriegstheologie im Ersten Weltkrieg* (Bielefeld, Germany: Luther-Verlag, 1974); Heinz Hagenlücke, *Deutsche Vaterlandspartei* (Düsseldorf: Droste, 1997); and Matthew Stibbe, *German Anglophobia and the Great War, 1914–1918* (Cambridge: Cambridge University Press, 2006).

18. Günter Brakelmann, ed., *Der Deutsche Protestantismus im Epochenjahr 1917* (Wittenberg, Germany: Luther-Verlag, 1974).

19. *Die Reformationsfeier zu Wittenberg 1917* (Wittenberg, Germany: Max Senf, 1918).

20. *Die Reformationsfeier zu Wittenberg 1917.*

21. Roger Ford, *Eden to Armageddon* (New York: Pegasus Books, 2010); and Lawrence James, *Imperial Warrior* (London: Weidenfeld and Nicolson, 1993).

22. "We used the Bibles" is quoted from Schweitzer, *The Cross and the Trenches,* 22; and for the biblical Armageddon, see Rev. 16:14–18. John D. Grainger, *The Battle For Syria 1918–1920* (Woodbridge England: Boydell and Brewer, 2013).

23. Throughout this chapter, I draw from Eitan Bar-Yosef, *The Holy Land in English Culture, 1799–1917* (Oxford: Clarendon Press, 2005).

24. Bar-Yosef, *The Holy Land in English Culture.*

25. Raymond Savage, *Allenby of Armageddon* (London: Hodder and Stoughton, 1925).

26. Quoted from Savage, *Allenby of Armageddon,* 227; compare A. P. Wavell, *Allenby* (London: Harrap, 1940), 274; F. H. Cooper, *Khaki Crusaders* (Cape Town: Central News Agency, 1919); and of course by no means all the ordinary soldiers involved in these campaigns shared the crusading passion: James E. Kitchen, "Khaki Crusaders," *First World War Studies* 1, no. 2 (2010): 141–60.

27. M. M. Harris, "Chanukah with Judah Maccabee and General Allenby in Jerusalem," reproduced at http://szyk.com/pics/iLrg-hs-print-chanukah-maccabee-allenby.jpg.

28. For modern versions of the rabbi's prophecy, see "Rabbi Judah Ben Samuel Prophecy," March 14, 2010, http://endtimesforecaster.blogspot.com/2010/03/rabbi-judah-ben-samuel-prophecy.html; and Savage, *Allenby of Armageddon,* 233.

29. Gina Kolata, *Flu* (New York: Simon and Schuster, 2001); Howard Phillips and David Killingray, eds., *The Spanish Influenza Pandemic of 1918–19* (New York: Routledge, 2003); John M. Barry, *The Great Influenza,* revised edition (New York: Penguin, 2005); Mark Honigsbaum, *Living with Enza* (Basingstoke, UK: Macmillan, 2009); and Nancy K. Bristow, *American Pandemic* (New York: Oxford University Press, 2012).

30. Holger H. Herwig, *Operation Michael* (Calgary, AB: University of Calgary Press, 2001); Ian Passingham, *The German Offensives of 1918* (London: Pen and Sword, 2008); and David Stevenson, *With Our Backs to the Wall* (London: Allen Lane, 2011), 53–55. For the development of radical new German tactics on the Eastern

Front, see Michael B. Barrett, *Prelude to Blitzkrieg* (Bloomington: Indiana University Press, 2013).

31. Quoted from Ernst Jünger, *Storm of Steel* (London: Penguin Classics, 2004), 255; and Thomas R. Nevin, *Ernst Jünger and Germany* (Durham, NC: Duke University Press, 1996).

32. Vera Brittain, *Testament of Youth* (New York: Macmillan, 1933), 411.

33. John Toland, *No Man's Land* (New York: Doubleday, 1980).

34. Stevenson, *With Our Backs to the Wall.*

35. Jünger, *Storm of Steel;* and Rudolf Binding, *A Fatalist at War* (Boston: Houghton Mifflin, 1929), 204–21.

36. Bryn Hammond, *Cambrai 1917* (London: Weidenfeld and Nicolson, 2008).

37. For the 1918 campaigns, see J. H. Johnson, *1918* (London: Weidenfeld and Nicolson, 1997); Peter Hart, *1918* (London: Weidenfeld and Nicolson, 2008); Charles Messenger, *The Day We Won the War* (London: Weidenfeld and Nicolson, 2008); Alexander Watson, *Enduring the Great War* (Cambridge: Cambridge University Press, 2008); Scott Stephenson, *The Final Battle* (Cambridge: Cambridge University Press, 2009); and Nick Lloyd, *Hundred Days* (London: Viking, 2013).

CHAPTER SEVEN: *The Sleep of Religion*

1. J. M. Winter, *Sites of Memory, Sites of Mourning* (Cambridge: Cambridge University Press, 1995); and Laurent Véray, *La Grande Guerre au Cinéma* (Paris: Éditions Ramsay, 2008).

2. Charles à Court Repington, *The First World War* (New York: Houghton Mifflin, 1920); Annette Becker, "Messianismes et Héritage de la Violence," in *Théologies de la Guerre,* ed. Jean-Philippe Schreiber (Brussels: Editions de l'Université de Bruxelles, 2006), 59–71; and Emilio Gentile, *L'Apocalypse de la Modernité* (Paris: Aubier, 2011).

3. In Britain, the reaction against the war is epitomized by C. E. Montague, *Disenchantment* (London: Chatto and Windus, 1922).

4. William Ralph Inge, *Outspoken Essays* (London: Longmans Green, 1920), preface; and Étienne Fouilloux, "Première Guerre Mondiale et Changements Religieux en Europe," in *Les Sociétés Européennes et la Guerre de 1914–1918,* eds. Jean-Jacques Becker and Stéphane Audoin-Rouzeau (Paris: Université de Paris X-Nanterre, 1990).

5. Michael Burleigh, *Sacred Causes* (New York: HarperPress, 2006); and for the "geostrategic audit," see Michael Burleigh, "God in the Trenches," *Tablet,* November 8, 2008, 11.

6. Martin Conway, "The Christian Churches and Politics in Europe 1914–1939," in *The Cambridge History of Christianity,* ed. Hugh McLeod, vol. 9, *World Christianities c. 1914–c. 2000* (Cambridge: Cambridge University Press, 2006), 151–78. The theme of remembrance and commemoration is one of the most active areas in research on the Great War era. See Annette Becker, *Les Monuments aux Morts* (Paris: Ed. Errance, 1988); George L. Mosse, *Fallen Soldiers* (New York: Oxford University Press, 1990); Adrian Gregory, *The Silence of Memory* (Oxford: Berg, 1994); Winter, *Sites of Memory, Sites of Mourning*; Jonathan F. Vance, *Death So Noble* (Vancouver: University of British Columbia Press, 1997); Lisa M. Budreau, *Bodies of War* (New York: New York University Press, 2009); Steven Trout, *On the Battlefield of Memory* (Tuscaloosa: University of Alabama Press, 2010); for Canada, see Vance, *Death So*

Noble; for Italy, see Oliver Janz, *Das Symbolische Kapital der Trauer* (Tübingen: Nie-meyer, 2009); and for remembrance as a cultic ritual, see several essays in Gottfried Korff, ed., *Alliierte im Himmel* (Tübingen: Tübinger Vereinigung für Volkskunde, 2006).

7. Keith Robbins, *England, Ireland, Scotland, Wales* (Oxford: Oxford University Press, 2008), 152–232; and Jonathan H. Ebel, *Faith in the Fight* (Princeton, NJ: Princeton University Press, 2010).

8. Christopher Capozzola, *Uncle Sam Wants You* (New York: Oxford University Press, 2008); and Barry Hankins, *Jesus and Gin* (New York: Palgrave Macmillan, 2010).

9. Matthew Avery Sutton, *Aimee Semple McPherson and the Resurrection of Christian America* (Cambridge, MA: Harvard University Press, 2007); and Matthew Avery Sutton, "Was FDR the Antichrist?" *Journal of American History* 98, no. 4 (March 2012): 1052–74.

10. Hardy is quoted in Pamela Dalziel, "Hardy and the Church," in *A Companion to Thomas Hardy*, ed. Keith Wilson (New York: John Wiley, 2009), 76; for spiritualism in the 1920s, see Winter, *Sites of Memory, Sites of Mourning*, 54–77; and Georgina Byrne, *Modern Spiritualism and the Church of England, 1850–1939* (Woodbridge, UK: Boydell Press, 2010).

11. For Germany's self-proclaimed prophets and messiahs in this era, see Ulrich Linse, *Barfüssige Propheten* (Berlin: Siedler, 1983); Ulrich Linse, *Geisterseher und Wunder-wirker* (Frankfurt am Main: Fischer, 1996); for French parallels in the same era, see Lucien Roure, *Au Pays de l'Occultisme,* 2nd ed. (Paris: G. Beauchesne, 1925). For Ehrenburg, see Efraim Sicher, *Jews in Russian Literature After the October Revolution* (Cambridge: Cambridge University Press, 1995).

12. Crowley is quoted in Philip Jenkins, *Mystics and Messiahs* (New York: Oxford University Press, 2000), 91.

13. For Weimar cinema and the experience of war veterans, see Anton Kaes, *Shell Shock Cinema* (Princeton, NJ: Princeton University Press, 2009); and Corinna Treitel, *A Science for the Soul* (Baltimore, MD: Johns Hopkins University Press, 2004).

14. Rev. 17; Gyan Prakash, ed., *Noir Urbanisms* (Princeton, NJ: Princeton University Press, 2010), 17–30; and Oswald Spengler, *The Decline of the West,* 2 vols. (New York: Alfred Knopf, 1926–28).

15. For the Russian church in wartime, see Scott M. Kenworthy, "The Mobilization of Piety," *Jahrbücher für Geschichte Osteuropas* 52 (2004): 388–401.

16. Dimitry Pospielovsky, *The Russian Church Under the Soviet Regime, 1917–1982,* 2 vols. (Crestwood, NY: Saint Vladimir's Seminary Press, 1984), i, 25–43; and Chris-topher Marsh, *Religion and the State in Russia and China* (London: Continuum, 2011), 47–80.

17. Richard Landes, *Heaven on Earth* (New York: Oxford University Press, 2011); Al-exander Blok, *The Twelve and Other Poems,* trans. Anselm Hollo (Lexington, KY: Gnomon, 1971); and John Garrard, "The Twelve: Blok's Apocalypse," *Religion and Literature* 35, no. 1 (Spring 2003), 45–72.

18. *The Cambridge History of Russia,* ed. Ronald Grigor Suny, vol. 3 (New York: Cam-bridge University Press, 2006), especially the chapters by S. A. Smith, "The Revo-lutions of 1917–1918," and Donald J. Raleigh, "The Russian Civil War"; Gregory L. Freeze, "Subversive Atheism," in *State Secularism and Lived Religion in Soviet Russia and Ukraine,* ed. Catherine Wanner (New York: Oxford University Press,

2012); and for the crisis of church and aristocracy, see Douglas Smith, *Former People* (London: Macmillan, 2013).

19. "Powerful screws" is quoted from Marsh, *Religion and the State in Russia and China,* 57; William C. Fletcher, *The Russian Orthodox Church Underground, 1917–1970* (New York: Oxford University Press, 1971), 26; and Scott M. Kenworthy, *The Heart of Russia* (New York: Oxford University Press, 2010).

20. Pospielovsky, *The Russian Church Under the Soviet Regime,* i, 98. This account draws on Aleksandr A. Valentinov, *The Assault of Heaven* (London: Boswell, 1925); and Dimitry Pospielovsky, *Soviet Antireligious Campaigns and Persecutions* (New York: St. Martin's Press, 1988), 1–60.

21. Valentinov, *The Assault of Heaven.*

22. Fletcher, *The Russian Orthodox Church Underground, 1917–1970;* Edward E. Roslof, *Red Priests* (Bloomington: Indiana University Press, 2002); and Jennifer Jean Wynot, *Keeping the Faith* (College Station: Texas A&M Press, 2004).

23. Robert H. Greene, *Bodies Like Bright Stars* (DeKalb: Northern Illinois University Press, 2010), 103–95; Pospielovsky, *The Russian Church Under the Soviet Regime,* i, 39; and Pospielovsky, *Soviet Antireligious Campaigns and Persecutions.*

24. Greene, *Bodies Like Bright Stars,* 160–95; for the Ukrainian events, see Kate Brown, *A Biography of No Place* (Cambridge, MA: Harvard University Press, 2004), 58–74; and "Religion is like a nail" is quoted from Paul Kurtz, *Toward a New Enlightenment,* eds. Vern L. Bullough and Timothy J. Madigan (New Brunswick, NJ: Transaction, 1994), 179. It is variously attributed to a number of Bolshevik leaders.

25. Burleigh, *Sacred Causes,* 38–122; William B. Husband, *Godless Communists* (DeKalb: Northern Illinois University Press, 2002); Paul Froese, *The Plot to Kill God* (Berkeley: University of California Press, 2008); and Christopher Marsh, *Religion and the State in Russia and China* (London: Continuum, 2011).

26. Ann Hagedorn, *Savage Peace* (New York: Simon and Schuster, 2007).

27. Burleigh, *Sacred Causes,* 38–122.

28. Philip Jenkins, *Hoods and Shirts* (Chapel Hill: University of North Carolina Press, 1997); and Kelly J. Baker, *Gospel According to the Klan* (Lawrence: University Press of Kansas, 2011).

29. Wilhelm Pressel, *Die Kriegspredigt 1914–1918 in der Evangelischen Kirche Deutschlands* (Göttingen: Vandenhoeck and Ruprecht, 1967), 295–311; Wolfgang G. Natter, *Literature at War, 1914–1940* (New Haven, CT: Yale University Press, 1999); Boris Barth, *Dolchstosslegenden und Politische Desintegration* (Düsseldorf: Droste, 2003); Jason Crouthamel, *The Great War and German Memory* (Exeter, UK: University of Exeter Press, 2009); and for the stab-in-the-back mythology, see Lars Broder Keil and Sven Felix Kellerhoff, *Deutsche Legenden* (Berlin: Christoph Links Verlag, 2002).

30. Jürgen Brokoff, *Die Apokalypse in der Weimarer Republik* (Munich: Wilhelm Fink Verlag, 2001).

31. Pressel, *Die Kriegspredigt 1914–1918,* 303–6; the Doehring quote is from Arlie J. Hoover, *God, Germany, and Britain in the Great War* (New York: Praeger, 1989), 120–21; and for the Berlin inscription, see Reinhart Koselleck, *The Practice of Conceptual History* (Palo Alto, CA: Stanford University Press, 2002), 360.

32. All quotes in this paragraph are taken from Hoover, *God, Germany, and Britain in the Great War,* 120–22; and Pressel, *Die Kriegspredigt 1914–1918,* 301–2.

33. Robert P. Ericksen, *Theologians Under Hitler* (New Haven, CT: Yale University Press, 1985); and John A. Moses, "Bonhoeffer's Germany," in *The Cambridge Com-*

panion to Dietrich Bonhoeffer, ed. John W. de Gruchy (Cambridge: Cambridge University Press, 1999), 7–9.

34. James M. Stayer, *Martin Luther, German Saviour* (Montreal: McGill-Queen's University Press, 2000).

35. Friedrich Andersen, Adolf Bartels, Ernst Katzer, and Hans Paul Freiherrn von Wolzogen, *Deutschchristentum auf Rein-Evangelischer Grundlage* (Leipzig, Germany: Weicher, 1917); Alexandra Gerstner, Gregor Hufenreuter, and Uwe Puschner, "Völkischer Protestantismus," in *Das Evangelische Intellektuellenmilieu in Deutschland,* eds. Michel Grunewald and Uwe Puschner (Bern: Peter Lang, 2008), 409–36; and Christopher J. Probst, *Demonizing the Jews* (Bloomington: Indiana University Press, 2012).

36. Friedrich Andersen, *Der Deutsche Heiland* (Munich: Deutscher Volksverlag, 1921).

37. Adolf von Harnack, *Marcion* (Leipzig, Germany: Hinrichs, 1921); Wolfram Kinzig, *Harnack, Marcion, und das Judentum* (Leipzig, Germany: Evangelische Verlagsanstalt, 2004); and the quote is from Hendrikus Berkhof, *Christian Faith,* trans. Sierd Woudstra (Grand Rapids, MI: William. B. Eerdmans, 2002), 227.

38. Jack Forstman, *Christian Faith in Dark Times* (Louisville, KY: Westminster John Knox Press, 1992); and Richard Steigmann-Gall, *The Holy Reich* (Cambridge: Cambridge University Press, 2003).

39. I have drawn repeatedly here on Ericksen, *Theologians Under Hitler.* Althaus is quoted from 85–86 and 106; Hirsch's "sunrise" quote is from 146; and Kittel is quoted from 60. For the 1933 commemoration of Luther's birth, see Christian Deuper, *Lutherfeier im Jahr der "Machtergreifung"* (Munich: GRIN Verlag, 2008).

40. James Bentley, *Martin Niemöller* (New York: Oxford University Press, 1984).

41. Burleigh, *Sacred Causes.*

42. Francis McCullagh, *Red Mexico* (New York: L. Carrier, 1928).

43. Dianne Kirby, ed., *Religion and the Cold War* (New York: Palgrave Macmillan, 2002); and Philip Jenkins, *The Cold War at Home* (Chapel Hill: University of North Carolina Press, 1999).

44. Robert A. Ventresca, *Soldier of Christ* (Cambridge, MA: Belknap Press / Harvard University Press, 2012).

CHAPTER EIGHT: *The Ruins of Christendom*

1. Karl Barth, *The Humanity of God* (Louisville, KY: Westminster John Knox Press, 1960), 14.

2. Throughout this section I have used Eberhard Busch, *Karl Barth* (London: SCM, 1976); J. B. Webster, *The Cambridge Companion to Karl Barth* (Cambridge: Cambridge University Press, 2000); and Gary J. Dorrien, *The Barthian Revolt in Modern Theology* (Louisville, KY: Westminster John Knox Press, 2000).

3. Robert Lejeune, ed., *Christoph Blumhardt and His Message* (Rifton, NY: Plough Publishing House, 1963); and Wilhelm Pressel, *Die Kriegspredigt 1914–1918 in der Evangelischen Kirche Deutschlands* (Göttingen: Vandenhoeck and Ruprecht, 1967), 251–67.

4. John A. Moses, "Justifying War as the Will of God," *Colloquium* 31, no. 1 (1999): 3–20; and Paul Bock, ed., *Signs of the Kingdom* (Grand Rapids, MI: William B. Eerdmans, 1984).

5. Busch, *Karl Barth,* 81–138; Jochen Fähler, *Der Ausbruch des 1. Weltkrieges in Karl Barths Predigten 1913–1915* (Bern: Peter Lang, 1979); Richard E. Burnett, *Karl Barth's Theological Exegesis* (Grand Rapids, MI: William B. Eerdmans, 2001), 1; and

A. Rasmusson, "Church and Nation-State," *Nederduitse Gereformeerde Teologiese Tydskrif* 46 (2005): 511–24.

6. "It was like the Twilight of the Gods" is quoted in Duncan B. Forrester, *Apocalypse Now?* (London: Ashgate, 2005), 1; for Herrmann, see J. P. Bang, *Hurrah and Hallelujah* (London: Hodder and Stoughton, 1916), 196–204; and Martin Rade, *Dieser Krieg und das Christentum* (Stuttgart and Berlin: Deutsche Verlags-Anstalt, 1915).

7. Thomas F. Torrance, *Karl Barth* (London: Continuum, 2004), 38.

8. Carl E. Braaten and Robert W. Jenson, eds., *A Map of Twentieth-Century Theology* (Minneapolis: Fortress Press, 1995), 38.

9. The "Gott ist Gott" quote appears in several variants. Michael Trowitzsch, Christian Link, and Michael Beintker, eds., *Karl Barth in Deutschland* (Zürich: Theologischer Verlag, 2005), 63; Cornelis van der Kooi, *As in a Mirror* (Leiden, The Netherlands: Brill, 2005), 389; and James M. Stayer, *Martin Luther, German Saviour* (Montreal: McGill-Queen's University Press, 2000).

10. Rom. 1:25.

11. "Burst like a bombshell" is quoted from Karl Adams in Terry L. Cross, *Dialectic in Karl Barth's Doctrine of God* (New York: Peter Lang, 2001), 82; the original is translated variously.

12. Karl Barth, *Epistle to the Romans,* trans. Edwyn C. Hoskyns (Oxford: Oxford University Press, 1933).

13. Barth, *Epistle to the Romans,* 353; "One drop" is from p. 77.

14. Rudolf Otto, *The Idea of the Holy* (New York: Oxford University Press, 1950).

15. Richard John Neuhaus, "Kierkegaard for Grownups," *First Things* 146 (October 2004): 27–33.

16. The *Church Dogmatics* appeared in print between 1932 and 1968.

17. Jonathan Brant, *Paul Tillich and the Possibility of Revelation Through Film* (New York: Oxford University Press, 2012).

18. John S. Conway, *The Nazi Persecution of the Churches 1933–45* (London: Weidenfeld and Nicolson, 1968).

19. John W. de Gruchy, *The Cambridge Companion to Dietrich Bonhoeffer* (Cambridge: Cambridge University Press, 1999); John A. Moses, *The Reluctant Revolutionary* (New York: Berghahn, 2009); Eric Metaxas, *Bonhoeffer* (Nashville: Thomas Nelson, 2011).

20. Ralph McInerny, *The Very Rich Hours of Jacques Maritain* (Notre Dame, IN: University of Notre Dame Press, 2003); Jean-Luc Barré, *Jacques and Raïssa Maritain* (Notre Dame, IN: University of Notre Dame Press, 2005); Stephen Schloesser, *Jazz Age Catholicism* (Toronto: University of Toronto Press, 2006); Philip Kennedy, *Twentieth-Century Theologians* (New York: I. B. Tauris, 2010); Brenna Moore, *Sacred Dread* (Notre Dame, IN: University of Notre Dame Press, 2012); and Teilhard is quoted from Ursula King, *Spirit of Fire* (Maryknoll, NY: Orbis Books, 1998), 77.

21. Jacques Maritain, *Integral Humanism* (Notre Dame, IN: University of Notre Dame Press, 1973).

22. Carl E. Olson, "Pope Francis and Henri de Lubac, SJ," *Catholic World Report,* March 28, 2013, www.catholicworldreport.com/Blog/2136/pope_francis_and _henri_de_lubac_sj.aspx#.UYlIwr_3Blo.

23. Michael Burleigh, *Sacred Causes* (New York: HarperPress, 2006).

24. For Catholic efforts at peacemaking between the wars, see Gearóid Barry, *The Disarmament of Hatred* (New York: Palgrave Macmillan, 2012).

25. See for instance Charlemagne, "Real Politics, at Last?" *Economist,* October 28, 2004, www.economist.com/node/3332056/print?Story_ID=3332056.

CHAPTER NINE: *A New Zion*

1. For Palestine in these years, see Amy Dockser Marcus, *Jerusalem 1913* (New York: Viking, 2007).

2. Richard N. Ostling and Joan K. Ostling, *Mormon America,* 2nd ed. (San Francisco: HarperOne, 2007).

3. Nathaniel Deutsch, *The Jewish Dark Continent* (Cambridge, MA: Harvard University Press, 2011); for the Habsburg lands, see Marsha L. Rozenblit, *Reconstructing a National Identity* (New York: Oxford University Press, 2001); and David Rechter, *The Jews of Vienna and the First World War* (Oxford: Littman Library of Jewish Civilization, 2007).

4. Paul R. Mendes-Flohr and Jehuda Reinharz, eds., *The Jew in the Modern World* (New York: Oxford University Press, 1995); Jonathan D. Sarna, *American Judaism* (New Haven, CT: Yale University Press, 2004); and Marc Lee Raphael, ed., *The Columbia History of Jews and Judaism in America* (New York: Columbia University Press, 2008).

5. Yohanan Petrovsky-Shtern, *Jews in the Russian Army, 1827–1917* (Cambridge: Cambridge University Press, 2008); and Michael Berger, *Eisernes Kreuz und Davidstern* (Berlin: Trafo Verlag, 2006).

6. Geoffrey Lewis, *Balfour and Weizmann* (London: Continuum, 2008); and Shulamit Volkov, *Walther Rathenau* (New Haven, CT: Yale University Press, 2012).

7. Rivka Horwitz, "Voices of Opposition to the First World War Among Jewish Thinkers," *Leo Baeck Institute Yearbook* 33 (1988): 233–59; and Christhard Hoffmann, "Between Integration and Rejection," in *State, Society, and Mobilization in Europe During the First World War,* ed. John Horne (Cambridge: Cambridge University Press, 1997), 89–104.

8. Joseph Wohlgemuth, *Der Weltkrieg im Lichte des Judentums,* 3rd ed. (Berlin: Jeschurun, 1915); and Uriel Tal, *Christians and Jews in Germany* (Ithaca, NY: Cornell University Press, 1975).

9. George L. Mosse, *The Jews and the German War Experience, 1914–1918* (New York: Leo Baeck Institute, 1977); and Michael Berkowitz, *Western Jewry and the Zionist Project, 1914–1933* (New York: Cambridge University Press, 1997).

10. "Hate Song Against England," http://www.hschamberlain.net/kriegsaufsaetze/hassgesang.html.

11. John D. Klier and Shlomo Lambroza, eds., *Pogroms* (Cambridge: Cambridge University Press, 1992).

12. Norman Cohn, *Warrant for Genocide* (London: Eyre and Spottiswoode, 1967); Ezekiel Leikin, *The Beilis Transcripts* (Northvale, NJ: Jason Aronson, 1993); Marvin Perry and Frederick M. Schweitzer, eds., *Antisemitic Myths* (Bloomington: Indiana University Press, 2008); and Phyllis Goldstein, *A Convenient Hatred* (Brookline, MA: Facing History and Ourselves, 2012).

13. Benjamin Nathans, *Beyond the Pale* (Berkeley: University of California Press, 2002); and Wayne Dowler, *Russia in 1913* (DeKalb: Northern Illinois University Press, 2010), 183.

14. Marc Saperstein, "British Jewish Preachers in Time of War," *Journal of Modern Jewish Studies* 4, no. 3 (2005): 255–71; and Todd M. Endelman, *The Jews of Britain, 1656 to 2000* (Berkeley: University of California Press, 2002), 184.

15. Maurice Barrès, *Les Diverses Familles Spirituelles de la France* (Paris: Émile Paul Frères, 1917); Philippe-E. Landau, *Les Juifs de France et la Grande Guerre* (Paris: CNRS, 1999); and La Rochelle is quoted from Emmanuel Le Roux, "Exhibition Honours Jewish Soldiers in First World War," October 24, 2002, www.aftermathww1 .com/parisexpo.asp.

16. *The Holy Scriptures* (Philadelphia: Jewish Publication Society, 1917); and Alan T. Levenson, *The Making of the Modern Jewish Bible* (Lanham, MD: Rowman and Littlefield, 2011).

17. Jonathan Schneer, *The Balfour Declaration* (New York: Random House, 2010).

18. Michael Keren and Shlomit Keren, *We Are Coming, Unafraid* (Lanham, MD: Rowman and Littlefield, 2010).

19. Isaiah Friedman, *The Question of Palestine, 1914–1918* (New York: Schocken Books, 1973).

20. Mendes-Flohr and Reinharz, eds., *The Jew in the Modern World,* 580–81; Yoram Hazony, *The Jewish State* (New York: Basic Books, 2001), 174–75; and "a mischievous political creed" is quoted from "Montagu Memorandum on the Anti-Semitism of the British Government," August 23, 1917, www.jewishvirtuallibrary .org/jsource/History/Montagumemo.html.

21. "Turks and other Mahommedans" is quoted from "Montagu Memorandum."

22. Isaiah Friedman, *Germany, Turkey, and Zionism, 1897–1918* (Oxford: Clarendon Press, 1977).

23. Paul C. Merkley, *The Politics of Christian Zionism, 1891–1948* (London: Frank Cass, 1998).

24. For "Moslem tyranny," see Henry Grattan Guinness, *The Approaching End of the Age* (London: Hodder and Stoughton, 1879), 375, see 558 for "the last warning bell"; Timothy Larsen, *Christabel Pankhurst* (Woodbridge, UK: Boydell Press, 2002); William E. Blackstone, *Jesus Is Coming* (Chicago: Fleming H. Revell, 1917); Shalom Goldman, *Zeal for Zion* (Chapel Hill: University of North Carolina, 2010); and Eric Michael Reisenauer, "Tidings Out of the East," in *End of Days,* eds. Karolyn Kinane and Michael A. Ryan (Jefferson, NC: McFarland, 2009), 142–72.

25. Andrew Wingate, *Palestine, Mesopotamia, and the Jews* (London: Alfred Holness, 1919).

26. Merkley, *The Politics of Christian Zionism,* 59–61; and M. P. Shiel, *Lord of the Sea* (London: Grant Richards, 1901).

27. Kenneth O. Morgan, *David Lloyd George* (Cardiff: University of Wales Press, 1963); Eitan Bar-Yosef, *The Holy Land in English Culture, 1799–1917* (Oxford: Clarendon Press, 2005); James Renton, *The Zionist Masquerade* (Basingstoke, UK: Palgrave Macmillan, 2007); and R. J. Q. Adams, *Balfour* (London: John Murray, 2007).

28. Merkley, *The Politics of Christian Zionism,* 99.

29. Schneer, *The Balfour Declaration.*

30. Bernard McGinn, John J. Collins, and Stephen J. Stein, eds., *The Continuum History of Apocalypticism* (London: Continuum, 2003), 528.

31. S. An-Ski, *The Enemy at His Pleasure* (New York: Metropolitan Books / Henry Holt, 2002).

32. Gershom Scholem, *Lamentations of Youth,* ed. and trans. Anthony David Skinner (Cambridge, MA: Belknap Press / Harvard University Press, 2007), 123.

33. Horwitz, "Voices of Opposition to the First World War Among Jewish Thinkers"; and Alan L. Mittleman, *Between Kant and Kabbalah* (Albany: State University of New York Press, 1990).

34. Both quotes from Kook are from Rabbi Abraham Isaac Kook, *Orot,* ed. Bezalel Naor (Northvale, NJ: Jason Aronson, 1993), 98–99; and Benjamin Ish-Shalom, *Rav Avraham Itzhak HaCohen Kook* (Albany: State University of New York Press, 1993).

35. Alan Dowty, *The Jewish State* (Berkeley: University of California Press, 1998).

36. Tom Segev, *One Palestine, Complete* (New York: Metropolitan Books, 2000).

37. Haim Gerber, *Remembering and Imagining Palestine* (New York: Palgrave Macmillan, 2008).

38. Cohn, *Warrant for Genocide;* and Richard Allen Landes and Steven T. Katz, eds., *The Paranoid Apocalypse* (New York: New York University Press, 2012).

39. J. P. Bang, *Hurrah and Hallelujah* (London: Hodder and Stoughton, 1916), 140; and Matthew Stibbe, *German Anglophobia and the Great War, 1914–1918* (Cambridge: Cambridge University Press, 2006).

40. James Retallack, *The German Right, 1860–1920* (Toronto: University of Toronto Press, 2006); Dietrich Orlow, ed., *A History of Modern Germany,* 7th ed. (Boston: Pearson, 2012).

41. Arnold Zweig, *Education Before Verdun* (New York: Viking, 1936), 219–20.

42. Roger Chickering, *Imperial Germany and the Great War, 1914–1918,* 2nd ed. (New York: Cambridge University Press, 2004); and Ina Zweiniger-Bargielowska, Rachel Duffett, and Alain Drouard, eds., *Food and War in Twentieth Century Europe* (Burlington, VT: Ashgate, 2011).

43. Werner T. Angress, "The German Army's Judenzählung of 1916," *Leo Baeck Institute Yearbook* 23, no. 1 (1978): 117–37.

44. Otto Armin [Alfred Roth], *Die Juden im Heere* (Munich: Deutsche Volks-Verlag, 1919); and Tim Grady, *The German-Jewish Soldiers of the First World War in History and Memory* (Liverpool: Liverpool University Press, 2011).

45. Rosenzweig is quoted in W. Gunther Plaut, *Eight Decades* (Toronto: Dundum, 2008), 321–22; Arnold Zweig "Judenzählung vor Verdun," *Die Schaubühne* 13, no. 5 (February 1917): 115–17; and Rivka Horwitz, "Franz Rosenzweig and Gershom Sholem on Zionism and the Jewish People," *Jewish History* 6 (March 1992): 104.

46. Zweig is quoted from Noah Isenberg, "To Pray Like a Dervish," in *Orientalism and the Jews,* eds. Ivan Davidson Kalmár and Derek Jonathan Penslar (Lebanon, NH: University Press of New England, 2005), 96.

47. For the Luther celebrations, see Friedrich Andersen, Adolf Bartels, Ernst Katzer, and Hans Paul Freiherr von Wolzogen, *Deutschchristentum auf Rein-Evangelischer Grundlage* (Leipzig, Germany: Weicher, 1917); Christopher J. Probst, *Demonizing the Jews* (Bloomington: Indiana University Press, 2012).

48. Berkowitz, *Western Jewry and the Zionist Project, 1914–1933;* Noah Isenberg, *Between Redemption and Doom* (Lincoln: University of Nebraska 1999); Ulrich Sieg, *Jüdische Intellektuelle im Ersten Weltkrieg,* 2nd ed. (Berlin: Akademie Verlag, 2008); for Buber's biblical endeavors, see Levenson, *The Making of the Modern Jewish Bible;* and Arnold Zweig, *The Face of East European Jewry,* illus. Hermann Struck, ed. and trans. Noah Isenberg (Berkeley: University of California Press, 2004).

49. Scholem, *Lamentations of Youth.*

50. *The Jews in the Eastern War Zone* (New York: American Jewish Committee, 1916); An-Ski, *The Enemy at His Pleasure;* William C. Fuller, Jr., *The Foe Within* (Ithaca, NY: Cornell University Press, 2006), 175–80; Jonathan Dekel-Chen, David Gaunt, Natan M. Meir, and Israel Bartal, eds., *Anti-Jewish Violence* (Bloomington: Indiana

University Press, 2011); and Timothy Snyder, *Bloodlands* (New York: Basic Books, 2010).

51. An-Ski, *The Enemy at His Pleasure;* and Nathan Schachner, *The Price of Liberty* (New York: American Jewish Committee, 1948).

52. Dekel-Chen et al., eds., *Anti-Jewish Violence;* and for pogroms in Poland in 1918–19, see Henry Morgenthau and French Strother, *All in a Life-Time* (Garden City, NY: Doubleday, Page, 1922), 405–37.

53. Kenneth B. Moss, *Jewish Renaissance in the Russian Revolution* (Cambridge, MA: Harvard University Press, 2009); Oleg Budnitskii, *Russian Jews Between the Reds and the Whites, 1917–1920* (Philadelphia: University of Pennsylvania Press, 2012); and Olga Bertelsen, "GPU-NKVD Repressions of Zionists," in *State Secularism and Lived Religion in Soviet Russia and Ukraine,* ed. Catherine Wanner (New York: Oxford University Press, 2012).

54. Volkov, *Walther Rathenau;* and Dietrich Orlow, ed., *A History of Modern Germany,* 7th ed. (Boston: Pearson, 2012).

55. Erich Ludendorff, *Destruction of Freemasonry Through Revelation of Their Secrets* (Torrance, CA: Noontide Press, 1977).

56. William I. Brustein, *Roots of Hate* (Cambridge: Cambridge University Press, 2003).

57. Michael Kellogg, *The Russian Roots of Nazism* (Cambridge: Cambridge University Press, 2005).

58. Goldstein, *A Convenient Hatred.*

Chapter Ten: *Those from Below*

1. Robert I. Rotberg, *The Rise of Nationalism in Central Africa* (Cambridge, MA: Harvard University Press, 1965), 55–92, see 81–82 for Chilembwe's manifesto; and George Shepperson and Thomas Price, *Independent African,* 2nd ed. (Edinburgh: Edinburgh University Press, 1987).

2. Joe H. Lunn, *Memoirs of the Maelstrom* (Portsmouth, NH: Heinemann, 1999); Gerhard Höpp and Brigitte Reinwald, eds., *Fremdeinsätze* (Berlin: Das Arabische Buch, 2000); Richard S. Fogarty, *Race and War in France* (Baltimore, MD: Johns Hopkins University Press, 2008); Santanu Das, ed., *Race, Empire and First World War Writing* (New York: Cambridge University Press, 2011); Marc Michel, *L'Afrique dans l'engrenage de la Grande Guerre* (Paris: Karthala, 2013); and for colonial veterans, see Gregory Mann, *Native Sons* (Durham, NC: Duke University Press, 2006).

3. Kees van Dijk, *The Netherlands Indies and the Great War, 1914–1918* (Amsterdam: KITLV Press, 2007).

4. Mariano Azuela, *The Underdogs* (New York: Modern Library, 2002).

5. Benedict Anderson, *The Spectre of Comparisons* (London: Verso, 1998).

6. Charles Balesi, *From Adversaries to Comrades-in-Arms* (Waltham, MA: Crossroads Press, 1999); Mahir Saul and Patrick Royer, *West African Challenge to Empire* (Athens: Ohio University Press, 2001); and for the 1917 revolt against French rule in New Caledonia, see Adrian Muckle, *Specters of Violence in a Colonial Context* (Honolulu: University of Hawai'i Press, 2012).

7. Patricia Bernstein, *The First Waco Horror* (College Station: Texas A&M University Press, 2005).

8. Benjamin H. Johnson, *Revolution in Texas* (New Haven, CT: Yale University Press, 2003). Charles H. Harris III and Louis R. Sadler, *The Plan de San Diego* (University of Nebraska Press, 2013).

9. Chad Millman, *The Detonators* (Boston: Little, Brown, 2006).

10. John Teraine, *To Win a War* (London: Cassell, 2000), 21–24.

11. Allan J. MacDonald, *The War and Missions in the East* (London: R. Scott, 1919), 3; compare Friedrich Katz, *The Secret War in Mexico* (Chicago: University of Chicago, 1981); and Sean McMeekin, *The Berlin–Baghdad Express* (Cambridge, MA: Belknap Press / Harvard University Press, 2010).

12. Philip Mansel, *Levant* (London: John Murray, 2010). See also the notes in Chapter 11, pages 345–47.

13. For the fevered conspiracy theories of wartime Russia, see William C. Fuller, Jr., *The Foe Within* (Ithaca, NY: Cornell University Press, 2006).

14. Lothrop T. Stoddard, *The Rising Tide of Color Against White World Supremacy* (New York: Scribner, 1920).

15. Maia Ramnath, *Haj to Utopia* (Berkeley: University of California Press, 2012).

16. Ramnath, *Haj to Utopia*.

17. Quoted in Khushwant Singh, "The Ghadr Rebellion," *Illustrated Weekly of India,* February 26, 1961, www.sikhpioneers.org/rebellion.html.

18. R. W. E. Harper and Harry Miller, *Singapore Mutiny* (New York: Oxford University Press, 1984); and Nile Green, *Islam and the Army in Colonial India* (Cambridge: Cambridge University Press, 2009).

CHAPTER ELEVEN: *Genocide*

1. Philip Mansel, *Levant* (London: John Murray, 2010).

2. Philip Jenkins, *The Lost History of Christianity* (San Francisco: HarperOne, 2008); and Nicholas Doumanis, *Before the Nation* (New York: Oxford University Press, 2013).

3. For Smyrna, see *Encyclopedia Britannica, 1911* edition, www.studylight.org/enc /bri/view.cgi?N=30877&search=homer; and for Trebizond, see *Catholic Encyclopedia,* www.newadvent.org/cathen/15028a.htm.

4. "The Diocese of Amida," *Catholic Encyclopedia,* www.newadvent.org/cathen /01429c.htm; and Jenkins, *The Lost History of Christianity*.

5. Peter Balakian, *The Burning Tigris* (New York: HarperCollins, 2003).

6. Richard G. Hovannisian, ed., *The Armenian Genocide in Perspective* (London: Allen and Unwin, 1985).

7. M. Şükrü Hanioğlu, *A Brief History of the Late Ottoman Empire* (Princeton, NJ: Princeton University Press, 2008).

8. Balakian, *The Burning Tigris,* 11.

9. Donald Bloxham, *The Great Game of Genocide* (Oxford: Oxford University Press, 2005); Michelle U. Campos, *Ottoman Brothers* (Palo Alto, CA: Stanford University Press, 2010); Daniel Allen Butler, *Shadow of the Sultan's Realm* (Dulles, VA: Potomac Books, 2011); and for the genocide as a component in a long-term strategy of "Turkification," see Taner Akçam, *The Young Turks' Crime Against Humanity* (Princeton, NJ: Princeton University Press, 2012).

10. Ryan Gingeras, *Sorrowful Shores* (Oxford: Oxford University Press, 2009); and Walter Richmond, *The Circassian Genocide* (New Brunswick, NJ: Rutgers University Press, 2013). George W. Gawrych, *The Young Atatürk* (New York: I. B. Tauris, 2013).

11. Sean McMeekin, *The Berlin–Baghdad Express* (Cambridge, MA: Belknap Press / Harvard University Press, 2010); and Mustafa Aksakal, *The Ottoman Road to War in 1914* (Cambridge: Cambridge University Press, 2008).

12. Aksakal, *The Ottoman Road to War in 1914;* Balakian, *The Burning Tigris;* and Sean McMeekin, *The Russian Origins of the First World War* (Cambridge, MA: Belknap Press / Harvard University Press, 2011), 141–74.

13. Roger Ford, *Eden to Armageddon* (New York: Pegasus Books, 2010).

14. Robin Prior, *Gallipoli* (New Haven, CT: Yale University Press, 2009).

15. A. J. Barker, *The First Iraq War, 1914–1918* (London: Enigma Books, 2009); and Charles Townshend, *When God Made Hell* (London: Faber and Faber, 2010).

16. For the progress of the campaign against the Armenians, see Henry Morgenthau, *Ambassador Morgenthau's Story* (1918; repr., Detroit: Wayne State University Press, 2003), 190–234; Balakian, *The Burning Tigris;* Grigoris Balakian, *Armenian Golgotha* (New York: Knopf, 2009); and Ronald Grigor Suny, Fatma Müge Göçek, and Norman M. Naimark, eds., *A Question of Genocide* (Oxford: Oxford University Press, 2011).

17. Morgenthau, *Ambassador Morgenthau's Story,* 216.

18. "Knew that" is from Morgenthau, *Ambassador Morgenthau's Story,* 212–13; and Viscount James Bryce and Arnold Toynbee, *The Treatment of Armenians in the Ottoman Empire, 1915–1916* (London: Gomidas Institute, 2000).

19. "Raging like a crazed bloodhound" is quoted in David Gaunt, *Massacres, Resistance, Protectors* (Piscataway, NJ: Gorgias Press, 2006), 74–75; and Uğur Ümit Üngör, *The Making of Modern Turkey* (Oxford: Oxford University Press, 2011).

20. Bryce's report is quoted from "Bryce Report into the Armenian Massacre, October 1915," http://www.firstworldwar.com/source/brycereport_armenia.htm.

21. Report of Leslie A. Davis, American Consul General at Kharpert, February 9, 1918, Gomidas Institute Armenian Genocide Documentation Project, www.docstoc.com/docs/41557320/Gomidas-Institute-Armenian-Genocide-Documentation-Project.

22. For parallels between the two states, see Michael A. Reynolds, *Shattering Empires* (Cambridge: Cambridge University Press, 2011).

23. "Root and branch" is from Lord Bryce, preface to Joseph Naayem, *Shall This Nation Die?* (New York: Chaldean Rescue, 1921); for the "terrorist regime," see Melvin E. Page, ed,. *Colonialism* (Santa Barbara, CA: ABC-CLIO, 2003), 1089; and R. S. Stafford, *The Tragedy of the Assyrians* (Piscataway, NJ: Gorgias Press, 2006).

24. David Fromkin, *A Peace to End All Peace* (New York: Avon Books, 1990); Morgenthau, *Ambassador Morgenthau's Story,* 222–23; and Carter Vaughn Findley, "The Ottoman Lands to the Post–First World War Settlement," in *The New Cambridge History of Islam,* ed. Francis Robinson, vol. 5, *The Islamic World in the Age of Western Dominance* (Cambridge: Cambridge University Press, 2010), 31–78.

25. Speros Vryonis, Jr., *The Mechanism of Catastrophe* (New York: Greekworks.com, 2005); Giles Milton, *Paradise Lost* (New York: Basic Books, 2008); and Mansel, *Levant.*

26. Bruce Clark, *Twice a Stranger* (Cambridge, MA: Harvard University Press, 2006); for analogies elsewhere, see Benjamin Lieberman, *Terrible Fate* (Chicago: Ivan Dee, 2006); Niall Ferguson, *The War of the World* (New York: Penguin, 2007); and Annemarie H. Sammartino, *The Impossible Border* (Ithaca, NY: Cornell University Press, 2010).

27. Jay Winter, ed., *America and the Armenian Genocide of 1915* (New York: Cambridge University Press, 2003).

28. *The Case of Soghomon Tehlirian,* trans. Vartkes Yeghiayan (Los Angeles: A. R. F. Varantian Gomideh, 1985).

29. Aurora Mardiganian, *Ravished Armenia,* trans. H. L. Gates (New York: International Copyright Bureau, 1919).

30. Adam Jones, *Genocide,* 2nd ed. (New York: Routledge, 2011); and Raphael Lemkin, "Acts Constituting a General (Transnational) Danger Considered as Offences Against the Law of Nations," www.preventgenocide.org/lemkin/madrid1933 -english.htm. Raphael Lemkin, *Totally Unofficial,* edited by Donna-Lee Frieze (New Haven: Yale University Press, 2013).

31. Franz Werfel, *The Forty Days of Musa Dagh* (New York: Viking Press, 1934).

32. George Antonius, *The Arab Awakening* (Philadelphia: J. B. Lippincott, 1939).

33. Jenkins, *Lost History of Christianity.*

CHAPTER TWELVE: *African Prophets*

1. Robert R. Edgar and Hilary Sapire, *African Apocalypse* (Athens: Ohio University Press, 1999).

2. Philip Jenkins, *The Next Christendom,* 3rd ed. (New York: Oxford University Press, 2011).

3. Elizabeth Isichei, *A History of Christianity in Africa* (Grand Rapids, MI: William B. Eerdmans, 1995); Adrian Hastings, *The Church in Africa, 1450–1950* (Oxford: Clarendon Press, 1996); Bengt Sundkler and Christopher Steed, *A History of the Church in Africa* (Cambridge: Cambridge University Press, 2000); and Ogbu U. Kalu, ed., *African Christianity* (Trenton, NJ: Africa World Press, 2007). Throughout this chapter, I have used the Dictionary of African Christian Biography, www.dacb.org.

4. Sean Hanretta, *Islam and Social Change in French West Africa* (Cambridge: Cambridge University Press, 2009); Roman Loimeier, "Africa South of the Sahara to the First World War," in *The New Cambridge History of Islam,* ed. Robinson, vol. 5, 269–98; and Rüdiger Seesemann, *The Divine Flood* (New York: Oxford University Press, 2011).

5. Ogbu U. Kalu, "Ethiopianism and the Roots of Modern African Christianity," in *Cambridge History of Christianity,* eds. Sheridan Gilley and Brian Stanley, vol. 8, *World Christianities c. 1815 – c. 1914* (Cambridge: Cambridge University Press, 2005), 576–92.

6. Gordon M. Haliburton, *The Prophet Harris* (London: Longman, 1971); and Sheila S. Walker, *The Religious Revolution in the Ivory Coast* (Chapel Hill: University of North Carolina Press, 1983).

7. In 1964, the land of Tanganyika became part of the state of Tanzania when it merged with Zanzibar. Isabel V. Hull, *Absolute Destruction* (Cambridge: Cambridge University Press, 2005); David Olusoga and Casper W. Erichsen, *The Kaiser's Holocaust* (London: Faber and Faber, 2010); and Sebastian Conrad, *German Colonialism,* trans. Sorcha O'Hagan (Cambridge: Cambridge University Press, 2011).

8. This account of the African war is based on Hew Strachan, *The First World War in Africa* (Oxford: Oxford University Press, 2004); Edward Paice, *Tip and Run* (London: Weidenfeld and Nicolscn, 2007); Benjamin Griffith Brawley, *Africa and the War* (New York: Duffield, 1918); Paul von Lettow-Vorbeck, *My Reminiscences of East Africa* (Uckfield, UK: Naval and Military Press, 2006); and Marc Michel, *L'Afrique dans l'engrenage de la Grande Guerre* (Paris: Karthala, 2013).

9. Allan Anderson, *African Reformation* (Trenton, NJ: Africa World Press, 2001).

10. J. D. Y. Peel, *Aladura* (Oxford: Oxford University Press, 1968); Harold W. Turner, *History of an African Independent Church* (Oxford: Clarendon Press, 1967); Afeosemime U. Adogame, *Celestial Church of Christ* (New York: Peter Lang, 1999); and Ogbu U. Kalu, *Christian Missions in Africa,* eds. Wilhelmina J. Kalu, Nimi Wariboko, and Toyin Falola (Trenton, NJ: Africa World Press, 2010).

11. Akinjide Osuntokun, *Nigeria in the First World War* (Atlantic Highlands, NJ: Humanities Press, 1979); J. Akinyele Omoyajowo, *Cherubim and Seraphim* (New York: NOK Publishers International, 1982); Samson Adetunji Fatokun, "I Will Pour Out My Spirit Upon All Flesh," www.pctii.org/cyberj/cyberj19/fatokun.html; "Orimolade Tunolase," www.dacb.org/stories/nigeria/orimolade_moses.html; and "Garrick Sokari Marian Braide," www.dacb.org/stories/nigeria/braide1_garrick.html.

12. Lamin O. Sanneh, *West African Christianity* (Maryknoll, NY: Orbis Books, 1983).

13. Frieder Ludwig and J. Kwabena Asamoah-Gyadu, eds., *African Christian Presence in the West* (Trenton, NJ: Africa World Press, 2011).

14. Allan Anderson, "African Independent Churches and Global Pentecostalism," in *African Identities and World Christianity in the Twentieth Century,* eds. Klaus Koschorke and Jens Holger Schjørring (Wiesbaden: Otto Harrassowitz Verlag, 2005), 63–76.

15. Denis Basil M'Passou, *History of African Independent Churches in Southern Africa, 1892–1992* (Mulanje, Malawi: Spot Publications, 1994).

16. Marie-Louise Martin, *Kimbangu* (Grand Rapids, MI: William B. Eerdmans, 1975); David Martin, *The Breaking of the Image* (Vancouver, BC: Regent College Publishing, 2006), 49.

17. Lothrop T. Stoddard, *The Rising Tide of Color Against White World Supremacy* (New York: Scribner, 1920).

CHAPTER THIRTEEN: *Without a Caliph*

1. Throughout this chapter, I have used *The New Cambridge History of Islam,* ed. Francis Robinson, vol. 5, *The Islamic World in the Age of Western Dominance* (Cambridge: Cambridge University Press, 2010).

2. Barbara Daly Metcalf, *Islamic Revival in British India* (Princeton, NJ: Princeton University Press, 1982); compare Usha Sanyal, *Devotional Islam and Politics in British India* (Delhi and New York: Oxford University Press, 1996); Justin Jones, *Shi'a Islam in Colonial India* (New York: Cambridge University Press, 2012); for Sarekat Islam, see Deliar Noer, *The Modernist Muslim Movement in Indonesia 1900–1942* (Singapore: Oxford University Press, 1973); and Kenneth M. Cuno, "Egypt to c. 1919," in *The New Cambridge History of Islam,* ed. Robinson, vol. 5, 79–106.

3. Nader Sohrabi, *Revolution and Constitutionalism in the Ottoman Empire and Iran* (New York: Cambridge University Press, 2011).

4. Nikki R. Keddie, *An Islamic Response to Imperialism* (Berkeley: University of California Press, 1983); M. A. Zaki Badawi, *The Reformers of Egypt* (London: Croom Helm, 1978); and Pankaj Mishra, *From the Ruins of Empire* (New York: Farrar, Straus, and Giroux, 2012).

5. Azmi Özcan, *Pan-Islamism* (Leiden, The Netherlands: Brill, 1997).

6. Quoted in Lothrop T. Stoddard, *The Rising Tide of Color Against White World Supremacy* (New York: Scribner, 1920), 72; and for the Dutch East Indies, see Martin van Bruinessen, "Muslims of the Dutch East Indies and the Caliphate Question," *Studia Islamika* (Jakarta) 2, no. 3 (1995): 115–40.

7. Achmed Abdullah, "Seen Through Mohammedan Spectacles," *Forum* 52 (October 1914): 484–97.

8. Sean McMeekin, *The Berlin–Baghdad Express* (Cambridge, MA: Belknap Press / Harvard University Press, 2010); Tilman Lüdke, *Jihad Made in Germany* (Berlin: Lit, 2005); "The time has come" is from Elizabeth Siberry, *The New Crusaders* (Burlington, VT: Ashgate, 2000), 102; and "in cities and villages" is quoted from Lothrop T. Stoddard, *The New World of Islam* (New York: Scribner, 1921), 186.

9. John Buchan, *Greenmantle* (London: Thomas Nelson, 1916), 17.

10. Stoddard, *The Rising Tide of Color Against White World Supremacy*. Stoddard was a racist campaigner warning of what he called a "rising tide of color," and it was in his ideological interests to make militant non-Western movements appear as threatening as possible. Oddly, though, his 1921 book *The New World of Islam* presents a surprisingly balanced view of that faith, and his observations about current world developments were well informed.

11. For India, see Alfred Crowdy Lovett, Sir George Fletcher MacMunn, and George Sydenham Clarke, Baron Sydenham of Combe, *India and the War* (London: Hodder and Stoughton, 1915); and Russell McGuirk, *The Sanusi's Little War* (London: Arabian Publishing, 2007).

12. George Antonius, *The Arab Awakening* (Philadelphia: J. B. Lippincott, 1939).

13. John S. Habib, *Ibn Sa'ud's Warriors of Islam* (Leiden, The Netherlands: Brill, 1978); Haifa Alangari, *The Struggle for Power in Arabia* (Reading, UK: Ithaca Press, 1998); Askar H. al-Enazy, *The Creation of Saudi Arabia* (New York: Routledge, 2010); and Paul Dresch, "Arabia to the End of the First World War," in *The New Cambridge History of Islam,* ed. Robinson, vol. 5, 134–53.

14. James Barr, *Setting the Desert on Fire* (New York: Norton, 2008); Roger Ford, *Eden to Armageddon* (New York: Pegasus Books, 2010); James J. Schneider, *Guerrilla Leader* (New York: Bantam Books, 2011); and Scott Anderson, *Lawrence in Arabia* (New York: Doubleday, 2013).

15. Patrick Seale, *The Struggle for Arab Independence* (New York: Cambridge University Press, 2010); James Barr, *A Line in the Sand* (London: Simon and Schuster, 2011); for the French role, see Christopher Andrew and A. S. Kanya-Forstner, *France Overseas* (London: Thames and Hudson, 1981); Carter Vaughn Findley, "The Ottoman Lands to the Post–First World War Settlement," in *The New Cambridge History of Islam,* ed. Robinson, vol. 5, 31–78; and Charles Tripp, "West Asia from the First World War," in *The New Cambridge History of Islam,* ed. Robinson, vol. 5, 336–71. John D. Grainger, *The Battle for Syria 1918–1920* (Woodbridge England: Boydell and Brewer, 2013).

16. Sina Akşin, *Turkey from Empire to Revolutionary Republic* (New York: New York University Press, 2007); and Reşat Kasaba, "Turkey from the Rise of Atatürk," in *The New Cambridge History of Islam,* ed. Robinson, vol. 5, 301–5.

17. Ilan Pappe, *The Rise and Fall of a Palestinian Dynasty* (Berkeley: University of California Press, 2011).

18. Nikki R. Keddie, *Modern Iran,* updated edition (New Haven, CT: Yale University Press, 2006); Sean McMeekin, *The Russian Origins of the First World War* (Cambridge, MA: Belknap Press / Harvard University Press, 2011), 175–93; Christopher de Bellaigue, *Patriot of Persia* (London: Bodley Head, 2012); and Ali M. Ansari, "Iran to 1919," in *The New Cambridge History of Islam,* ed. Robinson, vol. 5, 154–79.

19. Andrew M. Roe, *Waging War in Waziristan* (Lawrence: University Press of Kansas,

2010); Nazif M. Shahrani, "Afghanistan from 1919," in *The New Cambridge History of Islam,* ed. Robinson, vol. 5, 542–57; and Douglas James Jardine, *The Mad Mullah of Somaliland* (1923; repr., New York: Negro Universities Press, 1969).

20. Reeva S. Simon and Eleanor H. Tejirian, eds., *The Creation of Iraq, 1914–1921* (New York: Columbia University Press, 2004); Charles Townshend, *When God Made Hell* (London: Faber and Faber, 2010); and Abbas Kadhim, *Reclaiming Iraq* (Austin: University of Texas Press, 2012).

21. Ilan Pappe, *The Rise and Fall of a Palestinian Dynasty* (Berkeley: University of California Press, 2011).

22. Ali Abdullatif Ahmida, *The Making of Modern Libya* (Albany: State University of New York Press, 1994); John Wright, *A History of Libya,* revised edition (New York: Columbia University Press, 2012); and Kenneth J. Perkins, "North Africa from the First World War," in *The New Cambridge History of Islam,* ed. Robinson, vol. 5, 417–50.

23. David S. Woolman, *Rebels in the Rif* (Palo Alto, CA: Stanford University Press, 1968); and Paul Preston, *The Spanish Holocaust* (New York: W. W. Norton, 2012).

24. Shoshana Keller, *To Moscow, Not Mecca* (Westport, CT: Praeger, 2001); Nicholas Griffin, *Caucasus* (New York: Thomas Dunne, 2003); Robert D. Crews, *For Prophet and Tsar* (Cambridge, MA: Harvard University Press, 2006); Adeeb Khalid, "Russia, Central Asia and the Caucasus to 1917," in *The New Cambridge History of Islam,* ed. Robinson, vol. 5, 180–202; and Muriel A. Atkin, "Central Asia and the Caucasus from the First World War," in *The New Cambridge History of Islam,* ed. Robinson, vol. 5, 517–41.

25. Atkin, "Central Asia and the Caucasus from the First World War"; and Martha B. Olcott, "The Basmachi or Freemen's Revolt in Turkestan 1918–24," *Soviet Studies* 33 (1981): 352–69.

26. Alexandre A. Bennigsen and S. Enders Wimbush, *Muslim National Communism in the Soviet Union* (Chicago: University of Chicago Press, 1980), 79–81.

27. Robert W. Olson, *The Emergence of Kurdish Nationalism and the Sheikh Said Rebellion, 1880–1925* (Austin: University of Texas Press, 1989).

28. Madawi al-Rasheed, *A History of Saudi Arabia,* 2nd ed. (Cambridge: Cambridge University Press, 2010).

29. Michael Darlow and Barbara Bray, *Ibn Saud* (London: Quartet, 2010); al-Enazy, *The Creation of Saudi Arabia;* and David Commins, "Saudi Arabia, Southern Arabia, and the Gulf States from the First World War," in *The New Cambridge History of Islam,* ed. Robinson, vol. 5, 451–80.

30. Ayesha Jalal, *Partisans of Allah* (Cambridge, MA: Harvard University Press, 2011).

31. Brynjar Lia, *The Society of the Muslim Brothers in Egypt* (Reading, UK: Ithaca Press, 1998); Malak Badrawi, *Political Violence in Egypt, 1910–1924* (Richmond, UK: Curzon, 2000); and Joel Gordon, "Egypt from 1919," in *The New Cambridge History of Islam,* ed. Robinson, vol. 5, 372–401.

32. John Calvert, *Sayyid Qutb and the Origins of Radical Islamism* (New York: Columbia University Press, 2010).

33. Van Bruinessen, "Muslims of the Dutch East Indies and the Caliphate Question."

34. Peter Hardy, *The Muslims of British India* (Cambridge: Cambridge University Press, 1972); and Francis Robinson, "South Asia to 1919," in *The New Cambridge History of Islam,* ed. Robinson, vol. 5, 212–39.

35. Jaswant Singh, *Jinnah* (Oxford: Oxford University Press, 2010); and Santanu Das, "Imperialism, Nationalism, and the First World War in India," in *Finding Common Ground,* eds. Jennifer D. Keene and Michael S. Neiberg (Leiden, The Netherlands: Brill, 2011), 67–86.

36. Quoted in Stoddard, *The New World of Islam,* 84–85; Özcan, *Pan-Islamism;* and Sean Oliver-Dee, *The Caliphate Question* (Lanham, MD: Lexington Books, 2009).

37. Gail Minault, *The Khilafat Movement* (New York: Columbia University Press, 1982); M. Naeem Qureshi, *Pan-Islam in British Indian Politics* (Leiden, The Netherlands: Brill, 1999); Dietrich Reetz, *Islam in the Public Sphere* (Oxford: Oxford University Press, 2006); Oliver-Dee, *The Caliphate Question;* and Vali Nasr, "South Asia from 1919," in *The New Cambridge History of Islam,* ed. Robinson, vol. 5, 558–90.

38. K. N. Panikkar, *Against Lord and State* (New York: Oxford University Press, 1989).

39. Muhammad Khalid Masud, *Travellers in Faith* (Leiden, The Netherlands: Brill, 2000); and R. Michael Feener and Terenjit Sevea, eds., *Islamic Connections* (Singapore: Institute of Southeast Asian Studies, 2009).

40. Roy Jackson, *Mawlana Mawdudi and Political Islam* (New York: Routledge, 2011).

41. Misagh Parsa, "Iran from 1919," in *The New Cambridge History of Islam,* ed. Robinson, vol. 5, 481–516; and for the apocalyptic views of Khomeini and his radical contemporaries, see Jean-Pierre Filiu, *Apocalypse in Islam* (Berkeley: University of California Press, 2011), 70–79.

CONCLUSION

1. For a critical view of Adorno's remark, see Susan Gubar, *Poetry After Auschwitz* (Bloomington: Indiana University Press, 2003).

2. Gilles Kepel, *The Revenge of God* (University Park: Pennsylvania State University Press, 1994).

3. Andrew Chandler, "Catholicism and Protestantism in the Second World War in Europe," in *The Cambridge History of Christianity,* ed. Hugh McLeod, vol. 9, *World Christianities c. 1914 – c. 2000* (Cambridge: Cambridge University Press, 2006), 262–84.

4. Michael Burleigh, *Earthly Powers* (New York: HarperCollins, 2005).

5. "Text of Pope Benedict XVI's weekly audience," April 27, 2005, www.american catholic.org/news/BenedictXVI/TextAudience.asp.

6. Simon J. D. Green, *The Passing of Protestant England* (Cambridge: Cambridge University Press, 2011); and Grace Davie, *Europe: The Exceptional Case* (London: Darton, Longman, and Todd, 2002).

7. Nachman Ben-Yehuda, *Theocratic Democracy* (New York: Oxford University Press, 2010).

8. Norman Stone, *World War One* (London: Allen Lane, 2007), 35.

Index

Page numbers of illustrations appear in *italics*.